THE EARTHLY REPUBLIC

FRANCESCO PETRARCA

COLUCCIO SALUTATI

LEONARDO BRUNI

FRANCESCO BARBARO

POGGIO BRACCIOLINI

ANGELO POLIZIANO

THE EARTHLY REPUBLIC

ITALIAN HUMANISTS ON GOVERNMENT AND SOCIETY

EDITED BY BENJAMIN G. KOHL & RONALD G. WITT

WITH ELIZABETH B. WELLES

UNIVERSITY OF PENNSYLVANIA PRESS *upp*

Designed by Adrianne Onderdonk Dudden

Sixth paperback printing, 1991

Library of Congress Cataloging in Publication Data
Main entry under title:

The Earthly republic.

Bibliography: p.
Includes index.
CONTENTS: Kohl, B. G. and Witt, R. G.   General
introduction.—Petrarca, F.   How a ruler ought to govern
his state.—Salutati, C.   Letter to Peregrino Zambeccari.
Letter to Caterina di messer Viere di Donatino d'Arezzo.
[etc.]
    1. Renaissance—Italy—Addresses, essays, lectures.
2. Humanism—Addresses, essays, lectures. I. Kohl,
Benjamin G. II. Witt, Ronald G. III. Welles, Eliza-
beth, B.
DG532.E37   945'.05   78-53335
ISBN 0-8122-7752-X
ISBN 0-8122-1097-2 pbk.

Printed in the United States of America

CONTENTS

PREFACE

This new anthology of Italian humanist writings in English translation arose from our teaching Renaissance history for more than a decade to American undergraduates and our realization that the texts presently available in translation increasingly fail to reflect issues raised by advances in historiography. Since World War II, scholars of the Italian Renaissance, and especially Hans Baron, have brought to the attention of a wide reading public a number of writings on economic, social, and political problems by Italian humanists, works hitherto known only to specialists. These writings not only provide knowledge of how these thinkers viewed developments in the society of their day but reveal as well their methodology, their basic assumptions, and the general quality of humanistic thought.

In making the present selection we endeavored to choose texts written by major humanist authors dealing with a variety of issues. Most of the works translated here are found in modern critical editions. The exception is Poggio's *De avaritia,* where only the central part has been edited by a contemporary scholar. The notes identifying quotations and allusions to individuals or historical events have, in the main, been provided by the editors of the Latin texts. But we have checked the quotation in each case against the original, and, except for Scripture and classical authors, we have based the translation on a modern edition. None of the works has been translated before into English, except for Barbaro's *De re uxoria,* which exists in an inaccessible, late seventeenth-century anonymous English translation.

In translating these tracts, composing the introductions, and compiling the bibliographies, we have incurred several debts. Foremost, we would like to thank our collaborator, Elizabeth B. Welles, who did the Poliziano translation and introduction as well as a preliminary translation of one-third of Poggio's *De avaritia.* For aid on some of the knotty problems of translation we are grateful to James Day of the Department of Classics at Vassar and to Francis Newton of the Department of Classical Languages at Duke. Michael H. McCarthy of Vassar's Department of Philosophy provided references for allusions to ancient philosophical texts. Typing, in Poughkeepsie, was done by Pamela Golinski, Gail Gardner, and Susan M. Taylor while Dorothy Sapp did the portions of the volume typed in Durham. Our wives, Judith C. Kohl and Mary Ann Witt, have served generously as listeners and editors. At the University of Pennsylvania Press we have benefited from the editorial skills of Sheila F. Segal and John McGuigan, and we owe much to the Director, Robert Erwin, for his initial interest and continuing encouragement of this book, which has been some years in the making. Most of all, however, this volume is the product of the stimulation of our students over the years. Therefore, we dedicate it to them: To our students in Renaissance history at Duke, Harvard, and Vassar.

Benjamin G. Kohl
Poughkeepsie, New York

Ronald G. Witt
Durham, North Carolina

Candlemas 1978

THE EARTHLY REPUBLIC

ABBREVIATIONS

DBI *Dizionario biografico degli Italiani.* 20 vols. to date. Rome, 1960–77.

PG J. P. Migne, ed. *Patrologiae cursus completus, series graeca.* 161 vols. Paris, 1857–1903.

PL J. P. Migne, ed. *Patrologiae cursus completus, series latina.* 217 vols. Paris, 1844–1905.

RIS L. A. Muratori. *Rerum italicarum scriptores.* 25 vols. in 28. Milan, 1723–51.

RIS, n.e. *Rerum italicarum scriptores,* new ed. by G. Carducci, V. Fiorini, P. Fedele. Città di Castello or Bologna, 1900ff.

GENERAL
INTRODUCTION

1

Since Cicero the ancient Latin rhetorical tradition had been committed to the belief that man's essential characteristic was the power of speech.[1] Men enjoyed superiority over all other animals because of their ability to express their feelings and thoughts in words. By the same reasoning, men, differing as they did in their ability to speak well, differed in the extent to which they were truly human. The eloquent orator realized his human nature most fully. Outward speech, moreover, was believed to reflect the inner life. If the discourse of an individual was sober and even, then his soul was probably well-disposed and harmonious. One could stutter and still be virtuous, but the orator had a greater potential field for doing good. Basically a speaker, man required a society to fulfill his nature and this implied among other things certain obligations toward his fellow men and women. The orator's duty consisted not merely in cultivating his own virtue and influencing others by his conduct, but through his words he was responsible for moving the hearts and wills of his listeners toward good. Ancient Roman rhetoric, therefore, established an integral relationship between eloquence and moral virtue.

To attain eloquence the potential orator needed to receive an education that trained both the tongue and will. For Cicero and later Latin rhetoricians this meant the study of Greek arts and letters, to which they attributed a humanizing effect. Because of their role in making men more eloquent and more human, such studies were known as *studia humanitatis*.[2] In the centuries after

1. See the brief but excellent discussion of this conception in Jerrold Seigel, *Rhetoric and Philosophy in Renaissance Humanism* (Princeton, 1968), pp. 3–30.
2. Werner Jaeger, *Humanism and Theology* (Milwaukee, 1943), p. 21. Also see Paul O. Kristeller, *Renaissance Thought: The Classic, Scholastic, and Humanist Strains* (New York, 1961), pp. 9–10; the following discussion owes much to Kristeller's work on humanism and rhetoric.

the fall of Rome and the loss of Greek, medieval rhetoricians in their turn treated the writings of the Roman rhetorical schools as their basic texts. Subsequently, with the reintroduction of Greek in the fifteenth century, the essential program for training in rhetoric became clearly defined as Latin and Greek literature in prose and poetry, grammar, history, and moral philosophy.[3]

Like ancient Roman rhetoric, French rhetoric in the twelfth century stressed the close tie between eloquence and moral philosophy.[4] The rhetorician's duty was to use his eloquence to make men better human beings. Devoting themselves to close study of the ancient texts in an effort to capture both their thought and techniques of forceful expression, the writers of that century often produced elaborate commentaries on the Latin authors. Nevertheless, if dominated by the respect they held for the great texts of antiquity, rhetoricians like Peter of Blois and John of Salisbury, both clerics, seemed unable to put a truly Christian stamp on the moral teachings inherited from the pagans. On the other hand, while they introduced frequent quotations of ancient writers into their own works, the creations of twelfth-century French rhetoric were medieval both in style and syntax.[5] Living as they did in an agricultural, feudal society, they failed to capture the spirit of ancient rhetoric, reflection of a cosmopolitan, urban environment. For this reason they could not appreciate the context in which moral problems had been discussed by the ancients; statements

3. Kristeller, *Renaissance Thought*, p. 10. Helene Wieruszowski, *Politics and Rhetoric in Medieval Spain and Italy* (Rome, 1971), pp. 589–627, effectively argues for the significance of classical literature even for the thirteenth-century Italian rhetoricians who considered themselves "modern."

4. Wieruszowski, *Politics and Rhetoric*, p. 373, notes that the thirteenth-century Italian *dictatores*, who professed to teach moral philosophy, gave only superficial treatment to this subject. But see the qualification of Kristeller, *Renaissance Thought*, p. 106.

5. Hans Schaller, "Die Kanzlei Kaiser Friedrichs II," *Archiv für Diplomatik, Schriftengeschichte, Siegel-und Wappenkunde* 4(1958):274–77. The suggestion that the twelfth-century rhetoricians were unable to integrate ancient ideas with Christian doctrines suggests Erwin Panofsky's thesis regarding a discontinuity between form and content in the high Middle Ages; see his *Renaissance and Renascences in Western Art* (Stockholm, 1960), pp. 42–113. While Panofsky utilizes the idea to characterize art in this period, Seigel discusses the relationship between wisdom and rhetoric in these centuries in terms of "disjunction" (*Rhetoric and Philosophy*, pp. 174ff.).

and historical references drawn from the ancient texts often appeared twisted to fit very different purposes.

Thirteenth-century Italian rhetoric constituted a break with the Western conception of the nature and goals of rhetoric.[6] Rather, Italian rhetoricians were responding in their own way to the needs of a highly urbanized, international society ruled by a large number of different political powers, a society in which public speeches in assemblies and frequent epistolary communications between governments were common. Secular in its orientation, Italian rhetoric in that century was dedicated to attaining eloquence in making speeches and writing letters with very practical ends in view. With rare exceptions rhetoricians, usually laymen, wished to achieve eloquence in order to win favor for a person or a policy or accomplish the opposite result. Theirs was in effect an eloquence without a conscience. In contrast to the French tradition, which had reached its apogee in the previous century, Italian writers strove to establish their novelty. To the extent that they utilized quotations and imitated style, the Latin *Vulgata* was their authority. Biblical influence did not, however, effect the subject matter or the approach to questions. Biblical associations were formal elements in a rhetoric dedicated to worldly concerns. Where moral tendencies in these writings can be defined, they bear the mark of popular Stoic rather than Christian influence.[7]

To appreciate the nature of humanism, the principal intellectual movement concerned with rhetoric in the fourteenth-century, attention must be directed to the effect made on European thought by the recovery of Aristotle. Although Aristotle's corpus was almost completely in circulation by the beginning of the thirteenth century, it required decades for Western thinkers to appreciate the intricacies of his ideas. As this was gradually accomplished, Western philosophers and theologians became aware of a complete, systematic philosophy having something to say on almost every aspect of human experience, and yet derived by reason from a few basic principles. Because of its cohesion and comprehensiveness, Aristotle's writings made Europeans conscious as never before

6. Wieruszowski, *Politics and Rhetoric*, pp. 593–94.

7. See the forthcoming study by Ronald G. Witt, *Salutati: His Life and Thought*, chap. 3.

of the boundaries defining the natural world and natural knowledge.

This rediscovery of the Aristotelian corpus had enormous significance in the areas of ethics and politics. The older Augustinian-Gregorian view of temporal power was that its task was primarily negative, serving the faith by controlling overtly sinful acts. The secular ruler was to govern the material aspect of human life while the Church supervised the spiritual life. By contrast, the Greek philosopher considered service to the state to be the means by which the individual could develop his ethical capacity to the fullest. The political thought of Aristotle therefore suggested to some thinkers that the state also had a positive spiritual function. Indeed, the language subtly shifted: the contrast lay no longer between temporal and spiritual but rather between natural and supranatural.[8] On this basis Dante felt confident in maintaining a twofold happiness for man, one found within the earthly paradise and the other in the celestial realm. With this distinction implicitly as his wedge, Marsiglio of Padua was able to restrict ecclesiastical power within very narrow limits. Through Aristotle the natural world gained respectability.

Even though in a sense refuting the enthusiastic claims for the power of human reason inspired by Aristotle's achievement, the rise of critical philosophy in the fourteenth century made further contributions to the distinctions between nature and supranature. Put very simply, fourteenth-century thinkers were concerned with describing a world reconcilable with the Christian belief in God's absolute will. Their criticism of the thirteenth-century theologians and philosophers was that they frequently deduced from God's creation what the Creator must be like. God was accordingly treated as if within the universe rather than outside it. Therefore, these fourteenth-century philosophers and theologians, loosely identified as nominalists, proclaimed God's absolute will and the utter contingency of everything he created. While God would not

8. Walter Ullmann, *History of Political Thought: The Middle Ages* (Baltimore, 1965), pp. 174–99. On the effect of Aristotle on Italian scholars in the Renaissance, see Kristeller, *Renaissance Thought*, pp. 24–47. Baron convincingly argues that the real nature of Aristotle's lay ethic could not be understood until the advent of civic humanism at the beginning of the fifteenth century; see "Franciscan Poverty and Civic Wealth as Factors in the Rise of Humanism," *Speculum* 13(1938):20–37.

change the universe radically because, according to Revelation, He was good, nonetheless, He could do so in a split second were He to will it. Nothing in the universe had to exist or be the way it was, and thus there was no means of arguing from created nature to God. All knowledge of God came through His Divine Revelation, while experience with and study of nature's operations were the sources for knowledge of created beings. Despite their sincere effort to depict a world completely subject to God's will, these thinkers unintentionally encouraged the sense of a gap between natural and supranatural, each having its own realm of truths. Apart from infrequent intrusions of miracles, the natural world emerged as something approaching an independent system susceptible to analysis by human reason.[9] A rhetorical movement basically antagonistic to the claims of philosophy for precedence, humanism nonetheless became deeply influenced by ideas that pointed to a desacralization of the natural life.

Humanism in the fourteenth century revived the traditional view of the rhetorician as a moral philosopher, teacher, and champion of virtue. Moreover, like the twelfth-century French rhetoricians, Italian humanists looked to the ancient Roman pagan writers for their models. On the other hand, the humanists were products of a culture very different from that of the French. They were members of a society similar in many ways to that in which the ancient Romans lived. Because of their desire to learn from the ancients, the humanists soon gained a profounder appreciation of the writings of Livy, Cicero, Vergil, and Seneca than the French writers had had. They found ancient culture far more relevant and useful for conceptualizing their own moral problems and working out solutions to them.

The ability to grasp similarities also implied a capacity to understand differences. In this regard the recent evolution of a sharp distinction between the realm of the natural and supranatural

9. Heiko A. Oberman, "Some Notes on the Theology of Nominalism," *Harvard Theological Review* 53(1960):47–69. Also see his "The Shape of Late Medieval Thought: The Birthpangs of the Modern Era," in *The Pursuit of Holiness in Late Medieval and Renaissance Religion*, ed. Charles Trinkaus and Heiko A. Oberman (Leiden, 1974), pp. 11–15, and the provocative essay by Francis Oakley, "Christian Theology and the Newtonian Science: The Rise of the Concept of the Laws of Nature," in *Creation: The Impact of an Idea*, ed. Daniel O'Connor and Francis Oakley (New York, 1969), pp. 54–83.

was of vital importance. Starting with Petrarch humanists were increasingly able to view the culture of the ancient world as secular and develop the implications of this for themselves as Christians. A sense of historical perspective developed, affording the humanists the means to comprehend the difference between their own world and that of the pagans.[10] The result was the objectification of ancient culture, from which arose a power to control the past and to use it selectively as needed.

In Petrarch, Boccaccio, and Salutati the evolving conception of the world of nature as distinct from the world of grace encouraged an effort to utilize ancient ethical ideas, properly understood, for the construction of a truly Christian morality. Because the twelfth-century rhetoricians were unable to objectify the culture of the pagans, they could not appreciate the problems involved in such a project.[11] While the fourteenth-century humanists were not always successful, their works reveal a preoccupation with working out a morality closely related to Christ's teaching and cutting away some of the overlay of pagan philosophical doctrines, especially Stoicism.[12] However, by the first half of the fifteenth century humanist treatment of moral problems was decidedly less Christian in character. Secure in the knowledge of the inherent value of the natural world, the humanists of the first half of that century exhibited a consuming interest in considering problems accessible to natural reason to

10. For a general contrast between the medieval and renaissance approach to antiquity see Panofsky, *Renaissance and Renascences,* pp. 108–13. An excellent treatment of the Renaissance sense of historical perspective is found in Myron P. Gilmore, "The Renaissance Conception of the Lessons of History," in his *Humanists and Jurists: Six Studies in the Renaissance* (Cambridge, 1963), pp. 1–37.

11. Because they were unable to separate clearly the natural from the supranatural, medieval writers (those favorable to the ancient poets) tended to view ancient poetry as divinely inspired and foreshadowing truths of revelation. On the other hand, the humanists of the fourteenth century approached the ancient poets as men utilizing natural—although still God-given—talents. See Ronald Witt, "Coluccio Salutati and the *Poeta Theologus,*" *Renaissance Quarterly* 30(1977):538–63.

12. For the complexity of Petrarch's ethical position, see Klaus Heitmann, *Fortuna und Virtus; eine Studie zu Petrarcas Lebensweisheit* (Cologne, 1958). On the general problem of the effect of Stoicism and Augustinianism on the humanists, see the brilliant essay by William J. Bouwsma, "The Two Faces of Humanism," in *Itinerarium italicum,* ed. Heiko A. Oberman with Thomas A. Brady, Jr. (Leiden, 1975), pp. 3–60.

the neglect of supranatural matters. Of course, the clarity of the contrasting realms of nature and grace would be dimmed in the last fifty years of the century, at least temporarily, by the growing influence of Neoplatonism, which confused the two in the great chain of being.

But even when directing their rhetoric toward supranatural goals, the humanists of the fourteenth century, like those of the fifteenth, recognized the importance of the secular. If the practical orientation of thirteenth-century Italian rhetoricians had been primarily a product of circumstances without a theoretical basis, their focus still must have had some effect here. Moreover, once the secular or natural life had been infused with positive value, as happened in late-thirteenth and early-fourteenth-century thought under the influence of Aristotle, theoretical grounds were provided for justifying a concern with problems of daily lay life. Nevertheless, the humanists of the fourteenth and fifteenth centuries made a major contribution of their own to the construction of a framework of thought in which the secular life was seen as significant and worthy of pursuit by virtuous men. They furnished Italian society with a series of models for living a kind of life that had received almost no theoretical elaboration in the Middle Ages and thereby succeeded in justifying lay society to itself. While by no means denying that man had a destiny beyond the heavens, the humanists provided assurances that man was at the same time a citizen of an earthly republic to which he owed duties and from which he could derive legitimate satisfactions.

2

Approaching the past with an awareness of historic difference, the humanists developed a keen sense of stylistic changes in various periods of Latin. Consequently they were far more successful than their French predecessors in creatively imitating ancient style. Ancient Latin poetry and prose relied for its meters on the succession of long and short syllables. In the Middle Ages, however, the ear was no longer attuned to these quantitative aspects of words, and writers came to depend on patterns of accented and unaccented syllables as the basis of metrics. The particular patterns employed by a rhetorical school were known as the *cursus* of that group of writers.[13]

In the twelfth century the *cursus* of the rhetoricians of Orleans emerged as the preferred series of patterns both in France and Italy. Reflecting their reverence for antiquity, the rhetors of this school, in describing their *cursus*, borrowed the terminology of metric used by the ancients for different patterns of syllabic quantification—spondee and dactyl—but applied it to feet determined by accent. By contrast, Italian rhetoricians of the thirteenth century generally employed the *cursus* as it had been developed in the medieval Roman Curia.[14] Less difficult than the *cursus* of Orleans, the Roman *cursus* was easy to learn and did not seriously impede the notary pressed for time in composing official letters or documents. Although they encouraged use of the *cursus* throughout the work, the Italian rhetoricians insisted on its importance primarily for the final syllables of a period.

There were basically three preferred forms. The *planus* consisted of a polysyllabic word with the accent on the penultimate followed by a trisyllabic word with the accent also on the penultimate: *fórma tenéndi; expectatióne convérsi*. It was acceptable to divide the trisyllable into a monosyllable and a bisyllable: *inimícus est véster*. The *cursus velox* consisted of a polysyllable accented on the antepenultimate and a tetrasyllable with an accented penultimate: *sanctitúdinis pertinére; respéctibus adimplére*. The final four syllables, however, could be divided in various ways: *sensíbiles se osténdunt; celsitúdinem vestram ámant*. The third common form was the *tardus*, consisting of a polysyllable with penultimate accent followed by a tetrasyllable with an antepenultimate accent: *núper accépimus; nóstris defíciat*. As with the *planus* and *velox*, however, the writer could use several words to make up the final four syllables of the *cursus tardus*.[15]

13. On the *cursus*, see the studies of Francesco di Capua, *Scritti minori*, 2 vols. (Città di Castello, 1959); and Alfredo Schiaffini, *Tradizione e poesia nella prosa d'arte italiana dalla latinità medievale a G. Boccaccio* (Rome, 1943), pp. 11–24; and Gudrun Lindholm, *Studien zum mittellateinischen Prosarhythmus* (Stockholm, 1963).

14. Lindholm, *Studien*, pp. 13–26; Witt, *Coluccio Salutati and His Public Letters* (Geneva, 1976), 24.

15. As late as the early fourteenth century, rhetoricians of *ars dictaminis* insisted on three- and four-syllable words in final clauses; see Paul O. Kristeller,

The rules of the *cursus* and other regulations governing style were usually brought together in manuals of composition known as *ars dictaminis*. The prime concern of these manuals was instruction in writing eloquent letters, but the treatment was intended to apply to prose composition generally. Rhetoric was taught by studying the manuals of composition, the *ars dictaminis,* together with collections of letters appended to serve as illustrations of the rules. There seems to have been almost universal agreement in thirteenth-century Italy, at least in the first half of the century, on the use of a simplified *cursus,* on avoidance of citations from the ancients, on neglect of ethical considerations, and on the practice of teaching rhetoric through the use of modern textbooks of *ars dictaminis.*

Yet despite the points of agreement, Italian rhetoricians divided into at least two camps on series of narrower issues.[16] The rhetors of Bologna, led by Boncompagno, who flourished in the early decades of the thirteenth century, believed in simple sentence construction and vocabulary. Stress was placed on minimal use of figures of speech and on brevity. The resulting product, something of a business Latin, fell under the general rubric of a humble style or *stilus humilis.* So easy was this style to learn and use that by the opening decades of the fourteenth century, a hundred years later, varieties of *stilus humilis* inspired by Bologna dominated most of the chanceries of Italy, and gradually, in the course of the century, even the papal Curia came to rely almost solely on this form of expression.

The second style grew up in the South, primarily around the Hohenstaufen emperor and the papal court. The leaders of this style were Cardinal Thomas of Capua and Peter della Vigna. A more elaborate rhetoric, this southern style employed frequent biblical quotations and an exotic vocabulary, while numerous interjections and interrogatives created an impression of deep feeling. This intricate, often obscure, style of the imperial and papal court was called the *stilus rhetoricus* because of its vibrant oratorical quality. Spreading north in the last half of the thirteenth

---

"Un *Ars dictaminis* di Giovanni del Virgilio," *Italia medioevale e umanistica* 4(1961):194–97. A fourth meter, the trispondaic, also occurred frequently.

16. Wieruszowski, *Politics and Rhetoric,* pp. 592ff.; Witt, *Coluccio Salutati,* pp. 34–38.

century, the *stilus rhetoricus* influenced rhetoricians of the stature of Brunetto Latini and Dante but, because of its difficulty, gradually lost out to the Bolognese *stilus humilis* in the Italian chanceries in the fourteenth century.

Within the two general stylistic approaches themselves rhetoricians commonly distinguished between public or institutional rhetoric and private writings. The latter tended in both cases to be somewhat more ornate. This difference became far more marked with the humanists. When writing on behalf of a public authority, as Petrarch did infrequently or as Salutati, Bruni, and Poggio did regularly in their chancery positions, the humanists followed fairly closely the basic rules of the *ars dictaminis* of the thirteenth century. Because of the more formal, official character of this kind of rhetoric, stylistic innovation would have been most difficult. On the other hand, in their own writings the humanists endeavored to break with traditions of medieval rhetoric and create styles of expression built closely on antique models.

Subservience to Ciceronian usage became a characteristic of an important number of Italian humanists only in the last half of the fifteenth century. In the fourteenth century, by contrast, the influence of Senecan stylistic models was easily as important for humanists as those of Cicero. Petrarch regarded himself as a bee who drew honey from various flowers but transformed it through his own efforts into a unique concoction.[17] This eclectic attitude fairly well characterizes the approach to style taken by Petrarch's successors for the next century. Medieval vocabulary was weeded out along with numerous set expressions. *Tu*, the ancient Latin second person singular, reappeared, and *vos*, the second person plural in ancient usage, was no longer employed when addressing a single person, as was done in the Middle Ages. Incidence of the present active participle diminished while that of indirect discourse increased. The list of changes is long: the humanists were reshaping the language to serve as the vehicle for ideas, many of them inspired by the ancients.

17. Vittorio Rossi, ed., *Lettere familiari*, 4 vols. (Florence, 1933–42), 1:39–40. English trans. *Rerum familiarum, libri I–VIII*, trans. Aldo Bernardo (Albany, New York, 1975), pp. 41–42. An example of Petrarch's *stilus rhetoricus* is found *Variae*, 54, *Epistolae de rebus familiaribus et variae*, ed. Giuseppe Fracassetti, 3 vols. (Florence, 1859–63), 3:469–71.

The reform of medieval Latin by the humanists naturally was not a product of one generation. By the mid-fifteenth century humanists looked back on their fourteenth-century predecessors as pioneers but also as relatively crude in their attempts at achieving a level of diction comparable to that of the ancients. The changing relationship of humanists to the *cursus* in the two centuries illustrates the evolution. All the fourteenth-century writers and those belonging to the first half of the fifteenth were trained in the correct usage of the *cursus,* and, as suggested above, they demonstrated their ability to use it along with the rest of the rhetorical arsenal of *dictamen* in their official writings. At the same time all were basically opposed to the *cursus* as a corruption of good style. Nevertheless, the fourteenth-century writers exhibited in their personal work a decided tendency to retain the music of its meters, even if they failed to observe the strict rules requiring the employment of three- or four-syllable words in metric formation.[18] The music remained, but the pattern could be composed of words of any length, provided that together they satisfied the rhythm. On the other hand, by the fifteenth century, beginning with Leonardo Bruni, it seems clear that the aesthetic pleasure taken in the sounds of the *cursus* sharply diminished, and occasions of *velox, tardus,* and *planus* meters in period endings became fortuitous.[19]

However, even when reading the writings of humanists like Bruni and Poggio in the fifteenth century, the modern scholar has little difficulty distinguishing between their style and that of the ancient Roman writers. The ancient Latin sentence was normally periodic, that is, it was an elaborate construction composed of

18. Lindholm (*Studien,* pp. 88–140) analyzes the *cursus* in Petrarch, Boccaccio, and Salutati. Especially on Petrarch, see Guido Martellotti, "Clausule e ritmi nella prosa narrativa del Petrarca." *Studi petrarcheschi* 4(1961):35–46. Salutati specifically attacked the rules requiring final clauses to end in words of three or four syllables; see *Epistolario di Coluccio Salutati,* ed. Francesco Novati, 4 vols. (Rome, 1891–1911), 4:234. Despite his superb treatment of the *cursus* in the Renaissance, Lindholm seems to distort his presentation of the problem by failing to consider these requirements as an intrinsic part of the *cursus* of Italian *ars dictaminis.* Consequently, when he emphasizes the continuing use of the *cursus* in the fourteenth century, he does not indicate the extent to which the early humanists liberated themselves from tradition in their refusal to follow the stipulations governing the distribution of the clausula between words of a specific number of syllables.

19. Lindholm, *Studien,* p. 151.

various clauses in differing degrees of subordination to others with the meaning of the whole suspended until the final words. Although ancient rhetoricians recognized an occasional need to use sentence structures taken from daily speech, that is, short independent sentences or ones made up of series of independent clauses linked by conjunctions (*oratio perpetua*), they regarded the period as the normal form used in good writing and oratory.[20] The Italian humanists for their part indicated a marked preference for less intricate subordination and tended to follow the patterns of popular language to a greater degree. Sentences were shorter than those of ancient authors, and conjunctions like *et* (and) were relied on to join expressions of ideas as they occurred to the mind.[21]

Because of their ability to isolate and define the characteristics of Latin at particular stages of its growth, the humanists were in a position to adapt those elements of the ancient language which most pleased them and which most fitted the kinds of ideas they wished to express. Renaissance Latin, therefore, was in its time a modern language. Popular languages still had a long way to go to develop the kind of theoretical vocabulary needed for high-level abstract thinking. In the meantime Latin not only furnished these languages with a model but also served as a major instrument for intellectual advancement until these languages were rich enough in vocabulary and firm enough in structure to bear that burden.

3

Early in the fifteenth century Renaissance humanism received its programmatic definition in an unexpected fashion: Pier Paolo Vergerio's *De ingenuis moribus,* a treatise on education dedicated to Ubertino da Carrara, heir apparent to the lordship of Padua. Within a few years after the composition of the tract, the Carrara

20. Aldo Scaglione, *The Classical Theory of Composition; from its Origins to the Present* (Chapel Hill, N. C., 1972), pp. 26–32. For an outstanding example of *oratio perpetua,* see Cicero's *Epistulae ad Atticum.*

21. This and other important differences between ancient and Renaissance Latin are treated by Raffaele Spongano, "Un capitolo di storia della nostra prosa d'arte," in *Due saggi sull'Umanesimo* (Florence, 1964), pp. 39–78. This does not mean that many examples of periodic construction cannot be found in humanist prose.

dynasty was to suffer extinction in a Venetian prison, but Vergerio's definition of the liberal arts, known as the *studia humanitatis,* became the dominant educational ideal of the Italian Renaissance. For Vergerio, the foundation of a liberal education rested upon the verbal arts of grammar and rhetoric, which were shaped by the power of reasoning gained from logic. To these methodological tools in communication Vergerio added the study of history as the empirical datum of human action, moral philosophy as the guide to right action in this life, and poetics as the expression of the fundamental nature of man and the world, beyond rational discourse and expressing an intuitive cognition of truth. But moral philosophy, eloquence, and history were, for Vergerio, at the core of humanism:

> By philosophy we learn the essential truth of things, which by eloquence we so exhibit in orderly adornment as to bring conviction to differing minds. And history provides the light of experience—a cumulative wisdom fit to supplement the force of reason and the persuasion of eloquence. For we allow that soundness of judgment, wisdom of speech, integrity of conduct are the marks of a truly liberal temper.[22]

Vergerio's statement of the new educational goals crystallized much of earlier humanist thought. It announced goals of liberal studies—history, Latin eloquence, literature—that had already become the preoccupation of mature humanist thinkers. Early in the fourteenth century the notaries, lawyers, and judges who formed the professional classes governing the city-states of northern Italy, including Padua, Verona, and Milan, had begun an intensive study of Roman history and literature in order to improve their own knowledge of antiquity and provide models for their literary compositions. A few decades later, at the papal court at Avignon, the young Petrarch formed his interest in the Roman historians and planned his epic and biographical history dedicated to the glory of Rome. But Petrarch soon turned to problems of moral

---

22. *De ingenuis moribus,* ca. 1403, English trans. in W. H. Woodward, *Vittorino da Feltre and Other Humanist Educators* (1897; reprint ed., New York, 1963), pp. 106–7; Latin text, ed. A. Gnesotti, *Atti e Memorie della R. Accademia di scienze, lettere ed arti di Padova,* n.s. 34(1917):122.

philosophy and human existence in his *Secretum* and *De remediis utriusque fortunae*. In so doing he established the humanist's role as a critic of society, a student of human nature, and a commentator on traditional assumptions about politics and government. At the same time the utility of ancient examples in telling men what to follow and what to flee required that history remain the major object of humanistic study. Both Petrarch and Boccaccio composed large treatises on ancient heroes and villains in order to provide their readers with "inducements to virtue and dissuasions from vice."[23] To formal works on history and ethics the early humanists added the study of mythology and impassioned defenses of poetry and the poet's calling, as witnessed by Boccaccio's *Genealogie deorum gentilium* and Coluccio Salutati's *De laboribus Herculis*. But the bulk of humanist writings were *pièces d'occasion*—letters, epistolary tracts, orations, and short treatises composed for friends, acquaintances, or rulers for their information, improvement, or glorification. The humanist works presented here represent well these humbler, commoner genres of humanist discourse.

Petrarch understood the function of the epistle in keeping friends and correspondents informed of his thoughts, plans, and whereabouts as well as its more dignified role in diplomacy and moral instruction. In the dedicatory preface, written in 1350, to his first letter collection, *Familiares,* Petrarch averred:

> In this book little was written in a labored style but much in a familiar tone about everyday things, although occasionally, when the subject required, a single straight-forward story may be seasoned with a few moral reflections. This was Cicero's practice.[24]

As Petrarch grew older and more famous, more and more contemporaries sought his advice and wisdom. The lengthy letter to Francesco il Vecchio da Carrara, translated in this volume, is an example of the humanist's response to the almost obligatory request to provide a tract for his last patron. The result was a treatise on princely rule in which Petrarch maintained the informal tone of

23. Boccaccio, *The Fates of Illustrious Men,* trans. L. B. Hall (New York, 1965), p. 2; Latin text in *De casibus illustrium virorum* (Paris, 1520; reprint ed., Gainesville, Fla., 1962), p. 25.

24. English trans. in Morris Bishop, *Letters from Petrarch* (Bloomington, Ind., 1966), p. 21; Latin text in *Familiari,* Vittorio Rossi, ed. 1:11.

the private letter while he broached the important theme of good government and the just exercise of political power. At the same time the humanist embellished and informed his work with examples from ancient history and pungent observations on contemporary customs. The resultant homely political philosophy is at once a testament to the humanist's vast learning and his desire to improve the city of Padua.

Coluccio Salutati spent his life in public service, mainly as the chancellor of Florence, where he penned literally thousands of public letters. But at the same time Salutati kept up a massive private correspondence proffering advice in the Petrarchan tradition on ethical and cultural issues. In the two letters translated here the Florentine chancellor reveals his typical characteristics: a propensity to questions of vocation and moral decision, a use of a wide variety of Christian and classical sources, an ability to write in a vivid and interesting style, and a quick turn of mind that moved from philosophical questions to humorous descriptions of recent events. For Salutati the letter became a versatile instrument in which the author's rhetorical skills could be used to admonish, persuade, and inform.

In the Middle Ages the political speech had been a means of expressing government policy and stirring citizens to proper actions. The oration in its epideictic mode was also used to mete out praise or blame, to edify and exhort. Typical developments in the fourteenth century were the funeral oration to recount the deeds of leaders recently dead, the inaugural address made by public officials when they took office in cities or universities, and the praise of cities to provide citizen or subject with a sense of the homeland's special history and destiny. Leonardo Bruni's *Panegyric to the City of Florence* is a specimen of this last type—the medieval *laudes urbis*. But Bruni's oration differs from its medieval predecessors in at least two important respects: it was composed at a crucial moment of Florentine political success after the sudden death of Giangaleazzo Visconti ended the Milanese threat to Florence's liberty; and Bruni, a student of ancient Greek, was able to use a Hellenistic model, the *Panathenaicus* of Aristides, to give his own speech structure and classical sanction. Cast in the epideictic style of unstinting praise, the *Panegyric* argues for the superiority of Florence because of its site and magnificence, its Roman republican founding, its recent history as the defender of Italian liberty, and its equitable, open government guaranteeing justice to all.

As much as Bruni, the Venetian patrician Francesco Barbaro was in the early fifteenth century a student of the teachings of ancient Greek literature and moral philosophy as well as the Stoic doctrines of Cicero and Seneca. While Barbaro probably used as his model for his tract *On Wifely Duties* Cicero's famous treatise *De officiis,* he relentlessly mined the moral thought of Plutarch and Xenophon to formulate his own views on virtue, marriage, childrearing, and domestic management. Barbaro also evinced contemporary Venetian customs to illustrate his prescriptions for wifely duties as well as anecdotes from the lives of great ancients to carry forward his argument. In the end Barbaro's purpose was to further the power and delineate the responsibilities of the Venetian patriciate of which he was a member. In so doing he ascribed a major role to patrician wives in the bearing and upbringing of the future rulers of his state.

The provincial Tuscan Poggio Bracciolini spent most of his life as a papal curialist until he returned to Florence as its chancellor in his old age. Book-hunter, antiquarian, and avid student of Latin literature, Poggio inherited from his hero Petrarch a penchant for criticism and irony in his approach to treating important social issues and vices, including clerical corruption, hypocrisy, and the utility of wealth. In discussing these questions Poggio found the dialogue a more congenial vehicle than the formal treatise or letter because debate admitted the possibility of arguing both sides of a question and thereby arriving nearer to the truth. Poggio would have answered in the affirmative the questions that Bruni has Salutati ask in the first *Dialogue to Pier Paolo Vergerio,* written probably in 1401:

> For examining and discussing subtle matters what could be more efficacious than disputation, where the topic is placed, as it were, stage center and observed by many eyes, so that there is nothing in it which can escape or deceive the view of all?[25]

25. English trans. in D. Thompson and A. F. Nagel, *The Three Crowns of Florence* (New York, 1972), p. 21; Latin text in E. Garin, ed., *Prosatori latini del Quattrocento* (Milan and Naples, 1952), p. 48.

In *On Avarice* Poggio cast his discussion in the form of an imaginary dialogue among his fellow curialists precisely so that several sides of an important—perhaps insoluable—moral question could be examined. That the question of the naturalness of greed and the utility of wealth admitted of no definitive resolution probably troubled Poggio very little. Rather he was content to expose several views of the issue and to admit ultimately that human reason could not solve every human problem.

More than any Italian humanist of the Quattrocento, Angelo Ambrogini, called Poliziano, was the heir to the Petrarchan tradition of writing poetry in Italian and important historical and philological studies in Latin. Poliziano used themes from classical history and mythology to inform his poetic inventions while he deepened his knowledge of antiquity and perfected his own Latin style. The failed conspiracy of the Pazzi family and its supporters to murder the Medici rulers of Florence afforded Poliziano the opportunity to write contemporary history, after the ancient manner, and to defend the legitimacy of the rule of his Medici patrons. Humanist historiography in the first half of the fifteenth century had been applied to describing the evolution of liberty in Florence, as in the histories of Leonardo Bruni and Poggio Bracciolini. Now, in 1480, Poliziano turned his considerable talent to proving the depravity of the Pazzi and the greatness of Medici rule. Modelling his history on the trenchant, economical, and vivid style of the Roman historian Sallust, Poliziano conveyed well the rapid succession of events and the inevitable triumph of the Medici over the evil, misguided, bungling conspirators. All subsequent historians of Medicean Florence have had to take account of this highly skilled historiographical propaganda in assessing the nature of this most important challenge to Lorenzo de' Medici's rule.

4

By the second half of the fourteenth century humanism was well on its way to becoming fashionable in Italian society. Even before his death in 1374, Petrarch had become a culture hero. It is impossible to define the almost magical effect that this man had on his generation. His enormous gifts of eloquence and creative genius cannot be separated from the fascination exercised by his style of life, his personal beauty and charm, and his reputation as the lover of Laura. Dante in his own way was just as unique and compelling a personality. Yet the work of the great Tuscan poet did not launch a movement anything like that inspired by Petrarch's humanism. Here again, as in other periods, the times had to match the man.

Petrarch was not the first Italian rhetorician of the fourteenth century with interests in ancient history and style, but he was the first to demonstrate the rewards of fame and fortune that such interests could bring. His success stirred the ambition of countless bright young men to pursue a career in letters. It is no coincidence that of the six humanists represented here only Barbaro came initially from the ranks of the upper class. In fact, the major Italian humanists of the Renaissance were individuals who had to find their way to the top through and around the obstacles that society put in the path of newcomers. In this process of individual achievement the humanists learned to understand human nature and to exploit situations. Rulers appreciated men of this stamp and showered them with favors. Ineluctably the humanists were drawn into the chanceries and councils of city-states, the service of princes, and the curiae of powerful ecclesiastics, including the pope.

Yet, despite their closeness to power, the humanists on the whole remained critical of contemporary mores and corruption and true to the high ethical standards of ancient Stoicism and their Christian faith. Social criticism, moreover, was a vital part of the ancient rhetorical tradition to which they adhered. Their rich personal experience made them well equipped to criticize with accuracy and gave them flexibility in finding solutions to social problems. They united a deep knowledge of history with their personal experience and reflection. Besides absorbing the individual lessons that history taught, the humanists came to appreciate how men themselves are the creators of their past and, as such, how they also have power to mold the future.

Almost all the humanists were critical of the contemporary Church. For them many preachers, friars, and other ecclesiastics failed to meet the needs of the believers. Hence, they felt compelled to offer advice and instruction on many moral problems whose solutions had formerly been the sole preserve of the clergy. The humanists attached great importance to the informed exercise of the will, after the courses of possible action had been thoroughly investigated. They wanted the precepts of a Christian life, now open to the laity as well as the clergy, to be not simply taught but also lived. Their ambivalent view toward Christian institutions extended most of all to scholastic theology and the medieval desire for architectonic finality. They criticized the excessive reliance on logical demonstration of northern European theology, as Petrarch did when he inveighed against the "British barbarians," and they sought a more accessible, colloquial expression of fundamental truths through poetry and debate. They distrusted the vast, inclusive Thomistic system based on Aristotle and were mixed in feeling toward the closed system of Dante's *Divine Comedy*. Their thought had a more open-ended, searching quality based on a willingness to reject system in favor of experimentation, to reject syllogistic demonstration in favor of reasoned personal conviction. Hence, the humanists advanced tentative solutions to the enduring problems of lay society. Theirs was an earthly republic of letters bent on the amelioration of society through the application of ancient wisdom, shaped by Christian faith, to the almost quotidian solution of very human needs.

Especially in recent years, scholars have done extensive research in Italian economic, social, and institutional history in an effort to determine the material conditions and social fabric of the world in which the humanists wrote. In certain areas of this research it has been possible to utilize the services of the computer to amass and analyze large amounts of statistical data. Undeniably the humanists' ideas were able to exert the influence they did because Italy by 1300 was already in fact very secular and because the political, economic, and social character of the culture made rhetoric the central intellectual discipline. Humanism itself was to an extent an outgrowth of the values and institutions of Italian society.

The focus of this book, however, is not primarily to determine the effect of the Italian environment on the rise of humanism and to contrast the texts, largely normative in character, with the reality of Italian society and culture. Such a detailed analysis and comparison admittedly would afford an appreciation of the texts in their Italian historical context. While not overlooking the fact that humanist attitudes developed in a social matrix, this book is basically concerned with the history of ideas, with illustrating a new and original effort to justify in intellectual terms the pursuit of secular aims in a Christian society. As such, the texts stand at the beginning of the development of the secular ethic that has characterized much of modern Western thought.

FRANCESCO
PETRARCA

Introduction

BENJAMIN G. KOHL

The enthusiasms, prejudices, and enormous accomplishments of Francesco Petrarca (1304–74) are well known. Throughout his long life he offered, usually in the form of letters or epistolary tracts, advice on many subjects to a large variety of people—great, near-great, and ordinary. Petrarch engaged as well in polemics on several subjects: against medical doctors, against those who criticized Italy, and against those who criticized him or at least his concept of humanistic learning. He was at the same time the foremost love poet of his age and also was deeply committed to investigating the questions of religious belief and human existence. Precisely because of the complexity of his thought and the magnitude of his writings, Petrarch's inner beliefs and true convictions have been variously interpreted. He has been viewed as much a spokesman for medieval commonplaces as a harbinger of a new secular spirit. This ambiguity is reflected most of all in Petrarch's views on politics and social issues.

Born in Tuscany at Arezzo, the son of an exiled Florentine merchant, Petrarch grew up at Avignon on the banks of the Rhone, where the papacy had moved in 1305.[1] As a young man he soon made a reputation as a love poet and budding scholar. He

1. A sure guide to the events of Petrarch's life is E. H. Wilkins, *Life of Petrarch* (Chicago, 1961).

25

developed his distaste for the contemporary papacy, formed his love of solitude, and found his calling as a man of letters and social critic after studying law at Montpellier and Bologna. Early he developed his passion for the study of the Latin classics, especially the Roman poets Vergil and Ovid, the historians Livy, Valerius Maximus, and Suetonius, and the philosophical works of Cicero and Seneca.[2] This interest in Roman antiquity prompted Petrarch to undertake, at the age of thirty, two immense projects: the *Africa,* a Latin epic depicting the life of Scipio Africanus Major, and the *De viris illustribus,* a series of biographies of great Roman leaders and generals. At the same time Petrarch continued his search for lost works from Roman antiquity and editing and emendation of the texts of his favorite authors, especially Livy.[3] But this interest in classical thought, philology, and history was at times diverted by his concern for personal salvation, as discussed in the *Secretum,* his investigation of the nature of the religious vocation, as contained in his *De otio religioso,* and his defense of the tranquil, rural existence he had found at his country house at Vaucluse. Soon after the Black Death Petrarch resolved to undertake a new version of the *De viris illustribus,* this one broadened to include Biblical and mythical as well as Roman figures.[4]

In 1353 Petrarch removed to Milan, where, under the patronage of the Visconti lords, he wrote his major philosophical work *De remediis utriusque fortunae,* a treatise on how to cope with both favorable and adverse fortune. During his stay in Italy Petrarch returned to the more militant, secular classicism of his youth and undertook to revise his one historical work back into a series of Roman lives and bring to completion his Latin epic. In 1366, stung by criticism of his life and intellectual interests made by certain Averroist critics, Petrarch wrote an invective against contemporary scholasticism and its devotées, he used the teaching of

2. See B. L. Ullman, "Petrarch's Favorite Books," *Studies in the Italian Renaissance* (Rome, 1955), pp. 117–37.

3. On Petrarch's interest in Livy, see G. Billanovich, "Petrarch and the Textual Tradition of Livy", *Journal of the Warburg and Courtauld Institutes* 14(1951):137–208.

4. For Petrarch's intellectual development I rely on the interpretations in Hans Baron, *From Petrarch to Leonardo Bruni* (Chicago, 1968), pp. 7–50, and G. Martellotti, "Linee di sviluppo dell'umanesimo petrarchesco," *Studi Petrarcheschi* 2(1949):51–82.

Plato, Cicero, and Seneca to defend his own concept of the humanities. Three years later, in a defense of Italy written against a certain French critic, Petrarch's classicism had reached a point where he could chortle: 'What is all history except the praise of Rome?''[5]

In 1370 Petrarch settled in the village of Arquà in the Euganean Hills to the south of Padua, in a house he had built on property given him by his final patron, the lord of Padua, Francesco il Vecchio da Carrara (1325–93). In the last four years of his life Petrarch worked at revising and putting in final form his vast collection of letters and Italian poetry. He also endeavored to finish the Roman lives and the Latin epic, both of which were to remain uncompleted at his death. At the same time he kept up his prolific correspondence with old friends and new admirers. Late in 1373 he wrote his last long letter, a treatise on the duties of a ruler of a city-state, in response to request from his Carrara patron.

Petrarch's political sentiments were so various and often so contradictory that his views on government and rulership have often been ascribed little credence.[6] But despite differences in tone, interest, audience, and time of composition Petrarch's views on politics do possess certain common threads: a desire for peace in society, a belief in justice, a value placed upon the patronage of scholars by the powerful, and, most of all, the view that Italy should be a unified state free from war and reflecting its cultural unity and Roman heritage.

This passion for Italian unity compelled Petrarch to place his faith at various times in several different political leaders. Petrarch's first great hope Cola di Rienzo, the demagogic tribune of Rome who, in 1343, expelled the ruling Roman aristocratic families and established—or rather, in his view, reestablished— the Roman Republic with himself as head. From Avignon and Vaucluse, Petrarch wrote letter after letter urging Cola to reunite Italy, restore the papacy to Rome, and bring peace to the peninsula.[7] But Cola proved an inept politician and was soon forced into exile. After a visit to the Roman emperor Charles IV at Prague

5. *Invectiva contra eum qui maledixit Italie,* in *Prose,* ed. G. Martellotti et al. (Milan and Naples, 1955), p. 790.

6. For a discussion of various interpretations of Petrarch's political views, see R. de Mattei, *Il sentimento politico del Petrarca* (Florence, 1944), pp. 18ff.

7. See M. E. Cosenza, *Francesco Petrarca and the Revolution of Cola di Rienzo* (Chicago, 1913), which includes translations of Petrarch's letters to Cola.

and brief captivity at Avignon, Cola did return to Rome, only to alienate his subjects and perish at their hands while trying to escape the city.

Petrarch's next candidate for restoring Italian unity was the Holy Roman Emperor, Charles IV of Bohemia.[8] Starting in 1350, Petrarch wrote more than a dozen letters to the emperor exhorting him to come to Rome to receive the imperial crown. This Charles did in 1354, but, much to Petrarch's dismay, the emperor promptly returned beyond the Alps, leaving Italy in disarray as before. A few years later Petrarch visited Prague as an envoy for the Visconti of Milan, and this embassy occasioned the resumption of his exhortations to the emperor to bring peace and unity to Italy. In 1361 Petrarch wrote perhaps his most persuasive and eloquent plea to Charles IV. In it the humanist argued that "in the whole world there is nothing under heaven that can be compared with Italy, in respect either to the gifts of nature or to human achievement."[9] Hence the emperor must not delay his descent to bring peace to so fine a jewel. Besides, though Charles was a Bohemian by birth, Petrarch claimed that by his coronation Charles had been reborn and acquired another, finer homeland, namely Italy. Moreover, Charles belonged in Rome "because the City is the real home and the true homeland of the Caesars."[10] The letter ended with a peroration designed to move Charles to action. Action came with a second imperial descent in 1368, but it was no more successful than the first in bringing peace to Italy.

At other times Petrarch saw the rulers of the regional states of Italy as possible agents for his dream of Italian unity. As early as 1339, Petrarch wrote to a Milanese official hinting that his lord Luchino Visconti might bring unity to Italy.[11] In the early 1350s, troubled by the approach of war between Genoa and Venice,

8. On Petrarch's relations with Charles IV, see C. C. Bayley, "Petrarch, Charles IV, and the 'Renovatio Imperii,'" *Speculum* 17(1942):323–41; and for the first exhortation, *Familiari* 10.1, see the translation in J. H. Robinson and H. W. Rolfe, *Petrarch, the First Modern Scholar and Man of Letters,* 2d ed. (New York, 1914), pp. 361–69.

9. *Le Familiari,* ed. V. Rossi and U. Bosco, 4 vols. (Florence, 1933–42), 23.2, 4:158.

10. Ibid., p. 165.

11. Ibid., 3.7, 1:116–18; English trans. in A. S. Bernardo, *Petrarch, Rerum Familiarum Libri I–VIII* (Albany, N.Y., 1975), pp. 130–34.

Petrarch wrote to both governments urging peace.[12] In a later letter to the Venetian doge Andrea Dandolo, when war had already broken out, Petrarch argued for peace and suggested that Venice might head a united northern Italy.[13] All these plans and suggestions fell, however, on deaf ears. Late in his life Petrarch turned away from active appeals for Italian unity and concentrated instead on the moral improvement of his friends and on practical advice to ruling lords. The letter to Francesco da Carrara presented here is a product of the more realistic political opinions of Petrarch's later years.

In composing this epistolary tract, Petrarch for the first time employed the well-known medieval genre of the "mirror for princes."[14] But he did not rely much, if at all, on medieval antecedents such as the treatise *On Kingship* by St. Thomas Aquinas or the tract *On the Governance of Princes* by Giles of Rome. Petrarch may well have known these tracts, for they were much copied and available in most large libraries; but he typically eschewed medieval sources of inspiration.[15] Instead Petrarch used his favorite classical authors, such as Cicero and Seneca, and his reading of the Bible and the Church fathers as sources for his moral opinion. For historical anecdotes to illustrate the virtues of good rulers and the fates of bad ones, Petrarch turned to his early favorites, the historians of Imperial Rome, including Suetonius, Valerius Maximus, and the writers of imperial lives from the second and third centuries, known collectively as the *Scriptores Historiae Augustae*. In addition, Petrarch drew upon his knowledge

12. The letter to Venice was addressed to the Doge Andrea Dandolo, *Familiari* 11.8., in Rossi and Bosco, ed., 2:340–48. Two letters to the Doge of Genoa are *Familiari* 14.5–6, 3:118–26; the second letter is translated in E. H. Wilkins, *Petrarch at Vaucluse: Letters in Verse and Prose* (Chicago, 1958), pp. 182–85.

13. *Familiari* 18.16, 3:302–8; see also the discussion in J. H. Whitfield, *Petrarch and the Renascence* (Oxford, 1943), pp. 31–32.

14. On the "mirror-for-princes" literature, see L. K. Born, "The Perfect Prince: A Study in Thirteenth- and Fourteenth-Century Ideals," *Speculum* 3(1928):470–504, and W. Berges, *Die Fürstenspiegel des hohen und späten Mittelalters* (Leipzig, 1938), which includes a discussion of Petrarch's letter on pp. 273–88.

15. This is the opinion of A. Steiner, "Petrarch's *Optimus Princeps*," *Romanic Review* 25(1934):94–111, which is the only extended discussion of the letter in English.

of Paduan society gained from intermittent residence in the city from 1349 onwards. Finally, the whole work is informed by a reproving, exhorting spirit perhaps appropriate to an older, distinguished cultural figure writing to a younger patron who has requested advice.

The Carrara lord, then in early middle age, was probably much in need of Petrarch's instruction. Succeeding to the lordship of Padua in 1350 following the brutal assassination of his father Giacomo II, Francesco il Vecchio had turned from a policy of subservient friendship with Venice to a series of wars against his powerful neighbor; he had thus at once asserted the greatness and independence of Padua and burdened his subjects with military service and taxes to pay for his wars of aggression. To be sure, he brought several improvements to his city: the promulgation of a new code of municipal statutes in 1362, the creation of a court system in which the lord became the source of final appeals, fortification of Padua and the towns of the *contado,* and patronage of the university and the humanists. But in securing his power over Padua, Francesco created a palace clique of cruel and often rapacious advisers drawn from the Paduan *popolo* and the feudal nobility of northern Italy. Hence Petrarch's cautions on the evil effects of counselors were well-deserved. Yet no doubt Francesco strove to govern with justice, even though his foreign policy brought war more often than peace. The Carrara lord was not in every respect the ideal ruler that Petrarch depicted, but his government and rule were in many ways groping toward the decorum, benevolence, and justice that Petrarch urged.

Petrarch's letter is divided into two parts: the first treats the ideal character and general duties of a ruler, while the second concentrates on the practical benefits that the Carrara lord might bring to the city and district of Padua. In the first part the humanist stresses the morality and character of the ideal Italian *signore.* In a vivid series of examples, he shows that in Imperial Rome evil rulers received their just deserts, usually murder at the hands of the Roman people, while good emperors gained the affection, esteem, and admiration of their subjects. Petrarch avers that Francesco da Carrara has already provided such good leadership to Padua. Indeed, the whole institution of signorial rule was, for Petrarch, founded upon the mutual love of ruler and subjects. In a homely metaphor, Petrarch urges the Carrara lord to love his Paduan subjects as members of a large family, to reprove and instruct them with his example, as a father does his children. But there is no room for political unrest or even change in this ideal state. Rebels and the discontented are to be viewed as evil men and expelled. Rather, Petrarch's ideal posits a just ruler governing a static state in which there would be no need for change or cause for rebellion.

In the second part of the letter Petrarch turns to the practical benefit that the Carrara lord might bestow on his subjects. Here he adopts an aesthetic view of rulership stressing the duties of the lord to drain swamps, build walls, and keep the streets in good repair.[16] Petrarch also urges, with realistic insight, princely habits that keep subjects happy. Thus the Carrara lord was to refrain from imposing new taxes, and if he did, he was to pay some himself. Moreover, modesty in dress and informality of manner would win the approval of the people. Here Petrarch praises the Carrara lord for his democratic use of the familiar form of address, showing his lack of fearful pretension and his ease with his subjects.

Emphasizing his own political values, Petrarch praises Francesco da Carrara for ending his recent war with Venice and bringing peace to northern Italy. The humanist also stresses the benefit that lordly patronage can bestow on the city's scholars and how the university can prosper under a benevolent ruler. At two points Petrarch urges the correction of minor blemishes in the governing of Padua. He asks the Carrara lord to remove rampaging herds of pigs from the streets of the city and, in a vivid passage at the end of the letter, recommends the curtailing of funeral lamentations and the adoption of more decorous exequies.

Indeed, the entire tract stresses decorum, measure, prudence, and dignity. In much of his advice Petrarch relies upon common sense observation in forming his prescriptions for improving Padua. At the same time he often takes as evidence for great lordship the deeds and character of the great men of antiquity. Written perhaps hastily near the end of Petrarch's life, the treatise contains much of his earlier research and thinking.[17] The historical

16. Petrarch's aesthetic view of lordship is stressed in Berges, pp. 281–83.

17. Midway in the letter Petrarch confessed that he was writing down whatever came into his head; see below, p. 68.

anecdotes had often been told before in other works, especially the Roman lives, *De viris illustribus,* and in the collection of historical examples compiled to improve individual morality, *Rerum memorandarum libri.* Hence, the letter is at once a mature and vivid record of the writer's view on politics. Petrarch saw that the achievements and failures of the Roman past were of immediate relevance to contemporary affairs and that the values of ancient culture, as demonstrated in the decorum and dignity stressed by Latin authors, were of great utility in solving current problems and correcting abuses. The past was useful to contemporary rulers, he maintained, if only they would heed its lessons.[18]

After his death Petrarch's tract on lordly rule was overshadowed by his more famous philosophical and literary works. As an occasional letter written for a lord whose dynasty was soon to suffer extinction in a Venetian prison, the treatise did not receive wide circulation.[19] Nonetheless, it is the humanist's most extended and elaborate statement on the art of ruling a city-state, and it provides an additional insight into one of Petrarch's constant preoccupations—the improvement of the lot of his fellow men.

BIBLIOGRAPHY

Francesco Petrarca: Editions

Opera omnia. 3 vols. Basel, 1554, reprint Ridgewood, N. J., 1965.
Prose. Edited by G. Martellotti et al. Milan and Naples, 1955.
Rime, Trionfi e Poesie latine. Edited by F. Neri et al. Milan and Naples, 1951.
L'Africa. Edited by Nicola Festa. Edizione nazionale delle opere di Francesco Petrarca 1. Florence, 1926.
Le Familiari. Edited by V. Rossi and U. Bosco. Edizione nazionale delle opere di Francesco Petrarca 10–13. Florence, 1933–42.
Epistolae de rebus familaribus et variae. Edited by G. Fracassetti. 3 vols. Florence, 1859–63.

18. On Petrarch's views on the value of history, see B. G. Kohl, "Petrarch's Prefaces to *De viris illustribus*," *History and Theory* 13(1974):132–44, esp. 134–36.

19. Before the twentieth century, the work was published four times in the *Opera omnia* of the sixteenth century and once separately at Bern in 1604 under the title *De republica optime administranda.*

Rerum Senilium liber XIV. Ad magnificum Franciscum de Carraria Padue dominum. Epistola I. Qualis esse debeat qui rem publicam regit. Edited by V. Ussani. Padua, 1922.

"Rerum Senilium liber XIIII. Ad magnificum Franciscum de Carraria Padue dominum. Epistola II, ed. V. Ussani." *Atti del R. Istituto Veneto di scienze, lettere ed arti* 83(1923–24):295–301.

Rerum memorandarum libri. Edited by G. Billanovich. Edizione nazionale delle opere di Francesco Petrarca 14. Florence, 1943.

De viris illustribus. Edited by G. Martellotti. Edizione nazionale delle opere di Francesco Petrarca 2. Florence, 1964.

Le traité de sui ipsius et multorum ignorantia. Edited by L. M. Capelli. Paris, 1906.

Liber sine Nomine. Edited by P. Puir. In his *Petrarcas 'Buch ohne Namen' und die päpstliche Kurie.* Halle, 1925.

Invective contra medicum. Edited by P. G. Ricci. Rome, 1950.

De otio religioso. Edited by G. Rotondi. Vatican City, 1958.

Translations

Bergin, T. G. and A. S. Wilson. *Petrarch's Africa.* New Haven, 1977.

Bernardo, Aldo S. *Petrarca, Rerum Familiarum Libri I–VIII.* Albany, N. Y., 1975.

Bishop, Morris. *Letters from Petrarch.* Bloomington, Ind., 1966.

Cosenza, M. E. *Francesco Petrarca and the Revolution of Cola di Rienzo.* Chicago, 1913.

———. *Petrarch's Letters to Classical Authors.* Chicago, 1910.

Draper, W. H. *Petrarch's Secret, or the Soul's Conflict with Passion.* London, 1911.

Kohl, B. G. "Petrarch's Prefaces to *De viris illustribus.*" *History and Theory* 13(1974):132–44.

Mommsen, T. E. *Petrarch's Testament.* Ithaca, N. Y., 1957.

Nachod, Hans. "Petrarch's On His Own Ignorance and That of Many Others." In *The Renaissance Philosophy of Man,* edited by E. Cassirer et al., pp. 47–133. Chicago, 1948.

Robinson, J. H., and H. W. Rolfe. *Petrarch, the First Modern Scholar and Man of Letters.* 2d ed. New York, 1914.

Thompson, David. *Petrarch, a Humanist among Princes.* New York, 1971.

Wilkins, E. H. *Petrarch at Vaucluse: Letters in Verse and Prose,* Chicago, 1958.

Zacour, N. P. *Petrarch's Book without a Name.* Toronto, 1973.

Zeitlin, Jacob. *The Life of Solitude by Francis Petrarch.* Urbana, Ill., 1924.

Studies

Baron, Hans. "The Evolution of Petrarch's Thought: Reflections on the State of Petrarch Studies." *Bibliothèque d'Humanisme et Renaissance* 24(1962):7–41. Reprint in his *From Petrarch to Leonardo Bruni* pp. 7–50. Chicago, 1968.

Bayley, C. C. "Petrarch, Charles IV, and the 'Renovatio Imperii,' " *Speculum* 17(1942):323–41.

Berges, W. *Die Fürstenspiegel des hohen und späten Mittelalters.* Leipzig, 1938.

Bergin, Thomas G. *Petrarch.* New York, 1970.

Billanovich, Giuseppe. "Il Petrarca e gli storici latini." In *Tra latino e volgare, Per Carlo Dionisotti,* 1:67–145. 2 vols. Padua, 1974.

————. *Petrarca letterato. 1. Lo Scrittoio del Petrarca.* Rome, 1947.

————. "Petrarch and the Textual Tradition of Livy." *Journal of the Warburg and Courtauld Institutes* 14(1951):137–208.

Bishop, Morris. *Petrarch and His World.* Bloomington, Ind., 1963.

Born, L. K. "The Perfect Prince: a Study in Thirteenth- and Fourteenth-Century Ideals." *Speculum* 3(1928):470–504.

Bosco, Umberto. *Francesco Petrarca.* 2d ed. Bari, 1968.

Koertung, G. *Petrarcas Leben und Werke.* Leipzig, 1878.

Martellotti, G. "Linee di sviluppo dell'umanesimo petrarchesco." *Studi Petrarcheschi* 2(1949):51–82.

Mattei, R. de. *Il sentimento politico del Petrarca.* Florence, 1944.

Mommsen, T. E. *Medieval and Renaissance Studies.* Edited by E. F. Rice, Jr. Ithaca, N. Y., 1959.

Nolhac, Pierre de. *Pétrarque et l'humanisme.* 2 vols. 2d ed. Paris, 1907.

Scaglione, Aldo, ed. *Francis Petrarch, Six Centuries Later, a Symposium.* Chicago and Chapel Hill, N. C., 1975.

Steiner, A. "Petrarch's *Optimus Princeps.*" *Romanic Review* 25(1934): 99–111.

Whitfield, J. H. *Petrarch and the Renascence.* Oxford, 1943.

Wilkins, E. H. *Life of Petrarch.* Chicago, 1961.

————. *Petrarch's Later Years.* Cambridge, Mass., 1959.

Zardo, Antonio. *Il Petrarca e i Carraresi.* Milan, 1887.

FRANCESCO PETRARCA
*How a Ruler Ought to Govern His State**

Translated by BENJAMIN G. KOHL

For a long time now, distinguished sir, I have been meaning to write to you. And you have, in your usual way, gently reproved me, so that I am now aware that I have omitted your name from among the names of the many great men and men of middle rank to whom I have addressed letters. This omission is especially disgraceful when I consider the patronage that I have received from you and your father. Indeed, it would be an enormous act of ingratitude if I should let myself forget the thanks and affection that I should always hold for you. Therefore, I have decided to write to you even though I am still undecided where I ought to begin and on what topic. This indecision does not derive from the lack of a suitable subject matter, but rather from a perplexing abundance of material, so that I feel like a traveler poised at a crossroads. On the one hand, your great and constant generosity compels me to tender you my deepest thanks. Indeed, it is a time-honored custom to give thanks to friends and especially to princes for their gifts, and I have done so to you many times. On the other hand, you have so daily and continually laden me with gifts and honors that I, weighted down with the number and magnitude of your gifts, cannot ever hope to repay you adequately with mere

---

* Complete translation of *Rerum Senilium liber XIV. Ad magnificum Franciscum de Carraria Padue dominum. Epistola I. Qualis esse debeat qui rem publicam regit*, ed. V. Ussani (Padua, 1922).

35

words. Rather, I think that it would be better to pass over such generosity in respectful silence than to try and repay it with inadequate words.

So I leave aside this matter of gratitude and turn to the vast and easy task of singing your praises. Now and again it has been the custom of many men to praise princes (and indeed I have done so myself occasionally), not in order to gain favors from those who are praised as much as to pay homage to the truth and to spur the prince on to greatness with the very stimulus of praise to a generous mind, which is a spur more powerful than anything else. For in these matters of giving praise I find nothing more offensive than adulation or an inconstant attitude. There are those indeed who would praise unworthy men and there are others who, having praised their subjects, promptly begin to vituperate them with an incredible turn of mind. I know of nothing more dishonorable, more base, than this. And in this matter so especially notorious was Cicero (whom I esteem and admire more than any other ancient author) that I feel almost compelled to hate him. Cicero did this to many people, but, most significantly, he ladened and honored Julius Caesar with a wealth of praise and then subjected Caesar to insults and abuse. Read Cicero's letters to his brother Quintus, in which everything said there about Caesar is friendly and complimentary. But then turn to his letters to Atticus, in which you first will find mixed feelings toward Caesar and finally even hatred and reproach. Read Cicero's orations, spoken before Caesar alone or before him when he was present in the Senate; so great are these praises of Caesar that they seem unmerited by any mortal and beyond the capacity of a mortal genius to compose. But read further in the book *On Duties* and in the Philippic orations and you will find expressions of hatred equal to the former affection and base abuse comparable to earlier praise. What makes these great changes in Cicero's attitude even worse is that Cicero gave Caesar nothing but praise while he was alive and nothing but vituperation after he was dead. I would have been able to tolerate this much more easily if Cicero had criticized Caesar when he was alive and praised him after he was dead, because usually death either diminishes or extinguishes altogether hatred and envy. However, Julius Caesar had a companion in this situation (as he did in many things) in the person of his nephew and adopted son Caesar

Augustus, who was inferior to Julius Caesar in his military prowess but surely superior in his ability to rule. Cicero, likewise, at first praised Augustus immoderately, but then he began to criticize him strongly while still alive and even wrote fierce censures of him.[1] I am reluctant to speak thus of a man whom I esteem so much, but truth is stronger than admiration. I regret that it must be this way, but it is. And I do not doubt that if Cicero were present he would answer me easily with his overpowering eloquence, but the truth is not altered by mere words.

I think I shall never turn with a diseased mind from praise to vituperation. Now, as I return to my theme, this occurred to me at the very outset of my discussion with you: While true virtue does not reject merited glory, glory should follow it even if virtue is unwilling, just as the shadow follows the body. I said to myself: This man, you can easily see, prefers to be criticized rather than praised, and it is easier to acquire favor with him by finding fault than by giving him due praise. What, therefore, shall I do? What course shall I take? A man whom I do not hesitate to praise I would not fear to criticize if he would be as fine a subject for criticism as for praise. I confess that it is the condition of mortals that no one is entirely above reproach. A person who has a few small defects can be called perfect and very good. Therefore, give thanks to God who made you what you are, so that if your detractor and your praiser were of equal ability the praiser would naturally be more eloquent. This is like the case of the two farmers who are of equal ability and energy; the one who has the luck to own the more fertile land will appear to be the better farmer. Likewise, in the case of two ship captains equal in every other way, he will be the more fortunate who sails on more tranquil seas and is propelled by more favorable breezes.

But after I had decided to criticize you and selected this topic for my epistolary discussion, I had found nothing in you worthy of blame except for that one thing concerning which I had a private discussion with you some time ago. If in this matter you will be so kind as to pay heed to my humble and faithful advice, there is scarcely any doubt that you will soon derive healthy nourishment for mind and body and for the greatness of your

1. An allusion to the pseudo-Cicero *Epistola ad Octavium*.

present fame and future glory. So I will express it to you with the same words that Crastinus used with Caesar on the battlefield of Thessaly: "You will thank me either dead or alive."[2] I shall not speak of this any more. For what is the use of words to those who already understand and know? You know what I want, and I ought not to want, nor am I able to want, anything but your good. I do not doubt that you know this.

Since things are this way, I feel that I am relieved from telling at this point the long story that, as I have said, is not in the least pleasant for you and, in any case, is well known to everyone. I am referring to the fact that in the very flower of your young manhood you were deprived of your worthy and magnanimous father, by whose example and erudition you were able to learn everything that is noble and magnificent.[3] At the time when it seemed especially fitting for you to have your own mentor, you took up the reins of government and, with the city of Padua under your control, overcame the difficulties created by your youth. You ruled with such competence and such maturity that no rumor, no hint of rebellion, disturbed the city in that time of great change. Next, after a short time, you transformed into a large surplus the enormous deficit that debts to foreign powers had left in your treasury. And now the years and experience in government have so matured you that you are esteemed as an outstanding lord, not only by your own citizens but also by the lords of many other cities, who hold you up as a model. As a result, I have often heard neighboring peoples express the wish that they could be governed by you and nurture envy for your subjects. You have never devoted yourself to either the arrogance of pompous display or to the idleness of pleasure, but you have devoted yourself to just rule so that everyone acknowledges that you are peaceful without being feckless and dignified without being prideful. As a result, modesty coexists with magnanimity in your character. You are thus full of dignity. Although, because of your incredible

2. Julius Caesar *Bellum civile* 3.91.3.
3. An allusion to the assassination in December 1350 in Padua of Francesco's father, Giacomo II da Carrara, by a distant kinsman. As a result Francesco, then a young man in his twenties, succeeded his popular father to the lordship of Padua.

humanity, you permit easy access to yourself even to the most humble, still one of your most outstanding acts is to have at the same time contracted for your daughters very advantageous marriages with noble families in distant lands.[4] And you have been, above all other rulers, a lover of public order and peace—a peace that was never thought possible by the citizen-body when Padua was ruled by a communal regime or by any of your family, no matter how long they held the power—you alone constructed many strong fortresses at suitable points along the Paduan frontiers. Thus you acted in every way so that the citizens felt free and secure with you as a ruler, and no innocent blood was spilled. You also have pacified all your neighbors either by fear or by love or by admiration for your excellence, so that for many years now you have ruled a flourishing state with serene tranquility and in continual peace. But at last that adversary of the human race, that enemy of peace [the Devil], suddenly stirred up a dangerous war with that power you never feared. Consequently, although you still loved peace, you fought with Venice bravely and with great determination over a long time, even though you lacked the aid from allies that you had hoped for. And when it seemed most advantageous to do so, you skillfully concluded peace so that at one stroke you won twofold praise both for your bravery and your political wisdom.[5] From these facts and from many others I shall omit, you have been viewed as vastly superior to all other rulers of your state and to all rulers of other cities, not only in the judgment of your own subjects but indeed in the opinion of the whole world as well.

But praising you in detail when the facts speak so clearly for themselves would be only a pleasant exercise, and it is a useless chore to try and criticize you. Besides, because of the lack of material my speech would end in unbecoming silence as soon as I

---

4. Francesco da Carrara contracted marriages for several of his daughters with the scions of noble houses in Italy and Germany, including the count of Oettingen, the count of Veglie, and the duke of Saxony.

5. An allusion to the border war fought with Venice in 1372–73, which Francesco da Carrara ended by agreeing to the payment of an indemnity to Venice while he maintained substantially his original frontiers. See Paolo Sambin, "La guerra del 1372–73 tra Venezia e Padova," *Archivio Veneto* 5th ser., 38–41(1946–47):1–76.

began to talk. So I shall tell you what I have decided to speak about, a topic which I am sure is well known to you even without any further elaboration but which may be sometimes useful even to someone like yourself who has already been made aware of it. For even though the mind has grasped something well and learned it thoroughly and used that knowledge frequently, it can recall that thing when stimulated by another and, urged on by another's words, it follows more readily a path it would still take by itself. I shall discuss, therefore, something that almost everyone knows but that people often neglect, namely, what should be the character of a man to whom the task of governing a state has been entrusted. I am not unaware that such a subject could easily fill many volumes, and that I am content to write only one letter. Yet for some people a single word is more useful than a long speech is for others, and, moreover, the quality of the mind of the listener is much more important than the eloquence of the writer, whoever he may be. Indeed, let me repeat what I have often said: There must be within you a tiny spark that can be increased by fanning and will eventually burst into flame. Without this one will have only fanned dead ashes for no good purpose. I hope (or indeed I am certain) that in you there are not just faint embers but bright and burning coals or even an excellent flame of virtue and an able mind that is accustomed to utilize all it hears. I can recall how much one letter—a great one because it was the product of a great mind, namely the letter from Marcus Brutus to Marcus Tullius Cicero— stimulated you to excellence, so that for a long time you could scarcely speak of anything else.[6] And I often used to say to myself about you: If he were not such a true friend of virtue he would never have been stimulated so strongly by such a brief, though admittedly excellent, piece of writing. Moreover, it has often been a great source of pleasure to me that I had procured this letter for you, and thus rescued from oblivion and neglect a letter that had been previously lost for a long time.

But before I begin to discuss this subject that I have just proposed, I wish to recall for you a passage from Cicero that, I suspect, is not unknown to you. Surely a man like yourself, who wants to be a good ruler, will listen eagerly to this passage as soon

---

6. An allusion to Cicero *Epistolae ad Brutum* 1.4a.

as you know that a good ruler is as dear to God as the state itself is dear to God. Here, therefore, is the passage from the sixth book of *On the Commonwealth*:

> But, Africanus, be assured of this, so that you may be even more eager to defend the commonwealth: all these who have preserved, aided or enlarged their fatherland have a special place prepared for them in the heavens, where they may enjoy an eternal life of happiness. For nothing of all that is done on earth is more pleasing to that supreme god who rules the whole universe in justice, which is called the State. Their rulers and preservers come from heaven and to that place they return.[7]

Moreover, it is imagined that this conversation took place in Heaven. Who, therefore, could be so completely hardhearted, so opposed to excellence, and so contempuous of true happiness that he would not seek out the task of governing and strive after such rewards? For although it is a pagan who speaks, yet his thought is not opposed to Christian truth or religious belief, even though our way of thinking and theirs are quite different when it comes to such doctrines as the creation of man and the soul.

But now at last I shall do what I have promised, and I shall discuss those things that the lord of a state ought to do. And I want you to look at yourself in this letter as though you were gazing in a mirror. If you see yourself in what I am describing (as no doubt you will quite often), enjoy it. And may you become every day more devoted and more faithful to God, who has bestowed upon us every good and perfect gift and virtue; and may you, albeit with enormous effort, overcome every difficulty and rise to that degree of holiness beyond which you cannot at the present moment ascend. On the other hand, if sometimes you feel that it is difficult for you to meet the standards I describe, I advise you to put your hands to your face and polish the countenance of your great reputation written there, so that you might become more

7. Cicero *Somnium Scipionis* 13 (= *De republica* 6.13), which was known in the fourteenth century only by its inclusion in Macrobius, *Commentarii in somnium Scipionis*.

attractive, and certainly more illustrious, as a result of this experience.

The first quality is that a lord should be friendly, never terrifying, to the good citizens, even though it is inevitable that he be terrifying to evil citizens if he is to be a friend to justice. "For he does not carry a sword without good cause, since he is a minister of God," as the Apostle says.[8] Now nothing is more foolish, nothing is more destructive to the stability of the state, than to wish to be dreaded by everyone. Many princes, both in antiquity and in modern times, have wanted nothing more than to be feared and have believed that nothing is more useful than fear and cruelty in maintaining their power. Concerning this belief we have an example in the case of the barbaric emperor named Maximinus.[9] In fact, nothing is farther from the truth than these opinions; rather, it is much more advantageous to be loved than to be feared, unless we are speaking of the way in which a devoted child fears a good father. Any other kind of fear is diametrically opposed to what a ruler should desire. Rulers in general want to reign for a long time and to lead their lives in security, but to be feared is opposed to both of these desires, and to be loved is consistent with both. Fear is opposed both to longevity in office and security in life; goodwill favors both, and this affirmation is supported by that opinion that one can hear from Cicero (or from the mouth of a Cicero who is speaking the truth). He says: "Of all things, none is better adapted to secure influence and hold it fast than is love, and nothing is more foreign to that end than is fear."[10] And a little further on he states: "Fear is but a poor safeguard of lasting power, while affection, on the other hand, may be trusted to keep it safe forever."[11] Since you know well that this matter was important to Cicero, let me cite another passage: "To be a citizen dear to all, to deserve well of the State, to be praised, courted, loved is glorious; but to be feared and an object of hatred is invidious, detestable, and proof of weakness and corruption."[12]

Now it does not seem necessary to speak of security since there

8. Romans 13:4.
9. See *Scriptores historiae Augustae* 19.8.8.
10. Cicero *De officiis* 2.7.23.
11. Cicero *De officiis* 2.17.23.
12. Cicero *Orationes Philippicae* 1.14.23.

can be no one so stupid and ignorant of politics that he does not know that opinion is criticized by certain men affirming that security is always threatened and ultimately destroyed by fear. This fear is in subjects and not in the ruler, so that it is their security, not his, that is endangered. To which I answer with the famous words directed by Laberius, a Roman knight noted for his wisdom and learning, to Julius Caesar: "He who is feared by many must himself fear many in turn."[13] That this opinion might be more convincing, let me reinforce it with another similar statement by Cicero, whom I have often named: "Furthermore, those who wish to be feared must inevitably be afraid of those whom they intimidate."[14] He borrowed the essence of this idea, which we should not be ashamed to embrace, from Ennius: "Whom they fear, they hate. And whoever one hates, one hopes to see dead."[15] And I add that whatever one wants, one desires to become. What strong passions urge many to accomplish can scarcely be forestalled.

Now, although the truth of the matter is as I have just sketched, there still are those who say: "They may hate me, provided they fear me." This was the speech that Euripides gave to that cruel tyrant Atreus.[16] Daily did Caligula, who was certainly no more merciful than Atreus, say and practice this idea, which was beneficial neither to its creator nor to his followers.[17] In this last category many people have wanted to place even Julius Caesar. This would certainly be strange if true; for although Julius Caesar did, to be sure, have an enormous appetite for empire and glory, I would say too enormous, still he did everything with mildness and mercy, with munificence and an incredible generosity, so that he would be loved rather than feared. For example, he kept nothing for himself from the booty won in his numerous victories and military commands, except for the very faculty to lavish gifts on others, and to this the most authoritative writers give witness. Indeed, Julius Caesar was so prone to be merciful to others that Cicero himself wrote that Caesar was accustomed to forget nothing except past

13. Macrobius, *Saturnalia* 2.7.4. The same anecdote was told earlier by Petrarch in his *Rerum memorandarum libri* 3.34.3–4 (ed. Gius. Billanovich, [Rome, 1943], p. 126).

14. Cicero *De officiis* 2.7.24.

15. Cicero *De officiis* 2.7.23.

16. Cicero *De officiis* 1.28.97; 3.21.82.

17. Suetonius *Caligula* 30.

injuries.[18] It is indeed a splendid kind of revenge to pardon past wrongs; to forget them altogether is more splendid still. What is most amazing is that this quality was noted as Caesar's most noble trait by Cicero, who had as often viewed him as an enemy as seen him as a friend. Do you want more examples? I shall remain silent concerning Caesar's other excellent qualities, but I must say that he was endowed with many more virtues than anyone else, although they were not sufficiently acknowledged. Indeed, he was cut down by those very men upon whom he had heaped wealth and honors. On these men he had bestowed the privileges that came to him from his victories, and he had forgiven every one of his hostile acts and injuries. But neither his generosity nor his mercy aided Caesar in the end. So it was with good reason that at his funeral this verse of Pacuvius was sung:

> That ever I, unhappy man, should save
> Wretches, who thus have brought me to the grave.[19]

In this case it can be asked what were the causes that brought about this hatred, since the conspiracy against Caesar was surely not lacking in hatred. I myself can find no cause except a certain insolence and haughtiness of bearing that raised Caesar above the customs of his country because he enjoyed unwarranted honors and usurped extraordinary dignities.[20] Rome was not yet ready to endure the imperial pride that was so much increased by Caesar's successors, that compared to them Caesar seems to be the very soul of humility. If then even Julius Caesar was not protected by his power and wealth from the hatred of the many, it is an important question to ask in what ways are the love of one's subjects to be sought. Since hatred is the cause of ruin, so love is the cause of the contrary of ruin. The former casts one down, the latter protects a ruler.

What I can say is that the nature of public love is the same as private love. Seneca says: "I shall show you a love potion that is made without medicines, without herbs, without the incantations

---

18. Cicero *Pro Ligario* 12.35.
19. Suetonius *Divus Julius* 84, quoting Pacuvius.
20. See Suetonius *Divus Julius* 76.

of any poison-maker. If you want to be loved, love."[21] There it is. Although many other things could be said, this saying is the summation of everything. What is the need for magical arts, what for any reward or labor? Love is free; it is sought out by love alone. And who can be found with such a steely heart that he would not want to return an honorable love? "Honorable" I say, for a dishonorable love is not love at all, but rather hatred hidden under the guise of love. Now to return love to someone who loves basely is to do nothing other than to compound one crime with another and to become a part of another person's disgraceful deceit. On this topic I shall, therefore, speak no more, but let us return to the theme of honorable love of others.

Indeed, from the discussion of this topic nothing but immense and honorable pleasure ought to come to you since you are so beloved by your subjects that you seem to them to be not a lord over citizens but the "father of your country." In fact this was the title of almost all of the emperors of antiquity; some of them bore the name justly, but others carried it so injustly that nothing more perverse can be conceived. Both Caesar Augustus and Nero were called "father of his country." The first was a true father, the second was an enemy of both his country and of religion. But this title really does belong to you. There is no one among your citizens (that is, among those who really seek the peace and well-being of Padua) who looks upon you otherwise, who thinks of you as anything other than as a father. But you have to continue to strive so that you merit this dignity; it endures forever because of your noble efforts. I hope that, urged and encouraged, you will continue to rule as you already willingly have ruled for a long time. You should know, moreover, that to merit this kind of esteem you must always render justice and treat your citizens with goodwill. Do you really want to be a father to your citizens? Then you must want for your subjects what you want for your own children. I am not saying that you must love each of your subjects as much as you do one of your own children, but you should love each subject in the same way you do your child. For God, the supreme lawgiver, did not say: "Love your neighbor as much as you love yourself," but "as yourself."[22] This means love sincerely,

21. Seneca *Epistulae* 9.6.
22. See Matt. 22:39.

without deceit, without seeking advantages or rewards, and in a spirit of pure love and freely-given goodwill. I am, moreover, of the opinion (without disputing the opinions of others) that you ought to love not each individual citizen but the whole citizen body at the same time, not so much as you love a child or a parent, but as you love yourself. Whereas in the case of individuals there are individual feelings for each one, in the case of the state all feelings are involved. Therefore, you ought to love your citizens as you do your children, or rather (if I may put it this way) as a member of your own body or as a part of your soul. For the state is one body and you are its heart. Moreover, this act is to be manifested by kind words, especially in righteous actions, and above all (as I was already saying) with justice and devotion to duty. For who could not love someone who has always pleasant, just, helpful, and always showed himself to be a friend? And if we add to these fine qualities the material benefits that good lords are accustomed to bestow on their subjects, then surely there develops an incredible fund of goodwill among the citizens that will serve as a firm and handsome foundation for a lasting government.

So put away arms, bodyguards, mercenaries, bugles, and trumpets, and use all these things only against the enemy because with your citizens your love is sufficient. As Cicero says: "The prince ought to be surrounded not with arms, but with the love and goodwill of his subjects."[23] And I reckon as citizens those who desire the preservation of the state and not those who are always trying to change things, for these should be thought of not as citizens but as rebels and public enemies. These considerations call to mind that well-known saying of Augustus: "Whoever does not wish to disturb the present state of the city is a good citizen and a good man."[24] Therefore, I have no doubt that whoever desires the opposite should be viewed as evil and not worthy to bear the name of citizen and enjoy the community of good men. In any case, in these matters your own nature has always guided you well, so that you have already gained both the citizens' love and goodwill. These qualities are, indeed, not just a path to glory, but even a road to salvation. As the good father said to his fine son Scipio Africanus: "Love justice and duty, which are very important in

23. Cicero *Orationes Philippicae* 2.44.112.
24. See Macrobius *Saturnalia* 2.4.18.

regard to parents and kinsmen, and most of all, to your native country. Such a life is the road to heaven."[25] What lover of heaven would not love the road by which he may ascend to heaven?

Now there are innumerable examples of the fact that arms will not defend evil and unjust leaders from the wrath of their oppressed subjects. It will suffice to adduce here only the most interesting and notorious instances. What use to Caligula were his German bodyguards even though they hastened to his defense?[26] In extreme danger, Nero was informed that the soldiers had deserted their posts and his guards had fled.[27] But no cohorts of soldiers were necessary for Augustus, Vespasian, and Titus. Consider the death of Augustus: at his death bed you do not find armed bodyguards but rather friendly subjects, and, in conversation with friends amidst the embraces of his beloved wife, Augustus did not expire and die but rather was almost lulled to sleep.[28] Afterwards his remains were laid to rest with more honors than owed a human being, and his memory was cherished. Vespasian, who believed that it was not proper for an emperor to die standing up, expired held off the floor in the hands of his many friends.[29] Afterwards his son Titus met a premature but peaceful death with innumerable expressions of gratitude. As a result, Titus's death was viewed (as Suetonius says) as more of a tragedy for mankind than for himself.[30] Indeed, unless I am mistaken, all those princes who pass their lives in governing a state ought to consider and remember the following: the death of good princes is for them tranquil and happy while it is terrifying and dangerous for their subjects. For evil princes precisely the opposite is true. In that same city of Rome, where (as I have just mentioned) many emperors have died in complete peace and contentment and have had their names recalled by everyone with honor and admiration— in that city Domitian, the brother of Titus, was killed, and the Senate itself applauded his demise, besmirching his reputation (as I have seen written) with bitter denunciations and calumnies.[31]

25. Cicero *Somnium Scipionis* 16 (= De *republica* 6.16).
26. Suetonius *Caligula* 58.
27. Suetonius *Nero* 47.
28. See Suetonius *Divus Augustus* 99–100.
29. Suetonius *Vespasianus* 24.
30. Suetonius *Titus* 10–11.
31. Suetonius *Domitian* 23.

Further, the Senate decreed that his statues be taken down and destroyed, that his name be cancelled from inscriptions, and that the very memory of him be obliterated. Likewise, Galba's very head was detached, stuck on a spear, and carried about by camp followers and servant boys through the encampments hostile to him to the jeers and horror of all.[32] Vitellius was cut down with many blows on the Scala Gemonia in the Forum and hacked into many pieces. Finally, his remains were dragged around on a hook and thrown into the Tiber.[33]

I shall pass over examples of many others who met their end in horrible ways. But does not this vast difference in manner of death surely follow from a vast difference in manner of living? For this reason that very wise emperor Marcus Aurelius, who joined to the difficult task of governing an empire the name and learning of a philosopher, after he had discussed the fall of many emperors who preceded him, concluded by saying that each emperor met the death that was consistent with his manner of life. He predicted that he himself would be among those who died peacefully.[34] Indeed, his prediction came true. Now since this was the opinion of a great and wise personage, and since every wise man agrees that one should live as decently and well as possible in order to gain—besides the many other benefits from leading a good life— the additional benefit of dying well. Surely it is not too great a task to spend all the preceding years well for a worthy final hour, although, according to the best opinion, this passage into eternity requires only a moment. And we should not wonder at this. Nor should we be surprised since we enter an immense city through a narrow gate, and we penetrate the vast reaches of the sea in a tiny ship. Likewise, through that brief passage of death we enter into an eternity, and just as the soul is when death takes it, so it endures for all time.

Now I shall speak of justice, the very important and noble function that is to give to each person his due so that no one is punished without good reason. Even when there is a good reason for punishment you should incline to mercy, following the example

32. Suetonius *Galba* 20.
33. Suetonius *Vitellius* 17.
34. *Scriptore. bistoriae Augustae* 4.8.3.

of Our Heavenly Judge and Eternal King. For no one of us is immune from sin and all of us are weak by our very nature, so there is no one of us who does not need mercy. Hence, one who wishes to be just must also be merciful. Therefore, although mercy and justice seem, at first glance, to be opposites, they are in fact inseparably linked. Indeed, it is as St. Ambrose says so perceptively in his book *On the Death of the Emperor Theodosius*: "Justice is nothing other than mercy, and mercy is the same as justice."[35] Thus, the two qualities are not merely linked; they are one. Now this is not to say that you should let go scot-free murderers, traitors, poisoners, and other such miscreants, so that by being merciful to a few criminals you are actually harming the vast majority of your subjects. What I am suggesting is that you ought to be merciful to those who have gone astray a little and who have lapsed momentarily if it can be done without encouraging their example. But otherwise remember that too much mercy and indiscriminate leniency can lead to a greater cruelty.

Now, after justice, the best way to earn the affection of your citizenry is generosity. Even if the head of a state cannot benefit individual subjects, he may at least benefit the entire population. There is hardly anyone who esteems someone from whom he does not expect either private or public benefaction. Of course, I am speaking of that esteem in which princes are held; among friends and equals there is a different kind of love, which is sufficient in itself, neither asking for favors nor expecting them. In the sphere of public beneficence there is the restoration of temples and public buildings for which Caesar Augustus, above all others, is to be praised. Livy named him rightly "the builder and restorer of all temples."[36] Similarly, Suetonius says: "He boasted, not without cause, that he found a city of brick and left one of marble."[37] Just as important is the construction of the walls of the city, which gave fame to the name of Aurelian, otherwise a cruel and bloody emperor. In the less than six years during which he ruled, this emperor enlarged the walls of the city of Rome to their present dimensions. As a result, the historian Flavius Vopiscus, following,

35. St. Ambrose, *De obitu Theodosii imperatoris* 26 (= PL 16:1456).
36. Livy *Ab urbe condita* 4.20.
37. Suetonius *Divus Augustus* 28.

I believe, the system of measures of antiquity, was prompted to say: "The circumference of the walls was now nearly fifty miles."[38] But you, sir, have been relieved of the task of wall-building thanks to the great industry of your forebears. In fact, I do not know a city in all of Italy, or even all of Europe, that is ringed with walls more handsome than Padua's.

But the ancients were, I believe, as much concerned with the construction of highways as with the erection of walls. While walls give safety in time of war, roads are a very useful addition in peacetime. The chief difference between the two is this: walls last for a long time because of their great size, whereas roads are soon destroyed because of the continual traffic in men and horses and, above all, the traffic in those heavy Tartarean carts, which I strongly wish that Erichthonius had never invented.[39] These carts not only damage the streets, the foundation of buildings, and the peace of those living in them, but they also disturb the thoughts of those wanting to meditate on the good. Therefore, I ask you to turn your attention to the streets of Padua, which have for a long time been neglected and broken up and which, with their silent deformity, call out for your assistance. I think that you will want to tackle this difficult task, not just because you are responsible for the city and its inhabitants. I know that the beauty of Padua and the well-being of its citizens ought to be—as they are—close to your heart, but the repair of the streets is in your own interest as well. For I have never known anyone—and I am not only speaking here of princes but of every sort of men—except perhaps your own dear father, who liked to ride on horseback, as you do, into every part of his country for such long stretches of time. I am not criticizing this habit of yours since your first duty and care is clearly the good government of Padua, and the presence of a good prince is always pleasing to faithful citizens; but you ought to take care that what you do so eagerly you also do safely. Hence you should remove all danger and difficulties from this horseback-riding and turn it into an agreeable and pleasant recreation.

Entrust, therefore, the repair of Padua's streets to some good

38. *Scriptores historiae Augustae* 26.39.2.

39. An allusion to Erichthonius, the son of Vulcan, king of Athens, who is credited with being the first man to hitch four horses to a chariot; see Vergil *Georgica* 3.113ff.

man who is dedicated to your own welfare and that of the city. And don't be afraid that by appointing a well-known and noble man to this seemingly vile job you are inflicting harm on him. To an honest and upright citizen no duty that results in benefit to his country can ever seem base. History provides an example of this truth. There was in Thebes a very brave and learned man named Epaminondas, who was—if we count virtue alone and not just good luck, which often raises up the unworthy—the leading man, or at least one of the leading men, of Greece. Now this man, about whom it has been written truly that with him the glory of Thebes was born and with him it died, was opposed by his fellow citizens—such evils often occur in democratic states—who appointed him to the job of street cleaner, which was in Thebes regarded as the dirtiest job of all.[40] The citizens hoped thereby that they would diminish the glory and good reputation attached to this man. But Epaminondas did not respond to this punishment with force, or even with a harsh word. Rather, he readily accepted the task assigned to him and said: "I shall undertake this task not with the idea that an indignity has been visited upon me as a result of this job, but rather that it has brought me dignity so that in my hands something very noble will be created out of a task that has always been viewed as base and ignoble." And soon, indeed, the job gained such a good reputation under his splendid administration that a task which has previously been despised, even by the lowliest of the plebs, now became a post sought after even by the most illustrious citizens.[41] Now I hope you will entrust this same task to some industrious and honest citizen of Padua and that you soon will see that many compete for this job, and thus, aided by the zeal of the citizens, the old homeland will be made good as new.

Now I am going to write concerning a matter that seems almost ridiculous and that I have already discussed with you one day recently when you came to visit me in my study at Arquà, an honor that you have paid me often, even though I am unworthy of such

---

40. See Justinus *Epitome historiae Philippicae* 6.8.9.33; Cicero *Tusculanae disputationes* 1.2.4; and Valerius Maximus *Factorum et dictorum memorabilium libri IX* 3.7. ext. 5. Petrarch used the same sources in a discussion of Epaminondas in his *Rerum memorandarum libri* 1.7 (Billanovich, pp. 6–7).

41. See Valerius Maximus 3.7. ext. 5.

visits. Moreover, the very subject of the discussion stood before your very eyes. Indeed, Padua is a fine city on account of the noble lineage of its leading families, the fertility of its site, and its ancient origins that go back many centuries before the founding of Rome itself. Moreover, Padua is furnished with a good university, fine clergy and outstanding religious celebrities, and truly impressive shrines, including the churches of the bishop Prosdocimo, the friar Anthony, and the virgin martyr Justina. What I think is not insignificant—nor should you—I add immediately: that the city has you as lord and protector. Finally it is celebrated in some verses by Vergil.[42] This city, I say, so outstanding in its many glories, is being transformed—with you looking on and not stopping it, as you easily could—into a horrid and ugly pasture by rampaging herds of pigs! Everywhere one turns one can hear their ugly grunts and see them digging with their snouts. A filthy spectacle, a sad noise! These are evils that we have already borne for a long time, and those who came to Padua are amazed and scandalized by them. This state of affairs is repulsive to all who meet it and even worse for those who come on horseback, for whom the free-roaming pigs are always a nuisance and sometimes even a danger because an encounter with these stinking and intractable animals will frighten a horse and even throw its rider. Now I recall that the last time I spoke with you concerning this matter you said that there was an ancient statute that carried with it a heavy penalty that anyone could seize the pigs found roaming freely in the streets.[43] But who does not know that, just as men grow old, so do all human creations? Even the Roman laws fell into disuse and, if it were not for the fact that they have been studied assiduously in the schools, they would now be quite forgotten. So what do you think is the fate of municipal statutes? So that this old law may be applied again, let us have it drawn up again and announced publicly by the town crier with the same, or even a heavier, fine attached to it. Then send out some officials who will remove the wandering pigs so that these urban herders will discover at their own expense that they cannot flout what the law forbids anyone to do. Let those who own pigs keep them on a farm and those

42. Cf. Vergil *Aeneid* 1.241ff.
43. On this statute, see the essay by G. Tamassia, "Francesco Petrarca e gli statuti di Padova," *Atti della R. Accademia di Padova*, n.s. 13(1896–97):201ff.

who don't have a farm keep their pigs shut up inside their houses. Those who don't even own a house should still not be allowed to spoil the homes of other citizens and the beauty of Padua. Nor should these pig owners think that at will, without hindrance from law, they can convert the famous city of Padua into a pigsty! Now some might think this is a frivolous matter, but I don't think it is either frivolous or unimportant. On the contrary, the task of restoring Padua to its former noble majesty consists not so much in large projects as in small details. Partly, of course, these latter concern the task of governing the city, but you must also pay attention to the decorum of the city so that the eyes have their share of the common joy, the citizens are proud of and revel in the improved aspect of the city, and strangers feel that they are not entering a mere village but a real city. This is what you can do for Padua, and if you do it, I think you will have done something worthy of yourself. But concerning this subject I have already said more than enough.

From this issue there arises still another matter; after you have repaired the streets both within the city and leading away from Padua, I hope that you will undertake with every effort the draining of the marshes and bogs which lie near the city. In this way you will be able to improve the already beautiful countryside surrounding the city and to restore to their true worth the farms of the famous Euganean Hills, pitted with bogs that are already rich in the fruits of Minerva and Bacchus, so that the cultivation of the grains of Ceres, prevented now because of the foul, boggy ponds, can be restored.[44] With this project you will be able to combine utility with beauty, and thus, with a single act, you will gain multiple praise. Undertake this project, I beg you, and you will gain that kind of glory which all your forebears never enjoyed because they did not think of such projects or were afraid to undertake them. Good God will assist you in this noble undertaking. Nature will help you too, because almost all the bogs are situated in the higher altitudes, making it a very easy matter to drain the swamps by letting the water flow to lower ground, into

44. An allusion to the cultivation in the Euganean Hills of the grape (the product of Bacchus) and of the liberal arts (represented by Minerva), and emphasizing the lack of cultivation of cereals, such as wheat, barley, or oats (the products of Ceres).

the nearby rivers, and thence into the sea. As a result, the present generation will enjoy more fertile fields, a more handsome countryside, a healthier and more pleasing climate. And future generations will, because of this one project, always remember your name.

Although I have often been irritated when those who love laziness and leisure say that such a project would be impossible, I know from my own common sense, and from the judgment of the inhabitants of the Euganean Hills, that such an undertaking is not only possible but even very easy. So put your hand to this task, my generous lord; if you willingly undertake this project, then surely a happy outcome will result. And you should not consider this sort of project unworthy of your dignity for none other than Julius Caesar took pride in such tasks. Concerning this point, Suetonius writes that a little before he died Caesar planned to drain the Pontine Marshes and to dig a canal across the isthmus on which Corinth is situated so that seaborne trade to the north and east could be expedited.[45] I would wish that you were in a position to undertake similar monumental projects. But the marshes I'm talking about are not far away, as are the Pontine Marshes; they are nearby, right under your very eyes. So give the orders to clean and drain these fetid marshes while your health and strength are good and age not too far advanced. Now I don't want you to laugh, but lest you think I am prepared to offer nothing but words toward the completion of this project, I intend to offer you my little purse for part of the expenses, even though I am not a citizen of Padua. What should a lord contribute? What ought we to expect of a private person? If perhaps one wants to know exactly what I will contribute, the answer will be known in due time. For now I will give you the same answer that the freedman gave once to Augustus: "On my part, I will give to you, lord, what seems to you proper to my new status."[46] But as to the repair of the streets, which I mentioned earlier, you ought to do this before other projects since that project is fairly easy and clearly more honorable. I have heard that at one time public funds were appropriated for such projects so that these tasks could be completed without any

45. Suetonius *Divus Julius* 44.
46. Macrobius *Saturnalia* 2.4.24. The same anecdote is told by Petrarch in *Rerum memorandarum libri* 2.71 (Billanovich, p. 93).

additional taxes on the citizen-body and without reducing the communal treasury or your own private wealth.

Indeed, I do not deny, nor am I ignorant of, the fact that the lord of a city ought to take every precaution to avoid useless and superfluous expenditures. In this way he will not exhaust the treasury and have nothing left for necessary expenditures. Therefore, a lord should spend nothing and do nothing whatsoever that does not further the beauty and good order of the city over which he rules. To put it briefly, he ought to act as a careful guardian of the state, not as its lord. Such was the advice that the Philosopher gave at great length in his *Politics,* advice that is found to be very useful and clearly consistent with justice.[47] Rulers who act otherwise are to be judged as thieves rather than as defenders and preservers of the state. One should always remember that saying of the Emperor Hadrian, who was speaking I know not whether more as a prince or a citizen. In either case, Elius Spartianus wrote concerning him: "He discussed policy frequently both in the Assembly and in the Senate. Thus he seemed to run the government of Rome as though he knew that it was not part of his own private property but belonged to the people."[48] Thus, I repeat, he did everything so that he could render account of his spending to anyone, and it is clear that he had to give account, if not to men, at least to God. Similarly, it was very proper that on his deathbed Augustus rendered account of his rule to the Senate.[49] Likewise, whoever has led a good and honorable life—no matter what is his social station—or has acted in such a way that he weighed every possibility and, even if answerable to no one, he could still give full and honest account of his actions to anyone. In this action consists the definition of duty (as Cicero gives it): "Duty is the thing that one cannot neglect without neglecting virtue itself."[50] Why is it important that you have no one to whom to account since your soul must answer to itself and its conscience, which, if dissatisfied, leaves you sad and unhappy? Granted, he was not one of the best

47. Aristotle *Politica* 5.9. 1314b40ff, which Petrarch knew only in medieval Latin translation.
48. *Scriptores historiae Augustae* 1.8.3.
49. Suetonis *Divus Augustus* 28.
50. Cicero *De officiis* 1.29.101.

of princes, but the promise of Tiberius given in the Senate, full of
generous trust, deservedly was praised as excellent: "I will see to
it that you will always have an accounting of my actions and
words."[51] Thus he did more than we asked for, for he gave not
just an accounting of his actions but of the words. Concerning the
moderation that rulers ought to display in their programs of public
works, we may consider the example of the Emperor Vespasian.
Although that emperor undertook very generously to make certain
public improvements, still, when a workman wanted to transport
some very large columns to the Capitoline at little cost, Vespasian
thanked the man for the fair offer but would not allow the work to
be done. He said: "Let me provide bread instead to my poor
plebs."[52] Such is the righteous and laudable preoccupation of a
good prince: to reduce the hunger of the plebs with every effort
and to procure for his subjects plentiful foodstuffs and make
happiness their honest companion. In this context that saying of
the Emperor Marcus Aurelius is very appropriate: "When stuffed
with food, no people are happier than the Romans."[53] This opinion
can be applied to all nations: a people are always driven to despair
more from a lack of foodstuffs than from a deficiency in moral
qualities. Thus, the happiness of every nation consists more in
the well-being of the body than of the spirit.

From these concerns, however, derives not just the happiness of
the people, but the security of the ruling class as well. For no one
is more terrifying than a starving commoner of whom it has been
said: "the hungry pleb knows no fear."[54] Indeed, there are not
just ancient examples but contemporary ones, especially from
recent events in the city of Rome, which bear out this saying.[55] In
this matter the prudence of Julius Caesar is especially to be praised.
During both his Gallic and German wars he was always very
intent on providing foodstuffs, and so, returning to Rome, was
quick to send ships to seek grain from fertile islands for the precise

51. Suetonius *Tiberius* 28.
52. Suetonius *Vespasianus* 18.
53. *Scriptores historiae Augustae* 26.47.4.
54. Lucan *De bello civili* 3.58.
55. An allusion to a revolt—caused by famine—by the lower classes of
Rome against the senatorial families in 1353, just before the return to the city
of the demagogic Cola di Rienzo. See F. Gregorovius, *History of the City of
Rome in the Middle Ages*, trans. A. Hamilton, 8 vols. (London, 1898), 6:337ff.

purpose of meeting the needs of the Roman people. No less concerned was Caesar Augustus, of whom it is written that when grain was in short supply he used to distribute it at a very low price and sometimes gave it virtually free to the Roman people, one by one.[56] For this sort of policy a prince is really worthy of praise, for this policy is motivated by a true love of country and a desire to gain adulation so that the people will bear their taxes more happily, suffer more willingly, and bear hardships more readily. Such a love Augustus showed clearly when he alleviated the hunger of the Roman people (as I have said) by selling grain at a very low price or dispensing it free. But the same Augustus silenced complaints over the scarcity of wine with a stinging and somber reply, making it apparent that he had not provided the grain out of a desire to curry favor with the people but to provide for the well-being and health of his subjects. For he told them that for the needs of thirsty men the city of Rome had plenty of aqueducts, which had just been built by his brother-in-law Marcus Agrippa, and that, moreover, there was always the Tiber flowing past the city walls.[57] There is, to tell the truth, a vast difference between grain and wine: the former is certainly a necessity of life, while the latter is often harmful to it. Of course, wine is more pleasant than bread to the people who often seek what gives pleasure more than what is good for them. But, indeed, the good and prudent prince does not pay heed so much to what is pleasureful as to what is beneficial.

Now this concern over the grain supply is so much a part of a prince's duty that even evil and feckless leaders cannot avoid it altogether. Hence, good princes ought to be especially diligent in seeing that grain is provided. It is true that from such preoccupations you have been released by God and by nature since the regions over which you rule are so fertile that you are far more accustomed to selling a surplus of grain from your district to others than to importing grain. Nonetheless, I would advise you that even in time of good harvests you should prepare yourself for scarcity, so that you may predict by cautious consideration not what is available now but what the future may hold, thus protecting yourself and your state from unexpected changes of fortune.

Until now I don't know whether I have spoken too much or too

56. Suetonius *Divus Augustus* 41.
57. Suetonius *Divus Augustus* 42.

little concerning those things that a prince ought to do. Surely that indulgence in banquets and circus games and the exhibiting of wild and exotic animals is useless; these things may provide a brief delight and momentary pleasure to the eyes, but indeed they hold nothing honorable or worthy for the eyes of a good prince. Hence, I would recommend that a good prince avoid these things even though they are adjudged pleasing by the insane and vulgar mob. In this instance I cannot bring myself to admire the policy of the ancient Roman leaders who, even though they recognized the vanity of these things, staged these vulgar games in order to curry favor with the people, and thus depleted the treasury and diverted the money for other than intended uses. But if I were to speak of leaders who had lapsed in their own time into these sorts of errors and narrated the flights of madness of each one, my discussion would surely soon become disorganized and not at all germane to my topic. Therefore, I return at once to the main subject.

Now when a ruler has decreed that his people are to be burdened with some new tax, which he will never want to do unless in times of public need, he should make all understand that he is struggling with necessity and does it against his will. In short, he should argue that, except for the fact that events compelled him to levy the tax, he would gladly have done without it. It will also redound to his good reputation if he will have contributed some of his own money to the new tax. Thus he will show that he, the head of the people, is but one among them, and at the same time he will demonstrate his great moderation. This is exactly what the Roman Senate did during the Second Punic War, following the advice of the consul Valerius Laevinus, and this act has been remembered with great admiration by many generations.[58] However high it is, the exaction will always be judged lighter and milder. Although it was not spoken by a good prince, yet let us not forget the excellent advice he is said to have written to provincial officials who recommended burdening the provinces with new taxes: "Good shepherds ought to shear their sheep but not skin them."[59] And if such a saying applied to Roman provinces,

58. See Livy *Ab urbe condita* 26.34.
59. Suetonius *Tiberius* 32.

should it not also apply to one's homeland? Because I wish you to be compared only with the best and most outstanding of princes, I beg you to imitate this policy and follow the example of those just words and deeds which have merited great praise. When your tax collectors, therefore, offer you hope of large profits, follow the example of Antoninus Pius, of whom it is written that he was never pleased by any income gained at the expense of his provincial subjects.[60] How much less should you want to cause any harm to your own subjects? Similarly, Constantius uttered a laudable sentiment: "I would rather have the public wealth distributed among my subjects than closed up in my treasury."[61] Now his policy has two rationales. First of all, it is better for riches to be held and enjoyed by many than by one person, and, second, it is more useful for private citizens to earn money from their own industry. What is a treasury but an inert and useless mass of metal heaped up on account of greed? Who cannot see that the wealth of the citizens is also the wealth of the prince? And it is *vice versa*, as Lucan writes: "The poverty of a servant is harmful, not to the servant, but to the master."[62]

And there are other even easier ways of gaining your subjects' affections—ways that are, I admit, difficult for a haughty prince, but in those cases where the prince's temperament tends toward humane behavior these methods are easy and pleasant. For instance, you have a tale that is told as follows: "Hadrian liked to visit twice or three times a day the sick, now of the equestrian order, now of the class of freedmen. These he revived with consolation, and he raised up their spirits with encouraging words. He always invited some of them to dine at his own table."[63] Now who can there be with such a terrible disposition that he would not be moved by such solicitous acts by his lord? And no one is more well endowed with these qualities than you are. Hence, all you have to do is to follow your own good instincts and everything you want will come to you. So be compassionate to those who are suffering from sickness or some other misadventure, and, if you

---

60. *Scriptores historiae Augustae* 3.6.1.
61. Eutropius *Brevarium ab urbe condita* 10.1.
62. Lucan *De bello civili* 3.152.
63. *Scriptores historiae Augustae* 1.9.7.

can, you ought to give them some help. But I do not doubt that you already act in this way. For who except a barbarian would remain unmoved when exhorted to help those whom he loves.

Furthermore, just as the love of the people is gained more easily by mercy and generosity than by any other quality, so, conversely, nothing is more guaranteed to provoke a people's hatred than cruelty and greed. If you compare the two evils you will see that while cruelty is harsher, greed is much more common. Cruelty is harsher but it only afflicts a few people, while greed is not so harsh but it affects everyone. Innumerable tyrants and princes have been undone by these two vices and made themselves hated and maligned through the centuries. But it is not necessary to speak with you concerning the vice of cruelty at any length because you are not merely a stranger to it but positively opposed to practicing it. Thus I would judge that nothing would be more difficult than for a merciful person such as yourself to commit, or even to consider committing, a cruel act against someone else. Cruelty is the quality of an ignoble, capricious, and treacherous person—someone quite different from yourself—a person quick to wreak vengeance when the possibility is offered. This vice is foreign to human nature and especially alien to the dignity of a prince, whose power to mete out vengeance is sufficient revenge. For this reason that short saying of Hadrian has been admired for a long time. Speaking to one who had been his mortal enemy when he was a private citizen and who now, seeing Hadrian emperor, was justly afraid and awaited all kinds of punishment, Hadrian said with a placid brow: "You have escaped."[64] But no more about this need be said, except that it seems to me that humanity is the high expression of human nature. Without this a person is not only not good but, indeed, cannot even be called a man.

It is more difficult, however, to banish greed completely from one's character. What person is there who does not lust after something? But I beg and beseech you that since, by God's grace, you have the means of leading a magnificent style of life, you will always hold a lustful appetite in check. Greed is insatiable, inexhaustable, and infinite, and whoever is governed by greed loses his own property while he desires that of another. Do you, perhaps,

64. *Scriptores historiae Augustae* 1.17.1.

wonder at this opinion? This much is certain: whoever desires
something very much and does not get it often forgets what he
already has. Thus inattentive persons lose their way, and, intent on
riches, they do not perceive immediate dangers; indeed, I don't
think a mortal life can suffer an evil greater than this one. You
ought not say to yourself what so many others do: "I am all right
for the moment, but what is going to become of me later on?"
Isn't this worrying about what is going to happen many years
hence rather silly when no one knows what the next hour may
bring? Leave aside these useless preoccupations, for it is written:
"Abandon yourself to the care of the Lord and He will nourish
you, and He will never let the righteous be shaken."[65] Why do
you waver? Why do you fear? Why do you worry? Don't you
know that the Lord cares for you? You have a good shepherd; He
will never fail you, He will never desert you. Again, it is written:
"Reveal your needs and go to the Lord and place your trust in Him,
and He will care for you."[66] Now some may say that this is good
advice for monks but not for princes. Such a critic does not understand, however, that princes ought to adhere to God and love and
put their trust in Him because they have received more great
benefits from Him. It is a kind of ingratitude to expect only a little
from Him who has given you so much. God is the one who has
nurtured you from infancy and who will care for you until the last.
God will never abandon hope in you whom He did not abandon
even when you could not hope in Him; indeed, even while you
were growing larger in your mother's womb.

Once you have overcome this difficult evil of greed, I shall show
you another sort of greed that is generous and above reproach; you
must lust after the treasure of virtue and win the fame of outstanding glory. This is a property that moths and rust cannot corrupt,
nor can thieves steal it in the night.[67] Now, except in the case of
war (as has recently happened to you)[68] or in the event of some
unavoidable difficulty, you should avoid anyone who wants his
lord to take over property at the expense of others. Indeed, such

65. Ps. 54:22 (Vulgate numbering).

66. Ps. 36.5–6 (Vulgate numbering).

67. An echo from Luke 12:33.

68. Another allusion to the border war fought against Venice in 1372–73.
See n. 4 above.

urgings are the practice of almost all courtiers. Hence, you should view persons who advise such a policy as the enemies of your good reputation and mortal soul. Such evil courtiers arouse their lords so that as they steal and pillage the property of others, thus earning the hatred of their subjects and this iniquitous kind of men so oppresses the people and deceives their lords that they bring to ruin both their lords and themselves. Concerning such matters, there is that true and famous saying of Marius Maximus—as Elius Lampridius records it in his history of the Emperor Alexander— and these are his very words: "The state in which the ruler is evil is happier and almost more secure than the one in which he has evil friends; for, indeed, one evil man can be made better by many righteous men, but in no way can many evil men be held in check by one man, however righteous he may be."[69] Hence, this Alexander was a good prince, for, besides his own innate virtues of character, he also had, as the same historian writes, friends "who were up- right and respected, never spiteful, or thieving, or seditious, or cunning, or leagued together for evil, or hateful to the righteous, or lustful, or cruel, or deceivers of their prince, or mockers, or desir- ous of hoodwinking him like a fool. But, on the contrary, they were upright, revered, temperate, pious, fond of their prince, men who neither mocked him themselves nor wished him to become an object of mockery by others, who sold nothing, who lied in no matter, who falsified nothing, and who never tricked their lord so that he might love them."[70] So, according to this author, such are the friends whom a prince ought to want and seek out. The other type ought to be avoided like the plague by the prince and to be excluded from his circle as though they were public enemies. These courtiers are the masters of evil arts who have never known and always hated good morals. Moreover, these men are eager to teach the greedy ways they so like to their own princes, so that if the princes are persuaded to follow their evil ways, they can be transformed into the worst of men. For if greed is an evil in the private citizen, how much worse is it in princes.

Just as a prince has such a capacity for harming, and just as contempt for base things is a very fine quality in a prince, so a prince's greed and desire for treasure and riches is very ugly. Not

69. *Scriptores historiae Augustae* 18.65.4.
70. *Scriptores historiae Augustae* 18.66.2.

without good reason, that very wise emperor Marcus Aurelius (whom I have had occasion to mention earlier) used to say: "In an emperor avarice is the most grievous of all evils."[71] For this failing alone did Pertinax and Galba suffer on account of their cruelty. Therefore, all those who love virtue and wish to have a good reputation should avoid and despise the evil of greed. But, most of all, princes should avoid greed because they are the leaders of men and in their care has been placed vast sums and much property as well as the state itself. And if they will administer their governments properly, they are certain to consider wealth foul corruption and obtain the treasures that are most prized, namely, an easy and clear conscience and the love of God and of their fellow men. Those who follow their own desires will only come to ruin, for they will never satisfy their insatiable desires and they will surely earn the hatred of God and of men. Both the consensus of the wise and experience itself—that infallible mistress of truth—teach that greed for wealth is never extinguished but only grows stronger. Concerning this question the best advice was given by Epicurus, who said that to become rich one did not need to increase his property but rather to curb his own desires.[72] Hence it is obvious that those things that are called riches are not really riches, for if they were, they would really make one rich, but they do not. In fact, all the treasure under the sun will not make one rich. Rather, consider the brief and modest axiom that in abandoning greed we approach nature more closely.

Indeed, there are many ways of acquiring money (as Aristotle points out in the *Economics*),[73] and to these the courtiers of the princes of our own age have added innumerable other methods. Consequently, the Philosopher now seems to have been quite unlearned in these matters. But these talents ought to be despised and condemned by a good prince, just as he ought to hate anything instituted for mere expediency to the detriment of justice. Rather, he ought to keep in mind that precept of the most learned and wisest of men: Nothing can be useful that is not at the same time just and honorable.[74] In the case of some courtiers, when they are

---

71. *Scriptores historiae Augustae* 6.8.2.
72. Cf. Seneca *Epistolae* 21.7ff.
73. See Aristotle *Economica* 2. 1345b5–1353b41.
74. Cf. Cicero *De officiis* 3.3.11.

good no one could be better (but this is very rare), and when they are bad nothing could be worse (and this is often the case); on this subject you have had my final thoughts. No, not really my thoughts but those of the emperor Diocletian, for although Diocletian was very harsh in his persecutions of the practitioners of Christianity, still he may be considered among the outstanding emperors. Here are his words, written down, unless I am mistaken, as they appear in a book on the life of the emperor Aurelius: "Four or five men gather together and devise a plan for deceiving the emperor, and so they tell him to what policies he ought to give his approval. Now the emperor, who is shut up in his palace, cannot know the truth. He is forced to believe only what these men tell him. He appoints as judges men who ought never to be appointed to that office and he removes from public office precisely those officials whom he ought to retain." What more can be said? As Diocletain himself was wont to say: "The favor of even a good and wise and righteous emperor is often sold."[75] When for these and other reasons he was finally persuaded to step down from the throne, he concluded: "There is nothing more difficult than to rule well."[76] And indeed it is so. Princes should not think that they can enjoy both happiness and ease in governing; perhaps they will find happiness, but I don't think that it will happen very often. If you don't believe me, just ask some prince who has had a great deal of experience in governing.

From this question I proceed to a topic concerning which I cannot warn or advise you enough, namely, never act in such a way so as to give control of the state to one of your courtiers and thus give Padua a lord other than yourself. History has seen many instances of princes who wanted to exalt their followers but who actually debased themselves and became contemptible and despised in the eyes of their subjects and ultimately were jeered at and reduced to poverty by the very men they had promoted. Because of such a disaster the emperor Claudius, who preceded Nero, was regraded as vile. He accorded many favors to his worthless freedmen, Posides, Felix, Narcissus, and Pallas, and gave them control over the provinces so that they despoiled the Empire and Claudius himself. At last he was reduced to begging from his former ser-

75. *Scriptores historiae Augustae* 26.43.3.
76. *Scriptores historiae Augustae* 26.43.2.

vants, now affluent. "Dependent on these men and their wives," Suetonius says, "Claudius acted more like a vile slave than an emperor."[77] Guided and compelled by such men, he acted very stupidly and very cruelly. The same mistake was made by the emperor Heliogabalus, who, to the grief of all good men, let those around him have great power and put everything up for sale, while dishonest friends made the emperor, as Lampridius says, "even more of a fool than he was naturally."[78] And Didius Julianus merits the same condemnation because he gave the power to rule to precisely those men whom he ought to have kept under his own authority.[79] Of course, there are always stupid and mediocre princes under whom such a state of affairs has to be tolerated. I know, however, that there is nothing mediocre about you, nothing that is not singular and outstanding. Indeed, you will not fulfill my hopes or those of many others unless you at least reach or even surpass the achievement of many good and outstanding rulers. And if you fail to achieve this I will not attribute it to a lack of natural ability but to the failure of your will.

But why should we talk only about lesser emperors when we can cite the example of such an outstanding man as the Emperor Marcus Aurelius over whom mere freedmen exercised a great deal of control?[80] Because of this sort of example, it is proper to warn fervently anyone like yourself, who proposes to excel and govern, that you should watch diligently and not permit yourself (as many outstanding princes have) to fall into this vice using the benevolent disposition (which you possess) as an excuse. Although it is well to imitate illustrious men, you should not follow their example in every particular. There is no one who does not occasionally make a mistake and thus fall short of his potential for excellence.

But you will say, and perhaps you have already said to yourself, that I am advising you to be ungrateful to your courtiers. If I did that, how then would I be allowed to enjoy the gifts that you have already bestowed on me? Would I really advise you to be niggardly? Never! Nothing is more wicked in a prince, more wicked in a man, than ingratitude. Every virtue has some distractors, every vice some

77. See Suetonius *Claudius* 28.
78. *Scriptores historiae Augustae* 17.15.1–2.
79. *Scriptores historiae Augustae* 9.9.4.
80. Cf. *Scriptores historiae Augustae* 4.15.2.

defenders. Only ingratitude never pleases anyone, and, conversely, gratitude displeases no one. But there are a great many things that you can bestow on those who merit rewards: horses, clothing, arms, plates, money, dwellings, land, and so forth. Follow, however, what is written in the Bible: "Do not bestow your honor on another."[81] I know well that you are ready to share cheerfully with your friends not only your own power but even your very life. But I beg you—not only for your own sake but for the sake of your country, which God gave you to govern. Nothing could be worse, nothing more harmful to the Paduan people, than to obey many chiefly unworthy men placed above them. At present all the citizens regard you as their lord, they all respect, admire, and even venerate you, and they look upon your courtiers not as rulers but as representatives who have been sent out to execute your orders. They see the courtiers as private persons with neither the dignity nor the power that you alone ought to possess. And there are other reasons why what I am saying is important; I myself have observed the unbelievable patience with which several citizen-bodies have suffered the rule of harsh and demanding lords who ruled alone. Conversely, I have seen a people become indignant and rebellious when more than one lord tried to command their respect and obedience. Indeed, unless I am entirely mistaken, we discussed this very subject when you did me the honor to visit me in my rustic retreat a year or so ago.

Now it would be superfluous for me to write you concerning the other type of friends, the ones who are not seeking your wealth but who respect and honor you for what you are. This topic is really unnecessary because you are among the most faithful and upright cultivators of friendship, and since Cicero has already discussed that topic in his elegant little book.[82] Putting all this into a few words, we can say that in human affairs nothing is sweeter than friendship, and, after virtue, nothing is more sacred. Those who rule over others by their power and ability especially have need of true friends who will stick with them through thick and thin. You should never ask a friend to do anything dishonorable, nor should you ever do anything dishonorable on behalf of a

81. Prov. 5:9.
82. A reference to Cicero's *De amicitia,* from which Petrarch derived some of the ideas in this section.

friend. But nothing honorable is to be denied to a friend. Now you ought to adopt this principle: Among friends everything ought to be held in common, all should act with one accord and by common consent; and what friends agree to ought never to be changed simply because of other expectations, fear, or some imminent danger. Each person ought to love his friend as himself and to overlook any difference in status or wealth. In short, seek to act as Pythagoras orders: "Several persons are gathered in one."[83] Likewise, the conditions of true friendship are expressed in Holy Scripture, where in the Acts of the Apostles it is written: "The company of those who believed and who loved one another in Christ was of one head and one soul, and no one of them, whatever he possessed, claimed it for his own use, and all their property was held in common."[84] If someone were to define friendship as being faithful and lovers in Christ, I certainly would not contradict him, because I do not believe there can be friendship, or any firm or stable relationship for that matter, except that Christ be the foundation. At the same time, however, I am in agreement with the opinion of the pagan philosophers that there can be no true friendship without there being at the same time true wisdom and virtue. In saying this I am not following those who say with a foolish sophistry that there never has been nor ever will be anyone called wise. I am not discussing here impossibilities, but I am content with what the human condition is capable of creating,[85] and surely we must number among these things the sort of friendship that I have just been talking about. Although it is true that we can actually name very few pairs of friends who knew a perfect and consummate friendship such as the younger Scipio and Laelius were famous for, still there has often been practiced among men a pleasant and fine sort of friendship. In this relationship there was never any fawning adulation, nor disparaging remarks, nor back-biting, and no discord or reproach. In fact, there was nothing in these friendships that did not lead to the pleasure and honor of the friends and to peace, harmony, and good fellowship. In these friendships there was nothing false, no dissembling, nothing duplicitous, but only what was pure, candid, and open. In these

83. Quoted in Cicero *De officiis* 1.17.56.
84. Acts 4:32.
85. Cicero *De amicitia* 5.18.

cases many things were held or done in common: advice, work, honors, wealth, talent, and even life itself. We know that such friendships have been frequent in history, and they have often, and rightly, been praised. But I have already spoken at length concerning these things, so it ought to be now an easy matter to distinguish a true friendship from a false one. For the time being enough has been said.

From here on I shall proceed without any preconceived plan and treat what I deem important, setting down with my pen whatever topic may come to mind. I would like to add another topic to those things that I have been discussing about fellowship and generosity toward a friend. The saying of Martial is especially true today: "Wealth is given to none but the rich."[86] Indeed, there are many crafty and cunning men who do get rich. Cicero has described the system by which you make many benefactions at interest and especially generous ones to those whom you are certain will return your benefactions manyfold.[87] But you, on the contrary, who never seek any reward from your gifts except to give benefits and obtain from this the happiness of a mind at peace with itself, act contrary to the habits of the greedy. Always make donations to the neediest and do not simply give away your own wealth; when you receive voluntary donations from the rich you should give them to the poor. You have in this matter the precedent of Alexander, who (as I have said) made exactly such benefactions when he was still an outstanding youth and prince.[88] Nor am I unaware that in what I have just been advising I may seem to be speaking against my own case. Although I am not so rich a man as to arouse envy, as the recipient of both your own generosity and that of your father, I lack nothing, a condition that in my view means the highest wealth. But when I gave this advice I was thinking neither of myself nor of others, but only of your own best interests.

Now there is another thing I want to discuss with you, something that ought to please you very much. I know, of course, that generosity is praised in a prince more than humility. Perhaps this is as it should be. But I really do think that both qualities are

86. Martial *Satirae* 5.81.2.
87. Cicero *De amicitia* 9.31.
88. *Scriptores historiae Augustae* 18.21.2.

worthy of praise and that one quality does not necessarily exclude the other, as foolish men often think. For in this matter, as in almost all things, the mob of men is mistaken. They call magnificence pride, and they consider humility to be timidness; both opinions are wrong. I would like you to be a prince who is humble at home among his own people and in prosperity while being magnanimous facing his enemies in adversity. In neither case is such a prince acting timidly or proudly. Indeed, it seems to me that humility is in the first rank of all the virtues. However, some stupid and blind rulers do not feel that they can be truly great lords unless they are swaggering and prideful beyond human dimensions. This is really just the idiocy of ignorant princes. Caligula, that vilest of emperors, was not content with the honors due him as a man; he wished to be worshipped as a god. Consequently, he placed statues of himself in the temples so that he, who was certainly unworthy to be revered as a god, would be worshipped and venerated. He even established his own temple where priests sacrificed victims before his golden effigy.[89] Caligula did many other things that he thought would bring him greater honor but that really only served to disclose his own stupidity. Is there anyone more evil, more monstrous than the emperor Commodus? Indeed, sacrifices were even made to this most evil son of an illustrious father, just as one would offer to a god. Statues in the form of Hercules were raised to Commodus, who certainly was not a god nor even really a man, but a cruel and ferocious beast.[90] Even Heliogabalus himself, that vilest of princes and of men, began to be worshipped. All of these emperors merited being murdered on the spot and having their bodies thrown into the Tiber or into sewers.[91]

I must confess that I am reluctant to speak of these crimes, and I am saddened and ashamed that these men so polluted with sins were our emperors. I have been discussing this matter, however, not because I enjoy it but because the truth compels me to. In like manner, these northern barbarians of our own time ought to be less angry at me if, when I speak of them, I am moved by a

89. Cf. Suetonius *Caligula* 22.
90. Cf. *Scriptores historiae Augustae* 7.9.2.
91. Cf. *Scriptores historiae Augustae* 18.17.2–3.

desire to tell the truth more than by hatred.[92] For I do not hate men; I hate vice, and I hate it more (not less) in us Italians than in other people. Similarly, a farmer is bothered more by rocks, tares, and thistles on his own farm than he is by finding them in another man's field. Yet I must confess that I really cannot bear the vain boasting of that good-for-nothing northern people that is always ready to lie about its accomplishments and brag about what it thinks are its glorious achievements. But, lest I get into a new dispute with those who are not even present, I shall return to my topic.

After those bad emperors, Diocletian wanted to be worshipped like a god and encrusted his shoes as well as his clothing with gems. In this fashion he transformed the dress of Roman emperors into a new style,[93] a great novelty for a man otherwise serious and disciplined and one who finally abdicated his throne in order to enjoy a peaceful retirement. Hence, I can only think that this desire for pomp and circumstance derives not from a desire for true glory but from a weak mind. Now it often seems to base persons that when they have attained high office, they have reached heaven, so that losing their perspective they lose control. On the contrary, no earthly honor is of much importance to the truly magnanimous leader. He does not strive to seem more than he really is. For example, the greatest and best of emperors, Caesar Augustus, did not hanker after divine honors, nor did he allow himself to be worshipped.[94] Indeed, he did not want to be called "lord," even by his children or grandchildren. For he believed (as Suetonius says) that "the name of 'lord' ought always to be abhorred as a curse and an insult."[95] Hence he forbade the use of the term, and he reproved anyone who dared to use it with a threatening word, a look, or a gesture. Likewise, did Alexander—and I don't mean that king of the Macedons who surpassed everyone in vanity and pride and who, after he had conquered the Persians, was himself conquered by Persian customs. Then impelled by some madness, this Alexander came to want himself worshipped like a

92. Probably an allusion to a French critic of Italy, whom Petrarch had recently inveighed against in his *Invectiva contra eum qui maledixit Italie.*

93. Eutropius 9.26.

94. Suetonius *Divus Augustus* 52

95. Suetonius *Divus Augustus* 53.

god and the son of a god following the Persian belief much to the harm of true religious practice. No, I am speaking of that other Alexander, the Roman emperor, whom we have often mentioned today, and who not only forbade the worship of himself but even enjoined that he be greeted in no other way than "Hello, Alexander."[96] If anyone dared to greet him with a bow of the head or any grand title, he either banished him from his presence or ridiculed him harshly with a loud guffaw.[97]

Now if I know you and your beliefs well (and after so many years I cannot help but know them), I have no doubt that you bear the title of "lord" more with patience than with pleasure. I have heard you say more than once, and really affirm it almost under oath, that the lordship of Padua was not a pleasure to you and that you would gladly relinquish it if it were not for the fear that an intruder might invade the city and place the Paduan people under oppressive rule and compel you unwillingly to live under a lord. Otherwise, I would much prefer that you were a free private citizen than a ruling lord, for then you could live of your own wealth and you could—as an important man free of the cares of governing— enjoy a quiet and profitable prime of life and, when it came, an honorable old age. From all this it is abundantly clear to me that you do not take pride in something unless you value it very highly. But since it is difficult to change a people's habits and to abolish longstanding customs, you should bear with the Paduan people and let them call you "lord" if they want to. After all, you can always speak of yourself as you see fitting and proper. Now I know that you never apply to yourself in speech or writing the name, "lord." Thus you reject the present usage of most other lords and princes. You sign your name at the bottom of your letters without any title; you never use the plural but always the singular form of address— and not just with superiors but with equals and inferiors as well. Even to me (and there is no one more humble), you never say "we" (as other lords do), but rather you say: "I wish this, I beg this, I order this." When I read these phrases in your letters I am pleased, and I say to myself that if this man really had an inflated opinion of himself his style of writing would show it too. Other princes wish to appear as more than one person, but they are not

96. *Scriptores historiae Augustae* 18.18.3.
97. *Scriptores historiae Augustae* 17.4–18.1.

even one; in fact, they are nothing. You are doing in this instance a fine thing; unwittingly, and from your own sound instincts, you are imitating the great leaders of ancient Rome. Look at the letters of Julius Caesar and of Augustus (some of which you will find preserved in the works of Josephus and others in Suetonius) and you will never find "we" written there. You will never find "we wish" or "we command," but instead "I wish," "I command," and the like. Indeed, it is—just as you are accustomed to joke— that those who speak of themselves in the plural seem to be naming not just themselves but their wives, children, and servants as well. But you speak only in your own name, and it is you (and no one else) who commands and orders your followers. I have nothing but admiration for your character and your manner and your style of writing, practiced not only by the contemporary leaders I have mentioned but by almost all of the ancient Roman emperors as well. This we know from many letters found in many different books. I mention it in the hope that you will be proud of your style of address while other princes will be made ashamed of theirs, which they consider to be a mark of great status when, in fact, it is an obvious indication of their inferiority and timidity.

Further, to your modesty in speech there is joined another modesty, a modesty in dress that is obvious to everyone. Thus, one modest habit merits approval through the eyes of the beholder while the other comes through the ears, and both together convey through the intellect and the senses the impression of a very modest person and a complete gentleman. Many other lords display themselves before their subjects covered, and even ladened down, with gold and finery[98]—rather like altars decorated for a high feast day—and they consider themselves very important merely because they are laden down with precious clothing. You, on the other hand, are content with modest dress, so that you prove to be a lord on account of neither costly clothing nor display but from the dignity of your manner and the authority of your bearing. This is a double good, just as the opposite is a double evil. Vulgar display is hateful in itself, and it often leads to the dangerous disease of imitation. Every people strives to imitate the deeds and habits of its prince. Hence, there is that very true saying

98. See Cicero *Tusculanae disputationes* 1.14.34, quoting Ennius.

that there is nothing more harmful to the state than the bad example of its prince. And in complete truth, the poet says: "The whole world follows the king's example."[99] There you have it: the bad habits of princes are dangerous not just to themselves but to everyone. Concerning this there is a very apposite passage in the third book of Cicero's *On the Laws:*

> For it is not so mischievous that men of high position do evil—though this evil is bad enough in itself—as it is that these men have so many imitators. For if you will turn your thoughts back to history, you will see that the character or our most prominent men has been reproduced in the whole state; whatever change took place in the lives of the prominent men has also taken place in the whole people. And we can be much more confident of the soundness of this than of what so pleased our beloved Plato. He thought that the characteristics of a nation could be changed by changing the character of its music. But I believe that a transformation takes place in a nation's character when the habits and mode of living of its aristocracy are changed. For this reason, men of the upper class who do wrong are especially dangerous to the state, because they not only indulge in vicious practices themselves, but also infect the whole commonwealth with their vices, and not only because they are corrupt, but also because they corrupt, others and do more harm by their bad example than by their sin.[100]

So much for Cicero. Indeed, I myself, when I have been with you and others, used to say: "This prince will teach boasting to no one; he will lead no one into pompous ways." And I have often reflected upon what Livy wrote about Hannibal: "He was equal to all others in dress, he stood out only in arms and in horses."[101] However, this is not such great praise for a soldier in time of war, when, of necessity, all comforts must be excluded. You show modesty in times of peace and prosperity, which are the mothers of immoderation and luxury. Therefore, when I consider your dress, the matter

99. Claudian *De quarto consulatu Honorii Augusti* 299–300.
100. Cicero *De legibus* 3.14.31.
101. Cf. Livy *Ab urbe condita* 21.4.8.

ought not to be compared with that of Hannibal, which I have just been describing, but with that of Augustus, under whose reign all kings and people enjoyed a universal peace. Concerning him it is written that he wore only clothes made at home by his wife, his sister, his daughter, and his granddaughters.[102]

Now there are many topics that I still might discuss if I did not fear that I might exhaust your patience (perhaps already wearied with all that I have said up to now). But there is one topic that I simply cannot pass over, a practice that will make princes both respected and venerated (and indeed on this theme you need no exhortation). In short, I appeal that you honor famous men and hold them in esteem and friendship. You are so eager to do this that you could not do otherwise (even if you wanted to)—your very nature would stop you—for a leader does nothing better than what he does following his own nature. Custom is a strong force, training is stronger still, nature is more so, but if all three are joined together it becomes the most effective. Now I view as outstanding those men who are set apart from the common herd of humanity by some singular quality; this could be outstanding justice or holiness (which these days is virtually nonexistent), or military skill and experience, or profound learning in literature and science. Although (as Cicero says in the first book of *On Duties*) "most people think that military science is more important than knowledge of government, their opinion is really quite mistaken."[103] He has pointed out many Greek and Roman leaders who were examples of this fact; Themistocles and Solon, Lysander and Lycurgus, and from the Romans, Gaius Marius and Marcus Scaurus, Gneus Pompeius and Quintus Catulus, the younger Scipio and Publius Nasica, and since Cicero wanted fame and glory for himself, he also added his own name to the list.[104] And indeed this judgment is not without justice, for I do not doubt that Anthony did no more for the good of Rome when he defeated Catiline on the field of battle than did Cicero himself when he exposed Catiline's horrible conspiracy to the Senate and threw the conspirators into prison.

102. Cf. Suetonius *Divus Augustus* 73.
103. Cicero *De officiis* 1.22.74.
104. Cicero *De officiis* 1.22.75–76 provided Petrarch with this list of great leaders from antiquity.

Among those honored for their abilities in governing, the first place ought to go to learned men. And among these learned men, a major place should go to those whose knowledge in law is always very useful to the state. If, indeed, love of and devotion to justice is added to their knowledge of law, these citizens are (as Cicero puts it) "learned not just in the law, but in justice."[105] However, there are those who follow the law but do no justice, and these are unworthy to bear the name of the legal profession. For it is not enough simply to have knowledge; you must want to use it. A good lawyer adds good intentions to his legal knowledge. Indeed, there have been many lawyers who have added luster to ancient Rome and other places: Adrianus Julius Celsus, Salvius Julianus, Neratius Priscus, Antonius Scaevola, Severus Papinianus, Alexander Domitius Ulpianus, Fabius Sabinus, Julius Paulus, and many others.[106] And you too (as much as our own times permit) have by the patronage of your university added honor to your country. There are other kinds of learned men, some of whom you can depend on for advice and learned conversation, and (as Alexander used to say) invent literary tales.[107] One reads that Julius Caesar, in like fashion, used to confer Roman citizenship on doctors of medicine and on teachers of the liberal arts.[108] Now, among learned men there is no doubt that we ought to give preference to those who teach the knowledge of sacred things (or what we call theology), provided that these men have kept themselves free from any foolish sophistries.

That very wise emperor Augustus used to bestow patronage on learned men to encourage them to remain in Rome, and hope of such a reward stimulated others to study, for at that time Roman citizenship was a highly valued honor. Indeed, when St. Paul claimed that he was a Roman citizen, the tribune judging the case said to him: "I myself have at a high price obtained this status."[109] You, my great lord, do not have such rewards in your gift, but you can do this: you can give learned and distinguished men

105. Cicero *Orationes Philippicae* 9.5.10.
106. Petrarch derived this list of famous legal experts from the time of the Roman Empire mainly from his reading of the *Scriptores historiae Augustae*, passim.
107. *Scriptores historiae Augustae* 18.34.6.
108. Suetonius *Divus Julius* 42.
109. Acts 22:28.

dedicated to honorable studies a place among your citizen-body. So be generous and kind to scholars, and Padua will be filled with learned men and its university restored to its ancient glory. Nothing entices outstanding men so much as the friendship and patronage of a prince. Caesar Augustus gathered together his famous troop of scholars and artists with his hospitality and patronage rather than with the power of his empire. He numbered among his friends Cicero in the beginning, and then Asinius Pollio, Valerius Messala, and Parius Geminus, all great orators, as well as Vergil and Horace, outstanding poets to whom he wrote personal letters. It was clear from these letters that the supreme ruler of the inhabited world treated these two rustics—one from Mantua, the other from Verona—not just as his equals but even as his superiors. By his example Augustus taught others that no ruler should be ashamed to enjoy the friendship of commoners who had been ennobled by their own genius and learning. Who could possibly be ashamed of such a friendship if the Emperor Augustus were not ashamed of it? Later on he was also friendly with Tucca and Varius of Cremona and with Ovid of Sulmona, though Augustus did eventually find Ovid unworthy and banished him from his court. And there were others, including Marcus Varro, perhaps the most learned of all, and the Paduan Titus Livy, the father of history who, if he were alive today, would be your fellow citizen. So at this one moment in history these and many others were gathered around Augustus so that he was made glorious as much by these illustrious men as by the conquests of all his Roman legions. Can the thirty-five tribes of Rome or her forty-four valorous legions really be compared to that one great man, Vergil, who so honored Augustus with his friendship? Vergil still lives by his fame; the others have long since perished. Indeed, learned men attracted by this famous imperial generosity came from Greece as well as from Italy. Now I am asking you: where can a talented and intelligent man be happier and lead a better life than under the benevolent gaze of a just and generous prince? I sincerely believe that if it were not for the bonds of your own generosity, a great many scholars who have come to Padua would soon leave. For my part, I praise and laud your patronage. Although soldiers can at times be useful to you and perform good services in time of war, it is only learned men who can provide the right advice at the right moment, and thus ensure the fame of your name. Moreover, they can show you the proper road to heaven, you can mount on the wings of their expert advice, and, if you get lost, you can find your way again by following their counsel.

But I have said enough, I fear even too much. At the beginning of this letter I had intended that I would exhort you, at its end, to correct the morals of your subjects. Yet I now think this would be an impossible task, for it is always difficult to change what had evolved out of custom. It cannot be done by force of law or by kings. Hence, I have changed my aim because it is always useless to attempt the impossible. However, there is one custom among the Paduan people that I cannot overlook. And I will not simply ask you, but I shall implore you, to correct this public evil with your own hand. Now don't say to me that this evil that I want you to correct is not unique to Padua but common to many other cities. This is a question of your own dignity, and just as you have been the beneficiary of many individual gifts, so that you now excel your contemporaries, Padua has received many gifts from you so that it excels all the neighboring cities.

Now you should certainly know, best of men, that it is written in the Old Testament: "Everyone dies."[110] The New Testament says: "It is established that every man dies once."[111] And among the pagan authors you find: "Death is certain, which day it will happen is uncertain."[112] Even if it were not written in any book, still death is certain, as our common nature tells us. Now I do not know whether it is because of human nature or from some long-standing custom that at the death of our close friends and relatives we can scarcely contain our grief and tears, and that our funeral services are often attended by wailings and lamentations. But I do know that scarcely ever has this propensity for public grief been so deep-rooted in other cities as it is in yours. Someone dies—and I do not care whether he is a noble or a commoner, the grief displayed by the commoners is certainly no less manifest, and perhaps more so, than that of the nobles, for the plebs are more apt to show their emotions and less likely to be moved by what is proper; as soon as he breathes his last, a great howling and torrent of tears

110. 2 Kings 13:14.
111. Hebrews 9:27.
112. Cf. Cicero *Tusculanae disputationes* 1.48.115.

begins. Now I am not asking you to forbid expressions of grief. This would be difficult and probably impossible, given human nature. But what Jeremiah says is true: "You should not bemoan the dead, nor bathe the corpse in tears."[113] As that great poet Euripides wrote in Crespontes: "Considering the evil of our present existence, we ought to lament at our birth and rejoice at our death."[114] But these philosophic opinions are not well known, and, in any case, the common people would find them unthinkable and strange.

Therefore, I will tell you what I am asking. Take an example: Some old dowager dies, and they carry her body into the streets and through the public squares accompanied by loud and indecent wailing so that someone who did not know what was happening could easily think that here was a madman on the loose or that the city was under enemy attack. Now, when the funeral cortege finally gets to the church, the horrible keening redoubles, and at the very spot where there ought to be hymns to Christ or devoted prayers for the soul of the deceased in a subdued voice or even silence, the walls resound with the lamentations of the mourners and the holy altars shake with the wailing of women. All this simply because a human being has died. This custom is contrary to any decent and honorable behavior and unworthy of any city under your rule. I wish you would have it changed. In fact, I am not just advising you, I am (if I may) begging you to do so. Order that wailing women should not be permitted to step outside their homes; and if some lamentation is necessary to the grieved, let them do it at home and do not let them disturb the public thoroughfares.

I have said to you perhaps more than I should, but less than I would like to say. And if it seems to you, illustrious sir, that I am mistaken in one place or another, I beg your pardon, and I ask you to consider only the good advice. May you rule your city long and happily. Farewell. Arquà, the 28th of November.

113. Jeremiah 22:10.
114. Cf. Cicero *Tusculanae disputationes* 1.48.115, quoting Euripides.

COLUCCIO
SALUTATI

Introduction

RONALD G. WITT

Compared with Padua, Verona, Milan, and Bologna, Florence in the opening decades of the fourteenth century played only a secondary role in the early development of interest in intensive study of ancient Latin prose and poetry. Dante demonstrated his ability to imitate ancient pastoral poetry only toward the end of his life, after a decade and a half of exile from the city and after extensive contact with northern Italian intellectuals. By mid-century wherever Petrarch dwelt was the center of the new humanism, and Petrarch chose to make his residence in northern Italy. Petrarch had his admirers in Florence, a circle of scholars that included men like Zanobi da Strada and Giovanni Boccaccio. Yet their contribution to the new cultural movement was not of such significance as to make Florence, rather than Milan or Padua, the natural capital of humanism once the great master disappeared from the scene. That Florence attained the leading position by the end of the fourteenth century was owing largely to the efforts of Coluccio Salutati (1331–1406), the Florentine chancellor.

Coluccio Salutati was born in a frontier province of the Florentine Republic in 1331. In the months preceding his birth a Ghibelline faction supported by troops from Lucca overran his family's homeland, the commune of Buggiano, forcing Salutati's father, a leader of the local Guelfs, to flee into exile.[1] The family finally settled in Bologna, where the father, Piero, worked for the tyrant of Bologna, Taddeo dei Pepoli. Thus Salutati had the advantage of growing up in the greatest university city of Italy. Of his teachers, Pietro da Moglio seems to have had the most influence on his development. If Salutati's later personal style derived directly from imitation of Petrarch, his official or public style, through which he first achieved international fame, probably owed much to da Moglio's training. When Salutati was seventeen he started the two-year course of training to prepare himself to become a notary. With this education he would know enough law to prepare contracts and wills for private clients and to draw up the variety of legal documents needed by governmental agencies.

In 1350 the Pepoli regime collapsed, and the now widowed mother of Salutati returned with her children to Buggiano, which had been back under Guelf Florence's rule since 1339. Over the next sixteen years Salutati earned a living as a private notary or as secretary of various communes in the Florentine contado. After the first few years he began to take an active role in his own commune's political affairs, and by the mid-1360s he emerged as one of the political leaders of the area. Whatever free time he had from this busy life he devoted to the study of classical literature. He became a correspondent and friend of a number of the intellectuals in the capital, including Boccaccio, and in 1366 he married.[2]

His appointment in August 1367 to be chancellor of the commune of Todi in papal territory marked the beginning of five years of employment outside Florentine territory. After a brief term at Todi, Salutati spent two years in Rome working in the papal chancery. Then in August 1370, largely through papal patronage, he was appointed chancellor of Lucca. At the end of the year appointment, however, Salutati was not rehired, and, after briefly acting as judge of the Merchants' Court of Lucca, he returned to

1. In the thirteenth century the Ghibellines were partisans of imperial power in Italy, while the Guelfs supported the papacy. In the fourteenth century even though the issues at stake were usually local or regional, the terminology continued to be used by factions throughout Italy.

2. On Salutati's life in the Valdinievole, see my "Coluccio Salutati and the Political Life of the Commune of Buggiano," *Rinascimento*, 6 (1966):27–55. The best biography of Salutati in any language is the work of Armando Petrucci, *Coluccio Salutati* (Rome, 1972).

Buggiano in mid-1372. His wife had died in Lucca, leaving him with a small child, and his grief over this loss was compounded by his disillusionment over what appeared to be professional failure. In February 1374, however, he was elected to the newly created office of notary of the elections in Florence, and in April of the next year he added to this position the prestigious office of chancellor of the Florentine Republic. By this time Salutati had not only remarried, but his wife, Piera, had already given birth to the first of what were to be at least ten children.

His appointment to this office occurred at the very outset of Florence's war against the papacy, and in the course of the three-year struggle Salutati established himself as the leading propagandist in Western Europe. Throughout the thirty-one years he served as chancellor Salutati's public letters, written in the name of the Florentine government, were important weapons in the Republic's arsenal. Florence's later arch enemy, the Duke of Milan, who at one point tried to have Salutati murdered, acknowledged the power of the chancellor's rhetoric when he reportedly remarked that one letter by Salutati "was worth a troop of horsemen."[3]

Despite his active employment as chancellor of the city, Salutati found time to devote himself to scholarship and to exchange ideas with a large circle of correspondents. The limited free time at his disposal helps in part to account for the fact that his writings appear less polished than those of Petrarch. Whereas Petrarch's writings usually offer only the results of his meditations, Salutati's display the process of thought itself. But a more important explanation of the difference between the two men derives from Salutati's conception of his role; he thought himself more a teacher than a stylist. Salutati gave extensive treatment (awkward from a stylistic standpoint) to explaining the proper spelling of words or to describing the procedure used in establishing the correct reading of a text. At the same time he was driven by a wide-ranging curiosity and an unembarrassed eagerness to learn, which led him to seek answers from those he thought would know. Consequently he made others, even younger scholars, feel not so much disciples but rather colleagues in a common cultural enterprise.

3. *Epistolario di Coluccio Salutati*, ed. Francesco Novati, 4 vols. (Rome, 1891–1911), 4:247–48, 514, provides versions of this statement supposedly made by Duke Giangaleazzo Visconti.

Although he failed to realize his hope to create a public library where texts of the ancient authors would be available in corrected editions, he made an extensive collection of manuscripts that significantly expanded Florence's treasury of ancient authors. He was almost solely responsible for having a chair of Greek created in the Florentine university in 1396.[4] While he seems to have never advanced very far in the language, younger Florentines developed such proficiency that before his death Salutati was able to use their earliest translations of Greek authors for his own work.

As a philologist Salutati became the first to differentiate between various periods in the development of ancient Latin literature itself.[5] In part this awareness grew out of his discovery that ancient Latin was not, as scholars in the Middle Ages believed, an immutable language, but rather, like modern languages, it too had experienced significant change.[6] Close analysis of style and attention to detail permitted him in a number of instances to sort out confusions in the history of Latin literature.[7] Through a profound knowledge of the sources and keen historical judgment, Salutati also worked out a very convincing account of the origins of the city of Florence.[8]

4. Emmanuel Chrysoloras was invited by the *Signoria* in March 1396 to accept a ten-year appointment as professor of Greek in the *Studio*. He did not arrive in Florence until February 1397 and terminated his teaching late in 1399. *Epistolario,* 3:120–21.

5. Salutati, in *Epistolario,* 3:80–82, was the first to distinguish between the Latin style of the late Republic and the Augustan age as superior to that of the immediately succeeding period; see Franco Simone, *Per una storia della storiografia letteraria francese,* Memorie dell' Accademia delle scienze di Torino, 4th ser. 12(1966):62–64.

6. The medieval scholars generally believed that Latin had greater dignity than modern languages because it had been created artificially. Modern languages were subject to constant change and were consequently more imperfect. Early humanists as a whole believed that medieval Latin represented a degenerate form of ancient Latin, but Salutati realized that not only ancient Latin style changed but also the language itself; see *Epistolario,* 4:142, and my forthcoming *Salutati: His Life and Thought,* chapt. 10.

7. He managed, for example, to correct an ancient authority when he showed that Valerius Maximus had erroneously identified the Scipio Nasica, who had received the representation of the Cybele, with the leader of the senators who killed Tiberius Gracchus. Salutati observes that the first Scipio would have been 90 when he attacked Gracchus and 115 when he was elected consul; see B. L. Ullman, *The Humanism of Coluccio Salutati* (Padua, 1963), p. 98.

8. He rejected the medieval view that Florence had been founded by Caesar

Deeply religious, Salutati endeavored to utilize his rhetorical gifts to make others not simply virtuous but rather virtuous Christians. As a humanist he was vitally concerned with justifying the role of the pagan classics in Christian education. For him the importance of such training went beyond providing an elementary foundation for young men in grammar, logic, rhetoric, and the sciences, a foundation on which they themselves could build. Rather, he maintained, when interpreted allegorically ancient poetry revealed all sorts of moral, natural, and theological truths of use to a Christian. Until the last decade of his life he was willing to argue that in its highest form ancient poetry was the product of a direct inspiration of the Holy Spirit. His most extensive defense of poetry, the uncompleted *De laboribus Herculis,* attempts to demonstrate this position by an analysis of the ancient poetry written about the labors of Hercules. The letter to Zambeccari dealing with the destruction of Vergil's statue by Carlo Malatesta, translated here, reflects Salutati's mature attitude. In this letter he was content to present poetic truth as representing the highest strivings of the human mind.

The *De fato et fortuna,* written in 1396–97, depicts a universe in which God has decreed the complete order of causes and effects from all eternity yet remained responsive to human decisions and deeds. While the order of causes "proceeds by fixed and immutable reason" in obedience to God's eternal decree, still a realm of indeterminacy exists in the created world wherein the human will can exercise its powers.[9] Supporting his position with numerous theological and philosophical arguments, Salutati concedes in the final analysis that the existence of such absolute necessity with contingency, simultaneously in the same created object, really lies beyond the understanding of the human intellect.[10] It is nonetheless the case and thus justifies considering God as absolute power and man as responsible for his own acts of good and evil.

---

for a theory of a Republican foundation under Sylla; see my "Coluccio Salutati and the Origins of Florence," *Pensiero politico* 2(1969):161–72.

9. See the text in Biblioteca Apostolica Vaticana, Vat. Lat., 2928, *Proem.,* fol. 1 verso. On the dating see my "Toward a Biography of Coluccio Salutati," *Rinascimento* 16(1976):28–34. For a discussion of the contents of this work, see Charles Trinkaus, *In Our Image and Likeness,* 2 vols. (London, 1970), 1:76–102.

10. Vat. Lat., 2928, Tr. II, c.7, fol. 9.

The treatise's emphasis on the centrality of the will in man's relationship with God and the relative superiority of the will to the intellect as a human faculty became a basic theme of Salutati's work in the last decade of his life. Quite logically, the discussion of the merits of the will and intellect was closely tied to the problem of the best form of life. This latter issue had been the subject of Salutati's first full-length treatise, the *De seculo et religione,* written about 1381. Composed at the request of a friend who had recently become a monk, Salutati designed the work to prove that the life of withdrawal and intellectual contemplation was better than life in the world. His unhesitating endorsement of the medieval belief in the virtues of monasticism derived in part from the character of his task, but the argument drew some of its inspiration from Salutati's own beliefs.[11] Sympathetic in any case, Salutati found monastic retreat especially attractive in 1381, a year when Florence was deeply divided politically and he himself was accused of treason.[12]

The first clear indication that Salutati had reexamined the assumptions behind the traditional medieval preference for the contemplative life appears in a letter of 1393 in which he attempted to dissuade a friend who had suffered adversities from taking monastic vows.[13] There are many ways to go to heaven, Salutati explains, and the monastic life offers no more assurance than does the active life. Moreover, while the contemplative life profits only the person himself, the active life, because many witness it, exercises a beneficent influence on others. By 1398–99 Salutati developed more impressive series of arguments with which to justify the active life.

Because of the terms in which the discussion is phrased, how-

---

11. The text is published without reference to the source in A. Gherardi, ed., "Diario d'anonimo fiorentino dall'anno 1358 al 1389," in *Cronache dei secoli xiii e xiv* (Florence, 1876), p. 270. The charge against Salutati is found in Florentine State Archives, *Capitano,* 1392, fol. 69. The charges were revealed to be false, ibid., fols. 69–69 verso.

12. On two occasions in the treatise he assigned a hundredfold harvest of fruit to the good monk, sixty to the good secular cleric, and thirty to the layman. *Colucii Salutati: De seculo et religione,* ed. B. L. Ullman (Florence, 1957), pp. 92, 163.

13. *Epistolario,* 2:453.

ever, Salutati's most elaborate defense of the active life, the *De nobilitate legum et medicine*, published in 1399, fails to meet the issue of the active versus the contemplative life head on. The ostensible concern of the treatise is to determine whether the profession of law or medicine is the more useful to the individual and to the society. As Salutati presents the problem, the physician represents the life spent in the study of natural philosophy through use of the speculative intellect. This entails living in seclusion with one's books, detached from the duties and satisfactions of being a participant in the human community. The lawyer, on the other hand, practices the active life. The law is a product of human conscience, established by human will for the wise governance of human society. To serve the law, product of the human will, is therefore to work for the good of the whole body of citizens.[14]

Moreover, inasmuch as we know through revelation that no one will be saved without works and the law represents the measure of human action, the lawyer not only fosters earthly felicity but also earns his personal salvation in the process. Indeed, eternal beatitude itself is more properly linked with man's will than with his intellect.[15] To put one's trust in the intellect is never to attain fulfillment. The individual intellect can never know the infinite number of truths, nor can it have perfect knowledge of God, whose essence is infinite. The proper end of man is not to know God's essence but rather to enjoy him eternally, and this enjoyment is a function of the will inspired by divine grace. Having God as its direct object in whom are unified all the particular goods of the universe, the human will can completely satisfy its desire for the good and experience beatitude.

Salutati's praise of the active as opposed to the speculative life, avoids opposing directly the medieval preference for the contemplative life. By implication, of course, the conception of beatitude as within the power of the will rather than the intellect could have served as a foundation for vindicating the claim of the active citizen to be morally superior to the solitary contemplative of divine truths. But the fact that he stops short with the easy victory of law

14. *De nobilitate legum et medicine. De verecundia,* ed. Eugenio Garin (Florence, 1947), pp. 76, 98.
15. Ibid., pp. 164, 166.

over natural philosophy and refuses to draw out the further implications indicates the extent to which Salutati felt ambivalent about
the new direction he was taking. In contrast to the *De nobilitate,*
Salutati's letter to Zambeccari states the problem clearly as one
involving a choice between the active and contemplative life. Yet
even here Salutati's own hesitations are so apparent, his qualifications so significant, that his final position is difficult to define.

This letter to Zambeccari of April 23, 1398, was the final one
in a series to the Bolognese chancellor concerning his colleague's
wild infatuation with a Bolognese girl.[16] Ostensibly Zambeccari's
confession of error made in a recent letter proved the success of
Salutati's vigorous campaign to convince the desperate lover to
cease his pursuit of his beloved Giovanna. But, as Salutati implies,
Zambeccari's changed attitude was in fact a product of his sorrow
at having been abandoned by the young woman, who left Bologna
to follow her husband in exile. Knowing well the mercurial Zambeccari, Salutati cannot take seriously the lover's emotional profession of a newly found religious faith and his intention to leave
his family and work in order to become a hermit. Although not
without a note of humor—rare in Salutati's writing—the letter
moves from an analysis of Zambeccari's particular motivations to a
consideration of the whole problem of the active and the contemplative life.

Salutati introduces the discussion of the general problem by
pointing out to his correspondent that unless he has really given up
his earthly passion for Giovanna, solitude will offer Zambeccari no
relief and may even intensify his desires. On the other hand, he
writes, if Zambeccari's emotions are under the control of his will,
he can find tranquility of mind living in the midst of crowds.
Often men living in the world lead more Christian lives than
anchorites in their solitude. Indeed, the active citizen, serving his
family and the state, imitates closely the work of Divine Providence
which cares for all creation.

From this point on, however, Salutati's presentation bristles with
ambiguities. The contemplative life, he continues, is admittedly
more perfect in that its direct object is God. Participants in the

16. *Epistolario,* 3:3–52, 58–64.

active life, while acting with a view to God as their final object, still serve imperfect creatures. Furthermore, because the object of the contemplative life is eternal, such a life is less dependent on outward things; it is more peaceful, has greater continuity with life after death, and is nobler because it exercises the intellect, the nobler faculty of the soul. Based on an election of the will to rise above the needs of the body, the contemplative life is more elevated than the active life, which is devoted to necessities.

Having conceded the inferiority of the active life to a life devoted to intellectual contemplation of divine truth, Salutati swerves almost in the opposite direction. If linked to the acquisition of necessary elements of life, he says, the active life is still concerned with virtue, and it too opens a way to heaven. As later in the *De nobilitate legum et medicine*, where he uses the argument in favor of the superiority of the will to the intellect, Salutati then depicts the final beatitude of man as an act of loving and enjoying, which are functions primarily of the will. Therefore, if on earth the active life is inferior to the contemplative in that it deals primarily with daily necessities, after death, when all discursive activities of the mind cease, it is superior. For then we possess God eternally by an act of love.

In practice, however, the two forms of life cannot be sharply separated. The process of contemplation itself consists in a movement from act to act. The contemplative cannot eschew certain necessary actions of life nor, as a Christian, refuse to help his neighbor work for salvation. Nor should he strive to be without feeling; after all, Christ himself wept. Salutati cites the careers of Augustine and Jerome to demonstrate that the contemplative life must inevitably be mixed with action, but he stops short of providing a definite conclusion. Rather, as if ignoring all that he had said in defense of the active life, in the final lines of the letter he abruptly confesses that if Zambeccari one day deserts the world in true penitence and out of sincere love of God, he himself is ready to follow.

The second, shorter letter has been included in this volume to give some impression of the attitude of the great scholar toward the female. Salutati was not distrustful of women, as was Petrarch; rather, in his case a nine-year love affair in youth was followed by two successful marriages. He wept uncontrollably on the death of his first wife, and, if more restrained when Piera died, he was deeply affected by her loss. Caterina's intellectual pretensions must have irritated Salutati. His insistence that she return to her nunnery—ostensibly contradicting his advice to Zambeccari— nevertheless has nothing to do with Caterina's sex. As a young girl Caterina had personally taken a solemn vow to become the bride of Christ. Salutati viewed a promise to God as inviolable, and thus Caterina's desertion of the convent as a mortal sin. Because the issue was so clear-cut for him, there is no discussion in the letter of the comparative virtues of the active and contemplative lives. Of course, it is very possible that he considered the problem relevant only for the male half of the human race.

Nevertheless, Coluccio Salutati was a pioneer, the first thinker of the early Renaissance even to suggest that the active life of the layman could be equal or superior to the contemplative life of the monk.[17] His writings, especially the *De nobilitate legum et medicine,* served as a source of inspiration for a whole body of literature dealing with the question. Obviously, his intellectual allegiances to the past made it impossible for Salutati to present a coherent defense of the superiority of the active life to the contemplative or even their equivalent value as lifestyles. Moreover, the work of Salutati's most famous disciple, Leonardo Bruni, indicates that the next generation of Florentines was almost as unwilling to decide conclusively for the precedence of the active life of the citizen over that of the contemplative in seclusion.[18]

17. Writers such as St. Bernard had insisted on the need for the monk to seek God not only through contemplation but also through works of charity. St. Bernard particularly emphasized preaching in the monastery as a good work; see citations in Alfred von Martin, *Coluccio Salutati und das humanistische Lebensideal* (Munich, 1916), pp. 157–58, n. 3. Salutati was among the first to emphasize the contrast between active and contemplative life as a contrast between the life of the layman and that of the monk.

18. Late in life, in writing to the Venetian patrician Lauro Quirini, Leonardo Bruni, who throughout his mature life praised the virtues of the active life of the citizen, exalted the intellectual faculty of man over man's will and the intellectual virtues over the moral ones. Although attainable by few, the contemplative life was for him the highest form of felicity; see L. Mehus, ed., *Leonardi Bruni Arretini Epistolarum libri VIII,* 2 vols. (Florence, 1741), pp. 135–40. This letter is dated 1441 according to Hans Baron, *Humanistisch-philosophische Schriften Bruni* (Leipzig–Berlin, 1928; reprint Wiesbaden, 1969), p. 215.

BIBLIOGRAPHY

Coluccio Salutati: Major Editions and Translations

Epistolario di Coluccio Salutati, 4 vols. Edited by Francesco Novati, Fonti per la storia d'Italia. Rome, 1891–1911.

Colucii Salutati de seculo et religione. Edited by Berthold L. Ullman. Florence, 1957.

De nobilitate legum et medicinae. De verecundia. Edited by Eugenio Garin, with Italian translation. Florence, 1947.

De laboribus Herculis. 2 vols. Edited by Berthold L. Ullman. Zurich, 1951.

Tractatus de tyranno von Coluccio Salutati. Edited by F. Ercole. Berlin, 1914. Or *Trakat 'vom Tyrannen' Coluccio Salutatis: eine Kulturgeschichtliche Untersuchung.* Edited by A. Martin. Berlin, 1913.

Invectiva in Antonium Luschum Vicentinum. Edited by D. Moreni. Florence, 1826.

Il protocollo notarile di Coluccio Salutati (1372–1373). Edited by A. Petrucci. Milan, 1963.

E. Emerton. *Humanism and Tyranny. Studies in the Italian Trecento,* pp. 70–116, 290–337. Cambridge, Mass., 1926.

Invectiva in Antonium Luschum Vincentinum, Prosatori latini del Quattrocento, pp. 8–37. Edited by Eugenio Garin. Milan, Naples, 1952.

Il trattato "de tyranno" e lettere scelte. Edited by F. Ercole. Bologna, 1942.

Studies

Baron, H. "La Rinascità dell'etica statale romana nell'umanesimo fiorentino del Quattrocento." *Civiltà moderna* 7(1935):21–49.

———. "Cicero and the Roman Civic Spirit in the Middle Ages and the Early Renaissance." *Bulletin of the John Rylands Library* 22(1938):73–97.

———. *The Crisis of the Early Italian Renaissance.* Rev. ed. Princeton, 1966.

Bonnell, R. A. "An Early Humanistic View of the Active and Contemplative Life." *Italica* 43(1966):225–39.

Borghi, L. "La dottrina morale di Coluccio Salutati. La concezione umanistica di Coluccio Salutati." *Annali della r. Scuola Normale Superiore di Pisa* 3(1934):75–102, 469–92.

De la Mare, A. C. *The Handwriting of the Italian Humanists.* Vol. 1, pp. 30–45. Oxford, 1973.

Garin, Eugenio. "I trattati morali di Coluccio Salutati," *Atti e memorie dell'Accademia fiorentina di scienze morali 'La Columbaria'*, n.s. 1(1943–46):53–88.

———. "A proposito di Coluccio Salutati," *Rivista critica di storia della filosofia* 15(1960):73–82.

———. *Italian Humanism.* Translated by P. Munz. New York, 1966.

Gasperetti, L. "Il 'De fato, fortuna et casu' di Coluccio Salutati," *Rinascita* 5(1941):555–82.

Herde, Peter. "Politik und Rhetorik in Florenz am Vorabend der Renaissance. Die ideologische Rechtfertigung der Florentiner Aussenpolitik durch Coluccio Salutati." *Archiv für Kulturgeschichte* 7(1965):141–220.

Iannizzotto, M. *Saggio sulla filosofia di Coluccio Salutati.* Padua, 1959.

Kessler, Eckhard. *Das Problem des Frühen Humanismus. Seine Philosophische Bedeutung bei Coluccio Salutati.* Munich, 1968.

Martin, Alfred von. *Mittelalterliche Welt- und Lebensanschauungen im Spiegel der Schriften Coluccio Salutatis.* Historische Bibliothek, 33. Munich, 1913.

———. *Coluccio Salutati und das humanistische Lebensideal.* Berlin, Leipzig, 1916.

———. "Die Populärphilosophie des Florentiner Humanisten Coluccio Salutati," *Archiv für Kulturgeschichte* 11(1913):411–54.

Novati, Francesco. *La giovinezza di Coluccio Salutati 1331–1353.* Turin, 1883.

Petrucci, Armando. *Coluccio Salutati.* Biblioteca biographica, 7. Rome, 1972.

Rice, Eugene. *The Renaissance Idea of Wisdom,* pp. 36–43. Cambridge, Mass., 1958.

Rüegg, W. "Entstehung, Quellen und Ziel von Salutatis de Fato et Fortuna," *Rinascimento* 5(1954):143–90.

Seigel, Jarrold. *Rhetoric and Philosophy in Renaissance Humanism.* Princeton, 1968.

Ullman, Berthold L. *The Humanism of Coluccio Salutati.* Medioevo e umanesimo, 4(1963).

Walser, E. *Gesammelte Studien zur Geistesgeschichte der Renaissance,* pp. 22–37. Basel, 1932.

Witt, Ronald G. "Coluccio Salutati and the Political Life of the Commune of Buggiano (1351–1374)," *Rinascimento* 6(1966): 27–56.

———. *Coluccio Salutati and the Public Letters.* Geneva, 1976.

COLUCCIO SALUTATI

Letter to Pellegrino Zambeccari *

Translated by RONALD G. WITT

I owe you an answer about two matters, distinguished man, brother,
and dearest friend. The first, about which I will say a few words,
concerns both you and that very eloquent lord, Jacopo da Fermo.[1]
You will see that what you and he so bitterly complained of in
such great detail—alas too credulous—actually never happened.
Indeed, you both have written how the magnificent lord, Carlo
Malatesta, had the beautiful and venerated representation of our
Vergil taken from the palace of Mantua and how, having broken
in pieces the statue that Vergil's native city dedicated to him, he
ordered the memory of such a great poet abolished in his
homeland.[2]

Nor did both of you fail to furnish explanations with your
account. In order to convince me more easily that such a detestable
thing was done, you have maintained that this lord, outstanding
and famous for his many virtues, is the deadly enemy of the Muses

---

* The translation is based on the edition of the letter by Francesco Novati,
Epist., 3:285–308. I have relied heavily on Novati's extensive notes to his edition.

1. Pellegrino Zambeccari was a frequent correspondent of Salutati and served
as chancellor of the commune of Bologna. The identity of lord Jacopo da
Fermo is unknown.

2. Carlo Malatesta, commander of the troops of the League, had inflicted a
decisive victory on Giangaleazzo Visconti near Mantua in August 1397. It
seems almost certain that he destroyed the statue of Vergil while staying in the
city after his triumph. Vergil (70–19 B.C.) was born in Mantua.

and despises not only mediocre poets but superb ones as well. Not only does he despise them, you write, but he calumniates them to the point that everywhere he proclaims them to be actors. Really a new kind of criticism! If he wants poets to be actors as the latter are commonly defined, that is, players representing actions in appropriate costume, then he is completely wrong. Poets do not gesture but, rather, write what is to be conveyed by gesture. Thus they differ as much from actors as men from apes, for while apes frequently copy men and by a certain natural aptitude imitate many things men do, still they differ from men in such a way that although man is one of the most beautiful living creatures and in the carriage of its body and in many activities the monkey comes very close to having a likeness to man, the monkey is one of the ugliest. So it is a serious error for so great a lord to judge the poets in this way.

But if perhaps he meant that the poets are to be called actors because they exaggerate like jesters when they praise, he is just as mistaken. When it comes to praising they have nothing in common. Jesters praise so that they might deceive or ridicule others, or advance themselves and make money. The poets' object is very different from this. Since, as Horace says, "the poets wish either to be useful or delight,"[3] their praises are intended to another purpose; for if the praise is true, they wish to be useful and delight, and they in fact accomplish their goal. Since those who are highly lauded delight in glory, as Valerius writes, "there is no humility so great that it can resist the sweetness of glory."[4] Praise is also useful to the praised, for nothing is more effective than the reward of praise for reinforcing the desire for virtue and the desire to do things well. This is true because the one extolled is always afraid that he might diminish the reputation for glory that he has acquired, and he desires in reality to surpass that for which he is praised.

On the other hand, if the poets praise falsely, given that the poet should be a most virtuous man and that it is the task of the poet, as the Philosopher says, either to praise or blame,[5] these

3. Horace *Epistulae* 2.2.333.
4. Valerius Maximus *Factorum et dictorum memorabilium* 8.14.5.
5. Aristotle *Poetica* 4.1448b25; see Ezio Franceschini, *Studi e note di filologia latina medievale* (Rome, 1938), p. 16.

commendations are to be considered bitter reproofs or sincere criticisms of the man who feels free of blame. O what a sweet form of criticism! Nay, rather, what biting criticism it is to praise someone above his merits or when he has none. What is more shameful and full of recrimination than to hear someone praised for things that have nothing to do with him? Imagine how it would feel to be praised for qualities you know are not yours. What greater spur or more effective teaching for living the good life than to hear said of yourself things for which you wish to be known? Who is so empty-headed that if given exaggerated praise he does not feel he has been warned about the perversity of his life with a view to his reform or instruction? The Philosopher distinguishes between those he calls "witty," those who enjoy themselves honorably, moderately, and pleasantly, and the *vomolicos,* those who indulge in pranks.[6] In much the same way our poets differ from actors and are distinguished from them as virtue is from vice and the honorable from the disgraceful.

What I'd really like to know is if this learned and distinguished lord was ill-advised by others or developed the opinion by himself, because he committed a serious error. Indeed, I would make an effort to defend the poets whom the Apostle and the sacred doctors of theology (who do credit to the Catholic faith and defend it) cite themselves, and I would show that these authors are not to be rejected but, rather, are to be considered admirable and useful. What more stupid and asinine thing could be imagined than to damn, because of a wrong opinion, the very poets with whose sayings Jerome often waxes eloquent, Augustine gleams, and Ambrose flowers. Fathers Gregory and Bernard utilize them as well, and the "Vase of Election"[7] himself did not consider it foolish to rely on their writings. If he damns the poets, doubtless he damns at the same time all the luminaries of the Christian religion whom we see shine with the weighty opinion of the poets as if with various stars.

But if anyone thinks poorly of poetic embellishment, let him read that admirable work of father Aurelius, which in the space of twenty-two books constructs the edifice of the city of God. There he will see the poets not only utilized for the sake of enriching the

6. Aristotle *Nicomachean Ethics* 2.7.13.
7. This term refers to St. Paul.

diction but also summoned in numerous places to combat the religions of the Gentiles. Moreover, he will see that he or another cannot possibly understand the meaning of this very elegant work without extensive knowledge of the poets. To attain such learning I have often seen masters of theology of our time, not without blushing, seek out not learned men, whom they avoid out of shame, but boys, in order that they might borrow what they do not themselves understand from the knowledge of those still in school. Furthermore, I have heard that some, so as not to appear as seeking instruction, tested others, and especially boys, on some passages of Vergil or other poet. After they learned what they did not know, they would shamefacedly commend a boy for his quickness of mind and encourage him with flattering words to continue his studies. And I know certain ones who, when they did not grasp the answer very well or perhaps did not agree with the exposition of the true meaning, asked, as if amazed, in what way the meaning given could be true. Then, having understood, they replied that this had always seemed to them the true meaning and that they had never agreed with any other; but, they said, they had been in doubt as to how such an explanation could be supported.

But let us forget these men who strive to hide their ignorance and to demonstrate with a variety of arts that they know everything. By the majesty of immortal God, what is this lord or any other able to condemn in the songs of the poets? Do they blame the elegance that by itself usually makes the presentation pleasing? Do they dislike the judgments with which the speech is resplendent as if with stars? Do they abhor the exalted tone of the words, which are usually reserved expressly for things and persons of great significance and which on their own are able to exalt a lowly subject? Do they damn the variety that, since uniformity is the mother of boredom, generates refreshment and, so to speak, sparks the intellect and appetite of the readers? Or do they detest the musical melody without which metric language cannot be expressed? Let them beware, lest they deserve the criticism that Lady Philosophy vigorously leveled against our Severinus; as the Greek proverb says, and as I write in Greek ὄνος λύρας? This means: Are you like an ass before the lyre?[8]

---

8. Boethius *De consolatione philosophiae* 1.4.2.

But I see what they are against. For they say: Who would stand this exquisite mendacity of the poets with which they pervert history, confound the times and persons, and with which, as a covering, they hide what they wish to say? However, let those who criticize the poets' songs for such things beware that they not condemn for the same reason the body of Holy Scripture and especially the Old Testament. For notwithstanding that all things compiled and written in that most sacred volume are completely true— regardless of the extent to which they are accepted by religious men or ridiculed by the impious because of their impossible or wonderous nature[9]—we realize that they unquestionably constitute a figure and a sign of other things. The sacrifice of Isaac, predestined and commanded by God, was the figure of our Savior on the cross sacrificed for the salvation of mankind.[10] The selling of Joseph and the thirty pieces of silver for which he was sold represent the symbol and token of the price and the sale of the Son of God.[11] And there is really nothing literally read in the Bible as happening that is not instituted to signify something else. Who is so hardheaded and such an enemy of truth that he would deny or refuse to acknowledge that this is poetic in nature?

They may say: "We do not wish to deny the meaning since, as the Apostle admonishes, the letter kills and the meaning gives life;[12] but in this case the letter itself contains truth. On the other hand, your poets do too much damage to the truth, because they conceal it in falsity and what they can clearly express they obscure with coverings of fables." The second of these two characteristics is common both to poetry and to Divine Scripture. For divinity was able to articulate what it wanted without a mantle of figures. And as for that truth which we want to signify, it is of no consequence whether we express what we wish with realities or fictions.

If, however, we wish to make fine distinctions, it is appropriate that the Divinity, which is the highest truth, draws truth from truth. But poetry as a human creation deserves some praise since truth emerges from fictions and falsehoods. For it is written: The

9. The Latin in this passage is unclear.

10. Gen. 22.

11. Gen. 37:28. Joseph, however, was sold for twenty pieces of silver according to Genesis.

12. 2 Cor. 3:6.

day gives the word to the day because it is the most divine, and the night reveals knowledge to the night.[13] This knowledge, although it is human, is not to be deprived of its own reward of praise. But poetry is not to be favored at the expense of truths about divine things expressed through the poetic faculty. The latter take precedence and represent a higher level of truth than those that have to do with human affairs. It is, therefore, a characteristic of divine poetry that it takes truth for a sign concealing another truth hidden in its mystery that comes forth as a further truth. By contrast, although human poetry, which does not immediately spring from the pure truth, can take a truth to signify other things, it is appropriate that it not reject fictions and other foolish devices, even though its aim is to lead to and produce the truth.

Nor let anyone ask: Why do the poets have to adopt such almost monstrous inventions when those who have a passion for inventing could openly explicate what they want without recourse to any veil at all? In divine matters we must use figurative speech, for these matters are above us and remote from the power of human intelligence; but, since we understand more than we can explain, they are still more remote from our power of expression. Similarly, in human things we like to borrow a certain elegance of embellishment from language utilized for speaking of the Divinity. But whereas we do so of necessity for divine things, in human matters we do it because we wish to. The result is that just as in divine matters truth proceeds from truth, so in human affairs the truth itself derives not only from truth but also from fictions and human inventions. Like a light shining in the darkness, it comes forth unspoiled from the shadows of falsities.

Nor do I doubt that had those dealing with the true and pure truth been permitted to use fictions, they would have adorned their truths with exquisite inventions. But the integrity of pure truth, which is the origin and mother of all truth, thus refuses association with falsity of any kind. It cannot be born, as it were, from the heart of falsities or be generated by its contrary. Nor ought one think it vain to hide the truth, for, as Gregory says in commenting on Ezechiel: "The obscurity of those speaking about God is very useful because it exercises the mind so that it is expanded with

13. Ps. 19:2.

labor and becomes well-trained when it must work to understand."
And he adds: "It also has a better advantage: since the comprehen-
sion of sacred Scripture, if it were available to all, would become
despised, in certain more obscure places the meaning discovered
gives more pleasure the harder the mind has to work to find it."
These are literally the words of Father Gregory.[14] Defined in relation to Divine Scripture, none can deny that these are advantages
of secular letters as well.

Why do I go on with such a detailed argument? I know that this
prince, who is not the least lord of Italy, could not and ought not
be accused of breaking Vergil's statue to pieces. Nor is it less
certain that he never could have uttered the words about the poets
you write. For although I have heard that with excellent advice
he devotes himself to the study of divine letters,[15] yet it is not
believable that he has this great animosity against the poets who,
as he reads, were approved by the holy doctors for their style and
were cited by them many times when proving or disproving something. Wherefore, whatever you write, I will not believe you and
others until I receive or (to speak more correctly) discover other
proof that a man of such learning, virtue, and moderation as
Carlo Malatesta could say such reprehensible things against the
sacred poets.

But enough of this. I would like him to see these words, however, not that he amend an error that, I think, he has not made but,
rather, that he might strengthen himself in his correct intention if,
as is more credible, he has not erred. But what can I say to you
who so readily and naively believed someone or other in a matter
so patently false? Are you perhaps of that nation and race who are
said to take rumors for established facts. If this was a rumor, did
you not recall Vergil's words:

Messenger of truth, hoarder of mischievous falsehood
equally?[16]

If, however, there has been testimony, why have you not examined
whether it was hearsay or firsthand evidence? Why have you not

14. St. Gregory *Homiliarum in Ezech.* 1.6.1213 (*PL* 76.829).
15. Malatesta seems to have been seriously interested in theological studies.
16. Vergil *Aeneid* 4.188.

determined how reliable your information was in a matter of such importance? If there was one witness, why did you not await another? If two, why not many? Did that popular dictum never come to mind:

Reliability is so rare because many say many things?[17]

If I had been so credulous, you might have made me—nay, rather, perhaps you wanted to make me—an object of amusement. But because it is incredible, I am simply bewildered by you and your source of information. I have asked everyone coming from Mantua about it. Nor have I stopped until I found out the truth from many people. I was expecting, and have expected for a long time, that you would recant like Stesichorus, affected alternately as he was by good and bad fortune, depending on whether he blamed or praised Helen. Just as he lost use of his eyes in criticizing Helen, so he afterwards regained his sight in praising her.[18] But although I have waited in vain a long time for you eventually to become heralds of the truth after you had been witnesses to a lie, I see that, since you have remained silent, you were endeavoring to have me believe such a foolish thing. Whether you erred in writing what you did or hoped to obtain an effect by remaining silent, I want you to realize your irresponsible conduct, your hasty credulity, and your inconsiderateness.

Now, however, I shall come to that which concerns you. You write,[19] my Pellegrino, that you have left the confusions and ravings of vain love behind and have strengthened your resolve through Him who hung on the cross for the salvation of the human race. And you add, if I might cite your words:

I hope, if bitter fortune not vex and disquiet me, to choose within two years, when I am in control of myself, a form of

17. Cato *Disticha* 1.13.2.
18. Plato *Phaedrus* 243a.
19. This letter is not published among the known correspondence of Zambeccari, *Epistolario di Pellegrino Zambeccari*, ed. Luigi Frati, Fonti per la storia d'Italia, 40 (Rome, 1929). Salutati's earliest correspondence with his friend on this matter is found in Novati, *Epistolario di Coluccio Salutati*, 3, pp. 3–6.

life that will make me master of my own time, and I will flee cares and the pursuit of wealth, which have up to the present deprived me of true freedom. Time will not make me as much a slave as it does you. And that you might believe that I have become another Pellegrino: I have had an oratory constructed outside the gate of Saint Mammoli,[20] in which I shall leave the relics of that mad Cupid. I will cherish and love the Mother of our Redeemer instead of false Giovanna, and I will leave you behind in this confused world attempting to flatter everyone. Farewell and spend a part of your old age on my behalf so that, if I survive you, I might be educated with your sacred words of eloquence.

I have quoted your words in context so that you might know that you wrote not in dust, which the wind scatters, nor in ice, which melts in sun and fire. Responding to you with this letter, I quoted them to this extent so that they might remain for reference. If I might enter into a friendly argument with you about some of your remarks, have you not said: "Now I have left the confusions and ravings of vain love"? Have you strengthened your resolve in our Savior, you who hope to choose (if fortune permits) a new life within two years, when you will be ready to free time for yourself? Are you to deposit the relics of mad Cupid in this your oratory? Are you going to love the Virgin Mary instead of the false Giovanna?[21] Have you strengthened yourself in Christ, my Pellegrino, who loves not yet but who will love His mother, the Virgin? My Pellegrino, anyone who intended to do what you say you will do would be mad! You have not yet left the remnants of a foolish love and still maintain that you are firmly tied to Christ. Do you not feel that these things are like opposites that contradict each other? Do you wish for miracles for yourself? For my part, I do not simply hope but ardently long for them.

Nevertheless, I rejoice that you who were once the blind lover

20. The oratory dedicated to St. Pellegrino was founded by an act drawn up in July 1398. Apparently Zambeccari did not heed Salutati's advice, at least in this regard: *ibid.,* 3, p. 295, n. 2.

21. We do not know the identity of Giovanna. From earlier letters it appears that years before, as a single man, Zambeccari had tried to marry her, but she chose another. Taking a wife himself in 1384, he was never able to put Giovanna out of his mind.

of your Giovanna, and would not heed my warnings, have finally with open eyes confessed that this love was false. I am vexed and displeased, however, that, although you recognize your earthly love to be false, you have not yet given it up and not made that fruitful conversion. You still love Giovanna and not the Virgin Mary, whom you say you will cherish and love but do not love now. Why put it off, my Peregrino? Why not start today? Why draw things out by procrastinating? This commitment does not require an oratory, only your heart and mind; there is no need to postpone what can be accomplished in a moment. If you discard the foolish, false, and mad love of Giovanna, you will have to love something else. Our soul cannot not love. It is perpetual, it always grows, always thinks, always loves. If you do not come to love the Virgin Mary, it is necessary that you embrace another thing with love, or doubtless remain in love with Giovanna. Tell me, you still love Giovanna, don't you? I clearly believe you do, or you would show you loved something else. You will love Mary the Virgin instead of Giovanna. Oh happy Mary, whom you think alone worthy of this honor and on whom you direct the focus of your love, hitherto directed on Giovanna. Tell me, will you love Mary's starry eyes and the other things that once, wild with desire, you marveled at in Giovanna? If you do not love these things in Mary, she will not be loved in place of Giovanna.

But you will say: "You take my words too literally. Why do you twist everything? Why do you not understand them fairly? You plainly know what I meant." I twist nothing at all, nor do I think that one ought to neglect the significance of the words, except when it is manifest that the speaker meant something else, as Marcellus advised in the third collection of the material on legates.[22] Nor am I able to understand more than the words mean. How do I know what you want when you do not know how to tell me? I am perhaps able to know what you ought to want; however, who but the spirit within you[23] can know what you want?

The crux of my dispute with you is that you have confessed to me that you love Giovanna. For what else am I to believe since you have not yet established the life that you will elect, nay, hope to elect within two years if fortune does not hinder or disturb you.

22. Justinian *Dig.* 32; *De legatis et fideicomissis* 69.
23. 1 Cor. 2:11.

What else, when you write that you will deposit the relics of insane Cupid in your oratory and that you will cherish and love the
Mother of our Redeemer for the false Giovanna? O if your star
but returned from Ferrara, your Giovanna! O if you would see her
again armed with the usual weapons! O if you looked on her again,
beautiful, charming, all full of honesty and virtue, qualities that
you thought you saw in her and wanted to see, even if they were
not there! Then would you not say:

> This woman is the only one who has stirred my senses and
> sapped my will. I feel once more the scars of the old flame?[24]

Clearly your mind would say this; your heart, your intellect, would
say this; and your mouth, which speaks from a full heart,[25] would
not keep silent. O then you would be happy! O deserted oratory!
O invisible and deserted Mary! But why do I go on? I am very
certain that if mild Giovanna nodded with the array of her beauty,
if she showed herself swept away by your love, if she cried out as
in the Song of Solomon: "I swear to you, o daughters of Bologna,
if you find my beloved, my Pellegrino, that you tell him that I
languish for love!"[26] O, if you would hear this song, how you
would act and what height of madness you would reach! What
binding vow, what stipulations in your profession of faith, what
principles of conduct, what religious bonds you would not break,
would not abandon, would not belittle in importance, and would
not dissolve!

Remember that love conquers all![27] Remember that, whether it is
innate or caused by the stars or customs, it is common for you and
other Bolognese to love too much. Remember that this is a licentious habit and practice among you, common not only to men but
also to young women! Remember that when the suitor arrives he
is immediately given leave to see the beloved, nay, rather, they are
even allowed to join hands! Remember that young women are also
allowed to rebuke a suitor[28] (for this they call their lovers) if he

24. Vergil *Aeneid* 4. 22–3.
25. Matt. 12:34.
26. This is an echo of Song of Sol. 5:8.
27. Vergil *Eclogues* 10.69.
28. The word in the text is "intendens," which Novati (p. 298 n. 4) believes
was derived from the old Italian "intendersi" or "to fall in love."

neglects them. I am not maintaining that the Bolognese are im-
moral because of these things, but, rather, I mean that you as a
people pursue love hotly and with passion.

I shall tell you a true account, not a fable, of one of your
compatriots, a Bolognese citizen, so that I might demonstrate how
wildly your people fall in love. There was a man, whose name I
shall omit, comparable to you in regard to family and age, not
dissimilar to you in profession or in dignity, and, that I might speak
truly, quite like you, a kind of other Pellegrino. His fate was that he
loved his Giovanna. Like yours, she was married, beautiful, upright, and honorable. The same thing happened to her husband,
who was exiled because he killed another man. This lover of his
Giovanna obtained a favor for her husband, as you did for the
husband of yours. Finally, after considering many places for a
residence in exile, the husband chose Ferrara, where he would have
his permanent home with his wife. And, since he wished to have
Giovanna with him, he asked the lover's help or had his wishes
reported to him.

The latter, just like all lovers, or rather madmen, tending to
their own ruin, procures a safe conduct for the husband so that he
might please Giovanna and make himself a friend to the husband
as he is a lover to the wife. The husband comes, he is thankful to
everyone, and he thanks especially the lover of his wife. He packs
his bags. Not only does he make preparations to depart but he
leaves, taking with him his wife, who will never return.

This stupid citizen of yours, your alter ego, who helped make all
this possible because of his desire for Giovanna, finally, but in vain,
recognizes what he has done. Still he bears it all happily. But when
he sees his soul, his heart leaving, becoming wild, he puts on his
elegant and expensive imported clothing, which you call "ciambel-
lotti," and, like a madman, follows her to the docks on the left
bank of the channel from which those going to Ferrara by water,
moving through a muddy valley or series of valleys, sail to the
Reno or a branch of that river.[29]

There, having a breakfast prepared that certain people call a
"refreshment," he shows his generosity. He takes charge of all

29. The Reno is a river near Bologna. In the twelfth century a canal was built,
starting from the river at Casalecchi, passing through Bologna, and thereafter
meandering through a plain until it rejoined the Reno near Segni.

things, arranging that Giovanna might recline on a skiff that they call a "barclum," or little boat, in order that she reach the ship safely and might board without fear or risk.³⁰ After all things have been looked after, the sailor loosens the rope and seizes and fixes the tiller so that he might control the boat. Not content with fixing the tiller, he calls a friend and compells him to pole the boat, and he himself with a similar implement drives the ship away from the dock. Not only does he double the velocity of the water moving downstream, but he drives it even faster.

Alas, what then was the feeling of the lover? How burdensome, how intolerable was the departure? Your fellow citizen started to rave and was smitten, running along the bank, urging Giovanna not to be afraid and the boatman to be diligent. It is said, moreover—such was his depravity—that at one point he got into the boat, and I easily believe it. I would like to have seen him—crying out phrases, rolling his eyes, nodding his head, and warning with hands—so that I could describe him.

I would, however, speak of one happening that ought to be amusing. Perhaps the persistent rain had made the banks sodden, but he, following the little ship, ran along the very edge of the bank to be as close as possible to the ship. While speaking to those directing the ship, while jumping over the rough spots with a leap, stirring up muddy pools where he landed and covering himself with the mud of the bank—for the river banks are not only dirty but deep with mud—he tripped all filthy on the bank and, leaping up, besmeared with mud, fell into the Reno. Soiled with slime and drenched with water, he was laughed at not only by spectators but by the sailors, and even by the river banks and the river itself, the weeping willows and the other trees and by the fish, all witnesses of his stupidity. Finally, as we read about Menoetes in Vergil:

> All laughed at the sight of him going overboard, swimming,
> And now they laugh to see him wringing the muddy water
> from his clothes.³¹

I wish you would have seen this ludicrous spectacle, nay, I would have liked for you to have been this fellow I am describing: I wish

---

30. The Latin of this passage is obscure.
31. Vergil *Aeneid* 5.181, has 'Trojans' as subject. Second line is not Vergil.

you had seen him all slimey and dripping, entering the city and being pointed out as a foolish man, an example of mad love, and jeered at by all whom he encountered. I think you would have been equally moved and, taking this experience to heart, would have put yourself in his place like Aeneas, who, having witnessed the slaughter of Priam, thought about his own father's fate.

> Then first the full horror of it all was borne in upon me. I stood
> In a daze: the picture of my dear father came to mind,
> As I watched King Priam, a man of the same age, cruelly killed . . .
> Gasping his life away; I pictured Creusa
> Deserted, my home pillaged, and the fate of my little Julius.[32]

Perhaps if you had seen him with his dirty face, befouled with mud and drenched with water, you would have seen your turpitude as his and your stupidity as well, so that what you would not heed by reason you would see by example and with your own eyes.

I see, my Pellegrino, that among the errors conceived regarding Giovanna the light of truth shines in you and that you are drawn from one extreme to the other. But before you consider the extremes, I want you to bring yourself back to the mean. To love Mary the Virgin and to have loved Giovanna are two extremes that confront each other as if from opposite towers. You will not be able to love Mary as much as you ought. You have been given the capacity and are able to love Giovanna to a lesser extent so as not to exceed the proper limit in loving. You have loved the latter with physical love and to the point of madness, but Mary is necessarily loved for spiritual consolation and as an example of chastity. You marveled at your earthly love among transitory things; however, you shall learn that Mary is to be cherished among eternal objects that lead to eternal glory. When you love the Virgin above you, then you will be near the goal.

Hence, I urge you, my Pellegrino, and I admonish you, if ever you want to learn anything from me, abandon Giovanna com-

---

32. Vergil *Aeneid* 2.559–63. L.561 of Vergil differs slightly from Salutati's version.

pletely! Second, consider that you are obligated to the state and to your family, your sons and relations. After you have fulfilled these obligations, free from others, you will be able to prepare yourself for that final love and charity for Mary that does not puff up but edifies.[33] Therefore, paying your debt, you will learn how much you owe to the highest good and in what way you, who do not yet understand, may satisfy those claims.

God has appointed you father of many and, because of many blessings, the refuge and friend to many; He has made it so that in your commonwealth you are able to do more than generally anyone else. If you desert these obligations, will God not demand these things from you? You have received a talent; do not bury it but use it. Labor! Make yourself a useful servant! Pay back in kind what was given you![34] Perhaps it is not actually God's will that you convert to another life. It is good and honest to love Mary, but it is better to imitate her. Know, however, that for this purpose we have no need of a man-made oratory or of solitude. Our mind, our heart, and our soul make a perpetual temple of God built not by man's hand. There our conscience lives; there our affection is examined by Him who scrutinizes the reins and the heart;[35] by Him who wills these things from eternity, whatever they be, and not only with a good will but with the best, and who fashions them from eternity in the most equitable manner.

Indeed, He acts most justly in abandoning us so that we do evil deeds or in aiding us beforehand with his beneficent grace, that we do the good things that are done. This is the temple of the Lord that was destroyed and rebuilt in three days.[36] It was destroyed by the descent into sin; it is restored in the triple light of penitence, that is, in the bitterness of remorse, in recognizing sins and in the shame of confession, in divulging secrets, and in making satisfaction out of contrition and lamenting the evil done. This is called the house of prayer, with the buyers and sellers excluded,[37] that is, the commercial transactions of the temporal life in which only the acquisition of temporal possessions counts. In the doorways of this

33. 1 Cor. 8:1.
34. Matt. 25:15–30.
35. Ps. 7:9.
36. Matt. 27:40.
37. Matt. 21:12–13.

our temple stands pride, seeking superiority; avarice lies in wait, picking up what falls by chance; envy burns, desiring evil; anger rages, wanting to profit from injury; sadness mourns, seeking repose; the throat sticks, wanting to stroke the food tasted; and lust sordidly seeks the satisfaction of desire. The Lord expelled those buying and selling from the temple so that we might expel them from our temple doors. He prohibited such dealings so that we not admit them to the temple that we keep for secret matters.

Purge your temple, my Pellegrino. Wish for nothing transitory; but the more beautiful things are to the eye, the sweeter to the taste and the softer to the touch; lust for them the less not only in words but also in your feelings and in deed. Do not think about peace for yourself when you can have no peace in the flesh. There will be worry in the hermitage; it does not abandon you in the oratory nor when you are alone in bed. You do not know how full of stimulation solitude is, how beset by thoughts, and how it is a prey to dangers. We praise all those things that we have not learned to fear; the active man and the contemplative man alike have their troubles. Each shade endures his own sufferings;[38] each one is tied to something that impedes, troubles, and disquiets. Do not believe, my Pellegrino, that to flee the crowd, to avoid the sight of attractive objects, to shut oneself in a cloister or to go off to a hermitage is the way of perfection. Something in you sets the seal of perfection on your work, something that receives within those things that do not touch you, nay, that are unable to touch you if your mind and spirit will restrain themselves and not seek outside.[39] If it will not admit those external things, the square, the forum, the court, and the busy places of the city will be to you a kind of hermitage, a very remote and perfect solitude. But if remembering things absent or confronted with enticements, our mind reaches outside itself, I do not know how it is an advantage to live as a solitary. For whether it is comprehended by the senses, represented by the memory, constructed by the sharpness of intellect, or created by the desire of the feelings, it is a property of the mind always to think something.

Now, my Pellegrino, tell me: Who do you think was more

---

38. Vergil *Aeneid* 6.743. The shades are the spirits of dead men in the lower world.

39. Persius *Saturae* 1.7.

pleasing to God, the contemplative hermit Paul or the active man Abraham? Do you not think that Jacob, with twelve sons, so many flocks of sheep, and two wives, and so much wealth and property, was more acceptable to God than the two Macharii, Theophylac, or Hilarion?[40] Believe me, Pellegrino, for just as there are incomparably more who are busy in secular affairs than who are concerned with spiritual matters alone, so far more of this kind of men are accepted by God than of that group who are interested in spiritual things alone. But if you perhaps do not believe me, please believe Aurelius, who says about the title of the fifty-first Psalm:

> Observe two kinds of men: The one composed of workers, the other of those among whom they labor; the one of the earth, the other thinking of heaven; the one weighing their hearts down into the depths, the others joining their hearts to the angels; the one trusting in terrestial possessions wherein this world is rich, the other seeking celestial goods that a truthful God has promised. But these two kinds of men are mixed. Now I find a citizen of Jerusalem, a citizen of the kingdom of heaven having an office on earth. That is, he wears the purple; he is a magistrate, an aedile, a proconsul, an emperor; he rules the earthly republic. But he has his heart uplifted, if he is a Christian, if a believer, if pious, if he distains the things of this present world and trusts in those things belonging to the future life. That holy woman Esther was of this nature; who, although the wife of the king, faced the danger of entreating for her own people and when she prayed to her lord in the presence of God, where lying was forbidden, she said in her prayer that her regal vestments were to her like a menstruating woman's cloth.[41]

or, as our translation runs: "You know my necessity, that I abhor the sign of pride and my glory, which is upon my head in the days

---

40. Three of these can be identified as monks: St. Macarius of Alexandria (4th cent.), St. Macarius of Egypt (4th cent.), and St. Hilarion (4th cent.). Salutati probably meant the fourth, Theophylact, to be Theophylact of Alexandria, patriarch of the city in the fourth century and regarded as the friend of the monks of the desert.

41. St. Augustine *Enarratio in Psalmum* 51.6.4 (*PL* 36.603–4).

of my splendor, and I detest this like the cloth of a menstruating woman."[42] To these words father Augustine immediately added: "Therefore let us not despair of the citizens of the kingdom of heaven, when we see them do some of the business of Babylon, some terrestrial affair in the terrestrial republic; nor again should we keep congratulating all men who we see doing heavenly business." And after a few words he added: "Those amid earthly matters raise their hearts to heaven, these amid heavenly words draw their hearts to the earth."

I have quoted all these passages of father Augustine, so that you not keep flattering yourself about your man-constructed oratory or about your being closer to heavenly things, and that you not damn me for remaining in the world and justify yourself fleeing the world. Clearly your fleeing the world can draw your heart from heavenly things to earth, and I, remaining in earthly affairs, will be able to raise my heart to heaven. And you, if you provide for and serve and strive for your family and your sons, your relatives and your friends, and your state (which embraces all), you cannot fail to raise your heart to heavenly things and please God. Indeed, devoted to these things, you are perhaps more acceptable since you not only claim for yourself the coexistence of the first cause, but striving as hard as you can for things necessary to your family, pleasing to your friends, and salubrious for the state, you work together with that same cause that provides for all.[43]

I know, and at this point I do not wish to argue, that the life of those contemplating the divine object, which we ought to love above and before all things, is more sublime and more perfect than that of those devoted to activities. The former contemplate and love God. The latter, if they are perfectly motivated on account of God and love God, still minister and serve His creatures. I admit, of course, that those given to activity, because of error and crime, can be devoted to the creature on account of the creature. The contemplative is more perfect since it is of such continuous duration that, as the Truth says, Mary has chosen the best part that shall not be taken from her;[44] from the present time and into the future

42. Esther 14:16 (Vulg).

43. When Pellegrino serves his fellow men, God is not merely present, as he is when men do any act, but a special relationship arises. In helping others Pellegrino is imitating God's Providence.

44. Luke 10:42.

she will be linked with an uninterrupted love. Just as she contemplates eternal things here, so there will she cling to and enjoy eternal things.

I grant that the contemplative life is more sublime for its high level of thought; more delectable with the sweetness of tranquility and meditation; more self-sufficient since it requires fewer things; more divine since it considers divine rather than human things; more noble since it exercises the intellect, the higher part of the soul, which among living things is the unique possession of man. I grant, finally, that it is more lovable because of itself and, as Aurelius says, that it is to be sought for love of the truth;[45] nonetheless, the active life that you flee is to be followed both as an exercise in virtue and because of the necessity of brotherly love. Indeed, as the Philosopher has said, it is better to philosophize than to grow rich,[46] but philosophy is not to be chosen by one needing the necessities of life. The contemplative life is better, I confess; nevertheless, it is not always to be chosen by everybody.

The active life is inferior, but many times it is to be preferred. Although the contemplative life is a matter of choice and the active life concerns necessary things, the latter is not so attached and tied to existence that it does not care about or consider acting well. Therefore do you not believe that this way of life opens a path to heaven? Moreover, eternal beatitude is an act, not a possession, and is devoted to loving, viewing, and enjoying; all discursive operations of speculation and contemplation cease in it. When we die we will see the truth as it is. Would it not, therefore, be appropriate to say that the active life follows the contemplative after death, just as the active precedes it in act while we are alive, since on earth the former produces and begets the latter.

For it was not permitted Jacob to have Rachel unless he had bought and possessed Leah as a wife for seven years.[47] By Leah one understands the active life and by Rachel the contemplative. Now, however, just as Leah comes first in order in this life, so she comes after Rachel in the eternal life. She is always dim-sighted, however, since here below she thinks of temporal things even though with a view to God; and when she receives eternal happiness by grace she will not behold the beatific object. There is a mystery in this

45. St. Augustine *De civitate dei* 19.19.
46. Aristotle *Topica* 3, 2, 3, 118a.
47. Gen. 29:16–30.

since Rachel died first; after a time, however, Leah was buried with Isaac and Rebecca. However, Leah was buried after Rachel, that is, the active life after the contemplative. Where was she buried? Certainly with Isaac and Rebecca. What is Isaac if not, as interpreters say, laughter and joy; what is Rebecca but great wisdom, much patience, and long suffering?[48] From this reading and analysis of Genesis it is clear that Leah is buried with laughter and joy, with much wisdom, which is perfected in action, and much patience, which is made known through a continuation of works and labors, and with much suffering. These are the things in Isaac and Rebecca that represent the happy life.

Indeed, although we distinguish these two ways of life with words and argument, they are really mixed; no one can be so connected with material things that he does for God's sake that he entirely lacks a contemplative element; nor can a contemplative, if he lives as a man, be completely dead to secular matters. Since God is the end of all his actions, how else could he do this unless he has contemplated God and this is done from act to act? Since he must live and help his neighbor on God's behalf, the first because of his nature and the second by the order of divine law, can he always remain in a state of contemplation, unmindful of the necessities of life and doing nothing for the salvation of his fellow man?

Will he be a contemplative so completely devoted to God that disasters befalling a dear one or the death of relatives will not affect him and the destruction of his homeland not move him? If there were such a person, and he related to other people like this, he would show himself not a man but a tree trunk, a useless piece of wood,[49] a hard rock and obdurate stone; nor would he imitate the mediator of God and man who represents the highest perfection. For Christ wept over Lazarus and cried abundantly over Jerusalem,[50] in these things, as in others, leaving us an example to follow.

To conclude shortly, let us grant that the contemplative life is better, more divine and sublime; yet it must be mixed with action and cannot always remain at the height of speculation. Just consider father Augustine meditating and acting; now he is intent on

48. St. Hieronymus, *Liber interpretationis Hebraicorum nominum, Corpus Christianorum*, S.L., 72 (Turnhout, 1969), pp. 67, 68, 70.

49. A reminiscence of Horace *Sat.* 1.8.1.

50. John 11:35; Luke 19:41.

contemplating, now on instructing; now in a certain way enjoying serving his neighbor; now thinking of God, now writing what he thinks; now resting in God, now fighting with heretics. Believe me, he will seem greater to you as an active than as a contemplative man, not only because of the infinite services derived from his deeds, which have benefitted all men living in his time and in our own, but also because of the merits of the active life given him in gracious recompense.

Tell me, I pray, what will we be called to answer for in that last judgment if not works of mercy, whether neglected or unfulfilled? For the one who clothed the naked, fed the hungry, gave drink to the thirsting, buried the dead, freed the imprisoned, visited the sick, received the wanderer, will hear these happy words: "Come, blessed of my father, possess the kingdom prepared for you from the foundation of the world."[51] If you establish yourself in Christ, do not think of solitude, for Jerome merited incomparably more in the monastic congregation than in solitude. In solitude he wept; there, I confess, he laid down the burden of sinners; there, after his departure from the world, he became of such a nature that he could fight isolation. But in the brotherhood and the frequent human contact of the monastery, my Pellegrino, he fought with heretics; criticizing the clerics, he purified and instructed them; he resisted his adversaries; he created many things and translated the sacred treasury of letters for Christianity.[52] He not only had men for followers but even used a lion for a guardian and for a beast of burden, which he did not merit in retreat.[53]

I want you, however, if you change your form of life, to learn in society to please God not yourself, so that, departing from this confusion, you seek not your own quiet, nor any pleasure in such things even if they be honorable, but the tears of sins and the deepest affliction because of the beloved Giovanna, bewailing your errors and grinding in penitence. I hope that if you leave the world in this way you will not abandon me, as you threaten, "in this confused world attempting to flatter everyone." The latter words you spoke with great anger. In this case, since I have confidence in you, induce me to follow you or, if I would remain behind, force me by

51. Matt. 25:34.
52. St. Jerome translated portions of the Bible into Latin.
53. From the *St. Hieronymi Vita*, PL 22.193.

violence to stay with you. Nor will you, who began by admonishing your friend about certain matters, look forward to learning from me. Farewell, if those matters of which you write are true, and meditate on those things I have included in my answer to you. Florence, April 23 [1398].

COLUCCIO SALUTATI

Letter to Caterina di messer Vieri di Donatino d'Arezzo[*]

I know, Caterina, beloved daughter in Christ, that it arouses suspicion when a man writes to a woman, especially to a young one, and, committed to the worldly life as she is, one with whom he might hope to have contact.[1] The same slanders have been made about the most holy women when they have written to very devout men. However, not only my age—for I am now in my sixty-eighth year—exempts me from such charges, but more than this a right conscience and a sincere intention. This being so, I do not fear the tongues or depraved thoughts of those imagining evil in everything.

[*] The Latin original of this letter is found in *Epistolario di Coluccio Salutati,* 3:337–41. I am deeply indebted to Novati's detailed notes in making my own.

1. On the death of her father, under strong pressure from her mother, Caterina di messer Vieri became a nun of Santa Chiara in Montepulciano at the age of eleven. Her mother's motives are unclear, but Caterina herself seems to have had no religious vocation. Consequently, when an occasion presented itself she fled the convent and presumably left Tuscany. Because she already enjoyed some reputation for intellectual gifts rarely recognized in women of the time, her flight probably received wide attention. After wandering for a time, however, she resolved to return home, to marry, and to have children. She wrote Salutati, obviously hoping for some kind of approval of her intention from the leading Italian intellectual. Instead the old man roundly rebuked her. Undaunted, Caterina married within a short time and began to raise her family. After a few years, wishing to have her offspring recognized as legitimate, she appealed to the pope to have her childhood vow annulled. A favorable decision was rendered by a papal representative in Arezzo in 1403.

Therefore, I write to advise you, so that you might look at yourself; so that I might attempt to recall you to the road of salvation, to reason, and to your God whom you have left at such a distance. If God grants this—and he will if you have not entirely abandoned yourself to perverted ideas—I will be responsible for giving you a holier life, one full of glory and honor.

You may be a bit superior to other women in having some notion of letters; you may have seen Seneca and other, lowly authors[2] and cite them. But do not flatter yourself that you are adorned with eloquence or that you possess secular learning, which in God's eyes is foolishness.[3] Believe me, you are indeed far from both. You can boast of this among simple women and those who are not properly educated in these studies. If you encounter something of moral or poetic significance, do not think that it is automatically a sure basis for truth. For you say:

O fortune envious of strong men![4]

This is not the assertion of the Tragic Poet but rather of the crowd, the chorus! Why do you, woman, complain about fortune? Why do you blame it for your crime or your guilt as you do? You are badly instructed in the art of organizing a speech according to the nature and condition of the listener. You dare accuse fortune to me? You are not speaking to simple women who follow what you say with sighs, tears, and fawning acquiescence. Divine Providence, which is fortune, ruling and governing all things, and your precious mother, of whom you are unworthy, dedicated you to God, delivered you to him, and consecrated you in the most holy fashion as the bride of Christ. Had you sincerely followed this rule of life as your vow demands, and, laying aside the trifles probably learned with your natural genius in the convent, had you devoted yourself to love of God with all your heart, all your soul, and all your powers[5] as is fitting and as we are commanded—had you done these things you would not have left the cloister. You would

2. Oddly, Salutati seems to imply that Seneca is an *ignobilis auctor.*
3. 1 Cor. 3:19.
4. Seneca *Hercules furens* 528. Salutati is criticizing Caterina for ascribing an opinion to the author that Seneca put in the mouth of the foolish crowd.
5. Luke 10:27.

not have wandered over the earth, moved by unfulfilled desires, notorious, ridiculed, and despised like the daughter of Inachus who was turned into a cow, according to the poets. Now, however, warned by heaven, as you say, you have returned home, or rather to the cradle of your exile; for if you do not know it, this world is an exile, a way, not a homeland. Rather, our sublime home is Jerusalem, the vision of peace, the eternal and immeasurable fullness of peace that passes all understanding.[6] I want you to long for this true home, to direct yourself toward it, to prepare yourself for it, so that you do not disgrace your bridegroom. You labor in the vain confusion of the world, burdened with passions, fouled by infinite evil deeds.

Hear, I pray, the voice of your bridegroom! For he calls you and others: "Come to me all you who labor and are burdened and I will refresh you. Bear my yoke upon you and learn from me because I am mild and humble in heart and you will find rest for your souls. For my yoke is pleasant and my burden light."[7] By returning reconcile yourself with him whom you offended by leaving. See how sweetly he calls you. See how humanely he encourages you. See what he promises: refreshment and rest for your soul! O if you would decide to return to him! O if you could see the difficulties that await you on your present path! If you do not know, worse than incest, more serious than debauchery is the marriage that you so ardently desire. Although you call it marriage, you cover a crime with this name.[8] You are not able to be the legitimate wife of another. When you embrace this man, whoever he shall be, you will know that you embrace not your husband but a fornicator, an adulterer. I beg you not to listen to those who advise you badly, with a view to bodily delights. This approval, this flattery will not lead you to peace of mind or serve your honor but, rather, will bring you to infamy, confuse your mind, and vex your body.

Return to your husband, your beloved, your king! Leaving your depraved path of passion, let the winter and rainstorms of your labors pass,[9] so that you will merit hearing His sweetest voice:

6. Phil. 4:7.
7. Matt. 11:28–30.
8. *Aeneid* 4, 172.
9. Song of Sol. 2:11.

"Arise, hasten, my love, my dove, my fair one, and come."[10] You will merit being called "love" when, abandoning the world, you shall resolve to follow Christ. You will deserve the name "dove" when it can be truly said that you have vomited the gall of passion. You will indeed be fair when, devoted to the spirit, you do whatever you do for God's sake. Then you will hear what Christ added many words later: "Arise, my love, my beautiful one, and come, my dove, in the clefts of the rock, in the cave under the cliff; show me your face, let your voice sound in my ears; for your voice is sweet and your face comely."[11] Your husband calls you to show him your face, that is, your works, in the clefts of the rock and the cave under the cliff, that is, in the cloister and in the monastery built of stones. Your voice sounds in his ears with frequent prayers and devotions. Do not enter into the depravity and incest that you call marriage, but allow yourself to be brought back to the cloister, not to the service of a man but of Christ, not to carnal delights but to the joy and happiness of the spirit. Believe me, Caterina, the more things of carnal nature are possessed and known, the more they burden, the more they afflict. Things of the spirit give more pleasure, the more they are possessed; the more they are known, the more they are loved.

I will make an end here although my mind is alive with many thoughts and the subject demands that a good deal more be said. But I must consider my other obligations and you, unless you are otherwise disposed, should not be afflicted further. Farewell and be happy. And you will fare well if you open your ears to my sincere and salubrious warnings and meditate on them. Florence, May 14 [1399].

10. Song of Sol. 2:10.
11. Song of Sol. 2:13–14.

LEONARDO
BRUNI

Introduction

RONALD G. WITT

The life of Leonardo Bruni illustrates the extent to which Petrarca remained a vigorous source of inspiration years after his death. Born to a Guelf family of Arezzo in 1370,[1] Bruni, together with his father, was seized and imprisoned when Arezzo was captured in 1384 by exiled Ghibellines of the city with the help of a French army. Taken to the castle of Quarata, Bruni was held captive in a room by himself because of his youth. In the room hung a portrait of Francesco Petrarch, with whose writings the boy must already have had some acquaintance. The presence of the painting in the isolation of the prison had its effect on the young Bruni. "As I looked at it daily," he wrote in his *Rerum suo tempore gestarum commentarius,* "I became inflamed with an incredible passion for his studies."[2]

Bruni's once well-to-do family suffered financial losses in the civil war; his father died in 1386 and his mother in 1388.[3] Poor young men with Bruni's talents, such as Salutati and Poggio, commonly studied the notarial art, a course of training that required two years. However, enough family money must have

1. The date of Bruni's birth has been definitely established by Hans Baron in "The Year of Leonardo Bruni's Birth and Methods for Determining the Ages of Humanists Born in the Trecento," *Speculum* 52(1977):582–625.

2. *Rerum suo tempore gestarum commentarius,* ed. C. di Pierro RIS n.e. 19, 3 (Bologna, 1926): 428.

3. Baron, "The Year of Leonardo Bruni's Birth," p. 610.

remained for Bruni to think of taking the more expensive five-
to eight-year course required to become a Roman lawyer.[4] Therefore, having finished his Latin studies at Arezzo, Bruni at some
point in the early 1390s moved to Florence, which had purchased
the war-ravaged Aretine territory from its conquerors in 1385.[5]
Florence offered the twofold advantage of being the center of
humanistic studies in Tuscany and of having a law school.

Bruni appears to have spent two years in the school of arts at
the Studium, where he studied Aristotle's *Nichomachean Ethics,*
and then about four years in the law school.[6] Increasingly falling
under the influence of Coluccio Salutati, who came to look on him
as his favorite disciple, Bruni ultimately abandoned these law
studies to devote himself to humanistic scholarship. The initiation
of Greek studies in Florence early in 1397 played a decisive role
in this decision. For almost three years Emmanuel Chrysoloras, an
eminent Greek scholar, offered lessons in his home to a group of
brilliant men who included, in addition to Bruni, Palla Strozzi, Pier
Paolo Vergerio, Jacopo Angeli da Scarperia, and Roberto de' Rossi.
When forced to leave Florence early in 1400, Chrysoloras, a gifted
teacher, left behind him a number of students sufficiently trained to
proceed with Greek studies on their own.[7] Without question Bruni
was the most outstanding. Among his first translations from Greek
into Latin were Xenophon's *De tyranno* and St. Basil's *Homilia ad
iuvenes: De legendis libris gentilium,* both done before 1403.
These were followed by dozens of translations of historical,
philosophical, oratorical, and epistolary texts, culminating in 1438
with a version of Aristotle's *Politics.*[8] These translations were inspired by the idea that the translator should strive for literary

4. For the training of the lawyer, see Lauro Martines, *Lawyers and Statecraft
in Renaissance Florence* (Princeton, 1968), pp. 84ff.

5. For a probable chronology of Bruni's schooling in Arezzo, see Baron, "The
Year of Leonardo Bruni's Birth." pp. 610–14.

6. Ibid., p. 613.

7. For a discussion of the chronology of Chrysoloras's Florentine teaching and
a description of his methods and the students who attended the lessons, see
Giuseppi Cammelli, *I dotti bizantini e le origini dell' umanesimo,* vol. 1
(Florence, 1941), pp. 43–98.

8. The dates of these translations are found in Hans Baron, *Humanistisch-
philosophische Schriften* (Leipzig-Berlin, 1928; reprint Wiesbaden, 1969), pp.
160–79. Corrections and additions are found in Baron's *The Crisis of the Early
Italian Renaissance,* rev. ed. (Princeton, 1966), Index under "Bruni."

excellence in interpreting the original rather than make a literal, almost word-for-word rendition, as was the practice in earlier centuries. Bruni's work, together with that of a small but growing number of other students of Greek, gradually made available to an educated public, trained in Latin, a large number of Greek texts, especially in areas of literature and history that medieval translators had almost entirely neglected.

Bruni was the first writer of the Renaissance to utilize an ancient Greek model for his own work. Although a long literary tradition of *laudes,* or praises, of medieval writers existed, Bruni's *Laudatio florentinae urbis,* composed in 1403–4 in the aftermath of the death of Giangaleazzo and the collapse of his empire, represents a conscious imitation of Aelius Aristides' *Panathenaicus* of the second century A.D.[9] Like the work of Aristides, from which Bruni borrowed many formal elements and the topics for discussion, the *Laudatio* is a panegyric endeavoring to magnify the city praised above all other cities. Aristides' claim that Athens acted as the bulwark of Greek liberty against the threat of Persian despotism helped Bruni formulate his own interpretation of Florence's role in contemporary Italy in the period of the Milanese wars. Aristides' contention that Athenian political dominance in Greece led to a cultural preeminence is echoed by Bruni in his emphasis on the cultural leadership of Florence in Italy. For his geographical description of Florence and its countryside, moreover, Bruni drew on the image of rings geometrically surrounding a central point used by the Greek author in another context. Aristides believed

---

9. Baron has convincingly assigned the date 1403–4 to the writing of the *Laudatio;* see "Chronology and Historical Certainty: The Dates of Bruni's *Laudatio* and *Dialogi,*" in *From Petrarch to Leonardo Bruni* (Chicago, 1968), pp. 102–20. The *Panathenaicus,* together with an English translation, is published in *Aristides,* ed. C. A. Behr (Cambridge, Mass., 1973), pp. 6–275. On the medieval *laudes* literature generally, see J. K. Hyde, "Medieval Descriptions of Cities," *Bulletin of the John Rylands Library* 48(1966):308–40. Although there is some precedent in Florentine *laudes* for descriptions of magistracies, nevertheless the influence of Aristides probably was the direct cause of Bruni's inclusion of this section in his panegyric; see Nicolai Rubinstein, "Florentine Constitutionalism and the Medici Ascendancy in the Fifteenth Century," *Florentine Studies,* ed. Nicolai Rubinstein (London, 1968), p. 442 n. 2. The following paragraph is based on Baron's comparison of the Aristides panegyric with Bruni's work; see "Imitation, Rhetoric, and Quattrocento Thought in Bruni's *Laudatio,*" *From Petrarch to Leonardo Bruni,* pp. 157–71.

that Athenian superiority stemmed from the fact that Athenians, alone of all the peoples of the peninsula, were not immigrants but, rather, natives of the soil, and this view found its parallel in Bruni's more abstract assertion that Florence was founded by the Romans when they were still at the height of their power and from this descent inherited a claim to historical greatness. Bruni's introduction into his panegyric of an analysis of the Florentine constitution, a topic without precedence in medieval *laudes* literature, also seems clearly inspired by his Greek predecessor's description of the Athenian constitution.

Despite its dependence on a Greek model, this early work of Bruni makes an original contribution to the history of western political thought in its insistence that political liberty is only possible where citizens obey and rule themselves and in its use of an historical analysis showing the deleterious effects of the monarchy on the Roman Empire with the advent of the Caesars. The significance of this contribution can only be understood in the light of previous thought about the nature of political liberty.

It was generally conceded in the Middle Ages that liberty was good and tyranny bad, but liberty was so defined as to make monarchy the best form of government. In the Middle Ages the man living his life according to the dictates of reason was morally free and virtuous.[10] The rule of the passions over reason represented moral slavery. Yet to be morally free, to act virtuously, normally was possible only for the man who was also legally free. The man who was juridically free could lead a virtuous life, that is, a life according to reason, because he was not subject to the whims and appetites of a master.

But this ethical and judicial conception of freedom had political implications. Men legally free could only be so in a political society ruled by reason. Whether in the form of statutes, accepted customs, or the prince's commands, law had to conform to reason. Such law permitted and encouraged individuals to lead lives of virtue and protected their status as freemen from arbitrary demands. In a tyranny the ruler, a slave to his own passions, dominated free men under him like a master over bondsmen. In such a society morality was seen to degenerate and civic life became

10. See my characterization of the medieval conception of liberty in *Coluccio Salutati and the Public Letters* (Geneva, 1976), pp. 73–76.

corrupt. Of the various good forms of government, monarchy, rule of the wise prince, was regarded as the most certain to produce good law and thereby guarantee subjects maximum freedom while inciting them to virtue.

Bruni's position, as it developed from the *Laudatio* to the end of his life, represents a revival of Cicero's conception of political liberty lost in the Middle Ages. Cicero would have accepted the moral and juridical ideas associated with the concept of liberty. At one point he defined the relationship between liberty and law in this striking fashion (*Pro Cluent.* 146): "We are slaves of the law so that we might be free." But he would have replaced the political implications present in the medieval idea of liberty with a clear formulation of political liberty centering on the principle of *aequitas*, or equality. Where equality existed there was for Cicero true liberty (*De off.* I, 124): "The private individual ought to live on fair and equal terms with his fellow citizens, with a spirit neither servile and abject nor yet domineering." In other words, fundamental to liberty were equality before the law and equality of basic political rights. For Cicero republican government was not only relatively superior to monarchy: monarchy was incompatible with liberty; monarchy was tyranny; only popular government made men truly free.[11]

Bruni was not the first European to restate the view that true liberty was impossible where government lay in the hands of a single individual, no matter how beneficent. The Tuscan Dominican Ptolemy of Lucca, writing in the years around 1300, had previously articulated this view in his continuation of the unfinished treatise of St. Thomas, the *De regimine principum*. Ptolemy appears to have read both Cicero and the recently recovered political writings of Aristotle with fresh eyes. A vital factor inducing Ptolemy to reexamine these ancient works was his own experience growing up in one of the major communes of Tuscany, in which his family played a leading political role. The continuation of the *De regimine*, moreover, was perhaps written during Ptolemy's long residence in Santa Maria Novella in Florence. For Ptolemy, only where the conduct of the ruler was regulated by statute could

---

11. C. Wirszubski, *Libertas as a Political Idea at Rome during the Late Republic and Early Principate* (Cambridge, 1950), p. 11. The quotations from Cicero are taken from this author, pp. 7 and 12.

law prevail.[12] In a monarchy the king "discovered" the law in himself and what pleased him was legal. This meant that, however good the monarch was, he was still above the law. Thus Ptolemy was led to identify monarchy with despotism and to characterize it as a form appropriate for slaves and brutish men. By contrast, free, civilized peoples merited republican government, which permitted them to make the laws they had to obey.

The major difference between the theories of Ptolemy and Cicero was that the Dominican did not emphasize equality of basic political rights as essential for the maintenance of liberty. Besides this, he did not offer consistent historical proof for the superiority of republican government. Like Aquinas and some other thirteenth-century writers, he criticized the early Roman kings as tyrants and regarded Julius Caesar as a usurper. Unlike his predecessors, Ptolemy used this historical material to prove the inferiority of monarchy to republican government, but he did not extend his censure to the institution of the emperor. For him the imperial office constituted a sort of halfway constitutional form between regal and republican forms. More important, however, since he saw Christian history as intimately connected with Rome from the reign of Augustus, he interpreted Roman history after Caesar as ecclesiastical and the popes rather than the emperors as playing the central roles. In spite of these qualifications, Ptolemy seems to have been the earliest to relate elements of a republican interpretation of Roman history to a theoretical justification of republican government.

Ptolemy's ideas had no definable impact on succeeding generations, even among thinkers devoted to their local communal regimes. The ambivalence of Coluccio Salutati (1331–1406), Florentine chancellor, toward a republican conception of history and politics illustrates the difficulties involved in overcoming the medieval prejudice for monarchy in political theory.[13] While intensely loyal to Florence, Salutati was never to work out a republican theory of government. He had in fact no interest in doing so. His was a deep commitment to the medieval view of the Holy Roman Empire, which comprised a grouping of princely powers and communal governments like that of Florence ruling

12. For references to relevant passages of Ptolemy's work and to bibliography relating to it, see my *Coluccio Salutati*, pp. 77–79.

13. On Salutati's political ideas see ibid., pp. 80–86.

under the aegis of the emperor. While he doubtless preferred Florence's neighbors to be republics, he nonetheless had no desire to challenge the principle of monarchy itself, on which the legal structure of empire rested.

The readiness of Bruni's generation of Florentines to develop and accept a republican interpretation of history and political theory derives from a number of causes. The war between Florence and the Church (1375–78) had revealed the hollowness of Florence's traditional conception of its international role as a member of a holy Guelf alliance under the leadership of the papacy. The wars against Giangaleazzo Visconti (1390–1402), in which Florence stood as the major obstacle to Milan's southward expansion, deepened Florence's awareness of its political power. That the emperor was now totally without influence in Italian politics meant that Florence had to define its role as a leading member of an international society of totally independent states. Internally, while the number of families in the city actively engaged in politics steadily decreased after 1387, within these families power was divided more evenly than before between all male family members.[14] Earlier it was common for one of two men to represent a whole family in high state offices in each generation. This new emphasis on sharing of political offices within the families was coupled with a growing consensus among leading families on foreign and domestic policies. With political power concentrated from the 1390s on within less than a hundred families, never before in Florentine history had there been such concord among the ruling class and such importance given to equal distribution of offices to active citizens. That the regime had stood fast against Giangaleazzo and after 1402 witnessed the destruction of his hastily erected empire gave this class enormous confidence.

Bruni's *Laudatio florentinae urbis* provided Florentines with a

---

14. For a discussion of the internal evolution of Florentine politics in the last decades of the fourteenth century and the first years of the fifteenth, see John Najemy, *The Guilds in Florentine Politics, 1293–1394* (Diss., Harvard, 1972) and Ronald Witt, "Florentine Politics and the Ruling Class, 1382–1407," *The Journal of Medieval and Renaissance Studies* 6(1976):243–67. For a key conceptual approach to this period, see Anthony Molho, "Politics and the Ruling Class in Early Renaissance Florence," *Nuova rivista storica* 52(1968):401–20. Gene Brucker, *The Civic World of Early Renaissance Florence* (Princeton, 1977), presents a brilliant synthesis of Florentine politics and society from 1378 to 1434.

means of conceptualizing the new political situation. By boldly isolating the characteristics, advantages, and pedigree of republican liberty, Bruni clarified the muddled thinking of his contemporaries. Providing an elaborate defense of republicanism, Bruni freed the Florentines from subservience to medieval categories of thought and justified to them their strong feelings of loyalty toward the commune. Ptolemy of Lucca, a century before, had formulated a conception of republican liberty, but Ptolemy's own generation was not prepared to understand it. Bruni's republicanism became an historical force because his ideas had meaning for contemporary Florentines.

While Aristides' panegyric of Athens provided Bruni with categories and images for articulating his ideas, thus lending them a clarity they would not otherwise have possessed, Bruni had clearly utilized the Greek model because he was already searching for a vehicle through which to express certain general ideas. If he knew Ptolemy's work, which we may assume he did, the humanist went beyond the scholastic writer in consistently appraising the history of the Roman monarchy, whether in the period of the kings or the emperors, as one of stagnation or decay. If he did not yet distinguish an equality of basic political rights from an equality before the law, Bruni nonetheless followed Cicero in stressing equality as a basic ingredient of liberty. Salutati's discovery that Florence had been founded in the republican rather than imperial period provided Bruni with a means of linking Florence closely with the republican history of Rome and helped to set Florence's tradition of liberty in sharp relief. Despite its intellectual debts, therefore, Bruni's *Laudatio* constitutes an original work of seminal importance for the history of republicanism.

Lured to Rome by the prospect of a lucrative position in the Curia in 1405, Bruni became an important official in the chancery of the Roman pope Innocent VII. Apparently, in the first year of his papal service Bruni, still warmly attached to Florence, composed the second part of his two *Dialogi*.[15] Whereas in the first, written in 1401, Bruni's principal character, Niccolò Niccoli, attacks modern Florentine writers such as Dante, Petrarch, and Boccaccio as vastly inferior to the ancients, part two presents

15. Baron, "Chronology and Historical Certainty," pp. 120–37, and his *The Crisis.* pp. 245–69.

Niccoli retracting these accusations directed against the heroes of the Florentine literary tradition and praising their work highly. The five-year distance between the writing of the two dialogues covers the period of the writing of the *Laudatio* with its emphasis on the cultural vitality of Florence. If, as it appears, Bruni's attitude toward the three modern writers changed after 1401, then Bruni likely would have written the second dialogue to correct his ideas, already in circulation, by specifically rebutting the charges of inferiority and thereby vindicating Florence's claim to cultural superiority.[16]

Bruni remained almost continuously in papal employment for the next ten years. In 1409 he deserted the Roman pope, Gregory XII, successor to Innocent VII, for Alexander V, the pope recently elected by dissident cardinals of Rome and Avignon at Pisa. He remained with Alexander's successor, John XXIII, until 1414, when the Council of Constance deposed all three schismatic popes. With the dispersion of John XXIII's court, Bruni returned to Florence. He had married a Florentine in 1412, and from 1415 until his death in 1444 he remained in the city. He became a citizen in 1416 and held the post of chancellor of the Republic from 1427 until the end of his life.

Besides continuing his activity as a translator, in his last thirty years Bruni produced a wealth of historical, moral, and literary works in Latin and Italian. A number of these were entirely or in part dedicated to developing the republican concept of liberty and the implications it had for interpreting history and contemporary political, moral, and cultural life.

Apart from its many scholarly merits, Bruni's historical masterpiece, the *Historiae florentini populi,* presenting Florentine history as a significant aspect of the continuing struggle of free men against the forces of tyranny, provided documentation supporting his arguments for the advantages of republican over monarchical government. Bruni's research into Italy's Etruscan and Roman past had its most significant effects on theory in two important works

16. For the position that the *Dialogi* were written at the same time and that neither reflects the author's convictions, see Jerrold Seigel, " 'Civic Humanism' or Ciceronian Rhetoric? The Culture of Petrarca and Bruni," *Past and Present* 34(1966):3–48; for a rejoinder of Baron to Seigel: "Leonardo Bruni: 'Professional Rhetorician' or 'Civic Humanist'," *Past and Present* 36(1967):22–27.

written in his later life, a Greek treatise *On the Florentine Polity* (1438) and the *Oratio in funere Johannis Strozzae* (1428), dedicated to the Florentine patrician Nanni degli Strozzi, who had died as a general in the service of the Marquis of Ferrara, ally of Florence in her wars against Filippo Maria Visconti of Milan.[17]

From his studies of ancient Italian states, Bruni had learned that the vitality of republics derives from the equality of political rights enjoyed by their citizens. In both these later political works, therefore, Bruni was able to articulate clearly Cicero's conception of equality as referring not merely to equality before the law but also to equal access to public honors and offices, a distinction not developed in the *Laudatio*. Such access to honors in the state, Bruni argues in the *Oratio*, awakens the talents of the citizens, encouraging a high level of morality and industry.[18] The Greek treatise, composed shortly after Bruni's completion of his translation of Aristotle's *Politics*, reflects Aristotelian influence in the definition of the ideal political class as being men from "the middle condition" to the exclusion of the very greatest families and the poorest elements.[19]

In later life Bruni himself characterized the *Laudatio* as a "kind of game of imitation and the exercise of a young man."[20] Doubtless he would have conceded that there were exaggerations in the *Oratio* as well. But he and members of the Florentine ruling class, who eventually embraced his political and historical outlook, genuinely believed in the validity of Bruni's basic analysis. Within a decade of the publication of the *Laudatio*, Florentine leaders were using Bruni's ideas in an effort to formulate public policy in their discussions.[21] While modern scholarship has shown that the highest offices were not in fact available to relatively large numbers of men in "the middle condition," there is no more reason to accuse the Florentines of conscious deception than there is to level

17. Baron, *The Crisis*, pp. 412–14.

18. Baron, *The Crisis*, pp. 414–30. On the link between the discoveries of the *Historiae* and the *Oratio*, see pp. 424–25.

19. Rubinstein, "Florentine Constitutionalism," pp. 447–49.

20. *Leonardi Bruni Arretini Epistolarum libri VIII*, ed. L. Mehus, 2 vols. (Florence, 1742), 2:111.

21. Gene Brucker discusses this new political rhetoric in his *The Civic World*, pp. 283–318.

the same charge against the slave-owning signers of the American Declaration of Independence.

Bruni's writings on the Florentine constitution represented in effect a mingling of reality and ideal. As such they were to inspire his own and future generations. In his work Bruni effected a union of a variety of ideas—the republican appraisal of ancient history, the definition of liberty as self-government, the career open to talents, the psychological role of liberty in human creativity, the virtue of rule by the middling classes—and these ideas formed the core of the republican tradition in Western Europe down into the last century.

BIBLIOGRAPHY

Leonardo Bruni: Editions and Translations

Laudatio florentinae urbis. In Hans Baron, *From Petrarch to Leonardo Bruni,* pp. 232–63. Chicago, 1968. Another ed. by V. Zaccaria. *Studi medievali,* 3rd ser. 8(1967):529–54.

Dialogi ad Petrum Paulum Istrum. In *Prosatori latini del Quattrocento,* edited by E. Garin, pp. 39–99. Milan and Naples, 1952. English translation in D. Thompson and A. F. Nagel. *The Three Crowns of Florence,* pp. 19–52. New York, 1972.

Leonardi Bruni Epistolarum libri VIII. Edited by L. Mehus. 2 vols. Florence, 1741.

Historiarum florentini populi libri. Edited by E. Santini. *RIS,* n.e. 19(Città di Castello, 1914):3–288.

Rerum suo tempore gestarum commentarius. Edited by C. di Pierro. *RIS,* n.e. 19(Bologna, 1926):423–58.

De militia. In C. C. Bayley, *War and Society in Renaissance Florence: The "De Militia" of Leonardo Bruni,* pp. 360–97. Toronto, 1961.

"Leonardo Aretini ad magnum principem imperatorem." In Hans Baron, *Humanistic and Political Literature in Florence and Venice at the Beginning of the Quattrocento,* pp. 181–84. Cambridge, Mass., 1955.

"Oratio in funere Johannis Strozzae." In E. Baluze and G. D. Manzi, *Miscellanea novo ordine digesta et . . . aucta.* 4 vols. 4:2–7. Lucca, 1761–64.

Bruni, Leonardo. *Perī tēs tōn Phlorentīnon politeīas.* Edited by C. E. Neumann, with German translation. Frankfurt am Main, 1822.

Baron, Hans. *Leonardo Bruni Aretino, Humanistisch-Philosophische Schriften.* Leipzig and Berlin, 1928; rept. Wiesbaden, 1969. Includes editions of many of Bruni's shorter works.

Studies

Aurigemma, Marcello. "Leonardo Bruni." *Letteratura italiana. I minori* 1, pp. 405–25. Milan, 1961.

Baron, Hans. "Leonardo Bruni, 'Professional Rhetorician' or 'Civic Humanist'?" *Past and Present* 36(1967):21–37.

————. *From Petrarch to Leonardo Bruni,* pp. 102–71, 219–31. Chicago, 1968.

————. "The Year of Leonardo Bruni's Birth and Methods for Determining the Ages of Humanists Born in the Trecento," *Speculum* 52(1977):582–625.

Beck, Franz. *Studien zu Lionardo Bruni.* Abhandlungen zur Mittlerem und Neuern Geschichte, vol. 36. Berlin and Leipzig, 1912.

Bertalot, Ludwig. "Forschungen über Leonardo Bruni Aretino." *Archivum Romanicum* 15(1931):284–323.

Freudenthal, Jakob. "Leonardo Bruni als philosoph." *Neue Jahrbücher für das klassiche Altertum* 27(1911):48–66.

Garin, Eugenio. "La retorica di Leonardo Bruni." In *Dal Rinascimento all' Illuminismo,* pp. 21–42. Pisa, 1970.

Gilbert, Neal W. "The Early Italian Humanists and Disputation." In *Renaissance Studies in Honor of Hans Baron,* edited by A. Molho and J. A. Tedeschi, pp. 201–26. Florence, 1971.

Molho, A. "Politics and the Ruling Class in Early Renaissance Florence." *Nuova Rivista Storica* 52(1968):401–20.

Radetti, G. "Le origini dell'Umanesimo civile nel '400." *Giornale critico della filosofia italiana* 38(1959):98–122.

Rubinstein, Nicolai. "Florentine Constitutionalism and the Medici Ascendancy in the Fifteenth Century." In *Florentine Studies,* edited by N. Rubinstein, pp. 157–71. London, 1968.

Santini, E. "Leonardo Bruni Aretino e i suoi 'Historiarum florentini populi libri'." *Annali della R. Scuola Normale Superiore di Pisa* 22(1910):1–174.

"La produzione volgare di Leonardo Bruni Aretino e il suo culto per le tre corone fiorentine." *Giornale storico della letteratura italiana* 60(1912):289–339.

Seigel, J. E. " 'Civic Humanism' or Ciceronian Rhetoric? The Culture of Petrarch and Bruni." *Past and Present* 34(1966):3–48.

Soudek, J. "Leonardo Bruni and His Public. A Statistical and Interpretative Study of His Annotated Latin Version of the (Pseudo–) Aristotelian Economics." *Studies in Medieval and Renaissance History* 5(1968):49–136.

Ullman, B. L. "Leonardo Bruni and Humanistic Historiography." In his *Studies in the Italian Renaissance,* pp. 321–44. Rome, 1955.

Varese, Claudio. *Storia e politica nella prosa del Quattrocento.* Turin, 1961.

Vasoli, Cesare. "Bruni, Leonardo." *DBI* 14(1972):618–33.

Wilcox, Donald. *The Development of Florentine Humanist Historiography in the Fifteenth Century.* Cambridge, Mass., 1969.

Witt, Ronald G. "Florentine Politics and the Ruling Class, 1382–1407." *Journal of Medieval and Renaissance Studies* 6(1976):243–67.

LEONARDO BRUNI
*Panegyric to the City of Florence**

Translated by BENJAMIN G. KOHL

Would that God immortal give me eloquence worthy of the city of Florence, about which I am to speak, or at least equal to my zeal and desire on her behalf; for either one degree or the other would, I think, abundantly demonstrate the city's magnificence and splendor. Florence is of such a nature that a more distinguished or more splendid city cannot be found on the entire earth, and I can easily tell about myself, I was never more desireous of doing anything in my life. So I have no doubt at all that if either of these wishes were granted, I should be able to describe with elegance and dignity this very beautiful and excellent city. But because everything we want and the ability granted us to attain what we wish are two different things, we will carry out our intention as well as we can, so that we appear to be lacking in talent rather than in will.

Indeed, this city is of such admirable excellence that no one can match his eloquence with it. But we have seen several good and important men who have spoken concerning God himself, whose glory and magnificence the speech of the most eloquent man cannot capture even in the smallest degree. Nor does this vast superiority keep them from trying to speak insofar as they are able about such an immense magnitude. Therefore, I too shall seem to have

* Complete translation of Leonardo Bruni, *Laudatio Florentinae Urbis*, edited by Hans Baron in his *From Petrarch to Leonardo Bruni* (Chicago, 1968), pp. 232–63.

done enough if, marshalling all competence, expertise, and skill that I have eventually acquired after so much study, I devote my all to praising this city, even though I clearly understand that my ability is such that it can in no way be compared with the enormous splendor of Florence. Therefore many orators say that they themselves do not know where to begin. This now happens to me not only as far as words are concerned but also concerning the subject itself. For not only are there various things connected one with another, here and there, but also any one of them is so outstanding and in some way so distinguished that they seem to vie for excellence among themselves. Therefore, it is not an easy thing to say which subject is to be treated first. If you consider the beauty or splendor of the city, nothing seems more appropriate to start with than these things. Or if you reflect upon its power and wealth, then you will think these are to be treated first. And if you contemplate its history, either in our own day or in earlier times, nothing can seem so important to begin with as these things. When indeed you consider Florentine customs and institutions, you judge nothing more important than these. These matters cause me concern, and often when I am ready to speak on one point, I recall another and am attracted to it. Hence, they furnish me no opportunity to decide which topic to put first. But I shall seize upon the most apt and logical place to begin the speech, even though I do indeed believe that other topics would not have provided an improper point of departure.

1

As we may see several sons with so great a resemblance to their fathers that they show it obviously in their faces, so the Florentines are in such harmony with this very noble and outstanding city that it seems they could never have lived anywhere else. Nor could the city, so skillfully created, have had any other kind of inhabitants. Just as these citizens surpass all other men by a great deal in their natural genius, prudence, elegance, and magnificence, so the city of Florence has surpassed all other cities in its prudent site and its splendor, architecture, and cleanliness.

So we see that in the beginning Florence observed a principle of great wisdom: Do nothing for ostentation nor allow hazardous useless display, but instead use great moderation and follow solid proportion. This city was set neither in the high mountains, so that it would present itself impressively, nor in a broad plain of fields, so it would be open on every side. Rather, this city has both advantages according to the most prudent and best opinion, for one cannot live in high mountains without intemperate climate, without harsh winds, without storms, without great discomfort and hazard to the inhabitants; nor are immense and vast plains without the drenching rays of the sun, without impurity of air, without a hazy humidity. Therefore, having avoided these potential discomforts, Florence very prudently was situated where it is midway between the dangerous extremes (a proven principle for all things), both remote from the evils of the mountains and distant from the dangers of the plains. Hence, though Florence knows both kinds of environments, it possesses a mild and pleasing climate. The mountains of Fiesole face north like a kind of bulwark for the city and repel the immense force of the cold and the headlong rush of the strong northern wind. To the east, where the force of the wind is less, the hills are smaller. And in the other directions, the fields lay open to the sun and to the southern breezes. Therefore, in the area of the city there is a great tranquility and a fine climate, so whenever you leave Florence, in whatever direction you set out, you meet either a greater cold or a hotter sun.

This city, covering an area of both mountains and plains, is surrounded by an extensive crown of wall, not, however, of such a mass that the city would seem timid or fearful of its power, nor, on the other hand so neglected that it can be called imprudent or indiscreet. And what shall I say of the throngs of people, of the splendor of the buildings, of the decorations of the churches, and of the unbelievable and admirable magnificence of the entire city? By Jove, everything here is striking and decorated with outstanding beauty. But it is better to know things in comparison with other things than from themselves alone. Therefore, only those who have been away for some time and return to Florence fully understand how much this flourishing city excels beyond all the others. For there is no other city in the whole world that does not lack perfection in some important way: one lacks its population, another in the decoration of its buildings, still another suffers the least of these in that it does not have a healthful site. Moreover, every other city is so dirty that the filth created during the night is seen in the early morning by the population and trampled under foot in the streets. Really can one think of anything worse than this? Even if there were a thousand palaces in such a city and inexhaustible wealth, even if it possessed an infinite population, still I would always condemn that city as a stinking place and not think highly of it. In similar fashion, someone who is deformed in body will always be unhappy even though he might possess a great many outstanding qualities. Hence, filthy cities that may in other respects be very good can never be considered to be beautiful. Further, who cannot see that a city that is not beautiful lacks its highest and noblest adornment?

Indeed, it seems to me that Florence is so clean and neat that no other city could be cleaner. Surely this city is unique and singular in all the world because you will find here nothing that is disgusting to the eye, offensive to the nose, or filthy under foot. The great diligence of its inhabitants ensures and provides that all filth is removed from the streets, so you see only what brings pleasure and joy to the senses. Therefore, in its splendor Florence probably surpasses all the cities of the world, and, moreover, in its elegance it is without doubt far ahead of all the cities that exist now and all that ever will. Indeed, such unparalleled cleanliness must be incredible to those who have never seen Florence, for we who live here are amazed daily and will never take for granted this fine quality of Florence. Now what is more marvelous in a populous city than never to have to worry about filth in the streets? Moreover, however big a rainstorm, it cannot prevent your walking through the city with dry feet since almost before it falls the rainwater is taken away by appropriately placed gutters. Hence, the cleanliness and dryness that you find only in the rooms of private palaces in other cities, you find in the squares and streets of Florence.

Perhaps another city is clean, but it lacks beautiful buildings. Another will have beautiful buildings, but it lacks a good climate. Another has a good climate, but it lacks a large population. Only Florence can claim to have all these qualities that are necessary for a prosperous city. And if you are interested in things from antiquity, you will find a great many remains from ancient times in both the public buildings and private homes. Or if you are looking for contemporary architecture, there is surely nothing more splendid and magnificent than Florence's new buildings. Indeed, it would be difficult to say whether the river that flows through the city gives more utility or more pleasure. The two banks of the river are joined by four bridges magnificently constructed of squared blocks, and these are placed at such convenient intervals that the river never seems to interrupt the several main streets that cross Florence. Hence you can walk through Florence as easily as though it were not even divided by a river. Wherever you go you can see handsome squares and the decorated porticos of the homes of the noble families, and the streets are always thronged with crowds of men. Of the houses built near the river, some are actually on the river's edge so that they are bathed by the water, while others are set back from the river so that there is a street between these houses and the river bank. Here large crowds of people gather to do their business and enjoy themselves. Indeed, nothing is more pleasant than this area, for walking especially at midday in winter and at dusk in summer.

But why do I concern myself with just one part of the city? Must I (like some fisherman) just move up and down along the river? As if this were the splendid part of Florence, and the other quarters not are equally beautiful, or even more so. What in the whole world is so splendid and magnificent as the architecture of Florence? Indeed, I feel sorry for other cities when a comparison is made with Florence. In other places perhaps one or at the most two streets in the entire city are filled with important buildings, while the rest of the town is so devoid of architectural distinction that the townsmen are ashamed to have visitors see these parts. But in our city there is really no street, no quarter that does not possess spacious and ornate buildings. Almighty God, what wealth of buildings, what distinguished architecture there is in Florence! Indeed, how the great genius of the builders is reflected in these buildings, and what a pleasure there is for those who live in them. Among these many buildings in Florence nothing is more impressive in size and distinction of style than the churches and shrines, which are numerous and are (as is proper for places of worship) spread throughout the city. These have been marvelously revered by those who worship in their various parishes, and are treated with exceeding piety. Indeed, in all of Florence nothing is more richly appointed, more ornate in style, more magnificent than these churches. As much attention has been given to decorating sacred buildings as to secular ones, so that not only the habitations of the living would be outstanding but the tombs of the dead as well.

But I return to the homes of the private citizens, which were designed, built, and decorated for luxury, size, respectability, and especially for magnificence. Indeed, what could be more pleasant and more beautiful to the sight than the entrance courts, halls, pavements, banquet halls, and other interior rooms of these homes? And how beautiful it is to see the well-ordered spaciousness of many of the homes and to view the curtains, arches, the panelled ceilings and richly decorated hung ceilings, and (as in many homes) the summer rooms separated from the winter ones. In these living quarters you find beautiful chambers decorated with fine furniture, gold, silver, and brocaded hangings and precious carpets. But am I not silly to go on enumerating these things? Even if I had a hundred tongues, a hundred mouths, and a voice of iron, I could not possibly describe all the magnificence, wealth, decoration, delights, and elegance of these homes. If there is someone who would like to experience them, let them come here and walk through the city. But don't let him pass through like a temporary guest or a hurrying tourist. Rather, he should pause, poke around, and try to understand what he is seeing. Now, it is very important that in other cities a tourist should not stay too long. In those cities, what they have to show is all publicly displayed and is placed (as it were) on the outward bark. Whoever comes into these cities is seen as a stranger; but if these tourists leave the well-frequented places and try to examine the interiors as well as the exteriors of the buildings, there will be nothing to confirm their first impressions. Indeed, instead of houses they will find only small huts, and behind the exterior decorations only filth. But the beauty of Florence cannot be appreciated unless seen from the inside. Therefore, the sort of careful scrutiny that brings shame to other cities only serves to raise the esteem held for Florence, for behind the walls of the buildings of Florence there are no fewer ornaments and no less magnificence than there is outside; nor is any one street better decorated or more handsome than another, but every quarter shares in the beauty of the city. Hence, just as blood is spread throughout the entire body, so fine architecture and decoration are diffused throughout the whole city.

To be sure, in the center of the city there is a tall and handsome palace of great beauty and remarkable workmanship. This fine building bespeaks by its very appearance the purposes for which it was constructed. Just as in a large fleet it is an easy matter to pick out the flagship that carries the admiral who is the leader and head over the other captains and their ships, so in Florence everyone immediately recognizes that this palace is so immense that it must house the men who are appointed to govern the state. Indeed, it was so magnificently conceived and looms so towerlingly that it dominates all the buildings nearby and its top stands out above those of the private houses.

Indeed, I do not think that I ought to call this building simply a "fortress" but, rather, "fortress of the fortress." The minute you step away from the city walls you are surrounded on all sides by many buildings, so that the latter ought to be called the "city" while this thing surrounded by walls would more correctly be called the "fortress." And as Homer writes of the snow that it falls thickly on the mountains and hills and covers the ridges of the mountains and finally the fertile fields,[1] in like fashion handsome buildings cover the entire region outside the city and all the mountains, the hills and the plains, so that they seem more to have fallen from heaven than to have been constructed by the hands of men. How magnificent, how well designed, how well decorated are these buildings! Indeed, these country houses are even more spacious than those in Florence, for they were designed and constructed on very spacious sites and greater care was taken to make them comfortable and pleasant. As a result, no one who lives in them lacks room, or colonades, or gardens, or stands of trees. What can I possibly say of the rooms and banquet halls, which are more magnificent and ornate than anything imaginable? And near these homes you find wooded groves, flowery meadows, pleasant river banks, sparkling fountains, and—best of all—the nature of the place itself fit for delight. Indeed, the very hills seem to laugh and to exude a certain joyfulness, of which visitors never seem to tire and which never grows stale. Thus, this whole region is rightly

1. An echo of Homer *Iliad* 12.278–86.

considered and called a paradise—unequaled in grace or beauty by any other area in the whole world. Surely anyone who comes to Florence is amazed when at a distance he sees from the top of a mountain the massive city, beautiful and splendid, surrounded by many country houses.

Nor does Florence's beauty at a distance become sordid when you come close, which happens when something is not really beautiful. But all things are so arranged and gleam with such true beauty that the closer you come to this city, the greater grows your appreciation of its magnificence. Thus the villas are more beautiful than the distant panorama, the suburbs more handsome than the villas, and the city itself more beautiful than its suburbs. Hence, when newcomers enter the city they forget the beauties and architecture of the outlying area because they are so stunned in their admiration for the splendor of the city itself.

Now I want to discuss another topic that I usually consider one of the chief arguments for demonstrating the greatness of this city. Florence has fought a great many wars and has been victorious over some very powerful enemies. It has fought several growing and formidable powers, and by its sound strategy, by its wealth and sheer willpower, Florence has even overcome those enemies to which it was judged to be very inferior and even incapable of resisting under any circumstances. Very recently Florence fought for many years against a very powerful and resourceful enemy with such great force that it filled everyone with admiration. For this Duke,[2] who had by his resources and power been a source of fear to the nations north of the Alps as well as to the rest of Italy, and who was elated in his hopes, prideful in victory, and destroyed, like a storm, everything in his path with an incredible success, found himself confronted by this single city that not only repulsed the invader and delayed the impetus of his conquests but even overthrew him after a long war. To these things done by Florence we shall devote time and space a little further on. For the moment, however, let us return to our subject.

I say, therefore, that everyone was so amazed by the dimensions of this conflict and by the duration of the struggle that they were wondering how a single city could muster the great number of

2. An allusion to the recent war with Giangaleazzo Visconti, which Florence eventually won as a result of the dissolution of the Visconti empire following Giangaleazzo's death in September 1402.

troops and immense resources, not to mention the vast amount of money needed for the war. But this wonder, the great amazement of everyone, lasts only as long as men have not seen this beautiful city nor observed its magnificence. When men actually have seen Florence their amazement at its achievements ceases. Indeed, we see that this happens to everyone; no one ever comes to Florence who does not admit to this experience. As soon as they have seen the city and have inspected with their own eyes its great mass of architecture and the grandeur of its buildings, its splendor and magnificence, the lofty towers, the marble churches, the domes of the basilicas, the splendid palaces, the turreted walls, and the numerous villas, its charm, beauty, and decor, instantly everyone's mind and thought change so that they are no longer amazed by the greatest and most important exploits accomplished by Florence. Rather, everyone immediately comes to believe that Florence is indeed worthy of attaining dominion and rule over the entire world. For this reason one can understand how extraordinarily wondrous this city is whose beauty and magnificence cannot be adequately comprehended or related in words. For just as actual sight has more effect than a report, so opinion is inferior to a report.

Now I do not know what others might say, but, for my part, I think my argument is so persuasive that it alone is able to confirm conclusively the incredible excellence of Florence. Once someone has seen the city, it is no easy matter to cancel and erase the general impression of the city's greatness. The only way that this could happen would be if even stronger evidence of nobility and beauty in this very city not just weakened but even cancelled the impression of wonderment caused by the magnitude of its deeds. This would be analogous to the case of someone telling me of the incredible and unparalleled accomplishments of strength by a boxer in a series of contests; for example, I might hear that this one boxer wore out others with his fists and laid out others with his glove. If I heard that this one had knocked down and beaten a great many other boxers, or that he had stopped a speeding heavy chariot with his bare hands or carried a live bull for a hundred yards (a feat that is claimed for Milo of Croton[3]); or if I heard that when this boxer stood upon an oiled bronze shield no one was

3. This description of the feats of the Greek athlete Milo of Croton probably derives from Cicero *De senectute* 3.10.33, and Pliny *Naturalis historia* 7.28.83.

able to take him by force (a feat that we read was performed by Polydamas[4]); and if someone would tell me, already dumbfounded by these deeds, that these reported feats were really seen, and, more than this, add that, if someone actually saw and inspected this boxer's powerful body, no one would be greatly amazed about these stories, and even more fantastic ones would be believed. Now, I say, if someone were to relate and swear these things to me, immediately this image of a very strong man would necessarily come to mind, showing his powerful body and graceful movements and the strength of his members. In like fashion, once this magnificent and splendid city is seen, it dispels all doubts about its greatness and converts former disbelievers to the truth. To do so the city must have a peerless magnificence and grandeur in its construction. How would such a complete change of mind, judgement, and opinion happen if it were not for the fact that Florence is, in truth, more majestic and magnificent than the tongues of narrators can describe or the minds of the listeners comprehend? Indeed, let everyone praise this city, let them always praise it. There has never been anyone who actually saw Florence who did not find it much more impressive than he had imagined when he had merely had it described to him. For this reason I do not fear that many will condemn me for being rash and reckless in attempting to describe the greatness of Florence. Seeing such a city, I have never been able to control my total admiration for Florence, and admiring it thus, not to sing its praises. Therefore, if I cannot accomplish this goal adequately, which no one ever has been able to do, my failings should be excused rather than censured. But let us return to our subject.

Beyond the country houses there are the walled towns. And what should I say of these walled towns? Indeed, there is no part of the region lying beyond the country houses that is not filled with these impressive and splendid walled towns. The city itself stands in the center, like a guardian and lord, while the towns surround Florence on the periphery, each in its own place. A poet might well compare it to the moon surrounded by the stars, and the whole vista is very beautiful to the eyes. Just as on a round buckler, where

4. Perhaps known from the account of Polydamas, the great Thesselian athlete and victor in the olympic games of 408 B.C., in Valerius Maximus, *Memorabilia* 9.12.ext.10.

one ring is laid around the other, the innermost ring loses itself in the central knob that is the middle of the entire buckler. So here we see the regions lying like rings surrounding and enclosing one another. Within them Florence is first, similar to the central knob, the center of the whole orbit. The city itself is ringed by walls and suburbs. Around the suburbs, in turn, lies a ring of country houses, and around them the circle of towns. The whole outermost region is enclosed in a still larger orbit and circle. Between the towns there are castles—these safest of refuges for the peasants—with their towers reaching into the sky.

Now the number of farmers is so great that all the available land is under cultivation. What shall I say of the abundance and quality of the crops? What of the large harvests of the fields? Indeed, these things are known to everyone and obvious to the beholder, so that they do not require proof. But I shall say this much: It is not easy to find a region that grows such a great multitude of inhabitants! Now there are many cities that do not have as many inhabitants as the Florentine countryside; still, it gives this population together with the populous city not only the necessity of life but even makes them independent of outside help either for necessities or even for luxuries. For this reason Florence, both inside and outside the city walls, should be judged as the most fortunate city in the entire world.

Now if there is anyone who would say that Florence is deficient because it is not a seaport, he errs, in my opinion, and considers a vice what is really a virtue. Proximity to the sea is perhaps useful for buying and selling products, but otherwise it is too salty and offensive. Indeed, there are a great many inconveniences that beset seaports and, worse still, dangers that they must of necessity undergo. When Plato of Athens, without question the greatest of all philosophers, established in his book how a city might live well and happily and investigated diligently what must be present and what must be avoided, he believed it was very important for a city to be rather distant from the sea.[5] Nor did that very wise man consider that a city could ever be fortunate if it were placed either on the seashore or anywhere near the lappings of the waves. He discussed at length the harm and discomforts to a happy way of

5. Plato *Leges* 704–7, the beginning of book 4.

life that proximity to the sea entails or necessitates. Indeed, if we should wish to discover how serious it is for a city to be situated in such a position, we need only consider the danger felt by seaports from Tana and Trebizond all the way to Cadiz. Not only do these cities have to worry about what their neighbors are doing, what policies neighboring peoples debate, what they are planning, and what their attitude is toward us and be aware of their internal conspiracies as well as frontal attacks; but, in addition, these seaports have to reckon with possible dangers at the hands of the Egyptians, the Syrians, the Colchians of Greece, the Scythians, the Moors, the men of Cadiz, and many other strange and barbarian peoples besides. Indeed, it is sometimes difficult to know the policies of neighboring states; how much more difficult it is to know what distant peoples are planning. Land armies, which are usually very slow, sometimes arrive before anything is suspected. Therefore, what is to be expected from the speed of fleets? And even if seaborne attacks do not presently happen, we are not entitled to believe that they will never occur in the future since we know for certain that they occurred in the past. Moreover, it would be very foolish when you might live securely and quietly to throw yourself into the path of danger.

But if you who love the sea and its shore so much are not moved by this line of reasoning, perhaps you will be convinced by examples from antiquity. Read the Roman and Greek historians, and consider in those works how much ill fortune, how frequent the destruction of maritime cities, how many cities, even while they flourished with wealth, men, and money, have been captured by an enemy fleet before they could undertake their own defense. If the skeptics will reflect upon these examples, they will begin to understand that this city that is not a seaport lacks nothing but, rather, possesses (as it does in other matters) a gift of Divine Providence. Troy, "the most noble capital of all Asia" and (as the tragedian says) "an outstanding creation of the gods,"[6] was twice captured and destroyed by a fleet: the first time by the sudden arrival of Hercules and Thelamones, the second by the trickery of Agamemnon and Ulysses. That flourishing city could not have been captured in any way except for the opportunities afforded by the

6. Seneca *Troades* 7–8.

nearness of the sea. A decade had been consumed in useless land-based assault when finally the attackers left in a fleet upon the waves—a very useful element for disguising plots. Then the Trojans believed that they were at last free of the lengthy siege, and, since no hostile force appeared before them, they suspected nothing, "but the Argive host with marshaled ships was moved from Tenedos, amid the friendly silence of the peaceful moon."[7] And a little later: "Others sack and ravage burning Pergamum, are you only now coming from the tall ships?"[8] These are the rewards of the sea! For such reasons is proximity to the sea deemed praiseworthy.

But why do I discuss such a distant example? We read that the very fine Italian city of Genoa was captured and leveled to the ground during the Second Punic War by a single sudden assault by Mago, the son of Hamilcar.[9] Do I need to remind you of the destruction of the Phocaeans and the Syracusans, of Alexandria and Athens? Who does not know that at the time when the Roman people ruled over the entire earth the sea was infested for many years by predatory fleets, so that a number of cities belonging to the Romans suffered complete destruction? And this people who had conquered the entire world could not preserve its seaports from the incursions of hostile fleets. Add to this the polluted air, the changeable weather, the debilitating diseases that derive from the unhealthfulness of coastal regions, and the harshness of the entire area of the seashore. In view of these and so many other adverse conditions, is it not surprising that a prudent city avoids a harbor so that it would be as secure as a ship in port? It prefers to do without the waves of the sea in order to avoid undergoing waves of invasions?

What indeed would a city without a harbor lack? Although I fear how my views will be received, still I shall say what I feel. As in all other respects, in this matter Florence has benefited from sage advice and Divine Providence. Florence is distant enough from the coast to be entirely free from all the difficulties that proximity to the sea carries with it, yet near enough to seaports so that it is not at all deprived of the use of the sea. It is only in nearness to the

7. Vergil *Aeneid* 2.254–55.
8. Vergil *Aeneid* 2.374–75.
9. From Livy *Ab urbe condita* 28.46.

sea that Florence is vanquished by seaports, and in this matter the vanquished city is in reality the victor. To be sure, seaports derive some advantages from their harbors and beaches, but these advantages are always accompanied by dangers and alloyed with vexations. Indeed, Florence profits from its nearness to the sea but derives only pure advantage from its situation; it is never disturbed by misfortunes or threatened by dangers. The comfort of Florence is never vexed or threatened by pestilential climate, by fetid and impure air, by the humidity of the water, or by autumnal fevers. Rather, its utility is as pure as can be, not dangerous and total. Indeed, it seems to me that Florence is distant enough from the western Mediterranean to enjoy at the same time the benefits of proximity to the Adriatic. This happy situation cannot be praised enough. If Florence were situated on either coast in addition to being plagued with innumerable different vexations because of its nearness to the sea, it would be inconvenienced because it was too distant from the other. Hence, it would suffer from being at two extremes at the same time: both too near to and too far from the coast. But since Florence is equidistant from either coast, it seems not content with one of them but has sought to utilize both coasts at the same time; almost as the queen of Italy, Florence sits equidistant between the Tyrrhenian and Adriatic seas. It is set in a very healthy climate and is not far from either plains or mountains. Here lie very fertile fields, there arise smiling hills. Florence is further supplied by a river flowing through its midst, which is both of great beauty and of even greater utility. And in the city there are admirable splendors, incomparable beauty, stupendous architecture, and enormous magnificence. Moreover, the surrounding villas provide great and unheard of delicacies, amenities not of this world, and indeed complete joyfulness, pleasantness, elegance. Indeed, Florence is so filled with greatness and splendor that it excels by a long way not just the cities of Italy but even those of all the provinces of ancient Rome.

This abundance of beautiful things, which affords such rich material for easily describing the city, has seized me so completely and forcefully that I have not had any opportunity to rest. Perhaps I have constructed my speech so disjointedly that in attempting to describe all the fine ornaments of Florence I have passed over the first and best ornament of all. Occupied with describing the other beauty and magnificence of this great city, I had almost forgotten that I should really be talking about the people, the size of the population, and the virtue, industry, and kindness of the citizen-body, which is Florence's greatest treasure and among the first things that ought to come to mind. Therefore, it is time for me to return to my point of departure and to render those who inhabit Florence their due. So we ought to acknowledge that we have wandered a bit, and we ought to return to the subject of our speech. At this time we ought to collect our thoughts, leave behind those topics that we have already treated, and turn toward the subjects that we ought now to discuss, so that we don't persist in this error any longer.

2

Therefore, now that we have described what Florence is, we should next consider what manner of citizens there are here. As one usually does in discussing an individual, so we want to investigate the origins of the Florentine people and to consider from what ancestor the Florentines derived and what they have accomplished at home and abroad in every age. As Cicero says: "Let's do it this way, let's begin at the beginning."[10]

What, therefore, was the stock of these Florentines? Who were their progenitors? By what mortals was this outstanding city founded? Recognize, men of Florence, recognize your race and your forebears. Consider that you are, of all races, the most renowned. For other peoples have as forebears refugees or those banished from their fathers' homes, peasants, obscure wanderers, or unknown founders. But your founder is the Roman people—the lord and conqueror of the entire world. Immortal God, you have conferred so many good things on this one city so that everything—no matter where it happens or for what purpose it was ordained—seems to redound to Florence's benefit.

For the fact that the Florentine race arose from the Roman people is of the utmost importance. What nation in the entire world was ever more distinguished, more powerful, more out-

10. Cicero *Orationes philippicae* 2.44.

standing in every sort of excellence than the Roman people? Their deeds are so illustrious that the greatest feats done by other men seems like child's play when compared to the deeds of the Romans. Their dominion was equal to the entire world, and they governed with the greatest competence for many centuries, so that from a single city comes more examples of virtue than all other nations have been able to produce until now. In Rome there have been innumerable men so outstanding in every kind of virtue that no other nation on earth has ever been equal to it. Even omitting the names of many fine and outstanding leaders and heads of the Senate, where do you find, except in Rome, the families of the Publicoli, Fabricii, Corruncani, Dentati, Fabii, Decii, Camilli, Pauli, Marcelli, Scipiones, Catones, Gracchi, Torquati, and Cicerones? Indeed, if you are seeking nobility in a founder you will never find any people nobler in the entire world than the Roman people; if you are seeking wealth, none more opulent; if you want grandeur and magnificence, none more outstanding and glorious; if you seek extent of dominion, there was no people on this side of the ocean that had not been subdued and brought under Rome's power by force of arms. Therefore, to you, also, men of Florence, belongs by hereditary right dominion over the entire world and possession of your parental legacy. From this it follows that all wars that are waged by the Florentine people are most just, and this people can never lack justice in its wars since it necessarily wages war for the defense or recovery of its own territory. Indeed, these are the sorts of just wars that are permitted by all laws and legal systems. Now, if the glory, nobility, virtue, grandeur, and magnificence of the parents can also make the sons outstanding, no people in the entire world can be as worthy of dignity as are the Florentines, for they are born from such parents who surpass by a long way all mortals in every sort of glory. Who is there among men who would not readily acknowledge themselves subjected to the Roman people? Indeed, what slave or freedman strives to have the same dignity as the children of his lord or master, or hopes to be chosen instead of them? It is evident that it is no trifling ornament to the city of Florence to have had such an outstanding creator and founder for itself and its people.

But at what point in history did the nation of the Florentines arise from the Romans? Now I believe that in the case of royal successions there is a custom observed by most peoples, namely, that the person who is finally declared to be heir to the king must be born at the time his father possessed the royal dignity. Those offspring who are born either before or after are not considered to be the sons of a king, nor are they permitted to have the right of succession to their father's kingdom. Surely whoever rules when in his best and most flourishing condition also accomplish his most illustrious and glorious deeds. Indeed, it is evident that, for whatever reasons, prosperous times stimulate men's minds and call forth great spirits, so that at such moments in history great men are able to do only what is important and glorious, and what is accomplished then is always especially outstanding.

Accordingly, this very noble Roman colony was established at the very moment when the dominion of the Roman people flourished greatly and when very powerful kings and warlike nations were being conquered by the skill of Roman arms and by virtue. Carthage, Spain, and Corinth were levelled to the ground; all lands and seas acknowledged the rule of these Romans, and these same Romans suffered no harm from any foreign state. Moreover, the Caesars, the Antonines, the Tiberiuses, the Neros—those plagues and destroyers of the Roman Republic—had not yet deprived the people of their liberty. Rather, still growing there was that sacred and untrampled freedom that, soon after the founding of the colony of Florence, was to be stolen by those vilest of thieves. For this reason I think something has been true and is true in this city more than in any other; the men of Florence especially enjoy perfect freedom and are the greatest enemies of tyrants. So I believe that from its very founding Florence conceived such a hatred for the destroyers of the Roman state and underminers of the Roman Republic that it has never forgotten to this very day. If any trace of or even the names of those corrupters of Rome have survived to the present, they are hated and scorned in Florence.

Now this interest in republicanism is not new to the Florentine people, nor did it begin (as some people think) only a short time since. Rather, this struggle against tyranny was begun a long time ago when certain evil men undertook the worst crime of all—the destruction of the liberty, honor, and dignity of the Roman people. At that time, fired by a desire for freedom, the Florentines adopted their penchant for fighting and their zeal for the republican side, and this attitude has persisted down to the present day. If at other times these political factions were called by different names, still they were not really different. From the beginning Florence has always been united in one and the same cause against the invaders of the Roman state and it has constantly persevered in this policy to the present time. By Jove, this was caused by a just hatred of tyranny more than by the well-deserved respect due to the ancient fatherland. For who could bear that the Roman state, acquired with the kind of virtue that Camillus, Publicola, Fabricius, Curtius, Fabius, Regulus, Scipio, Marcellus, the Catos, and countless other very honorable and chaste men displayed, fell into the hands and under the domination of Caligula and other monsters and vile tyrants who were innocent of no vice and redeemed by no virtue?[11] To excel in this these monsters were in a competition of mighty proportions, striving with all their power.

As a result of these struggles, every means of cruelty was employed in the annihilation of the Roman citizens, as though the highest prize in the world would be given to them only if they left in Rome no nobility, no political vitality, and even no citizen-body. Therefore, when Caligula had committed as many crimes as he possibly could, and many citizens still survived in that great city, the emperor, weary of killing and massacring and unable in any way to have his cruel desires satisfied, finally uttered that evil saying that serves as a witness to his enormities: "Would that the Roman people had but one neck, so that I could chop it off with a single blow."[12] Clearly he did just that. Not yet satisfied with the blood of the citizen-body, he would have made the city empty had he lived a little longer. In addition, he drove a sword through the senatorial order, he cut down the most outstanding members of the consular ranks, he cut off families at their roots, and he daily slaughtered whatever plebs were still left in the city as if they were cattle in droves. To this monstrous cruelty he added even more monstrous outrages, which indeed are uncommon and unequalled through all the centuries and have never been recalled without a curse. Three of his own sisters were, in turn, ravaged by him, and then they were forced to live openly with their brother as his concubines. Are these the deeds of emperors? Are these our

11. The following anecdotes about Caligula and Tiberius are derived from Suetonius *Gaius Caligula* 24, 30; and *Tiberius* 43–44.

12. Suetonius *Gaius Caligula* 30.2.

splendid Caesars whom many think are worthy of praise? What crimes and outrages are these, and what monsters are these men! For these reasons who will wonder that the city of Rome had such hatred against the imperial faction and that this hatred has even lasted down to the present?

Now has there ever been a more just cause for indignation? Has anything ever touched the people of Florence more deeply than the sorrow of seeing the Roman people, its progenitor and founder, which only a short time before had ruled over the entire world with great ability, suddenly lose its own freedom at the hands of the most criminal of men? These were men who, if the Republic had survived, surely would have been counted among the lowest dregs of society. And what should I say of Tiberius Caesar, although he ruled before Caligula? (There is no need to proceed in chronological order when discussing those matters where there is neither order or reason.) Indeed, what more loathsome, more shameful things have ever been heard or seen than the brutality used by Tiberius in his torturing and extermination of Roman citizens on Capri? What could be worse than that same emperor's lovers and gigolos, who were given to such evil and unspeakable types of sexual behavior that it is, I think, to Italy's shame that such degenerates once lived there? But if these emperors were base and evil, were those who followed better? And who were these? Were they not Nero and Vitellius and Domitian and Heliogabalus? Yes, of course they were. Now it's not an easy thing to point out what was the nature of Nero's virtue and humanity. To be sure, his mother Agrippina praised the piety of her son to the skies; nor could one who showed piety toward his mother be thought capable of being impious and inhuman toward other men. Indeed, this is the same emperor who, in his great mercy, set fire to the city of Rome so his subjects would not be troubled by the cold!

O Gaius Caesar, what manifest crimes have you visited upon the city of Rome! But I will remain silent on this topic, for there are some who are irate that Lucan, a very learned and wise man, wrote the truth concerning those crimes. Perhaps they do so not without good reason, for although you displayed many and great vices, these were sometimes overshadowed by many and great virtues. Hence, the safest course is not to discuss you at all. For the same reason I shall not treat your adopted son, even though I am not ignorant of the reasons that led you to adopt him. But I am passing over all this. I shall not call to mind either his fatuous cruelty or his proscription and slaughter of innocent citizens or his treachery to the Senate or his adultery and sexual perversions; for there were in him—as there were in his father—the vestiges of certain virtues that made his faults more tolerable. But those monsters to whom you handed over the empire were redeemed from their vices by no virtues, unless it is perhaps a virtue to destroy the state with all one's might or never to refrain from the vilest crimes. For this reason I shall not recall your other deeds, but I cannot forget, nor do I think that I should not be angry, that you paved the way for so many evils and outrages that your successors perpetrated with every kind of iniquity and cruelty.

But to what end? someone will ask Really there are two reasons: first, to show that Florence has not, without good cause, developed its political allegiances; and second, to make it understood that at the time when Florence was founded the city of Rome flourished greatly in power, liberty, genius, and especially with great citizens. Now, after the Republic had been subjected to the power of a single head, "those outstanding minds vanished," as Tacitus says.[13] So it is of importance whether a colony was founded at a later date, since by then all the virtue and nobility of the Romans had been destroyed; nothing great or outstanding could be conveyed by those who left the city.

Since Florence had as its founders those who were obeyed everywhere by everyone and dominated by their skill and military prowess, and since it was founded when a free and unconquered Roman people flourished in power, nobility, virtues, and genius, it cannot be doubted at all that this one city not only stands out in its beauty, architecture, and appropriateness of site (as we have seen), but that Florence also greatly excels beyond all other cities in the dignity and nobility of its origin.

But now let us turn to another topic.

3

Since Florence derives from such noble forebears, it has never allowed itself to be contaminated by sloth and cowardice, nor has it

13. Tacitus *Historiae* 1.1.

been content to bask in the glory of its progenitors or rest on its laurels at ease and leisure. Since it was born to such an exalted station, Florence has tried to accomplish those things that everyone expected and desired it to do. Thus, Florence imitated its founders in every kind of virtue, so that in everyone's judgment the city seemed completely worthy of its fine reputation and traditions.

Moreover, Florence did not refrain from fighting to show that it stood out among the leaders of Italy. It gained for itself dominion and glory not by deceit or trickery, not by covering itself with crimes and fraud, but by wise policies, by a willingness to face dangers, by keeping faith, integrity, steadfastness, and, above all, by upholding the rights of weaker peoples. Nor did Florence strive to excel only in riches; it sought to promote its industry and magnificence even more. Nor did it consider it better to be superior in power than in justice and humanity. With these qualities in mind, Florence strove to be the greatest of states; with these it acquired its authority and its glory. If Florence had not followed this policy, it wisely and truly knew that it would be falling away from the virtues of its ancestors and that its noble forebears would be more of a burden than an honor.

But Florence chose the wisest and best course of action. The same dignity and grandeur of the parent also illuminates its sons, since the offspring strive for their own virtue. And you may be sure that if the descendants had been cowardly or dissolute or had in any way fallen away from virtue, the splendor of the ancestor would not so much have hidden their vices as it would have uncovered them. The light of parental glory leaves nothing hidden; indeed, the expectation that the virtues of the parent will be reduplicated in the son focuses all eyes on the offspring. Whoever fails in these expectations to live up to the brilliance of their ancestors seems to be not noble but rather notorious on account of their descent. However, just as the grandeur of the ancestors scarcely aids those who are degenerate, so this same grandeur magnifies many times those descendants who possess high and noble spirits. Indeed, as their dignity and influence grows, these men are carried up to heaven, and they are placed together with their forebears in one and the same place on account of their own virtue and because of the nobility of their ancestors. Indeed, we have seen it happen in Florence that many men stand out as examples of excellence because of their great deeds, so that it becomes very easy to recognize in them their Roman virtue and the greatness of spirit. On this account, while Florence has been honored by the accomplishments and the splendor of its descent, it is even more honored by its own excellence and achievements.

But I think that I have already said enough concerning the brilliance of the city's origins—indeed, this is clearly manifest of itself. Concerning the excellence of the state, that is, how Florence has prospered at home and abroad, we should now speak. But I shall be very brief, and this speech does not allow a complete history of Florence; rather, I shall limit myself to the highlights. Before I come to this topic, however, I think that it would be appropriate and advisable for me to explain something and alert the reader, lest anyone, having gotten a false impression, might condemn me for being rash or ignorant. The former derives from levity, the latter from stupidity, and both are to be avoided. Now I do not doubt that a good many foolish men will suspect me and think that I wish with this my panegyric to win the good graces of popular acclaim, that I want to curry the favor of the mob, and that I am trying to capture men's minds as much as possible. Thinking this way, they believe that I have overstepped the bounds of truth and that in embellishing my speech I have mixed the false with the true. I want to advise such men, or rather disabuse them, so they will no longer think this way and will banish all their suspicions of my motives. Although I certainly wish to be loved and accepted by everyone (and I openly confess that I wish and desire this), still I have never been so driven by this desire that I would pursue it by means of flattery and adulation. For my part, I have always thought that one ought to make himself esteemed by others through the practice of virtue; not of vice. And I have certainly never expected or asked for any favors as a result of this panegyric. Indeed, I would be very stupid if I thought that I would be able to purchase the favors of a large citizen-body with this literary trifle. But once I had seen this beautiful city, once I had come to admire its fine site, architecture, nobility, comforts, and great glory, I wanted more than I can tell to try and describe its great beauty and magnificence. This is why I am writing this panegyric— not to curry favor or win popular acclaim. Indeed, it is so far from being the case that I undertook this labor in order to gain favor so that I would consider myself to be very lucky if I didn't generate more ill-will than good feeling against myself as a result of this speech. Rather, the great danger, as I see it, is that all those who have hated to see Florence flourishing will become my mortal enemies as a result of this panegyric. In fact, even now I continue to fear this. Thus my panegyric will make me an enemy of all those who are envious of or hostile to Florence and of all those men who have ever been troubled, beaten, or conquered by the Florentines or whose forebears were so effected—all these men will hate me. Accordingly, I am very much afraid that this work of mine will cause only hostility toward me. But I shall strike a bargain that no reasonable person can refuse. If I say in this speech anything that is false, self-seeking, or impudent, I shall gladly suffer the hostility and enmity of my listeners. But if what I say is true and if I express it with a becoming moderation, my listeners have no grounds to be angry with me. What bargain could be fairer than this? Who could be so perverse and evil that he could be angry with me if all I were trying to do was to provide the city of Florence with an appropriate and true panegyric?

Now, from all that I have just been saying, it ought to be clear that I have not undertaken the composition of this speech to win favor, nor can anyone justify becoming angry with me. But such are the various natures of men that I do not doubt that there will be many who will hold that the line of reasoning I have just given is of little value. And, indeed, there will be others for whom truth itself is hateful and vexatious. There will be still others who, either because of the baseness of their natures or their ignorance of the subject matter, will hold nothing to be true except what accords with their self-interest. These men will accuse me of vanity and will bring charges that I have written nothing that is genuine. To these I say that they should not try to treat me cunningly nor hasten to accuse me rashly; rather, they should always realize that their views are reprehensible and should especially remember that I am not talking about the virtue or excellence of individual citizens but about the entire community. Indeed, if one or another citizen in Florence has lapsed into some small sin, this is no good reason to reprove and calumniate the entire city, especially since in Florence the deeds of evil citizens are not imitated but are criticized and corrected.

Indeed, no city has ever been so well governed and established that it was completely without evil men. But just as the good qualities of a few men cannot really free the foolish and perverse mob from its infamy, so the perversity and evil of a few ought not to deprive an entire nation of being praised for its virtuous deeds. Now there are both public and private crimes, and there is a great difference between the two. A private crime derives from the intentions of the individual wrong-doer; public ones are the result of the will of the entire city. In the latter case it's not so much a question of following the opinion of one person or another as it is of following what has been hallowed by law and tradition. Usually the entire city follows what the majority of the citizen-body would like. While in other cities the majority often overturns the better part, in Florence it has always happened that the majority view has been identical with the best citizens. For this reason these accuse me falsely and do not let them point out to me the evil deeds of a few individuals. This would be just as fallacious as reproving the law-abiding quality of the Romans because of the corruption of Verres or the bravery of the Athenians on account of the cowardice of Thersites.[14]

Now if my auditors want to comprehend how outstanding a city Florence is (and I have justifiably praised it at length), let them travel through the entire world and select any city they wish and compare it with Florence—not just in splendor and architecture (although in these things Florence is unrivaled in the whole world), nor just in nobility of its citizens (though all other cities cede to Florence first place in this category), but in virtues and accomplishments as well. If they will do these things they will begin to understand what a difference there is between Florence and other cities, for they will find no other city that can compare in any of these praiseworthy categories to our Florence.

I have said "any," and so I shall prove it forthwith. If they find some city that is judged in the common opinion of men to stand out in some kind of virtue, let them give proof of that same quality in

14. The corruption of Verres, the partisan of Sulla who exploited Sicily during his proconsulship there in 73–71 B.C., was known to Bruni probably from Cicero's famous *Orationes Verrinae*. It seems probable that Bruni is thinking of the Aeolian coward of the *Iliad*, Thersites, who was not an Athenian as Bruni suggests. The precise reference remains obscure.

which the city is said to excel. I do not think they will find any city that, even in its own specialty, is not inferior to Florence. In short, a city cannot be found that equals Florence in any given category—not in devoutness of belief, nor in economic might, nor in concern for fellow citizens, nor in the achievements of its people. Let them enter in this competition whatever city they like; Florence will take on all challengers. Let them search throughout the entire world for a city that is thought to possess great glory in one special kind of activity, and let there be a comparison of the most outstanding accomplishments in the field in which their city appears to excel; they will be unable to find anything—unless they simply want to deceive themselves—in which Florence is not far superior. Indeed, the excellence of this city is a real marvel, and as a city worthy of praise in every kind of activity, it is really without equal.

Now I'm not going to discuss practical wisdom, a quality that everyone has always conceded to Florence in any case and that we have always seen practiced here with great capacity. Was there ever such beneficence as this city has displayed and displays now? For this quality seems intended to help as many as possible, and all have heard of the city's liberality, especially those who have needed it most. Because of Florence's reputation for generosity, all those who were exiled from their homeland and uprooted by seditious plots, or dispossesed on account of the envy of their fellow citizens, have always come to Florence as to a safe haven and unique sort of refuge. Hence there is no one in the whole of Italy who does not consider himself to possess dual citizenship, the one of the city to which he naturally belongs, the other of the city of Florence. As a result Florence has indeed become the common homeland and quite secure asylum for all of Italy. Here everyone, when he has need, comes and is received by the Florentines with complete goodwill and supreme generosity. Indeed, the zeal for generosity and concern for others are so great in this state that these qualities seem to cry out in a loud voice and are openly acknowledged by everyone. Hence, no one will ever think that he really lacks a homeland so long as the city of Florence continues to exist. The acts of generosity performed actually are even greater than this policy might seem to require, for exiles are not only received with a welcome hand if they are not completely unworthy but also are often helped with gifts in kind and in money. Maintained by such gifts, the exiles can remain in Florence with complete dignity or, if they prefer, they can return to their own homeland and try and recover their property there. Are these not the facts? Have even the malcontents of Italy ever dared to deny it? No, this policy has been witnessed by an almost infinite number of people who, when they had been struck with poverty at home or had been exiled from their own cities, were helped from the public treasury and were restored to their homeland by the goodwill of the city of Florence.

There is, further, the example of many cities that, when they were oppressed by the conspiracies of neighboring states or the violence of domestic tyrants, were sustained by Florentine advice, aid, and money and thus brought through a difficult crisis. I shall omit the embassies sent wherever trouble has broken out to reconcile opposing viewpoints, for indeed this city has always been very prompt to use its authority in reconciliation. Can a city that has undertaken so much for the benefit of neighboring states not be called beneficent? Can it really be praised enough for its great virtue and many achievements? Florence has never tolerated injuries to other cities, nor has it ever allowed itself to be an idle onlooker while other states were in trouble. First Florence always tries with all its might and moral authority to settle disputes through negotiations and, if it can, to reconcile differences to persuade the parties to make peace. But if this cannot be accomplished, Florence always aids the weaker party, which has been threatened or harmed by the more powerful. Thus, from the very beginning Florence has always extended its protection to the weaker states, as though it considered its duty to ensure that no people in Italy would ever suffer destruction. Therefore, Florence has never in its history been led by a desire for leisure or has it, because of fear, allowed any other state to suffer great harm. Nor did it think that it had the right to remain at ease and at peace while any other city or ally or friendly state or neutral nation was in danger. Rather, Florence has always immediately stirred itself, taken up the cause of other cities, and shielded them from attack. Thus it has protected those states that seemed to be lost and aided them with troops, money, and equipment.

Who, therefore, could ever praise Florence enough for its beneficence and liberality? What city in the entire world can surpass Florence in this sort of achievement? Has not Florence expended vast sums and undertaken incredible risks for the defense of other states? Has it not protected many states when they were in danger? Since Florence has defended those states in time of peril, they have naturally begun to acknowledge it as their patron. And since Florence has become such a patron, who will deny that it surpasses other cities in dignity, might, economic power, and authority?

To this beneficence and liberality there has been added an admirable faithfulness to allies that this city has always preserved inviolate with complete constancy. It was with a commitment to this principle in mind that Florence always carefully considered whether it could really provide complete protection before it entered into any league. As a result, when Florence agreed to something it never went back on its promise. Therefore, when Florence has thought something out from the beginning and come to believe that its cause is just, no manner of expediency has ever been able to influence Florence to break any pact, treaty, league, oath, or promise that it has made. For nothing can be judged more proper to the dignity of a state than a reputation for observing all its commitments. Conversely, nothing is worse than betraying promises. The latter is the action of evil criminals who are the greatest enemies of the states. They are the sort who (according to Cicero) say: "I have sworn with my tongue, but in my mind I have sworn no oath."[15] That is a deceit that a just city can never tolerate. Therefore, a good city ought always to make its commitments after due consideration. And once it has committed itself to something, it should never consider permitting anything to be changed except for those things that are not in its power.

Moreover, since faithfulness and integrity have been so highly valued in this city, it has scrupulously observed agreements even with its enemies, and, as a result, Florence has never been accused of defaulting on its promises. On account of this it has happened that not even the enemies of Florence have doubted that the city would live up to its agreements, and among them the name of Florence has always carried great authority. This is the obvious reason for the fact that several men, though they had previously

15. Cicero *De officiis* 3.29.108.

been Florence's worst enemies, gladly committed their sons and wealth to the guardianship of this people. They believed in this city's good faith and humanity; they saw that the second quality prompted the Florentines to pardon former injuries and furnish all due services, while the first ensured that the city would scrupulously observe what it had promised. Nor were they disappointed in their expectation. Indeed, it happened that the Florentines administered the property with great diligence and restored it to those to whom it belonged, justifying those who had believed in the good faith of this people. Indeed, their example of committing property to Florence's care was soon followed by others, for this city has always taken pains to give each one his due and in all things to put honor before expediency in all its dealings. Indeed, it has been the case that Florence considers nothing useful that is not at the same time honorable.

But of these many fine qualities with which I find this city has been endowed, I consider none greater or more outstanding or more consistent with Roman virtue and character than a certain loftiness of spirit and contempt for danger. Whose virtue could this be except the Romans? The Romans waged wars at every period in their history, and they engaged in enormous struggles and great military campaigns and—what is very rare and more incredible still—they never, even in times of greatest danger and difficulty, wavered from their purpose or permitted the debasement of their lofty principles. The emperor[16] was angry at the gates, threatening the ruin and destruction of Florence, and there followed him a group of Florence's enemies, resolute and ready to kill. This enemy was encamped within a mile of Florence, and the city resounded throughout with the sound of steel and the shouts of enemy troops. Nor even Hannibal approached the Porta Collina in Rome with more hostile intentions than did this monster plan his assault before the walls of Florence. What was worse, that part of the city most exposed to the enemy was not, at that time, well

16. A reference to the Emperor Henry VII, who pitched camp before the gate of Florence during his descent into Italy in 1312. See the modern account in F. Schevill, *History of Florence from the Founding of the City through the Renaissance* (New York, 1936), pp. 189–191. Cf. Bruni's later account in his *Historiarum Florentini populi libri XII*, ed. E. Santini, *RIS*, n.e. 19, 3(Città di Castello, 1914):107–11.

fortified. Consequently, it was believed that no Florentine there dared to use his arms or offer resistance. Indeed, this valorous city only showed contempt for the emperor's threats and menaces. While the enemy revealed for several days outside the walls, those inside Florence felt no fear; rather, everyone went about his business as though no danger threatened or no enemy army was nearby. Every workshop, store, and warehouse was open; there was no slackening of industry, certainly none of government. When the emperor discovered this he marveled at the high morale and greatness of the city, and he gave up the siege.

This city has been powerful not only in resisting attacks; it has been even more formidable in applying force in response to previous attacks. Now although Florence has never tried to harm anyone except when it was attacked first, yet when it has been subjected to an attack the city has shown itself to be a most valorous fighter in maintaining its dignity. Every time Florence has taken the offensive, the city has been transformed by its amazing desire for praise and glory. Therefore, Florence has always willingly undertaken great and difficult causes. It has never shunned any cause because of the greatness of the danger or the difficulty of the task. I can call to mind some very well-fortified towns that Florence has captured and innumerable trophies of neighboring cities that the Florentines have seized. There also have been some outstanding feats of military skill performed by Florentine people fighting outside their country. But this is not the place to describe many different wars, nor would it be possible to relate so many great feats. That would require a book of its own, and indeed a big one, which I hope I shall undertake some time in the future[17] and commit to paper, and therefore to memory, how single feats were accomplished by the Florentine people. At present I shall content myself with one or two examples on the basis of which one can readily understand how great has been the virtue of Florence in other events.

Volterra is an ancient and noble town in Tuscany, but because it is situated on a high mountain top, even men who carry no burdens scarcely ever go there. The Florentines undertook a mili-

---

17. A reference to the *Historiae Florentini populi,* which Bruni later wrote while chancellor of Florence.

tary campaign against this town,[18] for virtue accustomed to over-coming the greatest difficulties did not fear the harshness of the terrain nor the disadvantages of the combat. Therefore, when the Florentine forces sent there began to ascend the mountain, they were met by the defenders rushing down from their higher position, and the two armies were soon locked in mortal combat. The number of troops was about equal, but the Florentines possessed an advantage in fighting ability, while the nature of the terrain greatly favored the Volterrans. They used their superior position not simply to stop the Florentine advance with spears and swords; they also rolled large stones down the slopes. The Florentines, with a great effort of their own, struggled up the slope, and neither the weapons nor the stones nor the enemy troops nor the difficulty of the terrain could stop their assault. So, having fought their way step-by-step to the top of the mountain in the face of the enemy, the Florentines drove the Volterrans behind their walls. With the first assault the Florentines entered the town, although it was defended with very strong fortifications. The Florentine army did all this without any outside help; fighting only with its own troops, Florence courageously covered itself with glory and honor.

This accomplishment ought to seem remarkable to others and especially those who have actually seen Volterra are especially amazed by it, for it is obvious that no town in all of Italy is better fortified. Moreover, the town was being defended by brave men who were fighting valiantly for hearth and home. Yet they were overcome by an even greater valor. Who, therefore, cannot but admire those who captured this well-fortified city in a single day? Who would not praise to the heavens the valor of those who captured Volterra? Such are the deeds accomplished by this city! Such are its virtues and its bravery! With this same high morale, Florence has often conquered the Sienese, laid low the Pisans, and vanquished powerful enemies and tyrants.

Still, what is really remarkable is that Florence has undertaken military campaigns and endured great hardship more often for the benefit of others than for its own profit. It especially ought to redound to its credit and honor that Florence has suffered many dangers for the freedom and security of other states and that it has

18. The campaign against Volterra in 1254 is mentioned in Schevill, p. 122, and in Bruni, *Historiae*, p. 30.

safeguarded the welfare of many others out of its own resources. The Pisans, a nation rarely at peace with Florence, began a war against the people of Lucca who were friends and allies of the Florentines.[19] Finally, it happened that the long-awaited battle was joined between the two peoples, and in this conflict the troops of Lucca were defeated and many of them captured. The Florentines were at that moment making camp in the countryside near Pistoia, and when they heard what had happened to their friends they did not lose courage, nor did they fear the Pisans, who were fired up by their recent victory. Rather, the Florentines immediately broke camp and hurried to catch the victors, so they were able to intercept the Pisan forces before they had reached safety inside the walls of their city. The Florentines immediately joined battle with the Pisans and changed the fortunes of war so that the Lucchese, who had formerly been prisoners, now captured a great number of the Pisans who survived the slaughter and led them in chains back to the city of Lucca. In this way the military prowess of the Florentines saved the Lucchese, overturned the victory of the Pisans, and won for themselves laud and honor.

But what ought to be praised most in this outstanding Florentine triumph? Their military skill, which enabled them to win; or their high morale, which prompted them to pursue the victorious Pisans; or their generous spirit, which led them to undertake so great a battle on behalf of their friends? I think that the three ought to be viewed as one and the same deed that is to be praised. But I cannot laud every great deed with appropriate praise. Not only do I fear that there is not enough time, but larger topics demand my attention.

It has been not simply to this or that city that Florence has shown its beneficence but to the whole of Italy. Indeed, it would be judged properly an act of small import if Florence has undertaken these endeavors only for its own safety, but it is a glorious matter if a great many states have known and enjoyed the benefits of the Florentines' efforts. Indeed, it is a fact that Florence has always been motivated by a desire to protect the safety of neighbor-

19. An allusion to Florence's defeat of Pisa in 1252 when under the Primo Popolo the Florentines extended their power in Tuscany. See Schevill, *History of Florence*, pp. 120–21, Bruni, *Historiae*, p. 28, and Giovanni Villani, *Cronica*, ed. by F. Dragomanni, 4 vols. (Florence, 1844–45), 1:274.

ing cities that found themselves at war. Whenever such a state was threatened by some neighboring tyrant or the greedy desires of a nearby republic. Florence always opposed the aggressor, so it has always been clear to everyone that Florence treated these states as its own homeland and fought for the liberty of all Italy. Nor indeed would Florence, so motivated, have accomplished its goal except that many times the pious and just will of God favored the course of action taken by this city. I do not want to go back to old examples but, rather, shall relate what our own age has just seen. I think that it is obvious in any case that the whole of Italy has been liberated from the yoke of servitude by Florence on more than one occasion. But let us omit these other instances and consider only what was done very recently.

Can anyone so feeble of intellect or so devoid of truth be found who would deny that all Italy would have fallen under the power of the Duke of Lombardy had not this one city resisted his power with its troops and sound strategy?[20] Who in all Italy then had either power or resources comparable to that enemy? Who would have endured to the end the attacks of an enemy whose very name brought terror to every mortal? Indeed, his reputation struck terror not only in the Italians but in peoples north of the Alps as well! He was well provided with resources, money, and men, but, most of all, he possessed cunning and political wisdom. And he had great and formidable power. All of Lombardy, and nearly all of the cities on the peninsula between the Alps and Tuscany and the Romagna, were under his rule and obeyed his orders. In Tuscany, he held Pisa, Siena, Perugia, and Assisi in his grip, and eventually he even occupied Bologna.[21] Besides many cities and many powerful noble houses followed his name and fortune, either out of fear or motivated by hope for booty or perhaps led on by his trickery. His followers did not lack in financial rewards, gifts, and counsel. Indeed, the Duke could have been a happy—a very happy—man if he had but put his resources, his energy, and his genius to good purposes. No man ever possessed a shrewder or cleverer mind. He

20. Another reference to the recent war against Giangaleazzo Visconti, which ended in 1402.

21. The chronology of these events is as follows: Giangaleazzo occupied Pisa early in 1399, Siena during the summer of the same year, Perugia early in 1400, Assisi in May 1400, and Bologna in June 1402. See H. Baron, *From Petrarch to Leonardo Bruni* (Chicago, 1968), pp. 116, n. 257.

was present everywhere, he left nothing unnoticed, nothing un-
tried. And he acquired friends: some with money, others with expensive gifts, and still others with the promise or semblance of his
friendship. Sowing seeds of discord, he set the nations of Italy at
one another's throat, and when they had worn themselves down, he
stepped in and occupied them with his overwhelming power. So
eventually his cunning ways prospered everywhere. Hence many
governments, seeing these great powers, became very frightened
and began to temporize. But the stout Florentine heart could never
know fear, nor could it ever consider surrendering any part of its
honor. Florence knew that it was a Roman tradition to defend the
liberty of Italy against its enemies, precisely as its ancestors had
dared to fight against the Cimbri, the Teutons, and the Gauls.
These ancestors had not feared the ferocity of Pyrrhus or the de-
ceits of Hannibal, nor had they ever avoided any undertaking that
would preserve their dignity or their grandeur. Rather, they underwent great hardship in order to gain great glory. So the Florentines
were ready to do anything if they felt it would vouchsafe for
them the good reputation that had been handed down to them by
their ancestors. It was with these things in mind that the Florentine people set out for war in great and high spirits. So this
people thought that it would live with great glory or perish fighting valiantly for its principles. Moreover, the Florentines believed
that the position inherited from their ancestors had to be protected,
so that they could never place concern for their wealth before their
own self-esteem. Indeed, they were prepared to lose money and
life itself to maintain their freedom, considering their situation
both realistically and courageously. Now wealth and money and
such things are the rewards of the victors. But those who think
that in war they should conserve their wealth, since they think they
make themselves more secure with this wealth, are in fact serving
the interests of the enemy more than their own. With such a high
morale was this city endowed, with such a measure of military
skill did it meet its powerful and resourceful enemy in combat,
that Florence compelled him who shortly before had menaced all
Italy and believed that no state could resist him to wish for peace
and to quake behind the walls of Pavia. In the end he not only
abandoned the cities of Tuscany and the Romagna, but he even
lost a large portion of northern Italy.

O incredible magnificence and excellence of Florence! O Roman people and race of Romulus! Who would not now esteem the name of Florence with great honor on account of the excellence of its spirit and the vast dimensions of its deeds? What greater thing, what more outstanding feat could this city accomplish, or in what way could it better prove that the virtue of its forebears was still alive than by liberating the whole of Italy, by its own efforts and resources, from the threat of servitude? As a result of this feat, Florence daily receives congratulations, praises, and thanks from all nations. But all these accomplishments have been credited by Florence to the will of Almighty God. Always possessing a certain modesty, Florence has preferred to credit its deeds to divine intervention rather than claim them on account of its own virtue. Consequently, Florence has never become inflated in its successes, nor have its victories been accompanied by retribution against those states that Florence could, by right, have hated. Rather, it has always maintained complete humanity toward those whom it has conquered, so that those who knew Florence's courage in time of war experienced its mercy in time of victory. Of the many great virtues of this city this one stands out: to maintain its dignity at all times. Florence has shown no greater concern than making sure that it maintained its dignity in the process of accomplishing great feats. Therefore, Florence did not exult immoderately at its successes, nor did it collapse in times of adversity. It showed modesty in success, constancy in adversity, and justice and prudence in all of its actions. Hence, its great name had acquired even greater glory among men.

4

As Florence is admirable in foreign affairs, so it has outstanding civil institutions and laws. Nowhere else do you find such internal order, such neatness, and such harmonious cooperation. There is proportion in strings of a harp so that when they are tightened, a harmony results from the different tones; nothing could be sweeter or more pleasing to the ear than this. In the same way, this very prudent city is harmonized in all its parts, so there results a single great, harmonious constitution whose harmony pleases both the eyes and minds of men. There is nothing here that is ill proportioned, nothing improper, nothing incongruous, nothing vague; everything occupies its proper place, which is not only clearly defined but also in right relation to all the other elements. Here are outstanding officials, outstanding magistrates, an outstanding judiciary, and outstanding social classes. These parts are so distinct so as to serve the supreme power of Florence, just as the Roman tribunes used to serve the empire.

Now, first of all, great care is taken so that justice is held most sacred in the city, for without justice there can be no city, nor would Florence even be worthy to be called a city. Next there is provision for freedom, without which this great people would not even consider that life was worth living. These two principles are joined (almost as a stamp or goal) to all the institutions and statutes that the Florentine government has created.

Indeed, the magistracies were created to carry out justice; they have been empowered to punish criminals and especially to ensure that there is no one in Florence who stands above the law. Thus, all conditions of men must submit to the decisions of these magistracies, and they must pay due respect to the symbols of these offices. In many ways care has been taken that these upholders of the law to whom great power has been entrusted do not come to imagine that, instead of the custodianship of the citizens, a tyrannical post has been given to them. Many provisions are made so that these magistrates do not lord it over others or undermine the great freedom of the Florentines. First of all, the chief magistracy that is commonly viewed as possessing the sovereignty of the state is controlled by a system of checks and balances. Hence there are nine magistrates instead of one, and their term is for two months, not for one year. This method of governing has been devised so that the Florentine state may be well governed, since a majority will correct any errors in judgment, and the short terms of office will curb any possible insolence. Moreover, the city is divided into four quarters so that each section can never lack its own representative, and from each quarter two men are elected. And these men are not chosen by chance, but they have the approval of the citizens for a long time and are judged worthy of such a great honor. Now, in addition to these eight citizens, the task of governing the state is entrusted to one man, outstanding in virtue and authority and chosen in rotation from these same quarters. He is the chief of the priorate and bears the standard that is the symbol of the rule of justice over unruly men. The nine men, to whom the government of Florence is entrusted, can live nowhere except in the Palazzo Vecchio, so that they may be in a better position to govern the city. They are not to appear in public without their sergeants, for their dignity demands that they be treated with respect. Indeed, because it sometimes happens that there is a need for a larger council, the Twelve Good Men are added to discuss public matters together with the nine priors. Besides, to these are joined the standard-bearers of the Companies whom the whole population supports and follows since it is necessary to protect liberty with arms. These standard-bearers are also part of the council, and, like the higher magistrates, they are elected by quarter. They hold office for a term of four months.

These three colleges do not have power over all matters to be decided. A great many decisions, once they have been approved by these magistracies, are referred to the Council of the People and Council of the Commune for final action. Florence thinks that what concerns many ought to be decided by the action of the whole citizen-body acting according to the law and legal procedure. In this way liberty flourishes and justice is preserved in this most holy city. In this system nothing can be resolved by the caprice of any single man acting in opposition to the judgment of so many men.

These men oversee the government, uphold justice, repeal laws, and ensure equity. The power to dispense justice according to the legal procedure, and especially the power of life and limb, is given to minor magistrates who are not citizens but foreigners brought to Florence from distant cities and states. This custom is followed not because Florentines don't know how to act as judges (indeed they are employed daily in this capacity in many foreign cities) but, rather, to ensure that, from the judicial system, enmity and feuding will not arise among the citizens. For it often happens that, led on by their desire to be lenient, judges mete out some punishment other than what the statutes allow. Such judges, although they may, strictly speaking, have been judging correctly, cause a great deal of hostility toward their office. More than this, it seems objectionable for one citizen to stand in judgment over the life of another in a free city such as Florence, for whatever a native judge does, even if he is very just, will be viewed by the other citizens as abominable and horrible. Because of this our judges are imported from distant cities, and for them the procedures are carefully prescribed so that they cannot deviate from them in any way. They enter their office with an oath that, like stewards, they will render account of their administration of justice to the people when they have finished their term of office. Thus, in every particular, the people enjoy freedom and are in control.

Moreover, in order to make it very easy for each person in this vast city to receive his due, that is, so that while the magistracies are busy with some individuals will not lack justice and law, the authority to judge and hand down sentences concerning disputes among their own members has been given to certain groups. In this fashion, the heads of the guilds of merchants and bankers and other guilds have the right to hand down sentences on their members. There are still other magistracies that have been established to ensure the public good and the piety of the people: among these are numbered the officials of the gabelles, the heads of the Monte, and the guardians of wards' property. These are among the more useful offices because they attend to promoting public and private welfare and health and piety in this great city.

But of all the magistracies, and there are many in this city, none is more illustrious, nor founded on loftier principles, than that called the heads of the Parte Guelfa. Perhaps it would not be pointless to say something about the origins of this organization. Hence, a short digression will not be completely useless, I hope, and perhaps worthwhile.

After the defeat of the Florentines in pitched battle at Montaperti, it seemed certain that the city could not be defended on account of this great blow to the state.[22] Therefore, all citizens of high and noble spirits, so they would not be ruled over in the city by those who had obviously been traitors to Florence, left their homes and hearths, and went to Lucca with their wives and children. In doing this they followed the outstanding and laudable example of the Athenians, who abandoned their own city during the Second Persian War in order to be able to live there someday

22. The defeat of the Florentine Guelfs by the Tuscan Ghibellines at the battle of Montaperti in 1260 is discussed in Schevill, pp. 127–30, and the historical situation is described at length by Bruni in his *Historiae*, pp. 34–40.

in peace and freedom.[23] Therefore, with this in mind, these out-standing citizens, who survived that great battle, left Florence, thinking that by doing this they would have a better chance for revenge than if they remained starving and waiting their fate shut up behind the city walls. So they went to Lucca, and there they joined up with other Florentines who had been scattered in the course of the battle. Very soon they brought together arms, horses, and military equipment, so that everyone marvelled at their energy and resolve. They performed many feats of bravery throughout Italy. The exiles often fought to aid friends and to defeat men of opposing political allegiance by their courage and military skill. Moreover, from every endeavor they always emerged victorious, so that it finally seemed that the time was ripe for what they wanted most: to remove utterly the stain and blot on their home-land. Hence they set out against King Manfred of Sicily, who was leader over different factions in Italy and who had contributed knights to the enemy army at the battle of Montaperti. The Floren-tine exiles were under the leadership of a great and skillful general whom the Pope had brought from France to curb the insolence of this same Manfred.[24] After a while the army came to Apulia—and I would really like to describe in detail the great courage that the Florentines displayed on that occasion, but this is not the place for a lengthy narrative. To put it very briefly, the Florentines fought so well that even their most bitter enemy felt compelled to praise their skill and bravery. Thus, after they won at Tagliacozzo in Apulia and destroyed their enemy, honored and laden down with spoils and booty, the Florentine army returned to Tuscany. Im-mediately they expelled from Florence those who a little while before had governed the city so evilly, and they wreaked a splendid vengeance on their enemies in nearby cities. At this point the Florentines established a college composed of the chief men who had been the leaders of the Parte Guelfa and had taken a leading role in this noble and just campaign.

23. An allusion to the evacuation of Athens in 480 B.C. under the direction of Themistocles.

24. An allusion to Charles of Anjou, whom Pope Urban IV brought to fight against the Hohenstaufens in southern Italy in 1265. See Schevill, *History of Florence,* pp. 135–40.

From its very foundation, this magistracy has always had great authority in Florence. For almost everything has been placed under its care and vigilance so that Florence would never be turned away from the sound policies established by its forebears, nor would it ever come under the control of men of different political sentiments. What the censors were to Rome, the areopagites to Athens, the ephors to Sparta, these heads of the Parte Guelfa are to the city of Florence. This is to say that these are the chief men who oversee the constitution and who are elected from among those citizens who love the Florentine state.

Therefore, under these magistracies this city has been governed with such diligence and competence that one could not find better discipline even in a household ruled by a solicitous father. As a result, no one here has ever suffered any harm, and no one has ever had to alienate any property except when he wanted to. The judges, the magistrates are always on duty; the courts, even the highest tribunal is open. All classes of men can be brought to trial; laws are made prudently for the common good, and they are fashioned to help the citizens. There is no place on earth where there is greater justice open equally to everyone. Nowhere else does freedom grow so vigorously, and nowhere else are rich and poor alike treated with such equality. In this one also can discern Florence's great wisdom, perhaps greater than that of other cities. Now when very powerful men, relying on their wealth and position, appear to be offending or harming the weak, the government steps in and exacts heavy fines and penalties from the rich. It is consonant with reason that as the status of men is different, so their penalties ought to be different. The city has judged it consistent with its ideals of justice and prudence that those who have the most need should also be helped the most. Therefore, the different classes are treated according to a certain sense of equity; the upper class is protected by its wealth, the lower class by the state, and fear of punishment defends both. From this arises the saying that has been directed very often against the more powerful citizens when they have threatened the lower classes; in such a case the members of the lower class say: "I also am a Florentine citizen." With this saying the poor mean to point out and to warn clearly that no one should malign them simply because they are weak, nor should anyone threaten them with harm simply because someone is powerful. Rather, everyone is of equal rank since the Florentine state itself has promised to protect the less powerful.

Florence not only protects its own citizens in this way, but it extends the same protection to foreigners. No one here, citizen or foreigner, is allowed to suffer harm, and Florence strives to ensure that each is given his due. Moreover, the justice and spirit of equity in Florence promote toleration and humanity among the citizens since no one can be prideful or disparage others while all men experience the same benign rule. But who can be skillful enough to describe fully, in the short time remaining, the honorableness of life and high moral standards in this city? Certainly there are many men of great genius in this city, and whenever they agree to do something they easily achieve more than other men. Whether they follow the profession of arms or devote themselves to the task of governing the state, to study and scientific knowledge, or to business—in every profession and in every endeavor they undertake they excel far beyond all other mortals. No other people surpass them in any respect. Here they remain patient in their labor, ready in time of danger, eager for glory, brilliant in giving advice, industrious, generous, magnificent, pleasant, affable, and, above all, civil.

Now what shall I say of the persuasiveness of their speech and the elegance of their discourse? Indeed, in this category the Florentines are the unquestioned leaders. All of Italy believes that this city alone possesses the clearest and purist speech. All who wish to speak well and correctly follow the example of the Florentine manner of speech, for this city possesses men who are so expert in their use of the common vernacular language that all others seem like children compared to them. The study of literature—and I don't mean simply mercantile and vile writings but that which is especially worthy of free men—which always flourishes among every great people, grows in this city in full vigor.

Therefore, what ornament does this city lack? What category of endeavor is not fully worthy of praises and grandeur? What about the quality of the forebears? Why are they not the descendants of the Roman people? What about glory? Florence has done and daily continues to do great deeds of honor and virtue both at home and abroad. What about the splendor of the architecture, the buildings, the cleanliness, the wealth, the great population, the healthfulness and pleasantness of the site? What more can a city desire? Nothing at all. What, therefore, should we say now? What remains to be done? Nothing other than to venerate God on account of His great beneficence and to offer our prayers to God. Therefore, our Almighty and Everlasting God, in whose churches and at whose altars your Florentines worship most devoutly; and you, Most Holy Mother, to whom this city has erected a great temple of fine and glimmering marble, where you are at once mother and purist virgin tending your most sweet son; and you, John the Baptist, whom this city has adopted as its patron saint—all of you, defend this most beautiful and distinguished city from every adversity and from every evil.

FRANCESCO
BARBARO

Introduction

BENJAMIN G. KOHL

Venetian humanism in the early fifteenth century was shaped by three important factors. One was the rich legacy of Petrarchan humanism with its emphasis on moral philosophy, correct Latin style, and its prescriptions for "the art of living well and happily" as Petrarch borrowed the phrase from his model Cicero. This influence came mainly through scholars of the late Trecento, such as Giovanni Conversini da Ravenna (1343–1408), who had admired Petrarch in their youth and who later often served as tutors to the sons of the Venetian aristocracy. Another factor was the close rapport with Greek scholarship and classical studies in Constantinople. The Greek emigré scholar Emmanuel Chrysoloras (1350–1415) first came to Venice before finding teaching posts elsewhere in Italy, and while still in Constantinople Chrysoloras had hosted the native Italian scholar Guarino da Verona (1374–1460), who sought to acquire a knowledge of ancient Greek literature during a visit to the Byzantine capital. The result was that aspiring Venetian humanists received instruction in Greek both from emigré Byzantine scholars and well-trained Italian Hellenists, and they were able to discover Greek moral thought directly through the study of the works of Plato, Plutarch, Xenophon, and others. A third factor derived from the social position of the Venetian humanists. Almost all these humanists were members of the ruling class of their city; hence, their thought was strongly colored by the ideals of state service and family solidarity inculcated in the Venetian patriciate and embellished by the congenial influence of ancient moral philosophy that preached similar values. All three of these factors are represented in the life and works of the Venetian humanist and statesman Francesco Barbaro (1390–1454).

Born into a long-established, wealthy Venetian noble family, Francesco Barbaro was raised, after his father's premature death, by his widowed mother and later in the household of his elder brother Zaccaria. From 1405 to 1408 the young Barbaro studied Latin literature and rhetoric under the tutelage of Giovanni Conversini and later under a master of Ciceronian Latin, Gasparino Barzizza (1360–1431).[1] In 1409 Barbaro followed his teacher to the University of Padua, the center of learning for the Venetian state. At Padua he received the degree of *magister artium* in 1410 and his doctorate in arts two years later.[2] There Barbaro also came under the influence of the learned Venetian rector of the city, Zaccaria Trevisan (1370–1414), who instructed Barbaro in the rudiments of Greek, directed his reading in such Roman authors as Cicero and Livy, and provided the young Venetian with a fine model of the humanist-statesman. Barbaro never forgot his debt to Trevisan, which he acknowledged several times in the *De re uxoria*; further, he extolled the virtues of his mentor in two letters of consolation written shortly after Trevisan's death.[3]

In July 1414 Barbaro returned to Venice, where he came under the spell of Guarino da Verona. Bringing Guarino into his own household, the eager Venetian scholar applied himself to the study of the Greek language and its literature. His competence grew quickly, and, at Guarino's prompting, Barbaro undertook the translation into Latin of Plutarch's lives of two great ancient statesmen, Aristides and Cato the Elder. Barbaro completed these translations within a year after beginning his studies under Guarino, and he

1. On Barbaro's early life, see Percy Gothein, *Francesco Barbaro: Früh-Humanismus und Staats-Kunst in Venedig* (Berlin, 1932), chap. 2. This exhaustive biography is the source for much of this introduction.

2. See G. Zonta and G. Brotto, *Acta Graduum Academicorum Gymnasii Patavini ab anno 1406 ad annum 1450*, 3 vols. (2nd ed., Padua, 1970), 1:31, 108, 111, for the record of Barbaro's degrees taken at the University of Padua.

3. See Percy Gothein, "Zaccaria Trevisan," *Archivio Veneto*, 5th ser. 21(1937):1–59, for Barbaro's friendship with Trevisan and texts of the letters of consolation.

dedicated the two lives to his brother Zaccaria in the summer of 1415.[4] That same summer Barbaro widened his acquaintance with other Italian humanists when he accompanied Guarino on a trip to Florence. There Barbaro was a guest in the home of Lorenzo and Cosimo de' Medici, sons of Giovanni de' Bicci, and he soon formed friendships with a circle of Florentine literati, including Leonardo Bruni, Niccolò Niccoli, Ambrogio Traversari and the Medici tutor Roberto Rossi. In Florence Barbaro became aware of Poggio Bracciolini's recent discovery of several of Cicero's speeches and made a copy of the *Pro Roscio Amerino* for his mentor Guarino. At the same time he probably read the translations of some of Plutarch's lives made by Leonardo Bruni. But Barbaro's closest friendship developed with his fellow aristocrat Lorenzo de' Medici. In Florence Barbaro conceived of composing the *De re uxoria* to celebrate the approaching marriage of Lorenzo and Ginevra Cavalcanti; soon after he returned to Venice Barbaro wrote a letter to Lorenzo expressing his gratitude for the hospitality of the Medici family and his affection for his newfound Florentine friends.[5] In the autumn of 1415 Barbaro began composing the treatise, and the following spring he presented a dedicatory copy to the newly-married couple.

In composing the *De re uxoria*, Barbaro made good use of his recently-acquired knowledge of ancient Greek literature. In addition to drawing upon the translation of Plutarch's *De liberis educandis* made by Guarino in 1410 and his mentor's translation of the lives of Dion and Brutus which Guarino dedicated to him early in 1416, Barbaro probably also had Guarino's translation of the pseudo-Isocrates *Ad Demonicum* and a Latin version of Xenophon's *Oeconomicus*. He used as well Leonardo Bruni's Latin translation of Plutarch's lives of Aemilius Paulus and Demosthenes. But the majority of his citations of Plutarch, Xenophon and other Greek authors came directly from the Greek texts: it seems certain that Barbaro had studied carefully Xenophon's *Cyropaedia* as well as several parts of Plutarch's *Moralia,* including the *Coniugalia*

4. On Barbaro's study of Greek under Guarino, see R. Sabbadini, *Vita di Guarino Veronese* (Genoa, 1891), pp. 29–33.

5. See Sabbadini, "La gita di Francesco Barbaro a Firenze," In *Miscellanea di Studi in onore di Attilio Hortis,* 2 vols. (Trieste, 1910), 2:615–27, where the text of Barbaro's thank-you letter is published.

praecepta, before he composed the treatise. Clearly the classical inspiration and anecdotes in the *De re uxoria* were heavily Greek. In book 2 of the tract quotations or paraphrases from the works of Plutarch and Xenophon number more than seventy out of about ninety citations from ancient Greek literature. The remainder come from Homer's *Iliad,* Hesiod, Herodotus, and the Greek tragedians. From Latin authors Barbaro mainly quoted Cicero, the Roman historian Valerius Maximus, and the encyclopedists Aulus Gellius and Macrobius. Of contemporary works he utilized Pier Paolo Vergerio's *De ingenuis moribus,* a treatise on the proper education of a young prince composed a decade earlier for Ubertino da Carrara, heir to the lordship of Padua.

This massive reliance on historical anecdotes and moral precepts drawn from Greek and, to a lesser extent, from Roman antiquity would have given Barbaro's treatise a ponderous bookish quality if it were not for his lively allusion to contemporary Italian mores. In this context the author also drew examples from the customs of Venice's Cretan subjects, whose mores he had discussed with Zaccaria Trevisan, the Venetian captian of Candia on Crete before Barbaro came to know him in Padua.[6] Barbaro also took pains to make his moral lessons from antiquity consistent with Christian ideals of marriage and family responsibility. He had studied carefully St. Augustine's tracts on marriage, and from this and other sources Barbaro emphasized that the purpose of marriage was the procreation of children. Indeed, this theme of the need for a wholesome, continent relation between man and wife premeates the treatise. From this premise that marriage entails family life and childrearing followed the precept that the management of the household and the education of children were the chief responsibility of the wife.

But the *De re uxoria* was intended as more than simply instructions to wives on their personal and domestic obligations. Barbaro wanted to extol the family as the basis for the aristocratic polity of his native Venice. Although written for an aristocratic Florentine friend, the tract provides a fine insight into the values of the Venetian ruling class. In book 1 of the treatise (which is not included in the translation) Barbaro discussed two key topics: the

6. See P. Gothein, *Zacharias Trevisan, Leben und Umkreis* (Amsterdam, 1944), pp. 60–61.

nature of marriage and the choice of a wife. In his treatment of the
first he emphasized the inherited right of the Venetian aristocrat
to govern and his responsibility to provide sons who would become
the future rulers of the state. As a result, Barbaro viewed sexual
intercourse within marriage solely as the means of procreating
offspring who would fill the important offices of the Republic. In
discussing the selection of a wife, Barbaro stressed that aristocratic
marriage should be contracted only with other members of the
ruling class. In this way the purity of lineage would be assured,
and only those who were entitled to govern by descent and status
would continue in their privileged position. Although the choice of
a wife might entail some consideration of political alliance, business interests, and social standing of the bride's family, Barbaro
maintained that the chief factor in selecting a wife was her innate
virtue. This quality would ensure that the wife would bear fine
children and that she would be capable of educating them to meet
the demands of governing. Other considerations, such as beauty,
charm, and great wealth, were of secondary importance for Barbaro.
Hence, the theme of personal virtue, moderation, and sense of duty
that permeates the second book is foreshadowed in the treatment of
the selection of a wife in book 1.[7]

In book 2 of the *De re uxoria,* translated here Barbaro treats the
duties of the wife toward her husband, household, and children.
In the earlier chapters the author stresses the development in a wife
of the personal qualities that permit the well-ordered domestic life
that is requisite for the success of the aristocratic rule of the Republic. Continence in marriage, companionship with the husband,
and submission to his needs are stressed, for these attitudes allow
him to pursue his worldly career of public service without undue
attention to family matters. Further, Barbaro writes, modest demeanor and the avoidance of ostentatious display in dress reflect
the total devotion of the wife to the happiness and well-being of
her mate. Hence, Barbaro emphasizes dignity of comportment,
reticence in social situations, temperance in food and drink, and
modesty in dress as proper qualities in a wife. He describes the
two principal wifely duties as management of the household and

7. For much of this interpretation I draw on M. L. King, "Caldiera and the
Barbaros on Marriage and the Family," *Journal of Medieval and Renaissance
Studies* 6(1976):19–50, at 31–35; see also Gothein, *Barbaro,* chap. 4.

rearing of children. In these spheres Barbaro permitted considerable responsibility. Domestic cares included the training and overseeing of the servants and the provisioning and daily management of
the household. But the bearing, nursing, and training of children
were viewed as even more important duties. Nursed at their mother's
breast or, in case of absolute necessity, given over to a well-trained,
temperate nurse, the children of the patrician Venetian family
were to receive from birth the care proper to their status and future
responsibilities.[8] In their upbringing they were to be inculcated
with the ability to withstand hardships and attain the dignity in
behavior and learning in the humanities that were indispensible
to their future roles. For Barbaro the aristocratic mother was the
crucial vehicle in ensuring that the future rulers of the aristocratic
polity of Venice were properly nutured and educated.

Barbaro's treatment of wifely duties struck a responsive chord
among contemporary humanists and aristocratic friends. As he had
hoped, copies of the tract soon began to circulate among a wide
circle of friends and were studied by members of leading families
in Venice, Florence, and other Italian cities. From Constance in
December of 1416, Poggio Bracciolini wrote to Barbaro reporting
that he had read the treatise through twice and had passed it on to
other papal secretaries at the council held there. Poggio greatly
approved the dignity of style and exhaustive, well-ordered treatment of the subject. With fulsome praise, he explicitly compared
the work to Cicero's De officiis, remarking that, however, this tract
was one on duties written especially for wives.[9] Early the next year
Pier Paolo Vergerio wrote to one of Barbaro's Venetian friends
praising the treatise and noting the author's fine command of
Greek literature, his profound knowledge of the institution of
marriage, and, with rhetorical exaggeration, his excellent Latin
style.[10] Guarino also lauded the effort of his star pupil. In two
letters written in July 1417, the Veronese humanist mentioned
Barbaro's competence in Greek and his growing ability in Latin

8. Barbaro's insistence that mothers nurse their own babies accords well with
other treatments of family management in the fifteenth century; see J. B. Ross,
"The Middle-Class Child in Urban Italy, Fourteenth to Early Sixteenth Century,"
in The History of Childhood, ed. L. de Mause (New York, 1974), pp. 184–99.

9. See Poggio Bracciolini, Opera, 4 vols., ed. R. Fubini (Turin, 1964–1969),
3:30–31.

10. See Pier Paolo Vergerio, Epistolario, ed. L. Smith (Rome, 1934), pp.
126–28.

composition as evidenced in the *De re uxoria*.[11] But despite such encouragement, Barbaro did not continue his humanist writings; in 1419 he married the young Venetian noblewoman Maria Loredan. The same year he began his career as a Venetian states-man with his election to membership in the Senate at the exception-ally early age of twenty-nine.

Until his death thirty-five years later, Barbaro pursued a brilliant career of service to the Venetian Republic. Early in that career he served as the podestà, or chief magistrate, of the Venetian main-land cities of Treviso, Bergamo, Verona, and Vicenza, where he oversaw a new codification of the municipal statutes. Later he served as Venetian ambassador on a number of occasions, includ-ing several legations to the papal courts of Martin V and Eugenius IV. In 1437 Barbaro became a member of the Venetian magistracy overseeing the mainland empire (the *Savi di Terraferma*), and three years later he won the esteem of his fellow countrymen by directing the defense of Brescia against an invading army from Milan. In 1449 he became the presiding officer over the Venetian Senate, and in 1452 he was made a Procurator of St. Mark, an office inferior in dignity only to the dogeship itself.

But throughout his active career of public service Barbaro re-tained his interest in classical studies and became a friend and patron of several younger humanists. He was instrumental in bringing the Greek scholar George of Trebizond from Crete to Venice, where he lived for a time in Barbaro's household. While podestà of Vicenza, Barbaro secured the appointment of Trebizond as teacher of Greek in the school there. He made the noted hu-manist Flavio Biondo his personal secretary and tried to secure for him the post of chancellor of Bergamo. Barbaro's personal letters reveal a continuing lively interest in questions of politics, religion, and classical learning. For example, in a youthful letter to his friend Santo Venier at Zara, Barbaro recommended the study of Cicero's letters to Quintus for their precepts of governing provinces.[12] In later letters Barbaro continued to express his belief in the utility of the *studia humanitatis* and their application to the political and social problems of his age. To be sure, Barbaro evi-

11. See Guarino da Verona, *Epistolario,* ed. R. Sabbadini, 3 vols. (Venice, 1915–19) 1:133–34, 136–38.

12. See *Centotrenta lettere inedite di Francesco Barbaro,* ed. R. Sabbadini (Salerno, 1884), pp. 65–66, letter of 31 May 1417.

denced little interest in what he took to be the sterile debates of formal philosophy, but he did believe that the classics provided training not only in oratory and rhetoric but in moral philosophy as well.[13]

Barbaro was greatly pleased by a continuing interest in his youthful *De re uxoria*. In a letter of December 10, 1447, replying to praise of his treatise by a fellow Venetian, Luigi Barozzo, Barbaro admitted: "I cannot help but be delighted that, even now, this treatise, composed by the beginning of my studies, is approved by many learned and outstanding men."[14] Indeed, the work did enjoy a wide circulation even during Barbaro's lifetime. There survive in Italian libraries more than fifty manuscript copies of the tract, almost all made in the fifteenth century.[15] Its popularity continued unabated into the sixteenth and early seventeenth centuries; an Italian translation appeared in 1538, and two French versions and an English version followed in the late seventeenth century.

Instruction on Christian ideals of marriage stretched back to the time of the Church fathers with St. Augustine's fundamental treatise, *De bono coniugali*. The Middle Ages continued with writings on marriage by such scholastics as Hugh of St. Victor. Advice to women on their studies and proper role in society was freely given by such humanists as Salutati and Bruni, and an Italian treatise on family life, household affairs, and childrearing was written by the Dominican friar, Giovanni Dominici, early in the Quattrocento. But with his emphasis in the *De re uxoria* on the family as the basic unit of state and society, and on the duties of wives in this context, Barbaro created a new literary genre. Aided by his study of works from Greek antiquity on similar themes, Barbaro gave the conventional treatise on family life a new twist. He was to be followed by such famous works as Leon Battista Alberti's *Della familia* and Vegio's treatise on the education of children, as well as several tracts on matrimony by hu-

13. See Barbaro's letter to Guarino of 1438, where he discusses the utility of humanistic studies, in *Francesci Barbari et aliorum ad ipsum Epistulae,* ed. A. M. Querini (Brescia, 1743), pp. 65–66. On Barbaro's career and continuing study of the classics in general, see N. Carotti, "Un politico umanista del Quattrocento: Francesco Barbaro," *Rivista Storica Italiana* 5th ser., 2 (1937), fasc. 2:18–37.

14. *Barbari . . . Epistulae,* ed. Querini, appendice, p. 115.

15. This figure is based on my count of the manuscript copies of the *De re uxoria* listed in P. O. Kristeller, *Iter Italicum,* 2 vols. (Leiden, 1965–67), *passim.*

manist friends, including Guiniforte Barzizza, Poggio Bracciolini, and Giovanni Antonio Campano. But the *De re uxoria* stands as a pioneering work on the subject of love, marriage, and family among the aristocratic classes of Europe in the early modern period.

BIBLIOGRAPHY

Sources and Translations

Barbaro, Francesco. "*De re uxoria,* edited by A. Gnesotto." *Atti e Memorie della R. Accademia di scienze, lettere ed arti di Padova,* n. s. 32 (1915):6–105; excerpts with Italian translation. In E. Garin, ed. *Prosatori latini del Quattrocento.* Milan and Naples, 1952, pp. 104–37.

———. *Das Buch von der Ehe.* Translated by P. Gothein. Berlin, 1933.

———. *Directions for Love and Marriage.* Anonymous English translation. London, 1677.

———. *Francisci Barbari et aliorum ad ipsum epistulae,* edited by A. M. Querini. Brescia, 1743.

———. *Centotrenta lettere inedite di Francesco Barbaro,* edited by R. Sabbadini. Salerno, 1884.

Alberti, Leon Battista. *The Albertis of Florence, Leon Battista Alberti's Della Famiglia.* Translated by G. A. Guarino. Lewisburg, Pa., 1971.

Barzizzi, Gasparino and Guiniforte. *Opera,* edited by G. A. Furietto. Rome, 1723.

Campano, G. A. *De dignitate atque fructu matrimonii.* In *Opera.* Leipzig, 1734.

Dominici, Giovanni. *Regola del governo di cura familiare,* edited by D. Salvi. Florence, 1860.

Garin, E., ed. *Il pensiero pedagogico dell'umanesimo.* Florence, 1958.

Vergerio, Pier Paolo. "*De ingenuis moribus et liberalibus studiis adulescentiae,* edited by A. Gnesotto." *Atti e Memoire della R. Accademia di scienze, lettere ed arti di Padova,* n.s. 34(1917):75–157. Translated in W. H. Woodward. *Vittorino da Feltre and Other Humanist Educators,* pp. 93–118. Reprint with introduction by E. F. Rice, Jr., New York, 1963.

Studies

Agostini, Giovanni degli. *Notizie istorico-critiche intorno la vita e le opere degli scrittori viniziani.* 2 vols., 2:28–134. Venice, 1752–54.

Carotti, Natale. "Un politico umanista del Quattrocento: Francesco Barbaro." *Rivista Storica Italiana,* 5th ser., 2(1937):fasc. 2, 18–37.

Chojnacki, Stanley. "Patrician Women in Early Renaissance Venice." *Studies in the Renaissance* 21(1974):176–203.

Cian, Vittorio. "La coltura e l'italianità di Venezia nel Rinascimento." In his *Scritti minori,* 1:171–203. Turin, 1936.

Diller, Aubrey. "The Library of Francesco and Ermolao Barbaro." *Italia Medioevale e Umanistica* 6(1963):253–62.

Geankoplos, D. J. *Greek Scholars in Venice.* Cambridge, Mass., 1962.

Gnesotto, A. "I codici marciani del 'De re uxoria' di Francesco Barbaro." *Atti e Memorie della R. Accademia di scienze, lettere ed arti di Padova,* n.s. 30(1913):105–28.

————. "Dei Mediceo-Laurenziani e del codice padovano del 'De re uxoria' di Francesco Barbaro." Ibid., pp. 281–94.

Gothein, Percy. *Francesco Barbaro. Früh-Humanismus und Staats-Kunst in Venedig.* Berlin, 1932.

————. "Zaccaria Trevisan." *Archivio Veneto,* 5th ser. 21(1937):1–59.

————. *Zacharias Trevisan: Leben und Umkreis.* Amsterdam, 1944.

Gualdo, G. "Barbaro, Francesco." *DBI* 6(1964):101–3.

King, Margaret L. "Caldiera and the Barbaros on Marriage and the Family: Humanist Reflections on Venetian Realities." *Journal of Medieval and Renaissance Studies* 6(1976):19–50.

Kristeller, P. O. "Un codice padovano di Aristotele postillato da Francesco ed Ermolao Barbaro: Il manoscritto Plimpton 17 della Columbia University Library." In his *Studies in Renaissance Thought and Letters.* Rome, 1956.

Lugli, V. *I trattisti della famiglia nel Quattrocento.* Bologna, 1909.

Monfasani, John. *George of Trebizond. A Biography and a Study of His Rhetoric.* Leiden, 1976.

Newett, M. H. "The Sumptuary Laws of Venice in the Fourteenth and Fifteenth Centuries." In *Historical Essays,* edited by T. F. Tout and J. Tait. Manchester, 1907.

Ross, J. B. "The Middle-Class Child in Urban Italy, Fourteenth to Early Sixteenth Century." In *The History of Childhood,* edited by L. de Mause. New York, 1974.

Sabbadini, R. "La gita di Francesco Barbaro a Firenze." In *Miscellanea di Studi in onore di Attilio Hortis,* 2:615–27. Trieste, 1910.

————. *Vita di Guarino Veronese.* Genoa, 1891.

————. *La Scuola e gli studi di Guarino Guarini Veronese.* Catania, 1896.

FRANCESCO BARBARO
On Wifely Duties[*]

Translated by BENJAMIN G. KOHL

Our ancestors, my dear Lorenzo, were accustomed to making gifts on the occasion of the marriages of their friends or relatives as a token of the obligations that they felt or the love they bore toward the couple. Now this custom (as has happened to many others instituted by our ancestors) is no longer observed among us. For it happens that many people, for a variety of reasons, often borrowed money so that they could give the finest presents to those who were usually very rich. And in sowing these gifts (if I may speak in this way), they seem to me to be imitating those Babylonian peasants for whom (as the father of history, Herodotus, writes) fertile fields were expected to return two-hundredfold, and often even three-hundredfold.[1] I would call these fields anything but fertile and fruitful; but even though they were very poor, these people sent presents to the very rich while they themselves lacked everything and the wealthy had plenty. For this reason, driven on by hope for gain or for money, they lent their property at high interest. But I think they deserve to be deluded in their hoped-

[*] Translation of the preface and book two of Francesco Barbaro, "De re uxoria, ed. A. Gnesotto," *Atti e Memorie della R. Accademia di scienze, lettere ed arti di Padova,* n.s. 32(1915):23–27, 62–100. In identifying Barbaro's sources I also have used the notes to the German translation of the tract by P. Gothein, *Das Buch von der Ehe* (Berlin, 1933).
1. Herodotus *Historia* 1.193.

for riches because they were trying to gain reward by means of a deceitful liberality and were striving for many and great advantages. But I find myself very different from these people, especially when I am dealing with you who has so many riches and such great wealth and has enjoyed so much good fortune in all your affairs that I do not see what could be the use of gifts. So I refrain from talking about the necessities of life since you have a great many precious clothes and elegant and rich furnishings in several places. Besides, when I recall the many pleasant discussions we have had, it seems to me that it would be more pleasant and welcome for you if you could be given something not from my fortune but from your friend Francesco.[2] Therefore, I have decided to write in dedication to you some brief comments on wifely virtues that I judge may be very useful on the occasion of your marriage, and perhaps not completely useless in the future. And if you will find what follows to be different from the usual precepts; it is on account of the mediocrity of my intellect that these precepts are not expressed in a more ornate style or explained at greater length. I have, for the most part, followed the ideas expressed by Zaccaria Trevisan, that very distinguished Venetian and learned man of our age, who is endowed with wisdom, justice, great experience in public affairs, and great learning, and who is closely bound to me by ties of friendship. When sometimes we had discussions on these matters, he elegantly summarized what the ancients had said on this matter.

Nor indeed do I undertake the composition of this tract just in order to instruct you yourself, but I am also attempting to teach several others of our age through you. Although I hope to instruct them in what they ought to be doing, you who have already followed these precepts, are now following them, and will continue to follow them in the future can see them more clearly in yourself for others. Really, how can I instruct you who have by nature been endowed with dignity, laud, and honor and have had such fine models at home? The very path to glory is clearly open to you who are filled with such instruction joined to nature. Indeed, you have imitated that outstanding man, your father Giovanni, and your most distinguished brother, Cosimo, and you have been abundantly

2. An allusion to Barbaro's trip to Florence in the summer of 1415 when he formed his close friendship with Lorenzo de' Medici.

fortified with their authority, wisdom, and advice.[3] In addition to these, you know several fine and very learned men with whom you have often spoken. Indeed, when I was with you I observed the great care and diligence with which you treated and esteemed that very learned man Roberto Rossi, from whose side you were almost never—and rightly—absent. Moreover, add to this your familiarity with that most eloquent man Leonardo Bruni, as well as with our very learned scholar, Niccoli.[4] From these men, I trust, you have heard and learned carefully a great deal on our theme as well as on many other topics. Even though you have already discussed the nature of marriage, yet I do not think it would be contrary to my love toward you if you understood just what I think on the same topic, for I have considered that it would be very pleasing for you to have something written on the subject in my own words. When Xenocrates refused to accept fifty talents of gold received from Alexander as a gift, as if the philosopher did not need royal presents, Alexander said: "Even if it is not right for Xenocrates to use the gifts of Alexander, still it is proper for Alexander to seem to be generous to Xenocrates."[5] Thus, although you have been so well instructed that you perhaps don't consider my advice especially necessary for you, writing this treatise still seemed to me a valuable thing to do, both in instructing young men and in honor of our close friendship.

Now, although all aspects of philosophy are both fruitful and profitable, and no part of it ought to be left uncultivated and undiscussed, still there is a field of it that is especially rich and fertile.[6] Thus marriage, from which all domestic duties follow, should be begun, practiced, and ended honorably, truly, and wisely, according to the best customs and the most sacred teaching. Indeed, for this reason you can easily see the bond of our will and the depth of our friendship. Indeed, I shall consider that I have

3. Stressing the distinction of the Medici family, Barbaro names Lorenzo's father, Giovanni Bicci de' Medici (1360–1429), and his older brother Cosimo (1389–1464), who in 1434 was to become the first Medici ruler of Florence.

4. The list is of Lorenzo's intellectual friends and mentors in Florence, whom Barbaro came to know in 1415: Roberto Rossi (ca. 1353–ca. 1420), who was Lorenzo's tutor, Leonardo Bruni, and Niccolò Niccoli.

5. Plutarch *Regum et imperatorum Apophthegmata, Alexander* 30; *Moralia* 181E.

6. Cf. Cicero *De officiis* 3.2.5.

won a great prize and singular reward if this, my small effort, is for you, to whom I owe everything, somewhat pleasant and profitable. My happiness will be doubled if the youth of our age will find good instruction in these brief comments. And so these precepts, which we have produced in our leisure, might be advantageous to those concerned with this matter, and those skilled in matters connected with marriage can take pleasure in seeing their views confirmed by learned men, or if they are unskilled in such affairs, they can be properly warned. Now if you find some of this treatment perhaps less than totally acceptable to you, still it is my desire and wish that you will be able to approve of the work on the whole. In like fashion at dinner parties, even though we sometimes avoid taking one of the many courses, still we are accustomed to praise the whole meal. Indeed, those few things that the stomach refuses to accept do not reduce the pleasure that the vast majority of the courses affords us. Therefore, I shall begin by talking about taking a wife, and I shall discuss this as briefly as possible. These are the same matters that, as I have said, I discovered to be especially important from that fine friend of mine Zaccaria and from many other outstanding men. Now I shall do what I have proposed. I know that you will listen to me carefully and favorably, and whatever sort of work it turns out to be, I know that you will accept it as evidence of our goodwill, representing the kind of outstanding present that you ought to receive on the occasion of your wedding.

BOOK 2. ON WIFELY DUTIES

Chapter 1. On the Faculty of Obedience

This is now the remaining part to be done here, in which if wives follow me, either of their own free will or by the commands of their husbands, no one will be so unfair as to think that I have not so established the duties of the wife that youth can enjoy peace and quiet the whole life long. Therefore, there are three things that, if they are diligently observed by a wife, will make a marriage praiseworthy and admirable: love for her husband, modesty of life, and diligent and complete care in domestic matters. We shall discuss the first of these, but before this I want to say something about the faculty of obedience, which is her master and companion, because nothing more important, nothing greater can be demanded of a wife than this. The importance of this faculty did not escape the ancient wise men who instituted the custom that when a sacrifice was made to Juno, who was called by the name Gamelia because of her governance of marriage, the gall was removed from the victim. They were wisely warning by this custom that it was proper to banish all gall and rancor from married life.[7] For this reason the Spartan woman's response has usually been approved by many learned men. When she was provoked by the slanderous reproaches of some mad old woman against her husband, she said: "Get out of here with such slanderous talk! When I was still a girl, I learned to obey the dictates of my parents, and now I realize that it is best to follow the wishes of my husband if I want to be what I ought to be."[8] Therefore, let the husband give the orders, and let the wife carry them out with an even temper. For this reason that woman called Gorgo is surely not to be censured when she gave this reply to the question of whether she made advances to the husband: "No, I have not, but he comes to me."[9] Cyrus, that great man and emperor, used to tell his troops that if the enemy advanced making a great noise, they should withstand the asault in silence, but if the enemy approached silently, then his men should go into battle with great noise and clamor. I would give the same advice to wives. If a husband, excited to anger, should scold you more than your ears are accustomed to hear, tolerate his wrath silently. But if he has been struck silent by a fit of depression, you should address him with sweet and suitable words, encourage, console, amuse, and humor him.[10] Those who work with elephants do not wear white clothes, and those who work with wild bulls are right not to wear red; for those beasts are made ever more ferocious by those colors. Many authors report that tigers are angered by drums and made violent by them. Wives ought to observe the same thing; if, indeed, a particular dress is offensive to a husband, then

7. Cf. Plutarch *Coniugalia praecepta* 27; *Moralia* 141F.
8. Cf. Plutarch *Lacaenarum incertarum Apophthegmata* 23; *Moralia* 242B.
9. Cf. Plutarch *Lacaenarum incertarum Apophthegmata* 25; *Moralia* 242C; *Coniugalia praecepta* 37; *Moralia* 143C.
10. Cf. Plutarch *Coniugalia praecepta* 37; *Moralia* 143C.

we advise them not to wear it, so that they do not give affront to their husbands, with whom they ought to live peacefully and pleasantly.[11] I think that ear guards (for so they are called because they protect the ear) are far more necessary for wives than for wrestlers, for the ears of the latter are only subject to blows, but indeed the former are subject to bills of repudiation accompanied by deep humiliation.[12] Hence, wives must take great care that they do not entertain suspicions, jealousy, or anger on account of what they hear with their ears. Indeed, wives can often prevent such errors if they will only follow the prudent example of King Alexander, who, when someone was accused and brought before him for trial, would always stop up one of his ears so that he might later open it to the accused who might want to defend himself.[13] Indeed, it seems that Hermione was speaking the truth when she testified that she was brought to ruin by wicked women with whom she had been on familiar terms. Therefore, if wives should at some time become suspicious, let them stay away from slanderous women, stop up their ears, and supress their mutterings, so that (as the proverb has it) fire is not added to fire. Let wives learn to follow that saying of Philip, that most outstanding king. This man was urged once by his courtiers to be harsher toward the Greeks who, though they had received many benefits from him, still criticized and slandered him. But he said: "What would they do if they were ever to receive bad treatment from us?"[14] In the same way, when troublesome women say, "Your husband esteems you, who are so obedient and affectionate, only very little," then wives should answer, "What if I willingly and actively lost my modesty with my shame and my great desire for him along with my love?" A certain master found his runaway slave in a workhouse, and because the slave had been punished enough the master said: "Would that I had found you somewhere else than in this place." The wife who is angry with her husband because of jealousy and is considering a separation should ask herself this question: If I put myself in a workhouse because I hate a whore, what could make her far happier and more fortunate than this? She would see me almost

11. Cf. Plutarch *Coniugalia praecepta* 45; *Moralia* 144E.
12. Cf. Plutarch *De recta ratione audiendi* 2; *Moralia* 38B.
13. Cf. Plutarch *Vitae Parallelae, Alexander* 42.2.
14. Cf. Plutarch *Coniugalia praecepta* 40; *Moralia* 143F.

shipwrecked, while at the same time she was sailing with favorable winds and securely casting her anchor into my marriage bed?[15] Euripides, in his usual manner, greatly criticized those who were accustomed to listening to the harp while they were at dinner, for such music was better fitted to soothing anger or sadness than to relaxing those already immersed in pleasure.[16] In similar fashion I would criticize wives who when they are happy and contented sleep with their husbands but when they are angry sleep apart and reject their husbands' affections, which through pleasantness and pleasure easily bring about reconciliation. The word Juno in Homer means "overseer of the nuptial ties," and if I remember correctly, when she spoke of Tethys and Oceanus, she declared that she would compose their differences and bring them together in lovemaking and nocturnal embraces.[17] At Rome when there arose any differences between husband and wife, they entered the temple of the appeasing goddess where, after the spectators had been ushered out, they discussed everything frankly, and, finally, they returned home reconciled.[18]

It was considered very good for domestic peace and harmony if a wife kept her husband's love with total diligence. At the olympic games that were dedicated to the great god Jupiter and attended by all of Greece, Gorgias used his eloquence to urge a union of all the Greeks. Melanthus said: Our patron attempts to persuade us that we should all join together in a league, but he cannot bring himself and his wife and her maid—who are only three people— to a mutual agreement (for the wife was very jealous because Gorgias was wildly enamoured of her maid).[19] Likewise, Philip was for a long time displeased with the queen Olympias and Alexander. And when Demaratus of Corinth returned from Greece, Philip eagerly and closely questioned him about the union of the Greeks. Demaratus said to him: "Philip, I consider it a very bad thing that you are spending all your energy in bringing peace and concord to all of Greece when you are not yet reconciled with your

15. Cf. Plutarch *Coniugalia praecepta* 41; *Moralia* 144A.
16. Cf. Euripides *Medea* 190ff.
17. Cf. Homer *Iliad* 14.205, 209.
18. Cf. Valerius Maximus *Factorum ac dictorum memorabilium libri IX* 2.1.6.
19. Cf. Plutarch *Coniugalia praecepta* 43; *Moralia* 144BC.

own wife and son."[20] Therefore, if any woman wants to govern her children and servants, she should make sure that she is, first of all, at peace with her husband. Otherwise, it will seem that she wants to imitate the very things that she is trying to correct in them. In order that a wife does her duty and brings peace and harmony to her household, she must agree to the first principle that she does not disagree with her husband on any point. But of this enough has been said.

Chapter 2. On Love

Now we shall speak of conjugal love, whose great power and high dignity almost always created—as we know from many great thinkers—a pattern of perfect friendship. I must omit a great many topics so that I may speak primarily about what is to be observed most. I should like a wife to love her husband with such great delight, faithfulness, and affection that he can desire nothing more in diligence, love, and goodwill. Let her be so close to him that nothing seems good or pleasant to her without her husband. Indeed, I think that true love will be of the greatest help in this matter. In all matters there is no better, no shorter path than being exactly what we seem to be.[21]

How much work, how much energy must an incompetent farmer expend if he would appear to be competent? How much learning, how much effort do unskillful physicians, or horsemen, or harp players need if they desire to seem to surpass others in fields where they are themselves completely without talent? It happens that many things generally intervene, so that the counterfeit practice of agriculture, medicine, horsemanship, and music comes to naught. If these persons take my advice, they will attain a solid and well-deserved reputation more easily, more quickly, and more surely if they suppress the spokesmen of false and overzealous praise. Since in every instance truth always overcomes imitation, the fact is that the farmer should take pains to till his fields with skill and hard work; the physician to heal men's diseases; the horseman to control unruly horses at his will; and the musician to give such

20. Cf. Plutarch *Regum et imperatorum Apophthegmata, Philippus.* 30; *Moralia* 179C.
21. Cf. Cicero *De officiis* 2.12.43.

delight with his song that nothing could be more pleasant or sweeter to the ears. Wherefore, if wives want to seem to love their husbands deeply, let them love them from their hearts.

In the first place, let wives strive so that their husbands will clearly perceive that they are pensive or joyful according to the differing states of their husbands' fortunes. Surely congratulations are proper in times of good fortune, just as consolations are appropriate in times of adversity. Let them openly discuss whatever is bothering them, provided it is worthy of prudent people, and let them feign nothing, dissemble nothing, and conceal nothing. Very often sorrow and trouble of mind are relieved by means of discussion and counsel that ought to be carried out in a friendly fashion with the husband. If a husband shares all the pressures of her anxieties he will lighten them by participating in them and make their burden lighter; but if her troubles are very great or deeply rooted, they will be relieved as long as she is able to sigh in the embrace of her husband. I would like wives to live with their husbands in such a way that they can always be in agreement, and if this can be done, then, as Pythagoras defines friendship, the two are united in one.[22] Now that this could be accomplished more easily, the people of Crete, who have for several centuries now lived under our dominion, used to permit their daughters to marry only those men with whom as virgins they had expressed mutual signs of love. The Cretans believe that those men would be more beloved by their wives if they were loved by them even before marriage. They recall that nature has so arranged and usage proven that all actions require time with few exceptions. It certainly happens that we may touch something hot and we are not immediately burned, or sometimes wood that is thrown into a fire does not always burst into flame right away. Hence, they think it is necessary for the girl to choose a husband suited to her own personality, just as one does in forming a friendship. The Cretans believe that a couple cannot properly know each other or fall passionately in love immediately. Whether the custom is a good one, I leave it to everyone to decide, but I cannot deny that it is well suited to the joy and constancy of love.[23] I cannot pass over in silence those who seek to arouse their

22. Cf. Cicero *De officiis* 1.17.56.
23. This argument for the gradual acquisition of love is drawn from Plutarch *De liberis educandis* 4; *Moralia* 2B.

husbands to love by means of potions and amorous incantations. I would compare such wives to fishermen who catch fish with poison bait (as they still do in certain parts of Tuscany), and in so doing make the fish tasteless and almost inedible. Really, such women seem to be scarcely different from travelers who prefer to lead the blind than follow these who can see.[24]

Therefore, mutual love should freely and diligently be acquired, nurtured, and preserved. This principle is illustrated by the lives and actions of the most distinguished women, and if wives imitate these they themselves will successfully meet the trials of virtue, love, and constancy. For example, Panthea wonderfully loved and delighted her husband, Abradatus, prince of Susa, and even as a captive she preserved her fidelity to him and made Cyrus a friend. In providing honorably for her husband, moreover, she did not squander his wealth but stored it. Abradatus fought valiantly against the Egyptians, who were the allies of Croesus, in order both to win the affection of Cyrus and to be a worthy husband to his wife Panthea. Then, performing his duty as a brave commander and stalwart soldier, he gave up his life in battle. Panthea, so that she might make him the most honorable sacrifice, desperately sought out his dead body and committed suicide upon it.[25] Likewise, Cassandane so loved Cyrus that when she was about to die she found it was more bitter for her to leave Cyrus than to depart this life. For this reason Cyrus, who did not want to act as an ungrateful husband, lamented her long after her death and ordered all those whom he governed to go into mourning in her honor.[26] The wife of Themistocles loved him so much that it was generally acknowledged that she thought of nothing except her affection and love for her husband. For this reason it happened that the most famous leader of Greece yielded to her in all matters. Hence she was able to bring about more changes than any other Greek of her time. For whatever she wanted Themistocles also wanted, whatever Themistocles wanted the Athenians wished as well, and whatever the Athenians desired the whole of Greece desired.[27] Thesta, the

24. Cf. Plutarch *Coniugalia praecepta* 5–6; *Moralia* 139A.

25. Barbaro's summary of the story of Panthea and Abradatus is taken from Xenophon *Cyropaedia* 6–7.

26. Herodotus *Historia* 2.1.

27. Cf. Plutarch *De liberis educandis* 2; *Moralia* 1CD.

sister of the elder Dionysius, was married to Polyxenus, who, after he had been treated as an enemy by his brother-in-law, fled from Sicily. Then Dionysius called upon his sister and accused her of failing to report the flight of her husband even though she knew about it. Thesta, relying upon her reputation for constancy and outstanding virtue, responded: O Dionysius, do I seem to you to be such a vile and terrible woman that if I had known of my husband's flight I would have refused to go with him as a companion and partner in his misfortune? Indeed, it would be more acceptable to me to be called the wife of Polyxenus, the exile, than the sister of Dionysius, the tyrant. The Syracusans so admired the loftiness of her character that, after the tyrant had been expelled, they conferred royal honors on her as long as she lived. When she died men of all sorts and conditions—indeed, the entire population of Syracuse—attended her funeral.[28] Armenia, the wife of Tigranes, is another noble example to women. For when Cyrus waged a campaign against the Assyrians, she was not able to bear the absence of her husband, so she followed Tigranes very willingly everywhere as his untiring companion through thick and thin.[29] In Homer, Andromache showed her great affection for Hector, on whom she bestowed all her love, as in this passage:

You are my sole father, and indeed my venerable mother,
you are my sweet brother, you are my spouse, admirable in
in all respects.[30]

Eventually driven insane by her husband's death, she ran through the city and wandered on the walls of Troy.

At this point I should speak of the virtue of the excellent wife Camma. Although her story is a long one, still its dignity, nobility, and distinction will be pleasing both to you and to others who will read this treatise. Therefore, we shall set about telling her story in detail. Sinatus and Sinorix, who were united to each other by blood, no doubt excelled the other tetrarchs of Galatia in power, renown, and glory. Of the two, Sinatus took as his wife Camma,

28. Cf. Plutarch *Vitae Parallelae. Dion* 21.
29. Cf. Xenophon *Cyropaedia* 3.37–41.
30. Cf. Homer *Iliad* 6.428; and Plutarch. *Coniugalia praecepta* 48; *Moralia* 145A.

who was outstanding not only in her bodily beauty but in her singular virtue as well. Thus endowed with chastity, goodness, prudence, and magnanimity, she bound the hearts of everyone to her with marvelous affection. That she was a priestess of Diana, who was especially worshipped by the Galatians, made Camma even more famous, and, on account of her own great status and that of her ancestors, she became the chief priestess. At their sacrifices, where she was always magnificently attired, she attracted everyone's eyes. For this reason Sinorix began to be smitten with her, and soon he began to plan the death of his kinsman since he feared that while her husband was still alive he would not be able to carry out his plan of seduction. Thus this evil man, blinded by his great passion, secretly succeeded in killing the unsuspecting Sinatus. Soon thereafter he urged marriage on Camma, who, courageously bearing her husband's death, waited the chance and opportunity for revenge of the impious deed of Sinorix. He continued to urge that the fatal marriage be made and he even admitted honest motives for the murder, if we may consider honest that which has been contaminated by the worst sort of crime. At first Camma rejected his entreaties, but soon her relations, who wanted to join their line forever with that of a powerful prince, urged her even more strongly to be content with marrying him. Then, as if persuaded, she agreed to marry him, and thereafter she received the young man at home and went with him to the temple of Diana, where they were to institute their marriage with a convenant and vows in the presence of the goddess. Taking a cup in her hand, as if about to make a toast, she put her lips to the rim and then gave the rest to Sinorix to drink. The cup had been filled with mead mixed with poison, and when she saw that Sinorix had drained the cup, her pleasure shone on her face and from her eyes and countenance. Turning to the statue of Diana, she spoke the following words: "O divine mother, I witness to you that I have not wanted to survive my beloved Sinatus because of love for life (because indeed the life I have led has only afflicted me with troubles, which now ended will release me from all pain) but because I was determined to survive to carry out the events of this day. Nor would I have taken any pleasure in continuing to live after the funeral of my husband, which was sorrowful to me and a calamity to his country? Only a certain hope for revenge has comforted me from time to time. And now that this vengeance had been exacted, I go to my dear and fine husband, Sinatus. And as for you, vilest of beasts, Sinorix, instead of a wedding bed, a tomb is being prepared." In a short time after the poison had spread through all the members of their bodies, first Sinorix and then Camma died.[31]

Stratonica loved her husband Deiotarus so much that she thought she should do nothing but follow her husband's commands and interests. Therefore, she was in great grief and mourning when she saw that Deiotarus was unhappy because she had given him no heir, and that there would be no successor for his kingdom. Hence, of her own free will she provided her husband with a woman named Electra, who was handsome of face and decent in her habits, and Stratonica urged, exhorted, and persuaded her husband, who much admired the affection and constancy of his wife, to meet privately with Electra. Afterwards she cared for, educated, and instructed honorably the children born of Electra as if they had been her own.[32]

It would be tedious if I were to recount here the earnest affection that Tertia, daughter of Aemilius Paulus, held for P. Cornelius Scipio, or if I were to call to mind the very great love of Julia, Porcia, Artemisia, Hypsicratea, and other fine examples, which are familiar to anyone who has any familiarity at all with ancient history.[33] There are also many things to be learned concerning the love of wives that I shall pass over intentionally. For we are confident in the great ingenuity with which wives will diligently and carefully seek out, of their own free will, ways to love and esteem their husbands. Still, we hope that those qualities which wives will develop naturally by practice will not differ too much from the precepts which have been described here.

Chapter 3. On Moderation

The next part is concerning moderation, from which very often an enduring love between man and wife is begun, always nurtured

31. The story of Camma is taken from Plutarch *Mulierum virtutes* 20; *Moralia* 257F–258C.
32. Cf. Plutarch *Mulierum virtutes* 21; *Moralia* 258D.
33. Cf. Valerius Maximus *Memorabilia* 6.7.1.

and preserved. This quality is not only pleasing to the husband but also seems very noble to all those who hear about it. Moderation in a wife is believed to consist especially in controlling her demeanor, behavior, speech, dress, eating, and lovemaking. We shall discuss briefly these things that we have perceived either by our natural powers, learning, or experience; and since the first two qualities mentioned above amount to the same thing, we shall discuss them together.

Now demeanor, which is above all the most certain expression of the personality and is found in no living creature except man, demonstrates signs of an honest, respectful, and abstemious character. In demeanor the habits that nature might otherwise have hidden completely are detected. One's demeanor declares and manifests many things without the use of words. From the face and its movement the disposition of an individual may be known. Even in dumb animals we discern anger, pleasure, and other such emotions from the movement of the body and from the eyes, which testify and make clear what kind of emotions there are inside. Wherefore many who trust in facial characteristics maintain that one can learn many things about an individual's nature in this way. But I digress too much.

I therefore would like wives to evidence modesty at all times and in all places. They can do this if they will preserve an evenness and restraint in the movements of the eyes, in their walking, and in the movement of their bodies; for the wandering of the eyes, a hasty gait, and excessive movement of the hands and other parts of the body cannot be done without loss of dignity, and such actions are always joined to vanity and are signs of frivolity. Therefore, wives should take care that their faces, countenances, and gestures (by which we can penetrate by careful observation into the most guarded thoughts) be applied to the observance of decency. If they are observant in these matters, they will merit dignity and honor; but if they are negligent they will not be able to avoid censure and criticism. Still, I am not asking that a wife's face be unpleasant, with a sour expression, but, rather, it should be pleasant. And her demeanor should not be clumsy but gracefully dignified. Moreover, I earnestly beg that wives observe the precept of avoiding immoderate laughter. This is a habit that is indecent in all persons, but it is especially hateful in a woman. On the other hand, women should not be censured if they laugh a little at a good joke and thus lapse somewhat from their serious demeanor.[34] Demosthenes used to rehearse his legal speeches at home in front of a mirror so that with his own eyes he could judge what he should do and what he should avoid in delivering his speeches at court.[35] We may well apply this practice to wifely behavior.

I wish that wives would daily think and consider what the dignity, the status of being a wife requires, so that they will not be lacking in dignified comportment. We know that Spartan wives used to go about with their faces covered, while Spartan virgins went about with their faces uncovered. When the Spartan Charillus was asked about this practice he answered: Our ancestors permitted this liberty to young virgins so that they might find husbands; but they prohibited it in married women so that they might understand that it was not their place to seek husbands but to care for and keep those they already had.[36] Indeed, our Cretan subjects permit a similar custom. They allow their young girls to stand in their doorways and sing and joke and play games with their suitors. But when their women are married they have to stay at home, just as do those women who are dedicated to the rite of Vesta; and they can scarcely even go out, as if it would be unlawful for them even to see strange men. Who would not agree that they took this custom from Xenophon? One can easily learn from the following anecdote how much Xenophon would control the gaze of women. For when Tigranes returned home from service under King Cyrus with his kinsmen and his beloved wife Armenia, many men praised the king's manners, the size of his body, and his gracefulness. Tigranes asked Armenia what she thought of Cyrus's beauty, but Armenia, swearing before the immortal gods, answered: "I never turned my eyes away from you. Therefore, I am quite ignorant of what Cyrus's size or shape may be."[37] That story is consistent with the principles of Gorgias, who wanted women to be shut up at home so that nothing could be known about them except their reputation. But Thucydides did not think that they merited such

34. These strictures on propriety are taken from Cicero *De legibus* 1.9.27, and *De officiis* 1.34–36.125–39.
35. Cf. Plutarch *Vitae Parallelae, Demosthenes* 11.
36. Cf. Plutarch *Apophthegmata Laconia, Charillus* 2; *Moralia* 232C.
37. Cf. Xenophon *Cyropaedia* 3.1.41.

treatment, for he declared he had the best wife, about whom there was not the least word praising or censuring her.[38]

We who follow a middle way should establish some rather liberal rules for our wives. They should not be shut up in their bedrooms as in a prison but should be permitted to go out, and this privilege should be taken as evidence of their virtue and propriety. Still, wives should not act with their husbands as the moon does with the sun; for when the moon is near the sun it is never visible, but when it is distant it stands resplendent by itself. Therefore, I would have wives be seen in public with their husbands, but when their husbands are away wives should stay at home.[39] By maintaining an honest gaze in their eyes, they can communicate most significantly as in painting, which is called silent poetry.[40] They also should maintain dignity in the motion of their heads and the other movements of their bodies. Now that I have spoken about demeanor and behavior, I shall now speak of speech.

Chapter 4. On Speech and Silence

Isocrates warns men to speak on those matters that they know well and about which they cannot, on account of their dignity, remain silent.[41] We commend women to concede the former as the property of men, but they should consider the latter to be appropriate to themselves as well as to men. Loquacity cannot be sufficiently reproached in women, as many very learned and wise men have stated, nor can silence be sufficiently applauded. For this reason women were prohibited by the laws of the Romans from pleading either criminal or civil law cases. And when Maesia, Afrania, and Hortensia deviated from these laws, their actions were reproved, criticized, and censured in the histories of the Romans. When Marcus Cato the Elder observed that Roman women, contrary to nature's law and the condition of the female sex, sometimes frequented the forum, sought a favorable decision, and spoke with strangers, he inveighed against, criticized, and restrained them as

38. Cf. Plutarch *Mulierum virtutes, Proemio; Moralia* 242EF.
39. Cf. Plutarch *Coniugalia praecepta* 9; *Moralia* 139C.
40. Plutarch *Quomodo adulator ab amico internoscatur* 15; *Moralia* 58B.
41. Isocrates *Ad Demonicum* 41.

was required by that great citizen's honor and the dignity of his state.⁴² We know that the Pythagoreans were ordered to be silent for at least two years after beginning their studies. In this way they were not able to lie, to be deceived, or to be in error—all of which are very shameful acts—and, moreover, they could not stubbornly defend those opinions that they had not yet sufficiently investigated.⁴³ But we require that wives be perpetually silent whenever there is an opportunity for frivolity, dishonesty, and impudence. When addressed, wives should reply very modestly to familiar friends and return their greetings, and they should very briefly treat those matters that the time and place offer them. In this way they will always seem to be provoked into conversation rather than to provoke it. They should also take pains to be praised for the dignified brevity of their speech rather than for its glittering proxility. When a certain young man saw the noble woman Theano stretch her arm out of her mantle that had been drawn back, he said to his companions: "How handsome is her arm." To this she replied: "It is not a public one." It is proper, however, that not only arms but indeed also the speech of women never be made public; for the speech of a noble woman can be no less dangerous than the nakedness of her limbs.⁴⁴ For this reason women ought to avoid conversations with strangers since manners and feelings often draw notice easily in these situations.

Silence is also often praised in the finest men. Pindar heaped praise on that outstanding Greek ruler Epaminondas because, though he knew much, he said little. In this matter, as in many others, Epaminondas followed the excellent teachings of nature, the mistress of life, who has clearly made known her thoughts on silence. She has with good reason furnished us with two ears but only one tongue, and this she has guarded with the double defense of lips and teeth.⁴⁵ Now Theophrastus and many other men say that nature has made us with this opening so that the virute planted in us may enjoy the most pleasant and best results. As for the other senses that nature has bestowed upon us as scouts and messengers, they sometimes are sources of reliable knowledge but are very

42. Cf. Livy *Ab urbe condita* 34.2–4; Valerius Maximus *Memorabilia* 8.3.1–3.
43. Cf. Aulus Gellius *Noctes Atticae* 1.9.3–4.
44. Cf. Plutarch *Coniugalia praecepta* 31; *Moralia* 142D.
45. Cf. Plutarch *De recta ratione audiendi* 3; *Moralia* 39B.

often only the conveyers of ignorance.[46] Yet a certain Venetian citizen, whom I don't think it is necessary to name at present, praises silence only in those who cannot gain approval by their genius, authority by their wisdom, or renown by their well-wrought speeches. To this man I usually answer that the principal consideration in every matter refers to the person and to the place as well as to the time. Even if I were to concede, following his opinion, that it is usually appropriate for men to speak, still I consider such speechmaking to be, in the main, repugnant to the modesty, constancy, and dignity of a wife. For this reason the author Sophocles, who is certainly no worse than the Venetian I am discussing—and most men consider him better—has termed silence the most outstanding ornament of women.[47] Therefore, women should believe they have achieved glory of eloquence if they will honor themselves with the outstanding ornament of silence. Neither the applause of a declamatory play nor the glory and adoration of an assembly is required of them, but all that is desired of them is eloquent, well-considered, and dignified silence. But what am I doing? I must be very careful, especially since I am treating silence, that I do not perhaps seem to you too talkative.

Chapter 5. On Dress and Other Adornments

This is the point at which to discuss dress and other adornments of the body, which when they are not properly observed, lead not only to the ruin of a marriage but often to the squandering of a patrimony as well. All authorities who have studied these matters bear witness to this fact. If indeed one is pleased by the always praiseworthy rule of moderation, women will be recognized for modesty, and care will be taken for personal wealth and, at the same time, for the city as a whole. Here this fine precept should be followed: wives ought to care more to avoid censure than to win applause in their splendid style of dress. If they are of noble birth, they should not wear mean and despicable clothes if their wealth permits otherwise. Attention must be given, we believe, to the condition of the matter, the place, the person, and the time; for who cannot, without laughing, look upon a priest who is dressed in

---

46. Cf. Plutarch *De recta ratione audiendi* 2; *Moralia* 38AB.
47. Sophocles *Aiax* 293.

a soldier's mantel or someone else girdled with a statesman's purple at a literary gathering or wearing a toga at a horse race. Hence, we approve neither someone who is too finely dressed nor someone who is too negligent in her attire, but, rather, we approve someone who has preserved decency in her dress.[48] Excessive indulgence in clothes is a good sign of great vanity. Moreover, experience and authorities have shown that such wives are apt to turn from their own husbands to other lovers. King Cyrus ought to be an example to our women that they should not strive too much to have expensive clothes, for Cyrus seems to be equal to his great name, which in the Persian tongue means "sun," both in his admirable wisdom and in his splendid moderation. When ambassadors came from the king of India to make peace with the Assyrians in the city of his uncle Cyaxares, the uncle wanted the choicest part of his army to appear before them. He sent orders to his general Cyrus to appear as soon as possible with all his troops in the courtyard of the royal palace and the large market square. Cyrus carried out these orders and came with order, dignity, and unbelievable speed, wearing only a thin garment, even though Cyaxares had sent him a purple robe, a precious necklace, and other Persian ornaments to wear so that his nephew, the general of his army, might seem all the more splendid and well-dressed. But Cyrus despised all these things greatly, and it seemed to others and to himself the highest decoration to be seen arriving ready to fight with the well-trained army almost before the royal messenger had returned to Cyaxares.[49] A similar disdain for fine apparel would bring great honor to our wives.

Dionysius, the tyrant of Sicily, gave two very precious garments to Lysander so that his daughters might be more finely dressed. But Lysander refused the gifts and ordered the garments returned to Dionysius, saying that his daughters would be even more finely attired without the garments.[50] Julia, the daughter of Caesar Augustus, imagined that her fine attire was sometimes offensive to

48. Barbaro took this idea from Pier Paolo Vergerio, *"De ingenuis moribus,"* ed. A. Gnesotto, *Atti e Memorie della R. Accademia di scienze, lettere ed arti di Padova,* n.s. 34(1917):145; English trans. in W. H. Woodward, *Vittorino da Feltre and Other Humanist Educators* (1897; reprint New York, 1963), p. 118.

49. Cf. Xenophon *Cyropaedia* 2.4.1–6.

50. Cf. Plutarch *Coniugalia praecepta* 26; *Moralia* 141E.

her father, so one day she put on a plain dress and went to pay him a visit. When Caesar greatly approved of her new attire, she acknowledged that she was now wearing clothes that would please her father while before she had been dressing to please her husband Agrippa.[51]

One may believe whatever he wishes. But still I think that wives wear and esteem all those fine garments so that men other than their own husbands will be impressed and pleased. For wives always neglect such adornments at home, but in the market square "this consumer of wealth"[52] cannot be sufficiently decked out or adorned. Indeed, a great variety of clothes is rarely useful and often harmful to husbands, while this same variety is always pleasing to paramours for whom such things were invented. I am wont to compare these men who are properly called "uxorious" to those who are so pleased with splendid exteriors on their houses while they are forced to do without necessary things inside. Hence, they present a golden facade to give pleasure to neighbors and the passers-by. Such husbands are also similar to unskilled but rich barbers whom middle-aged men frequent only if they wish to have their hair arranged. Their ivory tools and elaborate mirrors are no source of wealth to them, but rather of grief, when they see the most noble young men going, to their great sorrow, to the neighboring barbershops. Moreover, sumptuous attire, magnificent clothes, and luxurious apparel give pleasure to those who frequent porticos, open courts, and sidewalks or very often promenade through the whole city. Hence, it was wisely forbidden to the women of Egypt to wear ornate shoes so that they might be prevented from wandering about too freely. Indeed, if we were to deprive most women of their sumptuous clothes, they would gladly and willingly stay at home.[53]

Yet I think we ought to follow the custom—for good mores have so decayed,—that our wives adorn themselves with gold, jewels, and pearls, if we can afford it. For such adornments are the sign of a wealthy, not a lascivious, woman and are taken as evidence of the wealth of the husband more than as a desire to impress wanton eyes. I will not dwell on the fact that this sort of wealth is more

51. Cf. Macrobius, *Saturnalia* 2.5.5.
52. Terence *Eunuchus* 79.
53. Plutarch *Coniugalia praecepta* 30; *Moralia* 141E.

durable, and less likely to entail poverty than money put into rich clothing. Moreover, jewels and gold may often easily be of great use in business and public affairs. Who does not know how useful this sort of wealth was at a certain time to the ancient Romans, who in the time of peril during the Punic War raised money— which the ancients called the "sinews of war"—for their city, following the Oppian Law.[54] Still I think that wives ought to display their jewels even less than the present sumptuary laws permit. Therefore, I would like them to abstain from wearing very licentious apparel and other bodily adornments, not out of necessity but because they desire to win praise by showing that "they can do without those things that they are legally allowed."[55] But you have heard enough about attire.

Chapter 6. On Food and Drink

Now we shall discuss food, which, as anyone who wishes to consider such things agrees, is of the greatest importance in every regard. Who doubts that the very sinews of moral virtue are broken and quite destroyed by these luxuries that the great mob believes will lead to the good life? What asceticism cannot be ultimately corrupted in a very short time by indulgence in food. Whoever is lost in fleshly desires cannot win praise for himself by sobriety, care, and vigilance and acquire the profit and benefit of the moderate life.

Hence, so that the quality of moderation will not be lacking in wives, I should have them take care first of all to abstain from those things that encourage, instill, or increase the desires of the flesh. The holy virgins were instructed by the best and sagest of men to observe vigils and abstain from food and drink, lest carnal desires might contaminate their pure thoughts or weaken their firm resolve. In antiquity the use of wine was denied to Roman women,

54. The story of the use of the Oppian Law to confiscate jewels for the Roman treasury during the Second Punic War is recorded in Valerius Maximus *Memorabilia* 9.1.3.

55. The phrase is from St. Augustine *De bono coniugali* 3 (= *PL* 40.375). For a description of repeated efforts by Venice to enforce laws against luxurious dress, see M. H. Newett, "The Sumptuary Laws of Venice in the Fourteenth and Fifteenth Centuries," in *Historical Essays,* ed. T. F. Tout and J. Tait (Manchester, 1907), pp. 245–78.

just as it is now forbidden to the Syrians and the Persians. In order that any transgression of this rule might be easily detected, a kiss was instituted among members of the Roman family so that from the smell it could be discovered who had been drinking. Those women who broke the law were not only held in low esteem, but, as Cato tells us, they also had to pay a heavy fine.[56] This kind of intemperance very often leads to and invites the most illicit pleasures. For this reason some heathen peoples justly used to place statues of Venus and her father Bacchus together in the same temple, so that those who came in order to see the image of Venus would first have to pay honor to the statue of Bacchus.[57] Surely in such degenerates the mind and character become very weak, and they can understand nothing divine, can remember nothing honorable, and think of nothing sacred. Rather, their minds are devoid of reason and judgment, and they always define as the highest good what the prurient senses demand. As Cicero writes, if brutes could speak, they would call it sensuality.[58] Cyrus easily warded off the attack of Spargapises, the son of Tomyris, who had a very fine army, and weakened his desire to conquer and extinguished his will to resist. Indeed Cyrus, who was upright and ready to do battle, halted the advance of Spargapises, who had been destroyed by wine and reveling, seized and destroyed him.[59] Did not the luxuries of Capua weaken Hannibal's strength more than the defeat at Cannae troubled the Romans?[60] De we really need more examples? Unless a very moderate care is exercised over eating and drinking, the mind itself, trangressing the limits of moderation, becomes shipwrecked and falls into ruin.

Of all the various sorts and conditions of humankind, there are scarcely any brought up in the lap of luxury who will be able to observe decent behavior or even preserve a pretense of moderation. Those who follow nature as a guide require very little, but those who follow pleasure to a sumptuous satiety always desire what is immense and infinite. I admire the frugality of that Spartan who

---

56. Cf. Valerius Maximus *Memorabilia* 2.1.5; Aulus Gellius *Noctes Atticae* 10.23.1–5.

57. Pausanias *Descriptio Graeciae* 2.23.8.

58. Cicero *De finibus* 2.6.18.

59. Herodotus *Historia* 1.211.

60. Cf. Valerius Maximus *Memorabilia* 9.1. ext. 1.

having caught some fish gave them to a chef to be prepared. But the chef, in his manner, wanted cheese, oil, vinegar, and many other condiments so that the fish might be seasoned more delicately. To him the Spartan said: 'If I had all the things that you are asking for, I would not have needed the fish in the first place.'[61] Indeed, the vices of Venus and uncontrolled lovemaking do not simply follow but are the inevitable result of the delights of Alexandria and the feasts of Syracuse. As a fine custom, the Spartans used to exhibit drunken slaves at their banquets so that intemperance in drinking would appear as a deformity to their wives and children. For the slaves always attracted the attention of the onlookers with their folly, and they appeared not only worthy of pity but even miserable and most unfortunate. I do not believe that those fine ancients were pleased by the misery of their slaves. Rather, they considered that whatever was evil in a slave was even worse among free men.[62] Thus, wives should very carefully observe drunken maidservants so that they themselves can perceive just what they ought to avoid. For although, as Homer says, wine gives a great deal of vigor to weary bodies, immoderate consumption makes one weak in the mind and leaves the senses decayed as in senility.[63] The great power of wine in such that the heat that is naturally given to us is overcome by a more violent force, and our natural energy is not gradually but suddenly consumed.[64] Just how harmful that dangerous and tumultous vapor is to our correct understanding of things is obvious, for under the influence of drink we can neither reason, nor make a logical argument, nor refute, nor discourse well. What more need I say? The poets report that because of drink a great many men have become swine, asses, and lions. Indeed, one must be doubly careful to avoid drunkenness because women with dulled mind or neglectfulness of important matters become (as Aristotle reminds us) even more prone to other vices.[65] Moreover, moderation and naturalness in the mother's life will be an aid to the child, for whose benefit I have in large part

61. Cf. Plutarch *De esu carnium* 1.5; *Moralia* 995C.

62. Cf. Vergerio *De ingenuis moribus,* p. 108; Woodward, *Vittorino da Feltre,* p. 100.

63. Homer *Iliad* 6.261.

64. Cf. Aristotle *Problemata* 30.1:953b.

65. Cf. Aristotle *Politica* 1.13.8:1260a, and *Oeconomia* 1.3.4.

been writing these things. Therefore Diogenes, when he beheld a drunken boy, said very aptly: "Drunken parents begat you."[66]

How much a good upbringing by a temperant mother may aid her offspring we shall discuss a little further on. But in this matter we admonish and exhort our wives that they should follow nature, and that they should reject and despise pleasure, in whose realm virtue in no way exists. Rather, they should approve and imitate the frugal table of Lucretia instead of the sumptuous delicacies of the Etruscans and of Cleopatra. In this way they will preserve their own dignity and that of their children to whom they owe every care. Now at this point we ought to discuss lovemaking.

Chapter 7. On the Regulation of Lovemaking

Indeed, the fact is that as food and drink are to be regulated, so in its own fashion moderation in lovemaking ought to be observed. For lovemaking itself follows the rule of life, just as a young chick follows its mother. This fact is borne out by many examples, but we cannot at this point in our treatise begin more wisely or more aptly than from the example of nature itself. So we shall discuss briefly what we have in mind.

Indeed, the union of man and wife was first invented (as we said above), and ought to be esteemed especially, for the purpose of procreation.[67] The couple must mainly use intercourse in the hope of procreating offspring. We can perceive and understand well enough that in most beasts there is a natural urge that leads them to follow certain rules of copulation, so that through the seed of mortal animals these same beasts are made immortal by a perpetual succession. Thus, in this way animals provide an example for us who possess a freer and nobler appetite, that we should indulge in sexual intercourse not for pleasure but only for the purpose of procreating offspring. Using the words of Julia, the daughter of Augustus, I admonish you that when the ship is full it should admit no more passengers.[68] Therefore, we should certainly

66. Plutarch *De liberis educandis* 1.3; *Moralia* 2A.

67. See St. Augustine *De bono coniugali* 3 (= *PL* 40.375), and Xenophon *Oeconomicus* 7.19, for the Christian and pagan sources of the notion of procreation as the purpose of marriage, which is more amply discussed in book 1 of the tract.

68. Cf. Macrobius *Saturnalia* 2.5.9–10.

not consider beasts to be beasts for the very reason that they never
have sexual appetites when they are pregnant but only for the sake
of procreation. But if a woman should transgress these limits, I
wish that she will curb herself so that she will be, or at least seem
to be, chaste in that sort of temperance from which chastity is derived. It would be conducive to achieving this result if, from the
very beginning, husbands would accustom themselves to serving
as the helpers of necessity rather than of passion. And wives
should bear themselves with decorum and modesty in their married
life so that both affection and moderation will accompany their
lovemaking. Lust and unseemly desire are harmful to their dignity
and to their husbands, even when they later say nothing about it.
Herodotus writes that women lay aside their modesty together with
their undergarments;[69] if they make love with adulterers, let us
acknowledge that this is true, but if wives will listen to us they will
maintain their dignity with their husbands. When a certain woman
was being forcibly taken by King Philip to satisfy his lust and desires, she declared: "Give me any woman and take away the light
and you won't know one from the other." Now this can be justly
said of adulterers. But wives, even though the light has been far
removed, do not behave at all like these vile women.[70] Does not
Hesiod absolutely forbid that we should be uncovered at night?
Because, as he says, the nights also belong to the immortal gods.[71]
For at all times a wife ought to do her duty, and although her
body cannot be seen, still she ought always to observe decency so
that she will justly seem decent to her husband even in the dark.
Hence, when the wife of the famous Commodus attempted to en-
tice her husband to use unusual and improper pleasures on her, he
answered: "How far one can go in doing such things depends on
the woman, but the term wife is surely a name of honor, not of
pleasure."[72] Similarly Cato the Censor expelled Manilius from the
Senate because he passionately kissed his wife in the presence of
his daughters.[73] Now if it is true that it is a very base thing to kiss

69. Cf. Plutarch *Coniugalia praecepta* 10; *Moralia* 139C.
70. Cf. Plutarch *Coniugalia praecepta* 46; *Moralia* 144F.
71. Hesiod *Opera et Dies* 727–30.
72. Cf. Plutarch *Coniugalia praecepta* 29; *Moralia* 142BC, where Phocion,
not Commodus, is laying down the precept.
73. Cf. Plutarch *Coniugalia praecepta* 13; *Moralia* 139E.

or passionately embrace one's wife in the presence of one's children, how much more important is it that nothing immoderate, nothing wanton should take place before the eyes that wives ought especially to please? Hiero fined Epicharmus, the comic poet, very heavily because he publicly made an indecent remark in the presence of his wife; for the dignity of marriage is so venerable that it is proper that no access should be given to the eyes and ears of strangers.[74] The decency of the Athenians demonstrates this principle beautifully when they returned with the seals unbroken the letters they had intercepted that King Philip had sent to his wife Olympias; indeed, they held that it was completely wrong for a stranger, or even an enemy, to share the secrets exchanged between a husband and his wife.[75]

It is therefore proper that wives always be careful and thoughtful in such matters so that they may win praise, honors, and crowns of gold. Hence, nothing should seem so pleasant and delightful that it would ever keep them from their obligation to do everything in a modest manner. In this matter wives should follow the example of many illustrious women. I do not know if Brasilla was the first among these, but surely her great deeds should not be passed over in silence in our own age.[76] She was born of noble parents at Durazzo, as we know from the testimony of certain authors, and when she had been taken captive during a pirate raid she was in danger of being raped. But this beautiful woman, even in that great peril, preserved her sacred and uncorrupted chastity by the use of her wit, virtue, and lofty spirit; and with many words she stayed the aggression and repelled the fury of her captor, Čerič. And she struck a bargain with him that if she could preserve her chastity, she would provide him with a magic ointment that would render him immune to harm from military arms. Convinced by the argument of this fine and chaste woman and the virgin's reputation for magic, he put Brasilla under guard while she went out to

74. Cf. Plutarch *Regum et imperatorum Apophthegmata, Hiero* 5; *Moralia* 175C.

75. Cf. Plutarch *Praecepta gerenda reipublicae* 3; *Moralia* 779E.

76. The story of Brasilla and the Slavic pirate chief Čerič was known to Barbaro from one of his mentors, Giovanni Conversini da Ravenna. See V. Zaccaria, "Il *memorandarum rerum liber* di Giovanni di Conversino da Ravenna." *Atti dell'Istituto Veneto, Classe di scienze morali e lettere* 106, 2 (1947–48):221–50, at 239–40.

gather herbs, and he eagerly awaited the concoction of the ointment. Then, with great courage, she approached Cerič and promised that she would render him safe from harm not with mere words but with herbs. After she had annointed her own neck with the ointment, she offered her throat to him. Indeed, Čerič, who rashly believed that she was quite immune, cut off her head with his sword and was amazed at such a display of chastity. What more need be said? If wives would want to be as they ought to be, there would be no need of further examples and exhortations. So that we do not further delay the discussion of those matters that we ought to treat next, we shall end our treatment of modesty here.

Chapter 8. On Domestic Matters and the Managements of Households and Servants

Both the time and place require that we now speak with you concerning domestic matters, and I wish to talk with you about a few topics that we know by common experience to be the most useful of all. But I will not include in this small and limited space all the things that learned men have treated, since some do not pertain to our present topic in any case and besides these matters can be understood by reading their books. It will be enough if, out of many things, we treat as briefly and summarily as possible those topics that are absolutely essential to our little treatise. I therefore would treat the whole matter of domestic affairs as it concerns the management of the household and servants and dependents, and especially the education of the children. We shall discuss this last topic later, but first let us treat the two former matters.

We are interested in the care of our property and the diligence proper to our servants and staff because it is necessary to have both property and servants, without whose help family life itself cannot exist. Surely it is in these two things that the management of domestic matters primarily is involved, for unless a wife imposes her own judgment and precepts on these matters, the operation of the household will have no order and will be in great disarray. Men are naturally endowed with strength of mind and body; both for these and other reasons, they provision their homes by their labor, industry, and willingness to undergo hardships. Conversely, I think we may infer that since women are by nature weak they should diligently care for things concerning the household. For weakness can never be separated from cares nor cares from vigilance. What is the use of bringing home great wealth unless the wife will work at preserving, maintaining, and utilizing it? Nothing else has been written about the daughters of Danaus than that they were subjected to the eternally vain task of perpetually filling a leaky cask.[77] I am of the opinion, which, I hope you, Lorenzo, will approve, that no small utility derives from wifely concern for household management. Indeed, it has been well put by that most prudent man, Caesar Augustus, that Alexander would have obtained more renown and profit if he had been able to keep and preserve what he had gotten than in performing his great deeds aided by fortune.[78] Therefore, wives ought not to lack praise if they merely organize, as is their duty, the wealth that has collected in the home. They ought to attend, therefore, to governing their households just as Pericles daily attended to the affairs of Athens.[79] And they ought always to consider how well they are doing so that they will never be deficient in their care, interest, and diligence in household matters. They will surely be successful in this matter if they do what they should do, that is, if they are accustomed to stay at home and oversee everything there.

At this point there comes to mind the example of the very prudent groom who, when asked what mainly made a horse fit, replied: the eye of the master.[80] So that a wife's duty might be commended to posterity, there were affixed to the bronze statue of Gaia Caecilia, the daughter of Tarquinius, an ordinary shoe and a distaff and spindle, so that those objects might in some way signify that her diligent work at home ought to be imitated by future generations.[81] What neglectful landowner can hope to have hard-working peasants? What slothful general can make his soldiers vigilant for the state? Therefore, if a wife would like to have her maids working hard at home, she should not merely instruct them with words but she ought also by her actions to demonstrate, indicate, and show

77. Cf. Aristotle *Oeconomia* 1.3.4, 1344a; Xenophon *Oeconomicus* 7.40.
78. Cf. Plutarch *Rerum et imperatorum Apophthegmata, Caesar Augustus* 8; *Moralia* 207D.
79. Cf. Xenophon *Oeconomicus* 7.35.
80. This famous aphorism appears in Aristotle *Oeconomia* 1.6.3, 1345a; Xenophon *Oeconomicus* 12.20; and Plutarch *De liberis educandis* 13; *Moralia* 9D.
81. Cf. Plutarch *Quaestiones Romanae* 30; *Moralia* 271E.

what they should be doing. Indeed, there is surely nothing more excellent in household affairs than that everything be put in its place, because there is nothing more beautiful, more useful than order, which is always of the greatest importance. We consider that an army or chorus can be called anything but an army or chorus unless its organization is well preserved.[82] I would have wives imitate the leaders of bees, who supervise, receive, and preserve whatever comes into their hives, to the end that, unless necessity dictates otherwise, they remain in their honeycombs where they develop and mature beautifully. Wives may send their maids and manservants abroad if they think this would be useful to them. But if, indeed, these servants are required at home, they should urge, order, and require their presence. Wives should also consider it their duties to see to it that no harm comes to their husbands' winecellars, pantries, and oil cellars. Just as generals often review the size of their armies, so wives should frequently and diligently survey the provisions kept at home so that they will not learn, to their great detriment, that what ought to last for years is in supply for only a month.[83] Now Pericles' custom especially deceives the ignorant and often harms domestic plenty. He sold at one time all the crops he received from his fields, and afterwards he bought daily at the market whatever was needed at home.[84] But this daily provisioning with grain, wood, and wine is more proper for a traveler or unsettled soldier than for a citizen and the head of a family, for if he did this he would not be splendidly, generously, or comfortably looking after his own wealth. Whether someone contends that this practice was introduced by him on account of the irresponsibility of the steward, or whether, following my opinion, one blames the negligence of the wife or her staff more than the opinion of the most learned men, I think we should imitate the Roman custom that noble women not be employed in vile tasks. As a result of the pact instituted with the Sabines, noble Roman women were freed from the tasks of the mill and kitchen and from other servile duties.[85] But, indeed, they could undertake such jobs if their husbands or the need to entertain guests required them, for if it is

82. Cf. Xenophon *Oeconomicus* 1.3.
83. Cf. Xenophon *Oeconomicus* 7.32–36.
84. Cf. Plutarch *Vitae Parallelae, Pericles* 16.
85. Cf. Plutarch *Quaestiones Romanae* 85; *Moralia* 284F.

a question of the well-being of the husband, they should not merely not neglect such tasks but also should hate such neglect. I am happy to discover in the writings of that very learned poet and philosopher Homer that Andromache held such great love and affection for her husband Hector that she was very diligent and painstaking in everything that added to her husband's honor and welfare, even to the point of feeding hay to his horses.[86] Therefore, if a wife will be mindful of what duties are hers and how praise can be earned, she will realize she owes everything to her husband and will do her duties very well. If a generous husband wants to entertain others at home, the wife should not even avoid kitchen work, which was, after all, not completely unknown to such fine and valiant men as Achilles and Patroclus. For when Ulysses and Ajax came to him to be reconciled, Patroclus laid down his harp and eagerly undertook duties that would hardly have been worthy of an ordinary slave had they not been done for the sake of good-will and hospitality.[87] But enough of these matters. In any case I have proposed to treat them summarily and not to explain every detail, especially since these matters are discussed more fully and more expertly in the works of learned men than I am able to treat here. Therefore, let us turn to the topics remaining.

It is now proper to speak, as we have promised, about servants, who, provided they are not neglected, can add great luster to our houses and be useful and pleasant. So they will be if wives will instruct them carefully and if they will not get angry with them before, having warned them, they discover that they have made the same mistakes. I should like that wives, in these matters as in others, follow the example of the leaders of the bees, who allow no one under their control to be lazy or negligent.[88] Marcus Cato the Elder absolutely followed this precept in household management, so that he, a censor himself, was thought to have fallen slowly, acting the part of a good man in this regard: he immediately sold those too old to work and always believed that it was in no way proper to keep useless slaves in his household.[89] Wives should adopt this ancient custom as their own, so that they

86. Cf. Homer *Iliad* 8.186–89.
87. Cf. Homer *Iliad* 9.182–224.
88. Cf. Xenophon *Oeconomicus* 7.33.
89. Cf. Plutarch *Vitae Parallelae, Cato maior* 4.

might convert ignorant servants into skillful ones and then promote any maidservant who showed herself hardworking, faithful,
and diligent at lesser tasks to the custody of the cellars.

Thrifty wives constantly ought to seek out and appoint sober
stewards for the provisions and address them courteously and be
generous to them, so that by the great interest of the mistress the
industry of the steward daily increases. They should feed their
servants so that they will satisfy both their human needs and
reward their constant labor. Wives should clothe their servants
comfortably as befits the season, climate, and place. Moreover, as
Hesiod advises, they should always be careful that servants are not
separated from their children and families,[90] for servants will
always find a way to stay together with their own family, even
secretly. Furthermore, servants will be very grateful if especially
good medical care is provided when a member of their family is
taken sick. For these acts of humanity, this solicitousness will make
servants very conscientious and hardworking for the household.
We can see this, if we may return to the same example, in the case
of the bees who never desert their leader on account of his care and
provision for them. They always follow him wherever he goes as
a sign of their goodwill.[91] This practice should not seem strange
to anyone since similar expressions of gratitude are also to be
found in other animals. This will be made clear from the next
example which has been chosen out of many possible ones. During
the Persian War the Athenians, in order to provide for their own
safety, left the protection of the walls of their city and committed
their state to the sea. While they were hurriedly leaving the shore,
they saw the dog of Xanthippus the Elder consumed with desire to
accompany his master, which he showed by running about, wagging
his tail, whining, and barking. Therefore, Xanthippus, who was
fleeing in a ship, stopped and waited for his dog, who was in the
midst of the waves, swimming toward his master's ship, and he
finally gathered his anxious dog in the boat. Afterwards, when the
dog died, Xanthippus wished that such devotion that ought
not to be forgotten could be remembered, so he erected an honorable tomb for his dog in a certain high spot that for a long time
thereafter was called "Dog-Grave." In this way Xanthippus was

90. Probably an allusion to Hesiod *Opera et Dies* 373.
91. Cf. Xenophon *Oeconomicus* 7.37.

able to leave for posterity a perpetual monument of the mutual affection to be observed between masters and their inferiors.[92] In military affairs, legates, tribunes, and centurions, and in civil government, praetors, treasurers, and other magistrates have specific duties in particular matters; so in domestic affairs, when each servant is assigned only a few tasks, he is best able to perform diligently his duties. Hence, if wives want to provide well for the management of the households, they should separate the tasks of overseeing work from those of manual labor. In this way it will be clear what should be done by each servant and just what is expected of him. Unless a specific place is assigned to each person on a ship, everything would be confused, even if no storm were raging. We know that heaven itself, which is the final resting place appointed for us, is comprised of a concatenation of things where one part is joined to another until all the parts fit together in a harmonious whole.[93] If the strings of a harp are well played, they will make one harmony from different notes, so that no sound could be sweeter or more pleasant to the hearer. Hence, if wives will assign specific tasks to their servants and specific places for their supplies, they will see that such order contributes greatly to the splendor, utility, and pleasantness of their homes. Therefore, as I have already said, they should take in, store, and distribute with care, prudence, and diligence those supplies that are brought into the home. And they should work very carefully to put in order and improve with their diligence whatever is in the home. As a result, the general dignity of their household can be maintained and increased. But enough on this subject.

Chapter 9. On the Education of Children

It remains to speak about the education of children, which is surely a rewarding and certainly the most serious of a wife's duties. Diligence in accumulation of money for the family is really worth nothing (as ancient Crates used to say) unless a great deal of care and really extraordinary amount of energy is expended on the upbringing and instruction of the children to whom the wealth is to

92. Cf. Plutarch *Vitae Parallelae, Cato maior* 5.
93. An echo of Cicero *Tusculanae disputationes* 1.11.24.

be left.[94] For this care children, who owe everything to their parents, are especially obligated. But if parents do not perform the task of caring for and instructing children, the children must really and truly seem deserted and abandoned. If, indeed, we acknowledge that all things are due to the authors of our life, which all mortals naturally cherish and hold on to with good reason, and what should we do if to a noble upbringing we add training in living well? On this account, if you reflect upon all the aspects of the matter, you will find that unless mothers totally repudiate the rules of nature, the duty of educating their children is so incumbent upon them that they cannot refuse this duty without great harm. For nature assigns to them an overwhelming love for their children, which they simply cannot overlook.[95] So that this fact may be amply demonstrated, I will speak of the procreation of children before they see the light of day; but time does not allow me to digress for long, and Nature has so hidden and secluded those parts of the body that what cannot be viewed without embarrassment can hardly be discussed by us without loss of dignity. However, we shall treat those matters that we absolutely cannot omit.

In pregnancy the same blood of which women otherwise are cleansed in their monthly effusions is held back. This time, following the laws of nature, the fetus is nourished by this blood until the time of birth arrives. Then, as in all animals who give birth, the nourishment of milk is supplied. For this, Nature has made breasts, which, like bountiful fountains, nourish the young child and help it to grow gradually in all its parts. Moreover, women have been given two breasts so that if they have twins they may easily suckle and nourish them together.[96] All these things have been thus provided with great wisdom, but they still might seem to have been done in vain except that Nature has also instilled in women an incredible love and affection for their offspring.[97] Here the special care and diligence of Nature can be observed, for while she has placed the nipples of other animals under their stomachs, in women she has affixed them on their breasts so that they may

---

94. Cf. Plutarch *De liberis educandis* 7; *Moralia* 4E.
95. Cf. Plutarch *De amore prolis* 3; *Moralia* 495.
96. Cf. Plutarch *De liberis educandis* 5; *Moralia* 3D.
97. Cf. Plutarch *De amore prolis* 3; *Moralia* 496A.

feed their children milk and fondle them with embraces at the same time, kiss them easily and comfortably, and, as they say, receive them to their bosoms.

Thus Nature has assigned to women the duty of bearing and rearing children not only by necessity but also with her singular goodwill and love.[98] Moreover, we can see a good argument in favor of a mother exercising great care for her newborn babies if women will but follow the habits of the terrible she-bear and other beasts. After bears have given birth to their unformed cub, they form and clean the cub with their tongues, as if the tongue were a kind of tool, so they can be justly called not just the mother of the cub but even its artificer.[99] But why should we dwell on these small matters? Surely Nature has bestowed such good feeling toward newborn infants that we can see some animals who are timid become very brave on account of their offspring, others who are lazy become diligent, and others still who are slave to the stomach and gluttony become very abstemious. Did not even the Homeric bird endure hunger in order to provide for her young ones, and did she not cheat her own stomach to keep them fed?[100] Therefore, mothers merit the severest censure if they neglect the care of their children and live carelessly. I would have them avoid no hardship in order to ensure that they make their children the best companions, comforters, and helpers in their old age. Therefore, if mothers would be free from reproach they should not neglect their offspring, but they should provide for both the bodies and souls of their children, and they should nourish and suckle them at their breasts. And the ones they nourished with their blood while still unknown mothers now will raise, since they are now born and have become human beings and are known and dear, since they require greatly not simply the care of a nurse but that of a mother as well.[101] The wife of Marcus Cato the Censor fed her infant with her own milk, and this custom continues among Roman women down to the present age.[102] In fact, because the fellowship of food and nourishment always increases friendship and love,[103] in order

98. Cf. Plutarch *De amore prolis* 3; *Moralia* 496C.
99. Cf. Plutarch *De amore prolis* 2; *Moralia* 494C.
100. Cf. Plutarch *De amore prolis* 2; *Moralia* 494D.
101. Cf. Aulus Gellius *Noctes Atticae* 12.1.6.
102. Cf. Plutarch *Vitae Parallelae, Cato maior* 20.
103. An echo of Plutarch *De liberis educandis* 5; *Moralia* 3D.

to make the infants of her servants more loving to her own infants, a wife should sometimes feed them at her own breasts.[104] We beg and exhort the most noble women to follow this example of feeding her infant her own milk, for it is very important that an infant should be nourished by the same mother in whose womb and by whose blood he was conceived. No nourishment seems more proper, none more wholesome than that same nourishment of body that glowed with greatest life and heat in the womb and should thus be given as known and familiar food to newborn infants. The power of the mother's food most effectively lends itself to shaping the properties of body and mind to the character of the seed. That may be discerned quite clearly in many instances; for example, when young goats are suckled with sheep's milk their hair becomes much softer, and when lambs are fed on goats' milk, it is evident that their fleeces become much coarser. In trees it is certain that they are much more dependent on the qualities of both sap and soil than on the quality of the seed;[105] thus, if they are transplanted to other ground when flourishing and well leafed, you will find them changed enormously by the sap from the less fertile ground. Therefore, noble women should always try to feed their own offspring so that they will not degenerate from being fed on poorer, foreign milk. But if, as often happens, mothers cannot for compelling reasons suckle their own children, they ought to place them with good nurses, not with slaves, strangers, or drunken and unchaste women. They ought to give their infants to the care of those who are freeborn, well mannered, and especially those endowed with dignified speech. In this way the young infant will not imbibe corrupt habits and words and will not receive, with his milk, baseness, faults, and impure infirmities and thus be infected with a dangerous degenerative disease in mind and body.[106] For just as the limbs of an infant can be properly and precisely formed and strengthened, so can his manners be exactly and properly shaped from birth. Therefore, mothers ought to be especially careful in their choice of nurses for infants; at this tender age a child's unformed character is very susceptible to being molded, and, as we impress a seal in soft wax, so the disposition and faults of a

104. Cf. Plutarch *Vitae Parallelae, Cato maior* 20.
105. Cf. Aulus Gellius *Noctes Atticae* 12.1.11–16.
106. Cf. Plutarch *De liberis educandis* 5; *Moralia* 3DF.

nurse can be sealed upon an infant. That very wise poet Vergil showed how important a nurse's inclinations and nature are when he described how Dido called Aeneas harsh and unyielding. Thus he has her say: "The Hircanian tigers fed you at their breasts."[107] Likewise, that most pleasant poet Theocritus said that he detested cruel Cupid, not because he was born of his mother Venus "but because he suckled the breast of a lioness."[108]

Therefore, women ought to consider it best, very honorable, and commendable to suckle their own children, whom they should nourish with great love, fidelity, and diligence; or they may commit this part of their duty to well-trained nurses who will esteem and care for the infants, not with a pretended enthusiasm nor out of mercenary consideration. After their offspring have passed their infancy, mothers should use all their skill, care, and effort to ensure that their children are endowed with excellent qualities of mind and body. First they should instruct them in their duty toward Immortal God, their country, and their parents, so that they will be instilled from their earliest years with those qualities that are the foundation of all other virtues. Only those children who fear God, obey the laws, honor their parents, respect their superiors, are pleasant with their equals and courteous to their inferiors, will exhibit much hope for themselves. Children should meet all people with a civil demeanor, pleasant countenance, and friendly words. But they should be on the most familiar terms with only the best people. Thus they will learn moderation in food and drink so that they may lay, as it were, the foundation of temperance for their future lives. They should be taught to avoid these pleasures that are dishonorable, and they should apply their efforts and thoughts to those matters that are the most becoming and will be useful and pleasant when they become older. If mothers are able to instruct their children in these matters, their offspring will much more easily and better receive the benefit of education. Very often we see that the commands and gifts of rulers are welcomed by their subjects, yet when these same things are bestowed by private persons they hardly even seem acceptable. Who can be unaware of what great authority the mildest and shortest reproach of a parent has on his children? Whence that wise man, Cato the Elder,

107. Aulus Gellius *Noctes Atticae* 12.1.20, quoting Vergil *Aeneid* 4.366–67.
108. Theocritus *Idyllion* 3.15–16.

instructed his offspring diligently in many subjects, including literature, so he would not be lacking in his duties as a father.[109] Even the barbarous Eurydice ought to be judged worthy of great praise, for when she was advanced in years she applied herself to the study of literature, that monument of virtue and learning, so that, having done this, she would not only be considered the source of life to her children but could also instill in them through the bountiful condiments of the humanities the art of living well and happily.[110] Mothers should often warn their children to abstain from excessive laughter and to avoid words that denote a rash character. That is the mark of stupidity, the evidence of passion. Moreover, children should be warned not ever to speak on those matters that are base in the act. Therefore, mothers should restrain them from vulgar or cutting words. If their children should say anything that is obscene or licentious, mothers should not greet it with a laugh or a kiss, but with a whip.

Moreover, they should teach their children not to criticize anyone because of his poverty or the low birth of his lineage or other misfortunes, for they are sure to make bitter enemies from such actions or develop an attitude of arrogance. Mothers should teach their children sports in which they so willingly learn to exert themselves that, if the occasion arises, they can easily bear even more difficult hardships. I would have mothers sharply criticized for displays of anger, greed, or sexual desire in the presence of their offspring, for these vices weaken virtue. If mothers act appropriately, their children will learn from infancy to condemn, avoid, and hate these most filthy mistresses and they will take care to revere the names of God and will be afraid to take them in vain. For whoever has been taught at an early age to despise the Divinity, will they not as adults surely curse Him? Therefore, it is of great importance to train children from infancy so that they never swear. Indeed, those who swear readily because of some misfortune are not deserving of trust, and those who readily swear very often unwittingly betray themselves. Mothers ought to teach their children to speak the truth. This was well established among the Persians, and for that reason they decreed that there would be no market squares in their cities since they believed that such places were only fit for

109. Plutarch *Vitae Parallelae, Cato maior* 20.
110. Cf. Plutarch *De liberis educandis* 20; *Moralia* 14BC.

lying, or telling falsehoods, or for swearing falsely.[111] Mothers should teach their children to say little at all times, and especially at banquets, unless they are ordered to speak, so that children do not become impudent or talkative—qualities that ought to be especially avoided in the young. It will be an impediment to proper education if children try to explain impudently what they themselves have not yet sufficiently understood.[112] Therefore, you should recall that saying of Cato who, when he was as a youth blamed for his silence, said: "Then I shall not harm myself at all, until I shall say those things that are not worthy of being left unsaid."[113] If children will learn such precepts from their mothers as soon as their tender years permit, they will more happily and easily obtain the dignity and learning of their parents.

There are many other matters that I shall omit at present because they are peculiar to fathers, and I do so readily because I see that some people consider this subject of wifely duties to be so vast and infinite that the subject of fatherly duties can scarcely be sufficiently treated here. I can say nothing truer than that I never intended to discuss what might be done, but, rather, I have tried to describe what ought to be done. Therefore, who is such an unjust critic that if he will approve of a marriage done for the best reasons, (just as you have done) and will, in his choice of a wife, take a woman outstanding in her morals, suitable in her age, family, beauty, and wealth, loving to her husband, and modest and very skillful in domestic matters—who, I say, would be so pessimistic in these matters that he cannot wish for all these great qualities or imagine that wives so endowed ought not to perform all these important precepts? Therefore, my Lorenzo, your compatriots ought to be stirred by your example and follow you with great enthusiasm, for in Ginevra you have taken a wife who is a virgin well endowed with virtue, charm, a noble lineage, and great wealth. What more outstanding, more worthy model could I propose than yours? What more shining, more worthy example than yours, since in this outstanding city of Florence you are most eminently connected

111. Cf. Aulus Gellius *Noctes Atticae* 11.11.1–2, for this distinction between telling falsehoods and lying.

112. Cf. Vergerio *De ingenuis moribus,* p. 105; Woodward, *Vittorino da Feltre,* p. 99.

113. Cf. Plutarch *Vitae Parallelae, Cato minor* 4.

through your father, grandfather, and ancestors? You have taken a wife whose great wealth the entire world indeed admires but whose chastity, constancy, and prudence all men of goodwill esteem highly. They consider that you are blessed and happy to have her as a wife, as she is to have you as a husband. Since you have contracted such an outstanding and fine marriage, these same men ask God Immortal that you will have the best children who will become very honored citizens in your state. These matters might perhaps seem negligible since I am treating them, but indeed they are, in their own fashion, borne out in your marriage. Thus, surely young men who follow your example will profit more than only by following my precepts; just as laws are much more likely to be observed in a city when they are obeyed by its ruler, so, since your own choice of a wife is consistent with my teachings, we may hope that these precepts will be followed by the youth.

But, Lorenzo, as my treatise begins with you, so shall it end. You now have, instead of a present, my opinion on wifely duties, and I hope that whatever has been said by me, not to admonish you (as I made clear from the beginning) but to declare our mutual goodwill, will in large measure be kindly accepted by many others. I am certain that it will be well received by you, in whose name I undertook this endeavor. If when you are reading our little commentary you find anything that perhaps seems to be well or wisely stated, attribute it to that excellent man Zaccaria Trevisan, who is worthy of every sort of praise and whose memory I gladly cherish, and to my study of Greek literature.[114] From the latter I have culled some things that pertain to our subject and inserted them here. Although I have been occupied with this treatise for only a few months, I still am happy to think that it will bear abundant and pleasant fruit. For I have profited so much from the learning and talent of that fine and very erudite man, Guarino da Verona, who was my tutor and my closest friend from among all my acquaintances. He was a guide to me and to several other first-rate people, in understanding and advancing our study of the humanities. And he was such a fine guide that, with his help, these divine studies, to which I have devoted myself from boyhood, have

---

114. Another reference to Barbaro's debt to his Venetian model, Zaccaria Trevisan, and to his Greek teacher, Guarino da Verona.

become very enjoyable and profitable to me. Therefore, please accept gladly from me this wife's necklace (as I wish to call it), given on the occasion of your marriage. I know that you will esteem it greatly both because it is the sort of necklace that cannot be broken or destroyed by use (as others can) and because it is the product of my sincere friendship and of a mind that is entirely devoted to you.

POGGIO
BRACCIOLINI

Introduction

BENJAMIN G. KOHL

The question of the utility of wealth in the commercial but Christian society of early Renaissance Italy exercised the minds of many thinkers and humanists. In the thirteenth century the dominant Christian ethic was probably the Franciscan ideal of voluntary poverty, an ideal that held that the proper practice of the Christian life lay in simplicity, frugality, and the joyous acceptance of the gifts of God's creation. Dante gave approval to this view in canto 15 of the *Paradiso* of the *Divina Commedia,* where the poet's ancestor Cacciaguida praises the simple lives and virtue of medieval Florentines in contrast with the acquisitive spirit and conspicuous consumption of the early Trecento. In addition, in book 4 of the *Convivio* Dante explicitly argued against the medieval notion that nobility was based upon great wealth and ancient family. Trecento humanists, including Petrarch and Salutati, followed the teachings of Roman Stoicism, patristic learning, and Franciscan asceticism in finding that external riches did not lead to virtue. Critical of the greed and corruption of contemporary individuals and institutions, Petrarch especially deplored the luxury and vice that flourished at the papal court at Avignon. Rather, Petrarch advised that laity and clergy alike should seek only enough earthly goods sufficient for a life of dignity and avoid ostentatious display and crass materialism. Later humanists at the time of the Great Schism (1378–1417) continued to inveigh

231

against clerical corruption and hypocrisy, but, at the same time, they began to adopt new, more positive views toward the use of riches in serving the needs of state and society.[1] Chief among these lay spokesmen who criticized the evils of the clergy and grappled with the question of the utility of wealth was Poggio Bracciolini (1380–1459), famed as book-hunter, papal secretary, social critic, and historian.

Born at Terranuova near Montepulciano in Tuscany, Poggio received his early education in Arezzo and, at the age of about twenty, migrated to Florence to pursue studies in the notarial arts and Latin literature. There he formed a close friendship with another Tuscan scholar, Leonardo Bruni, and became a member of the circle of young humanists who looked to the Florentine chancellor Coluccio Salutati as their leader. After brief attendance at the Florentine Studium, Poggio set off for Rome in 1403. Armed with a warm letter of recommendation from Salutati, Poggio soon found employment in the papal curia. Employed by several popes as a copyist and secretary during the stormy years of the Great Schism, Poggio finally followed the papal entourage of John XXIII to the Council of Constance, where he remained from 1414 to 1418. In Switzerland, Poggio devoted himself to hunting down texts of ancient works in nearby libraries. During four separate sojourns visiting monasteries in eastern France and southern Germany, Poggio was able to discover a number of previously unknown Latin works, including a complete copy of Quintilian's *Institutio oratoria,* seven of Cicero's orations, and several late Latin epics—Silius Italicus' *Punica,* Valerius Flaccus' *Agronautica,* and Statius' *Silvae.*[2] Poggio soon became famous for his discoveries and circulated among his friends in the papal curia and in Florence copies made in his clear, elegant hand, which was to become the basis for humanistic script.[3]

1. This paragraph is based mainly on the important analysis of Hans Baron, "Franciscan Poverty and Civic Wealth as Factors in the Rise of Humanistic Thought," *Speculum* 13(1938):1–38.

2. See A. C. Clark, "The Literary Discoveries of Poggio," *The Classical Review* 13(1899):119–30. Poggio put some of these discoveries to use in the *De avaritia,* quoting from one of Cicero's speeches and the *Punica* of Silius Italicus.

3. On Poggio's contribution to the development of humanistic script, which forms the basis for italic type, see B. L. Ullman, *The Origin and Development of Humanistic Script* (Rome, 1960), chap. 2.

With the election of Martin V at the conclusion of the Council, Poggio followed Henry Cardinal Beaufort, Bishop of Winchester, to England. There Poggio continued his search for lost manuscripts and served as a secretary in his patron's household. The Italian scholar disliked the crude customs of the English and complained in letters to his Florentine friend Niccolò Niccoli of the harsh, humid climate and the lack of culture. Despairing of finding more manuscripts, Poggio turned to the study of the Bible, the writings of St. Augustine, and the homilies of St. John Chrysostom, which he read in a medieval Latin translation.[4] Homesickness for Italy and hope for preferment at the papal court at Rome prompted Poggio to quit England late in 1422 and return home.

Back in Rome, Poggio continued his search for lost manuscripts, began his study of Roman antiquities, and became a secretary and adviser to Pope Martin V. Always critical of contemporary society and ecclesiastical corruption, in 1417 Poggio had composed an oration against clerical vices, including avarice, which he sent to several of his acquaintances, among whom was the Venetian humanist Francesco Barbaro.[5] By the end of the 1420s, the Pope's disputes with the Observant Friars and the presence of the renowned Franciscan preacher San Bernardino da Siena in Rome gave Poggio the occasion to vent his criticism of the corruption of the mendicant preachers and, at the same time, try his hand at the composition of a Ciceronian dialogue investigating the questions of the value of wealth and the nature of avarice. Poggio was also able to use his wit on his fellow curialists, whom he made the interlocutors of the dialogue. In his choice of speakers he exercised his delight in irony by casting the well-known miser Cencio Romano dei Rustici as a critic of greed and making the Vicentine humanist Antonio Loschi, who was a very generous man, the principal

---

4. On Poggio's stay in England, see R. Weiss, *Humanism in England during the Fifteenth Century*, 3rd ed. (Oxford, 1967), chap. 1. His reports to Niccoli on his reading and on English customs are available in English translation in *Two Renaissance Book Hunters: The Letters of Poggius Bracciolini to Nicolaus de Niccolis*, trans. with notes by Phyllis W. G. Gordan (New York, 1974), pp. 43, 46–49.

5. See R. Fubini, "Un'orazione di Poggio Bracciolini sui vizi del clero fatta al tempo del Concilio di Constanza," *Giornale storico della letteratura italiana* 142(1965):24–33, which proves Poggio's authorship of the oration of 1417, entitled *De reformanda ecclesie*.

defender of avarice. Only in making the learned theologian Andrea of Constantinople the main spokesman against avarice did Poggio create a character who matched his human personality.

Poggio's conscious irony, his use of well-known contemporaries as interlocutors, and, most of all, the inherent complexity of the issue of the utility of riches have caused debate as to the correct interpretation of the dialogue. The Italian literary historian Eugenio Garin has held that *On Avarice* was an apology for the rising burgher ethic of Quattrocento Florence, with Loschi's speech most closely resembling Poggio's own views.[6] This interpretation has been followed and elaborated by other scholars, including G. Saitta, R. Roedel, and Christian Bec, all of whom emphasize that the dialogue was a defense of prevailing middle-class values and of the use of wealth in the defense of state and society.[7] But there is much evidence against such an interpretation.

First the dialogue arose from Poggio's desire to criticize the corruptions of society, especially the avarice and hypocrisy of the begging orders. The discussion begins with a consideration of the inability of Franciscan preachers to curb vice and to mend the troubled souls committed to their care. Of contemporary churchmen, only San Bernardino da Siena is viewed as a competent preacher, and even he, it is held, is not successful in overturning avarice and curbing usury. Second, the first main speaker against avarice, Bartolomeo da Montepulciano, emphasizes, through a vivid series of classical allusions and contemporary anecdotes, that avarice is the worst affliction besetting mankind. This position is only partially controverted by the subsequent speech of Antonio Loschi, who appeals to the needs of society and governments in his argument in favor of the acquisition and utility of great wealth. The third major speaker, Andrea of Constantinople, on account of his stature and reputation as a theologian, was clearly supposed to represent the orthodox Christian position on the problem. Andrea overturns Loschi's arguments point by point, appealing both to

6. See E. Garin, *Das italienische Humanismus* (Bern, 1947), pp. 43–44; English trans. by P. Munz, *Italian Humanism* (New York, 1966), p. 43.

7. See G. Saitta, *Il pensiero italiano nell'umanesimo e nel Rinascimento*, vol. 1: *L'umanesimo* (Bologna, 1949), pp. 316–20; R. Roedel, "Poggio Bracciolini nel quintocentenario della morte," *Rinascimento* 11(1960):51–67, esp. 55–56; and C. Bec, *Les marchands écrivains à Florence 1375–1434* (Paris and The Hague, 1967), pp. 379–82.

experience and the ways of nature and to biblical and patristic authority to make his case. Here Poggio put to use the study of the Bible and the writings of St. Augustine, and St. John Chrysostom, which he had made in England a decade earlier. In fact, the arguments of Andrea are so near Poggio's own views on avarice, expressed in his letters, that a few students of the dialogue have asserted that Poggio's own opinion is represented by the Byzantine theologian.[8] Indeed, in a contemporary letter to Niccolò Niccoli, Poggio averred that he used the words of St. Paul, St. Augustine, and St. John Chrysostom in Andrea's speech to clinch his argument.[9] But there is no real resolution offered at the conclusion of the dialogue. Although most of the papal secretaries assent to the arguments of Bartolomeo and Andrea, it seems that Antonio is still unshaken in his belief in the usefulness of riches.

Poggio's own position will probably never be known. Using as his model the colloquial Ciceronian dialogue, such as *De finibus*, Poggio was trying to present both sides of the question in a natural, conversational way. In a letter of 11 July 1429 to a Florentine friend Ambrogio Traversari, Poggio admitted that he purposely eschewed the flowery, persuasive eloquence of the epistle for presenting his views on avarice and instead opted for the plain, inelegant style of everyday speech.[10] Poggio employed the dialogue precisely because it admitted of no easy solution to a difficult social issue. In another letter written a decade after the composition of *On Avarice*, Poggio explained his affection for the use of the dialogue in his criticism of society: "For in a debate the truth will usually be elicited from both sides."[11] In his writings Poggio wanted to delineate real characters, present well-argued opinions, and achieve a simpler, more flexible Latin style. In this quest he was willing to sacrifice conclusiveness of argument in order to attain verisimilitude in diction and in portraying impromptu discussion.

8. See E. Walser, *Poggio Florentinus: Leben und Werken* (Leipzig, 1914), p. 129; and F. Tateo, *Tradizione e realtà nell'Umanesimo italiano* (Bari, 1967), pp. 259–60.

9. Letter of 11 June 1429 to Niccoli in Gordan, *Book Hunters*, p. 144.

10. See Poggio's *Opera omnia*, vol. 3, *Epistolae*, ed. T. Tonelli (1833, reprint ed. Turin, 1965), 1:282–83.

11. Letter of December 1442 in ibid., 2:267, where Poggio is paraphrasing Cicero *Academica* 2.3.7.

Poggio was not entirely satisfied with his first attempt at employing the dialogue form. In the dedicatory preface to Francesco Barbaro, Poggio depreciatingly called *On Avarice* "the first-born of my studies." He admitted the respect he held for the great scholars of his age and acknowledged his own inability to read in the original the ancient Greek texts that his contemporaries, including Leonardo Bruni and Barbaro himself, were then translating into Latin. Moreover, Poggio sought advice and criticism on the first version of the dialogue from his friend and mentor Niccolò Niccoli. Soon after the completion of this version, Poggio sent a copy to Niccoli asking for suggestions for improvements. Niccoli objected to the use of the Christian names of the discussants, the anticlerical tone of some of the speeches, and the allusion to San Bernardino. In a second version Poggio substantially altered the beginning and conclusion of the dialogue, but he retained his fellow curialists as the interlocutors.[12] In original or revised form, *On Avarice* won wide approval and about a dozen copies of each of the two versions exist today in European libraries. At least three editions of the work appeared in the early sixteenth century.

The accession of Eugenius IV (1433–1443) to the papal throne brought Poggio a willing patron and supporter. In those years, the humanist continued his study of ancient Roman inscriptions and monuments, began the study of ancient Greek, and formed his program of treatises and dialogues designed to point up the ills of society and examine problems of human existence. In 1436 Poggio married a young Florentine noblewoman; the event occasioned an apologetic tract on the reasons, pro and con, why an old man— Poggio was fifty-six at the time—should take a young wife. In other works the humanist treated the themes of the unhappiness of princes, the nature of true nobility, and the hypocrisy of monks. Toward the end of his life he broached the question of the power of fortune in human affairs in his works *On the Inconstancy of Fortune* (1448) and *On the Misery of the Human Condition* (1455).

The election of a close friend as Pope Nicholas V in 1447

12. On Niccoli's role in "correcting" the first version of the *De avaritia,* see H. Harth, "Niccolò Niccoli als literarischer Zensor, Untersuchungen zur Textgeschichte vom Poggio's 'De avaritia,' " *Rinascimento,* 2nd ser. 7(1967):29–53.

should have brought secure happiness to Poggio as the chief papal secretary. But criticism of his Latin style by a student of the brilliant contemporary humanist Lorenzo Valla caused Poggio great pain. At first Poggio fumed and tried to have Valla assassinated, but the quarrel soon settled down to a series of bloodless, though savage, invectives on correct Latin style, in which Poggio was clearly vanquished.¹³ His appointment as chancellor of Florence in 1453 permitted Poggio to leave Rome, but he soon became embroiled in disputes with a younger generation of Florentine humanists. Despite the duties of the office and his frequent quarrels, Poggio found time to follow in the historiographic tradition of his Florentine predecessors and composed a history of Florence narrating events from the middle of the fourteenth century to the Peace of Lodi (1453). But not even close friendship with the ruler of Florence, Cosimo de' Medici, could deter Poggio from resigning his office in 1458 and retiring to his rustic estate at Terranuova, where he died a year later.

Poggio was not popular with many of his contemporaries. Arrogant, mocking, quarrelsome, quick to criticize, quicker still to retort and refute with a fine, ironic wit, Poggio was redeemed by his powerful intellect, wide learning, and tireless service to the study of the classics through his discovery and copying of Latin texts. Toward the end of his life he mastered Greek well enough to translate several dialogues by the satirist Lucian and Xenophon's *Cyropaedia*. But Poggio remains best known today for his collection of salacious anecdotes, known as the *Facetiae*, which mainly criticized clerical vices, and for his capacity for vivid description and moving narrative, as demonstrated in his letter on the baths at Baden and his account of the trial and execution of the heretic Jerome of Prague at Constance.¹⁴ Always critical, often savage in his attacks on contemporary institutions and personalities, Poggio was *au fond* a pessimist. He realized his own frailty and the ultimate temporal, evanescent quality of all earthly things. He

13. See Walser, *Poggio Florentinus,* pp. 272ff.
14. There is an English translation of Poggio's description of the baths at Baden in Gordan, *Book Hunters,* pp. 25–30, and of his account of the trial of Jerome of Prague in J. B. Ross and M. M. McLaughlin, *The Portable Renaissance Reader* (New York, 1953), pp. 614–24.

also realized the capacity of men, no matter how well intended and instructed, to do the wrong thing. At the conclusion of *On Avarice,* Poggio has Andrea of Constantinople acknowledge that:

Despite the counsel of many fine men, despite so many authoritative opinions and sober judgments placed before our eyes, which ought to affect the minds of mortals, still there are those who, impervious to every argument, continue to dedicate themselves to avarice and worship it as a god.

Andrea then urges these sinners to "repent while there is still time and attend to their future life." To exhort misers to change their ways, Poggio quoted a passage from Cicero's *De officiis.*

In all of fifteenth-century humanist thought, there is perhaps no more poignant mixture of reasoned argument, ancient authority, and Christian morality than this passage.

BIBLIOGRAPHY

Poggio Bracciolino: Editions and Translations

Opera omnia, edited by R. Fubini. 4 vols. Turin, 1964–69.

"De avaritia." In *Prosatori latini del Quattrocento,* edited by E. Garin, pp. 248–309 (the central two-thirds of the dialogue with Italian translation). Milan and Naples, 1952.

Contra l'Ipocrisia, Edited by G. Vallese. Naples, 1946.

The Facetiae or Jocose Tales of Poggio. With English translation. Paris, 1879.

Two Renaissance Book Hunters: The Letters of Poggius Bracciolini to Nicolaus de Niccolis. Translated with notes by Phyllis W. G. Gordan. New York, 1974.

Studies

Aurigemma, Marcello. "Poggio Bracciolini." In *Letteratura italiana. I minori,* vol. 1, pp. 427–48. Milan, 1961.

Bec, Christian. *Les marchands écrivains à Florence 1375–1434.* Paris and The Hague, 1967.

Clark, A. C. "The Literary Discoveries of Poggio." *The Classical Review* 13(1899):119–30.

Gutkind, C. S. "Poggio Bracciolinis geistige Entwickung." *Deutsche Vierteljahresschrift für Literaturwissenschaft und Geistesgeschichte* 10(1932):548–96.

Harth, H. "Niccolò Niccoli als literarischer Zensor, Untersuchungen zur Textgeschichte vom Poggio's 'De avaritia.'" *Rinascimento,* 2nd ser., 7(1967):29–53.

Loomis, Louise Ropes. "The Greek Studies of Poggio Bracciolini." In *Medieval Studies in Memory of Gertrude Schoepperle Loomis,* edited by R. S. Loomis, pp. 489–512. New York, 1927.

Oppel, John W. "Peace vs. Liberty in the Quattrocento: Poggio, Guarino, and the Scipio-Caesar Controversy," *Journal of Medieval and Renaissance Studies* 4(1974):221–65.

————. "Poggio, San Bernardino of Siena, and the Dialogue *On Avarice,*" *Renaissance Quarterly* 30(1977):564–87.

Petrucci, A. "Bracciolini, Poggio." *DBI* 13(1971):640–46.

Roedel, R. "Poggio Bracciolini nel quintocentenario della morte," *Rinascimento* 11(1960):51–67.

Shepherd, William. *The Life of Poggio Bracciolini.* 2nd ed. Liverpool, 1837.

Ullman, B. L. *The Origin and Development of Humanistic Script.* Rome, 1960.

Walser, Ernst. *Poggio Florentinus: Leben und Werken.* Leipzig, 1914.

Weiss, Robert. *Humanism in England during the Fifteenth Century.* 3rd ed. Oxford, 1967.

POGGIO BRACCIOLINI
On Avarice *

Translated *by* BENJAMIN G. KOHL
and ELIZABETH B. WELLES

PREFACE

Since most mortals, my dear Francesco,[1] do not live but pass through life—indeed everyone passes through, while only a very few live it—those who have been so endowed by Immortal God that they can be said to have lived life ought to be viewed as indeed fortunate. I think this has happened to several men of our own time who have earned great renown by doing remarkable things, and their names will be known through the ages. They have translated various genres of Greek literature into Latin for us, and they have composed some works of their own with the greatest learning and eloquence.[2] As a result, the Latin Muses have become much

* Translation is based on the text of the *De avaritia* in the Basel edition of 1538, reprinted in Poggio's *Opera omnia*, ed. R. Fubini, 4 vols. (Turin, 1964–69), 1: 1–31. The central two-thirds of the dialogue appears with facing Italian translation and some notes in E. Garin, *Prosatori latini del Quattrocento* (Milan and Naples, 1952), pp. 248–309.

1. The recipient of the dialogue with its dedicatory preface was Francesco Barbaro (1390–1454), the author of *De re uxoria*, translated above, and a Venetian statesman and diplomat.

2. Poggio is alluding to the recent translation of ancient Greek works made by Leonardo Bruni, Guarino da Verona, and other scholars, including Barbaro himself.

more splendid and embellished. Although I think that it is not at all difficult for men learned in Greek eloquence and outstanding in all kinds of knowledge to publish something on the theme I propose, it is hard for me to do so because I can neither translate from the Greek language for our benefit, nor are my abilities such that I should wish to discuss in public anything drawn from these writings. But since it is true that sometimes "fortune helps the bold,"[3] I have been tempted to see whether I could contribute something to the public good, so that even if I am not regarded as "living" in the same way they are, at least I might be said not to have lived without doing anything. Therefore, I have assumed a task that is certainly pleasant to me, and, though I don't know whether it will be pleasing to most people, I think that it will not be useless to others. I have composed my treatise against avarice because I intend to relate a discussion regarding avarice that was held by some friends who are considered the equals of the wisest men of our age. My task is to set down in writing what they said in the way they said it. But I embark on this task more confidently because there are few scholars who devote themselves to the correction of vices. In any case, I have used these authors very attentively. Although there are many things that disturb our lives, vices, or rather this main vice from which "all crimes and misdeeds derive,"[4] form the subject of their discussion.

Now if it will seem to anyone that I have used too plain or humble a style, or that I have not undertaken to elaborate the theme of this work, he should understand, first, that I take delight in the sort of rhetoric that requires no greater effort at understanding than reading. Second, he should observe that I have not written all that might be written on this subject, but only what my poor abilities have allowed me to write about it. It has seemed to me enough to marshal in the fray a small number of troops, which are, however, my own. Others may be able to derive some good if perhaps they judge that my words merit some consideration, or some may wish to do something better on the same theme, emending or amplifying

3. The proverb, "Fortune helps the bold," goes back in Roman literature to Terence, *Phormio* 203, and was used by many other authors; see, e.g., Cicero *Disputationes Tusculanae* 2.4.11.

4. Cicero *Pro Sexto Roscio* 27.75, a text that Poggio had uncovered a decade earlier at the Council of Constance.

what I have said. However, it is to you, Francesco, my dear friend and most excellent scholar, who by your toil and industry have contributed greatly to our literature, that I have dedicated this treatise as the first-born of my studies. And I submit it for your skillful criticism. If you will approve it, then publish it, because I am confident that due to the power of your authority it will win approval from others as well. If you judge it poorly, cast it in the fire as a thing whose destruction will cause little harm, for it is better to suppress the errors of friends than to publicize them. So you can judge my work justly, however, you should now hear what these men have said together in this discussion, for they are the same with whom I had the great pleasure to associate when you were here.[5] When you have heard them talking, although they did not write it, I think you will not reject this little gift, if only for the sake of those who are engaged in conversation. I ask you to take this treatise under your protection, and do not act as a harsh judge or severe critic but, rather, as an eloquent and polished advocate who will want to take this case as his own and even defend its errors.

DIALOGUE ON AVARICE

Once Antonio Loschi, Cencio Romano, and several other papal secretaries were dining together with Bartolomeo da Montepulciano, who had invited them, as was the Roman custom on summer days, to his little country house near the Basilica of St. John the Latern. As often happened, the guests this time sat around discussing various topics, and they began to speak in praise of Fra Bernardino, who was then preaching in Rome.

Antonio, who had often heard Bernardino preach, praised him generously.[6] He said: Of all the preachers whom I have heard, Bernardino is the one who, in my opinion, is the most polished

5. An allusion to Barbaro's recent (1426) visit to Rome as a Venetian envoy, where he renewed his friendship with Poggio and evidently made the acquaintance of the papal curialists of the dialogue. See P. Gothein, *Francesco Barbaro: Früh-Humanismus und Staats-Kunst in Venedig* (Berlin, 1932), pp. 183–86.

6. St. Bernardino da Siena preached about eighty sermons in Rome during the summer of 1427, and Antonio Loschi must have attended at least some of them.

and learned. But I think he excels most of all in that one thing that is a chief concern of rhetoric; he has the power of persuasion, for he can work up the emotions of the people, moving them to tears or to laughter, as it is appropriate.

Then Cencio spoke: I would like this preacher to stay continually in Rome, for his words help the people a great deal, and he has been a good influence, sometimes correcting the people's morals, sometimes helping to settle the many dangerous disputes within the city. As you say, he has great power to change and convert the minds of men. But Bernardino and other such preachers do seem to me to err, if I may say so, in one matter; although they speak long enough, they do not tailor their sermons to our needs but to their own loquacity. They do not care in the least whether they heal the troubled souls that are committed to their care, but they only want to get in good with the plebs and win the plaudits of the crowd. So they have learned by heart certain set speeches that they are wont to speak in all places. Sometimes they speak before the ignorant of recondite and obscure matters that the audience cannot understand. At other times they pour forth words too freely, tending to confuse women and rustics, who, you can see, leave even more ignorant than they came. Some of these preachers criticize vices in such a manner that they themselves seem to be teaching them. They do not weigh their words depending on the help they give but on how they will affect housewives whose gifts and services they desire. Indeed, very few, or rather none, of these people are actually improved by these sermons. I have often laughed at the foolishness of those who often praise some topic or another they have heard preached but, when asked what they heard that was so praiseworthy, they stammer and fall silent or answer that they do not know.

Then Antonio spoke: You should not be surprised at this. To this day I have heard none of these preachers, except for Bernardino, who would satisfy in any matter that really pertains to eloquence. The whole art and faculty of eloquence consists in three things: to instruct the audience, to please it, and to move it to action.[7] But many of these preachers instruct in such a way that they seem to be upholding the art of ignorance and teaching the

7. A commonplace medieval definition of the purpose of oratory, which derives ultimately from Quintilian *Institutio oratoria* 3.5.2.

doctrine of foolishness. They please in such a fashion that nothing is more harmful than their own words and rhetoric, and they move the minds of their hearers so that they do not so much render them vigilant and attentive as they induce yawning and sleep.

Cencio said: It is just as you say, Antonio. All things are lacking in many, and even the preacher you wish to exclude lacks much. But I do not require genuine eloquence from these preachers because they admit that quality is quite unknown to them. What amazes me so much is that these men who claim they are so concerned with teaching, upbraiding, correcting, and improving others are themselves completely lacking in the ability to do this and in the very qualities they are professing. In fact, after they have proclaimed and railed for an entire year, we still can't find a single person who has been the least bit improved by the effect of their sermons. This is so for one reason especially, namely, that they do not adapt their words to curing the infirmities that vex our minds. Rather, they wander hither and yon and discourse on a variety of ills, going on as though their urge to speak did not permit them to pause at any particular problem. If they were to imitate the method of good physicians, all their labor would bear some fruit. For when doctors are summoned to sick people, they carefully examine the nature of the person and the power of the disease so that they may more correctly effect a cure. But these preachers who are charged with the salvation of souls—unless they diligently scrutinize and examine in what way each person is infected with vice and furnish them aid—can talk long and hard, and still they will not be able to help any more than an ignorant physician can cure a disease.

Bartolomeo spoke: You are correct in this. In fact, though our life is subject to all sorts of troubles and filled with various problems that ought to be remedied, still we know that some vices are more widespread and harmful than others, and among these are avarice and lust, which are so pernicious that it is difficult to remain unaffected by them. These are, so to speak, the two cruelest plagues that infect the human race. They never really leave anyone unstained, and since they require the gravest remedies, they are never easily cured. Preachers make only passing mention of these vices. And if they do indeed reprove avarice, they do so in the most jejune, arid, and insipid fashion and never with dignity of expression or conviction, so that it would have been better for them to have remained silent. They do not engender a hatred, but rather a desire, for sinning. In this fashion they occasionally discuss what are clearly great evils. I know of many people who have attended such sermons zealously, attentively, and for a long time, but they never derived from their attendance any advantage in their life and morals. Nor did it help their defects. It simply did not remedy their particular disease. But what use is medicine that is not fitted to the disease? There are certain people who forget what they hear before they have left; they have, as the saying goes, been making an effort in vain. But, indeed, if preachers would attack these two vices that afflict the great part of mankind, if they were to persevere against them, if they would execrate them, then their sermons would be very beneficial to their audience. For I firmly believe that avarice and lust are, as it were, the seat and foundation of all evils, and I hold that the following saying of M. Porcius Cato is very true: "The cities are suffering from avarice and luxury, which have been the destruction of every great empire."[8] Even though it seems that one of these vices has its origins in our natures, still reason can curb it and, indeed, control can be exerted so that it does not grow but is contained within certain limits. But the other vice is the enemy of nature; it cannot be ruled by reason, nor is this kind of evil controllable. It must be uprooted. And although wise men have said that lust is the cause of many evils, still it can be, in a sense, a kind of pleasant evil that is involved in the procreation of children. It is harmful to itself alone and not to others, and it is related to the continuance of the human race. But avarice is a despicable crime, harming everyone, and aimed at the subjugation of all mortals. It is harmful to all, injurious to everyone, and hostile to everyone. It is joined to nothing that is praiseworthy or honorable. It is a horrible, dreadful monster born to ruin people, to destroy fellowship among men.[9] You can believe me that nothing is more loathsome, nothing baser, nothing more horrible than avarice. If we were able to see its face, it would terrify us more than an army of Furies invading from deepest

8. Livy *Ab urbe condita* 34.4.2–3.

9. The depiction of avarice as a monster was a commonplace in late medieval literature; see, for example, *Les Auctoritates Aristotelis un florilège médiéval,* ed. J. Hamesse (Louvain and Paris, 1974), p. 280.

Hell. I won't give any examples so that my words will not offend anyone. But if I were to show you, I would soon instruct you that there is no evil, no disgraceful act that avarice does not incite and bring with it. The man who is seized by avarice possesses nothing that is good. He is utterly stripped of every virtue; he is completely devoid of friendship, benevolence, and charity. He is filled with hatred, fraud, malevolence, impiety—making him a monstrous and cruel criminal instead of a man, so that all the other vices are united in him. His cruelty is so great that I cannot conceive of any single being who can be compared with the avaricious person.

Antonio, your Bernardino, whom you have praised so much, never treated avarice. Once he did speak against usurers, but he moved the audience to laughter rather than making it aware of the horror of such a crime. Indeed, he left untreated the avarice that the moneylender generates. Rather, he ought to have inveighed against it, to have excited the natural forces of virtues if his ardor were in some way to restrict or diminish avarice. But since these wrangling preachers say nothing of these vices or only hold them up to ridicule, it seems to fall to us, who wish to avoid avarice and be good men, to discuss them. And now, since we have satisfied our hunger, I would have us discuss this topic—either both vices or one or the other—for this would be helpful to the mind. But night is drawing near, and it is time for us to return to our public duties that the Pontiff demands from us.

Antonio spoke: I think some time remains for discussion, and while we are so engaged, we will also be treating public matters, which should be judged of no small value. Indeed, Seneca, that outstanding preceptor of morals, has written in his work *On the Tranquility of the Mind:*

> For men who do good to the state are not just those who help others, who defend the accused, and who vote for peace and war, but they are also those who instill the mind with virtue, and resist or restrain those who rush about in pursuit of money and luxury.[10]

Therefore, let us ourselves try and see if we can be of some use in this discussion, and if we cannot help others, at least we can

10. Seneca *De tranquillitate animi* 3.4.

help ourselves. I am certainly glad that we have happened upon this topic, so that we may debate for a while about the power of these vices and their nature, and in what way they may be recognized. In this way we may more easily avoid the crimes and blame connected with them. Now, although I frankly confess to you that I am not able to be lustful at my age, I do not want to practice the other vice because it is alien to my character and to my education and training. I would like, however, to have us criticize avarice because I fear that we may, of necessity become greedy men on account of the smallness of our incomes, which are so reduced that we can scarcely maintain the dignity of our office. Therefore, Bartolomeo, continue what you have started and bring us to a conclusion.

Bartolomeo said: I think either you or Cencio ought to speak. It has been my duty to see that you have dined sufficiently and elegantly. Now it is only decent for you to act as though you have dined well, and this is usually indicated by discussion and sometimes by debate. Moreover, there is that saying of the ancients that the well-inflated pipes make the better sound.

Cencio spoke: The host of our dinner party has spoken in jest and divided the duties properly. Since he has looked after the needs of body, we ought to contribute something for the mind.

Antonio said: Then let that be your duty, seeing that you approve of your assigned portion.

Cencio replied: I see that you, filled with food, are trying to escape your obligation to speak. But I, who am also stuffed from the meal, would relieve you of the duty to speak did it not seem an offense to our host, a very fine man, whom prudence requires that he have no less diligence in exercising our minds than in filling our bodies. Our dinner party will be entirely perfect if the intellect also derives some benefit from it, and it is surely proper for you, Bartolomeo, to satisfy this need.

Bartolomeo said: I shall humor you, though you will all have to follow my rules. Moreover, I intend to say whatever comes to mind. Now this is the first rule: Antonio, you will follow me in speaking. Second, none of you should expect any polished speech or wise opinions from me, for after dinner no learned or dignified discourse or well-ordered oration should be required.

While he was saying this, in came Andrea of Constantinople,

a man learned in both literature and theology, who had been invited to the dinner but had been detained by official duties so that he arrived late. When he entered everyone gave him a round of applause.

Then Andrea said: I have already eaten, but I came over for the sake of a walk and to join in the discussion. But all have fallen silent. Why are you so quiet after your meal? Have I done something to make you so quiet?

Antonio replied: It's the latter. We were about to begin a discussion in which Bartolomeo has promised to say something about avarice. He had just reached that point in his talk where he was attacking avarice and lust for several reasons and asserting that he hated both but that he hated avarice more since it almost always seemed to accompany old age. And I was saying that I would like to hear something about avarice since it seems to pose the greater danger. Indeed, we fell to silence at your entrance because we were afraid that you would be critical of our absurd remarks. But even if what we have been saying may be silly or foolish, we ought to be pardoned for it and lay the blame on Bartolomeo, who plied us with strong local wine at dinner. Let him take the blame for his mistakes.

Andrea said: Now you would be speaking the truth, Antonio, if you were acting like those I have read about in Plato's *Symposium*—yawning, drunken, and half-asleep.[11] But I see that you are all quite sober. Therefore, Bartolomeo, please continue and let me be a participant in your discussion.

Then Bartolomeo spoke: Now this is the real reason we were silent; we all view you as a very learned scholar and theologian.

Andrea replied: But I didn't come here invited to an academic disputation. I came remembering the drinking bouts that used to take place here.

Antonio said: Don't you think we are ready, filled with food and wine? We are not looking for anything philosophical or difficult but for what's proper to the time and place. Even Andrea wouldn't oppose this. Since the time is very short for discussion, let us continue our silly debate. Go on, Bartolomeo, continue what you have started. We can at least ask that much.

11. An allusion to the state of the discussants as depicted at the end of Plato's *Symposium*; 223B–D.

Bartolomeo said: I shall do as you say, not so much to give a discourse as to provoke discussion from one or another of you. As Andrea says, I want to hear from you.

Bartolomeo continued: With all the things that have been written on this subject, whether by the most learned Christians or by Greek and Latin pagans, it seems superfluous to say more, especially since our words can scarcely be thought of much importance. But because we enjoy discussing the subject among ourselves and saying something about it for our own good, it seems to me that one must ask in the first place how the term "avaricious" is derived, from which "avarice" also derives. I think that those were called avaricious who were greedy for bronze,[12] so that those who coveted bronze excessively and put the greatset effort and energy into acquiring it were called avaricious.

Antonio then spoke smiling: But if this is true, there are no longer any avaricious men. Men of our age are driven by their desire for gold and silver, not bronze.

Bartolomeo answered: This term was introduced by men when neither gold nor silver money was in use. Only bronze was held precious by the Romans until the First Punic War. In fact, five years before the war, in the 585th year after the founding of Rome, silver coins were first struck showing chariots drawn by two or four horses. Sixty-one years later gold coins were first minted. Moreover, Servius Tullius was the first to stamp bronze money with a figure of herding animals, from which it is called money.[13] Before that unstamped bronze coins were used. Thus, even while the metal used in money changed, the term avaricious remained the same, so that those who are desirous of gold, silver, or bronze, who put all their effort into amassing wealth, who are always seeking it, always wanting it, who are reluctant to spend money and despise no means to satisfy their desire for profit, who judge everything from the standpoint of their own benefit and reckon success always in terms of money—these persons are rightly called

12. The etymology of the miser as "greedy for bronze (*avidus aeris*)" is taken from Aulus Gellius *Noctes Atticae* 10.5.1.

13. Poggio derived his knowledge of early Roman minting practices from Pliny *Naturalis historia* 33.13.42–43, and his etymology of money from the same source, 18.3.11, which reads "money derives from herding animal (*pecunia a pecore*)."

avaricious. Therefore, avarice is a boundless desire to possess, or better still, a kind of hunger to accumulate wealth. The soul of the greedy man is concerned with getting rich and is abandoned in his zeal for treasure; he is dominated by his greed and becomes a slave to money, with whose care and protection he is tortured day and night. As you know, his thirst for gain is never quenched; it is always growing and never satisfied. According to the old proverb, the greedy man lacks what he has as much as what he does not have. He will suffer the continual thirst for riches; no day, no hour will pass free from this preoccupation. He will seethe and writhe, anxious to satisfy his ever-growing hunger for gold. Therefore, he will be a slave to his own private interests and mold himself to them in thought, word, and deed, attentive only to his own affairs, unmindful of public duties. For this reason it happens that this vice is repugnant and contrary to nature, whose law tells us to put the common welfare before our own, so that we may bring help to as many people as possible. A propos of this, the Stoic Cato, as cited by Cicero, said: "It is no less worthy of blame to desert the public welfare for private advantage than to betray one's own country."[14]

Hence, the avaricious man, who is dedicated only to himself and looks out only for himself, not only deserts but even opposes the public welfare and is its enemy. In the interest of his own profit, he never brings benefits to many but hurts everyone. It is certain that, just like a traitor to humanity, he departs from the law of nature itself; for avarice is distant from nature's law and opposed to the public good, for whose protection and preservation we exist. Therefore, it follows that the avaricious man can, on no account, be a good man, because, as Cicero claims in his book *On Duties:* "Whoever does whatever he does for his own advantage, is in no sense a good man."[15] And there is no doubt that the avaricious man puts everything that he does to his own advantage. Therefore, no avaricious man will ever be a good man. Moreover, not only will he not be good, indeed he will be very evil, because the word avaricious itself refers to a vice, so it represents evil. For no one can practice greed without being a detriment and danger to many. The greedy man especially offends justice,

14. Cicero *De finibus* 3.64.
15. Cicero *De legibus* 1.18.49, not from *De officiis,* as the text states.

queen of the virtues, since all the acts and workings of greed
derive from injustice. "For when the miser desires to increase his
wealth and attempts to amass money and possess property, he
casts all justice aside," as St. Ambrose says.[16] Therefore, suppress-
ing justice, the miser will overlook no crime; hoping for profit,
he will seize every opportunity to defraud the poor, cheat the
rich, exploit his fellows, harm strangers, extort from the weak,
deceive the ignorant. There is no foul or evil deed imaginable, no
shameful act to which he will not stoop, nothing he will not
perpetrate when hope for gain is in sight.

Hence, he is able neither to cultivate friendship nor be moved
by kindness. For what kindness can there be in someone who holds
nothing more dear than money? Or who can love if he hates himself? That old proverb is very true: The miser is kind to no one
but worse to himself. What friendship can he keep who is always
acting only for his own advantage in whatever he thinks or does?
How will he aid others with his money when he is ruining his
own life with it? In what fashion will he lighten the poverty of
others, who considers himself destitute? Nor is he moved by
petitions or tears and weeping. Indeed, he will walk right through
those weeping in hardship in order to amass his fortune. Harsh,
cruel, and impious, the miser will trample the bodies of the
wretched if he thinks he can squeeze anything out of them. For
this reason he deserves our common hatred as a public enemy of
all, and he should be expelled from the fellowship of men as the
source of all evil. In no way is it fitting that we should love someone who, leaving aside everything, takes from us love and kindness, the two bonds of human society without which no public or
private undertaking can endure. What else is the purpose of the
miser except to destroy the very foundations of the human race?
But the avaricious man should himself be destroyed and be out-
lawed[17] since he is useless to the city and ruinous to the state. It is
not fair that he have a place in the city. If we all were to imitate
him, we would soon have no city at all. If goodwill and friendship
are suppressed, men will fight one another and everything will be
overturned by plunder and slaughter.

16. St. Ambrose *De officiis ministrorum* 1.28.137 (= *PL* 16.68).

17. The text reads literally "to deprive of fire and water," which is the
phrase in Roman law meaning "to outlaw."

But consider, I ask you, the nature of this evil and how much it should be feared in every age of life. Men are usually more prudent and wise in old age than in the rest of life, for both the use and experience of the many things with which we deal over a long life give us prudence, just as reading and studying over a long period give us wisdom. In this way the longer we live, the nearer we come to wisdom. For this reason a wise and learned Greek, while dying, complained that he was leaving life just when he was beginning to know something. But this wicked stain, avarice, powerfully possesses the old, conquering them at an age when they ought to be able to oppose it with the greatest strength and vigor.[18] Moreover, this weakness so dominates their minds that when they should be satisfied with very little—for what remains of their journey is brief—they actually desire more as they require less. The poets tell us that there are many monsters on the earth, but the avaricious old man surpasses the deformity of any monster. So that you may truly see the face and likeness of the avaricious, I would like to refer to those famous lines of Vergil where he described the Harpies, for these lines depict the very nature and shape of greed. You know them by heart, I think:

Winged things with maidens' countenance, bellies dropping filth, and clawed hands and faces ever wan with hunger.[19]

How could anyone personify anything more vividly than Vergil has this vice in these lines? He speaks of birds with "maidens' countenances," implying that the miser is not a man but a monster, a vicious beast ready for any crime hiding behind a human face. The maidens' faces suggest an ever-fresh desire, for it grows daily and becomes more powerful with time and more vigorous with each passing day. It grows as the body weakens, untouched by age, but emerging strengthened by it. The poet used "winged things" because of the mobility and velocity of their appetites. The mind of a greedy man, likewise, is never quiet, never rests, but always yearns for wealth and is always concocting some plan for obtaining it. The term "bellies" aptly describes immense cupidity, an image that has made this verse famous. The greedy

18. Cf. Cicero *De senectute* 18.66.
19. Vergil *Aeneid* 3.216–18.

man is satisfied by no amount of profit, no abundance satisfies him; he stands with his mouth agape, not starving but mad like Cerberus, ready to seize and devour whatever is thrown his way. The poet also speaks of their great "filthiness," not simply on account of the indecency of the vice but because of their filthy life and sordid habits. They are dirty, savage, and uncouth; they wear the most vile and shoddy clothes and are afraid of the smallest expense, shunning even the barber. We see men known for avarice who wear their hair and beards longer than customary and who do not cut them unless admonished by others or driven by shame. We often laugh when they appear before us with long-flowing beards like peasants. The poet has rightly added the "clawed hands" to show the rapacity of the greedy man—he snatches, grabs, and extorts. He touches nothing from which he will not derive a profit; he impoverishes acquaintances and strangers alike. And when the poet depicted him with a "face wan with hunger," he could not have said anything truer, for the greedy man is tormented by a hunger to accumulate and amass his treasure, and the worry and effort exhaust him. But he allows himself no rest from these preoccupations that always afflict him, and the more his wealth grows, the more his desire for it increases.

Also, he is tormented by hunger for food and drink that he rarely satisfies, except with cheap and plain fare. For how will such a wretch procure fancier or more expensive dishes? There once was a Florentine, a miserly nobleman, who, it is told, was served two leeks for supper at one time. Although he was rich, he ordered that one be taken away to be served the next day, scolding his steward as a spendthrift. One of our acquaintances declared that when he ate at home he prefered onions and garlic, but not when he dined at others' homes. Another, when he was sick and his doctor asked him what foods he ate, answered veal and beef. Reproved because he did not eat chicken, he answered that it did not agree either with his character or his illness because it would cost more. But later, when he was given some chickens as a gift by a friend who had heard of his ailment, he devoured them voraciously. To be sure, the avaricious man is wan not only because of hunger but also because he likes to gorge himself.

Furthermore, when the poet described the three Harpies, I believe he meant to symbolize **Pride**, **Cruelty**, and **Envy**. For the avaricious do not suffer from a single vice, but since they lack every virtue, many vices are joined in them.

You have here almost a true portrait of avarice. If it could be viewed with the eyes, it would strike terror in the hearts of men and would seem an even more horrible monster than the Harpies just described. Before Vergil wrote down those verses, he realized that he could not render the deformity of avarice in words, and so he wrote:

No deadlier monster nor any fiercer plague of divine wrath has issued from the Stygian waters than these.[20]

What more terrible monster can be imagined than a public plunderer, burning with desire, who always devotes himself to making money, yearns for gold, shuns no profit; he strives, seizes, extorts, destroys. He lives in insatiable longing, piling up money without respite, and, once gotten, he guards it with extreme anxiety. He is miserly in his spending, starving, neurotic, and turns everything to his own advantage; shaggy and unkempt, the miser tramples upon everyone and comes to the aid of no one. I confess that he surpasses in excess and cruelty any monster in the legend of Hercules. Thus, if you will consider carefully what I have just said, you will judge the avaricious monsters of the human race, who should be removed from among us and dispersed elsewhere like the filthiest refuse of the cities, so that they will neither sicken us with their stench nor infect us with their contagion.

When Bartolomeo had finished speaking, Andrea said: What do you think about that, Antonio? Do you agree with what he has argued? Or, rather, what has struck you? For I saw while he was speaking that you were fixed in some deep thoughts.

Antonio replied: Are you asking what I think? I'll tell you. Bartolomeo has said many things that, in my opinion, ought not to be despised at all. For these I praise his intelligence. Even though he is very busy with the business of the Curia, still he has

20. Vergil *Aeneid* 3.214–15.

been able to devote enough time to his studies, so that he could make this argument, and not without subtlety either. But I am not certain whether I should completely approve or disapprove of each individual thing. Even if it is, as he says, still following the customs of the Academics,[21] who customarily disputed what had been said by others, I shall bring up certain points different from what he has argued. These you may accept according to your judgment.

I have heard many men, and not men to be despised either, who would in no way have agreed with Bartolomeo. In my opinion Bartolomeo has treated serious matters lightly in his discussion and has given matters of little importance great weight in his argument. I don't doubt that if one were to seek the opinion of the common people they would judge very differently from us, for although there are many laws and penalties made by the people against lust, there are none against avarice. However, since we should not discuss the judgment of the people, but instead rely upon reason, I will explain why lust seems to me a horrible crime and avarice does not. Indeed, the vice that weakens and corrupts both body and soul should be judged worse and more abominable. Certainly lust, more than avarice, enervates the body and confounds the soul. Therefore, lust is the baser vice. And it is well known that lust breaks down the body and dissolves the virtue of the soul. From lust the intellect loses its toughness and the body its strength, to the point that the lustful become foolish, effeminate, and cowardly. It harms ability, destroys health, removes judgment from the mind, and deprives it of reason. For this reason, the distinguished Seneca declared in the preface to his *Declamations:* "Nothing is more harmful to natural ability than lust."[22] It hinders the study of literature, weakens the limbs, reduces a man into a woman, a scholar into an ignoramus, a sage into a fool, and is very injurious to the memory. So you see, those who devote themselves to lust are wanting in energy, vigor, prudence, and reason and are contemptible and abject. On the other hand, the avaricious are strong, prudent, industrious, tough, temperate, great in intellect, but greater still in judgment. Besides, lust is always harm-

21. Poggio probably took this definition of the method of the Academics from Cicero *De officiis* 2.27.
22. Seneca *Controversiae* Praefatio 1.7.

ful, while avarice, sometimes, is beneficial. The former is not restricted to any age of life, while the latter seems almost a common ailment of old age, and in this age it can even be tolerated. Avarice does not subvert the soul, upset the mind, or impede the study of literature and the acquisition of knowledge. We know of excellent men in every field, even men able in the affairs of state, who were avaricious. We realize, moreover, that kings and princes, whose virtue shone forth brightly, were avaricious, so that if I had to choose one vice, I would rather be considered avaricious than lustful. I would not be ashamed to be counted as a member of that group where there are so many kings. The most learned of philosophers, Aristotle and many other ancients, eminent in their scholarship and dedicated to philosophy, were designated by the Greek author Lucian as avaricious.[23] Their authority and dignity are so great that the very mention of their names ought to be enough to defend the cause of avarice without further argument or advocacy. But let us lay aside authority and discuss the way you have upheld your argument with reason.

You have affirmed that those who greatly covet bronze, gold, and silver are called avaricious, but if this is so, then all those who desire money strongly should be called greedy, and almost all men will be judged as such. In fact, everything we undertake is for the sake of money, and we are all led by desire for gain, and not a small profit either. If you were to remove that profit, all business and work would entirely cease, for whoever undertakes anything without hope of it? The more evident the profit, the more willingly we enter into the enterprise. All follow gain, all desire it. Whether you consider the military profession, or business, or agriculture, or the arts, both liberal and mercenary, the desire for money is innate in everyone. Everything we treat, work at, or undertake is directed at getting as much profit as possible. For its sake we undertake hazards and run risks. The more we profit, the more we rejoice, and those profits are almost always measured by money. Therefore, everything is done for money, that is, because of avarice. For what motivates those practicing law (not to mention the humbler professions whose function is obvious), what else if not the desire for money and the means of making a large

23. Lucian *Hermotimus* 16.

income? What else leads on physicians or others who dedicate themselves to the study of the liberal arts?[24] Are they not spurred on by the avid desire for gain when they advertise their skills and offer them for hire as soon as they can? Do they not show that they have pursued knowledge only out of avarice, that is, the desire for gold and silver. Consider the more sacred disciplines, philosophy and theology; do you think so much effort is put into them out of pure love of knowledge or, rather, out of desire for gain? What shall I say of our priesthood, whose zeal for money is only too obvious? Why else do they seek, ask, and court (under the mantle of the faith), except so that they can get rich with very little work? More with importunity and impudence than with good intentions do they seek benefices, which I would rather call curses of the soul.[25] And we see that, thanks to this desire for riches, the more a benefice is worth, the more competition and effort goes into procuring it. You might think that all energy was being expended for the purpose of saving souls, instead of spending one's life in sin. Those priests are the same ones who hypocritically pretend to spurn and act as though they had not sought them, but in fact they had freely received them on account of their own merits and virtues. You can review every profession, whether intellectual or manual, and you will find not one that is immune from inborn greed. Whatever you see mortals accomplish, whatever risks they undergo, it is for the purpose of digging out gold and silver.

Indeed, I don't think this ought to be disapproved on any account. For money is very advantageous, both for the common welfare and for civic life. As Aristotle related, it was necessarily invented for commerce and for mutual exchange among men.[26] If you condemn this appetite for money, you must also condemn the other appetites that nature has given us. In fact, I ask you, why is it less permissible to have a desire for gold and silver than for food and drink and the other things with which we sustain life? Certainly

24. In Italian universities the faculties of medicine and arts were often joined; hence, physicians studied the liberal along with the healing arts. See H. Rashdall, *The Universities of Europe in the Middle Ages,* ed. F. M. Powicke and A. B. Emden, 3 vols. (Oxford, 1936), 1:233–37.

25. Poggio's conscious punning on *beneficia* (ecclesiastical benefices) and *maleficia* (curses) cannot be adequately reproduced in English.

26. Cf. Aristotle *Politica* 7.8; 1328a25–b5.

nature has instilled an instinct for survival in all living creatures; for this reason, we seek food and whatever else is necessary for the care and nurture of the body. And unless we are quite foolish, we buy these things with money. So is it surprising if I am covetous, if I seek bronze, gold, or silver, without which one cannot have the necessities of life? If this be avaricious, then (as it was asserted before) avarice is not against nature but instilled in us and imprinted on us by nature itself, just like the other desires with which we are born. Moreover, what exists in us by nature should not be criticized in any way. Hence, you must acknowledge that the desire for money is present in all men by their very nature. Everyone in every age, condition, rank, or estate is dominated by the desire for gold, that is, by avarice, and they rejoice in wealth as a recognized and appropriate good. Look at the situation in children; they are delighted to receive gifts of money. Look at the case of adolescents, the middle aged, and the elderly, the rich and the poor, kings and princes—all alike take pleasure in money and pursue wealth. They do this for no other reason except that nature has formed and taught them to buy whatever maintains and nourishes life. Therefore, since nature urges and exhorts everyone to follow this desire, avarice should not be condemned.

But you say that there have been some who were not driven in the least by this desire. There are also those who are born with a pig's head, but, despite some rare freaks, we are still usually born with a human head. It is not proper to hold up the example of the perversity or deformity that uncouth and fearful peasants might do; what concerns us here is the civic life that we ought to follow and preserve. I shall add this besides so I can make clearer what I feel. Saint Augustine, a very learned man among the Latin authors, wrote in his book *On Free Will* more moderately than you have written: "Avarice is the desire to have more than enough."[27] If this is true, we must admit that we are avaricious by nature. In fact, what everyone wants must be thought to emanate from nature and result from its influence. And indeed you will find no one who does not desire more than is sufficient; there is no one who does not wish to have an excess. Therefore, avarice is a natural thing. Go around the whole city, if you like, and walk through the markets,

---

27. St. Augustine *De libero arbitrio* 3.17.48 (= *PL* 32.1295).

streets, and churches, and if someone declares that he does not want more than enough—nature is, in fact, happy with little—then you should think that you have found the phoenix. And don't hold up to me crude, rough, and hypocritical fools who go about under the guise of religion to make a living without toil or sweat, preaching poverty and scorn for material goods to others, because it is very profitable for them to do so. It is not with these lazy worms of men, who live in ease off our labors, that we can preserve our cities. We need those who are fitted for the preservation of the human race. If no one exerted himself to work for anything beyond his own needs, all of us here, not to mention others, would be forced to become farmers. Suppose no one did anything except to provide the necessities for himself and his family. You soon would see what total confusion would result if we wanted only enough to provide for ourselves. The people would be deprived of fine virtues such as mercy and charity, for undoubtedly no one could be generous and liberal in those circumstances. After all, what can anyone give away if he has nothing in excess to give? How can anyone be munificent who has only enough for himself? Every splendor, every refinement, every ornament would be lacking. No one would build churches or colonnades; all artistic activity would cease, and confusion would result in our lives and in public affairs if everyone were satisfied with only enough for himself. But we know that this appetite for gain has been common to all ages, classes, and peoples from the beginning of history, since people want and work for more than is sufficient for themselves to insure against the accidents of the future and the reverses of fortune and to give aid to friends and neighbors, who would doubt that we should all be termed avaricious according to St. Augustine's definition. With such people the villages, towns, and cities are populated, and if you think that the avaricious ought to be expelled, you might as well (I might add) forsake and raze the cities. In fact you say this. But who will live in those places once the avaricious have been expelled? Indeed, we ourselves would be thrown out because, according to your argument, all of us are defined as avaricious or greedy. The cities should be left then, according to your opinion, empty and deserted by their inhabitants. But why discuss single cases? What are cities, states, provinces, and kingdoms, if you consider it carefully, if not the workshops of avarice?

This city, which is run by a communal government, gets its authority from public consent. I ask you, Cencio, in the Rome of antiquity and in states centuries later, how many kinds of taxes were imposed upon the subjects, how many unusual burdens forced on a conquered people, how many well-devised schemes were made to exact money in order to fill an empty treasury? Does this demonstrate liberty to you, or the height of greediness? When Jugurtha said that "the city was up for sale, if a buyer could be found,"[28] do you think he was referring to one greedy man or another or to the whole citizen-body? If that city, Rome, where they say virtue made its home, was avaricious, what should we think of the cities of our own age, which daily devise new laws in order to mulct the people? Look at princes and kings. What do you find in them except the public proof of a significant, not small, degree of avarice? A certain Robert, king of Sicily in the memory of our ancestors, was said to be very avaricious. He amassed an enormous quantity of gold, yet he was a man of great valor. Even today is there anything more illustrious than the memory, fame, reputation, and glorious deeds of that king? Francesco Petrarca, a man of the highest genius and the greatest learning, would not have praised Robert so greatly if his avarice had extinguished the merit of his virtue.[29] Wherever you turn your inquiring mind, you will find not unworthy examples of public and private avarice so that if you think that the avaricious ought to be censured, then the whole world should be censured, and all mankind should change its ways and adopt other rules for living. Desire for money has grown, so that avarice is not considered a vice but a virtue; the richer a man is, the more he is honored. A little earlier I said that someone who dedicates himself to civil or canon law turns to learning not for its own sake but out of a desire for gain. You see how popular such disciplines are, just like a real gold mine. And when doctors of law have assumed the insignia of the doctorate, which are signs of greed and avarice, you know how everyone visits, honors, and cultivates them, even though many of them are uneducated. They

---

28. Sallust *Bellum Jugurthinum* 35.10.

29. An allusion to Petrarch's eulogy of the wisdom and learning of King Robert of Sicily in his *Rerum memorandarum libri* 1.37, ed. G. Billanovich (Florence, 1943), pp. 39–42; English translation in D. Thompson, *Petrarch, A Humanist Among Princes* (New York, 1971), pp. 46–50.

wear the finest clothes, and it is their right to wear a gold ring,[30] but it is clearly understood that this profession is undertaken only to make money. If they heard from you that avarice is one of the most despicable vices, I am sure that they would not refrain from assaulting you and would assert that it is not a vice at all, or only a very trivial and common vice, and that there are many that are much worse.

I will not even concede to you what Bartolomeo said a little while ago, that all the vices taken together cannot be compared to this one alone. If this were so, the first law-givers and founders of states would be worth little to us since, having instituted a punishment for every crime and misdeed that can disturb a city or harm society, they left avarice unpunished. For they established by law that thieves, robbers, assassins, adulterers, murderers and other evil men ought to be punished, while the greedy are subject to no penalty and are restrained by no law. This is so because those very wise men understood that the seed of avarice is in men's character and necessary for the preservation of the cities and civil law. Instead, you would rid the cities of the avaricious as if they were accused of many crimes. But tell me, I beg you, if avarice were a vice, and if the cities were purged of all vices, would it not be better to expel ambition instead of avarice? We have often heard that aid was given to the state by the avaricious, but the ambitious brought only evil. Marcus Crassus was avaricious; Caesar was generous but hungered for power. What destroyed the Roman Republic? Was it Crassus' immense greed or Caesar's ambition?[31] See how far I am from your opinion!

If some are more greedy than others and desirous of wealth beyond the norm, you think they ought to be expelled from the cities. On the contrary, I think they should be invited into the cities as a proper support for the people. For when money abounds the sick and wretched may be helped, many in dire straits may be benefited, and both private citizens and the state may be aided. In

30. An allusion to the gold ring and purple robes awarded to doctors of law in Italian universities; see Rashdall, *The Universities of Europe*, 1: 195, 228.

31. Poggio's allusion to the First Triumvirate of Caesar, Crassus, and Pompey, formed in the First century B.C., could have been derived from many works on Roman history. There is a discussion of Caesar's ambition and Crassus' wealth in Cicero *De officiis*, 3.19–21.75–83, which Poggio doubtless knew and may have been his source.

some well-governed cities public storehouses for the charitable distribution of grain have been set up for the populace. In the same way it would be convenient to bring together many avaricious men in the cities to serve as a kind of private storehouse, which could be used to aid any of us while the funds would be managed privately. Money is necessary as the sinews that maintain the state. Hence, where many are avaricious, they must be considered its basis and foundation. If sometimes the city requires a subsidy, shall we run to indigent day laborers or some despiser of wealth, or instead to the rich, that is, to the avaricious (since rarely can one make a fortune without avarice)? Which type is it better to have populate the city? The rich, who with their means can protect themselves and others, or the poor, who can support neither themselves nor others. It seems to be preferable to have many avaricious men whom we can depend on in times of difficulty like a stronghold or a citadel. Not only do they support us with money but also with advice, wisdom, protection, and authority. We have seen many who were considered avaricious consulted on state policy and elevated to powerful positions of authority on account of their counsel. In no way have the avaricious been harmful. I might add that they have often brought great ornament and embellishment to their cities. Not counting antiquity, how many magnificent houses, distinguished villas, churches, colonnades, and hospitals have been constructed in our own time with the money of the avaricious? Without these ornaments our cities would be deprived of their largest and most beautiful monuments.

You said that the greedy are deserted by friends, never satisfy their hunger, and are barbarous, pitiless, always intent on their own profits. I do not deny that avarice may be viewed as a vice in some people. We say there is some justice that constitutes injustice— whence the old proverb: greatest justice, greatest injustice. There are many men whom even I criticize, not as avaricious, but as doltish, stupid, foolish, wretched, troublesome, stubborn. These are the worst dregs of humanity, who derive their harsh and cruel ways not from avarice but from a malignant nature. I also have known many avaricious noblemen—splendid, decorous, liberal, humane, and witty—whose homes are filled with guests and friends. Granted you are right, one cannot count on receiving monetary help from them. But are not other things appropriate,

such as friendship, counsel, solicitude, hard work, help, and protection? Does the strength and function of friendship reside in
money or, rather, in duty and kindness? And if these qualities
cannot be found in abundance in an avaricious man, I don't know
why. Money plays a small part in preserving friendship. Certainly
the friendship of the Pythagorean youths is not famous in
literature because one saved the other with money but because
one voluntarily offered up his life so that his friend and
companion might escape.[32] You have criticized the life of the
avaricious as filled with vices. But the kind of avaricious men I
have been discussing are not the same at all. You will find many
humble, courteous, benign, virtuous, and not in the least annoying.
You, on the contrary, find many evil, unjust, quarrelsome, ill-
mannered, and haughty. I can say the same about poets, orators,
philosophers, jurists, some of whom have turned out very bad.
While you may find those men lustful, thieving, rapacious, covetous, and criminal, they have never been suspected of being
avaricious. Thus, if some of the avaricious live evilly in licentious-
ness, sin, and deceit, it is not to be attributed to avarice but to their
own worthlessness, lust, and wrongdoing. So if you affirm that
avarice has caused much evil, I say it has brought about great good.
What do we have that is more beneficial than fire and water?
Nonetheless, have we not heard of regions devastated by floods
and many fine cities consumed by fire?

Your objection that the avaricious take interest only in what is
to their advantage, forgetting the public good, is not the habit just
of the greedy but of everyone. Is there any among you who puts
aside private advancement to promote the public good? To this
day I know of no one who could do this without harming himself.
Philosophers are wont to speak about preferring the common
welfare over private gain, but these arguments are more specious
than true.[33] Earthly life is not weighed on the scales of philosophy.
It is a custom established by common use and practiced from the
very beginning of the world that we strive more for our own good
than for that of the community. This we will all admit unless we

32. Cf. Valerius Maximus *Factorum et dictorum memorabilium libri IX* 4.7.
ext 1.
33. Poggio probably had in mind the famous argument in Plato *Republica*
4.1–2; 419–423B.

prefer pompous opinion to common sense. But, on the contrary, if you hold avarice offensive since it may cause the downfall of many men, you must also despise trade, commerce, and whatever else is done for the sake of profit and to amass wealth. For there is no gain without injury to someone else, since whatever adds to the profits of one man takes away from another. And as to your final, really odious, opinion—you say that old men slip very easily into avarice—I think they should be praised, and I do not think that their avarice derives from vice or old age but from planning ahead. Like persons making a voyage across a tempestuous and stormy sea, our elders take into account the risks and dangers that surround us and the destitution that besets us. They know that money is very useful in order to protect oneself, and since they are anxious not to fall again into those difficulties that they have already experienced, they make and save money and provide for themselves and family. Learning by experience, they accumulate those means that they have recognized as most important for others. Therefore, they do not amass wealth out of weakness of mind but out of strength of character, not out of error but on account of prudence, the mistress of this life. In this way they construct a very strong and safe citadel against poverty, famine, sickness, and the rest of the calamities that afflict humanity. On account of this, old men do not seem to err if they amass and save money, but, rather, they demonstrate great wisdom. If anyone still considers avarice dishonorable in old men, he should not blame the judgment of those men who fortify themselves against unexpected and unforeseeable events. Rather, he should blame the frailty of human nature, which subjects so many of us to danger, burdens us with so many needs, surrounds us with so many difficulties; all these things, if we wish to philosophize with deeds instead of empty words, make recourse to wealth necessary. As it turns out, avarice is not only natural, it is useful and necessary in men. It also teaches them to provide for themselves those things that they know are necessary for sustaining the frailty of human life and avoiding many troubles.

When Antonio has said this everyone looked at Andrea, who seemed to be the one who had to answer Antonio. He said: I cannot remain silent any longer. I am moved to speak by this shameful defense of a savage monster, for it would seem base for us to let him go unchallenged.

Then Andrea continued smiling: Besides, I believe that Antonio has not set forth his own opinion but that of others. Only when he defended the avarice of old men did he seem to be arguing his own case. He is indeed a learned and wise man who has read in Terence that "with age men become a little more covetous of material goods than is necessary."[34] And since he is afraid that, as an old man, he might come under suspicion of avarice, he has undertaken a defense of the avarice of old men. We know that a certain man has, as a rhetorical exercise, praised the Sicilian Dionysius, a tyrant of the worst kind of life, and has criticized Plato, one of the holiest of men.[35] I see that you, a very generous man, have in like fashion undertaken the defense of a vice that you know ought to be opposed before everything else. I am certain, in fact, that you have said these things not in defense of avarice but in accusation of it. As a result, you have given me the greater opportunity to refute what could be said in favor of greed, to reveal the deformity and baseness of so great an evil; for we know that you, Antonio, are a most liberal man who is not only far removed from the crime of avarice but even from any suspicion of it. If anyone would say that you have certain desire, he would not perhaps be lying, since this can happen without blame. At this point I should like you to recognize two things: first, that you may have been mistaken in the meaning of the words avarice and desire, terms that are themselves distinct but that you seem to mix together as though they signified the same thing;[36] second, and I shall be discussing this later on, whether it is correct, as you have argued, that avarice is according to nature.

The term avarice obviously expresses one quality, while desire denotes another quality. Every avaricious man burns with desire,

34. Terence *Adelphoe* 834.

35. The unnamed critic of Plato and defender of Dionysius whom Poggio had in mind was probably the Syracusan historian Philistus; see Plutarch *Vitae Parallelae, Dion* 9.2–3; 13.

36. Andrea is intent here on making a clear distinction between the two Latin words *avaritia* and *cupiditas*, for much of his subsequent argument hinges on showing that avarice is not a natural, inborn trait. For the sake of clarity we have almost always rendered *avaritia* as "avarice" or "miserliness." *Cupiditas* has usually been translated as "desire," though occasionally it has been translated as "greed." *Avarus* has been translated variously—as "greedy man," as "avaricious man," or as "miser." The rarely used *cupidus* has been rendered as "desirous man."

but not every desirious man with avarice. If someone were to call me a desirous man, or apply the same term to good men, I would not deny it. As philosophers maintain, there are certain natural appetites, which are free from blame. For example, there is the desire to have those things that permit one to live with dignity, as when someone desires food and necessary clothing. Everyone desires money for the necessities of life, for charity, for largesse, and for the support of the needy. There is nothing reprehensible in such measured and temperate desire that you would not be mistaken in calling natural. But there is another immense desire, an insatiable lust for having more than is proper, more than is necessary; this is a violent desire that exceeds measure, and when there is a thirst for stealing and piling up, when there is a zeal for money and an anxious state of mind, then there is avarice—and the larger it grows the more despicable it becomes.

To say that this conforms to nature is, if I may say so, the utterance of a man who has scarcely observed the workings and ways of nature. In fact, if avarice were really natural to us, we could certainly complain greatly about the iniquity of nature; for it would be evil and shameful of nature, the parent and creator of all things, if man, whom she made the unique attendant of her handiwork and even appointed to command part of it, were rendered by her inferior to all the things she had created. In this case man, whom she had endowed with a soul and reason, would be placed lower than those things that she had made soulless and deprived of reason. Please, look at the sky, the sea, the earth and all that is contained therein, and not the least trace of avarice will be found there. Rather, everything overflows with largesse and munificence. What is the sky that bestows on us the sun and the moon and its great variety of stars but that from whose influence come the causes of our birth and destiny? What is the air but that spirit that gives us life? Does water with its great variety of fish and its great bounty ever ask for anything in return? Does not the earth with its many species of crops, vegetables and fruits, and many kinds of animals feed the human race? And when you bestow some benefit upon it, does it not return it with high interest? Does nature ever show us any sign of avarice or stinginess? Actually, every act of nature yields multiple gifts, so that she seems to be not only generous and beneficent but even prodigal. Just look in any direction, wherever you may turn, you will find nothing in the things of nature that is linked to avarice. Rather, avarice is entirely opposed to and quite removed from nature. Nature gives and bestows; avarice robs and steals. Nature donates freely and open-handedly; avarice snatches away. Nature feeds us; avarice destroys our food. Nature fills everything with her gifts; avarice empties by robbing, so that at times it can be rightly said that everything *but* avarice operates according to nature.

But observe, I ask you, how reason itself opposes you. You will not deny, I think, that all of us come into the world with certain natural appetites fixed in our souls—not just a desire for freedom but also a desire to rule, so that if we are well formed by nature, we do not want to be under others but, rather, to rule others ourselves. One may discern this trait not only in men but in animals as well, as when they break their chains so that they may run about and enjoy their freedom. Therefore, does someone who submits to voluntary servitude follow nature, or is he forsaking nature's law? But it is scarcely to be doubted that the greedy man submits freely to the servitude of concupiscence and becomes the slave and obedient servant of someone whom he has made his own master. Listen to what Chrysostom says on this matter:

Indeed, lust for money to which the miser is addicted is crueler than any tyrant. It permits no pleasures but brings many hardships and all things that oppose virtue. It makes its children even worse than hired slaves, for they are not the slaves of other men but of the worst passions and anxieties of mind—emotions that make them hateful to both God and their fellow men. O bitter slavery and satanic domination.[37]

From this passage I want you to learn what is the miser's slavery and what is his grim fate. How dare you assert, therefore, that avarice and lust for money follow nature? For by this vice the very laws of nature are subverted. If avarice were a product of nature, everyone would be born avaricious. For natural instincts come into the world with us, and once they are implanted no training can remove them; no instrument can destroy them. Following our

37. Cf. St. John Chrysostom, *Homilia 59 in Johannem*, 4 (= *PG* 59.326).

natural instincts, we laugh, we shudder at the sudden sight of dreadful things, we blanche at unexpected fear. But who, sane of mind, has ever held that avarice is innate within us? Indeed, a few men are avaricious, but they are not born that way; they become so out of distorted opinion. Besides, those qualities that are natural in men should not be censured. Indeed, we never ascribe a vice to someone born blind or lame. But avarice has always been judged as a great crime in any man, whatever his dignity or estate.

Now the whole night would not be long enough if I were to give in detail every single thing that has been written against avarice by the most learned and wisest Greek and Latin authors. And in all their writings you will never find a single word written in praise or defense of avarice, not even from those very men who were themselves notorious misers. I realize that Aristotle was viewed as a miser. I know, too, that some claimed he held that one ought to add the advantages of wealth to the good life, lest if he considered that happiness lay solely in the virtue of the mind (as did his master Plato), he would deprive himself of the ability to request gifts from Alexander, who was very generous to him. Yet in no part of Aristotle's writings do you find him praising avarice, for he always placed it among the vices quite removed from any virtue. Moreover, even if he were a miser, still compelled by the power of truth, Aristotle always called avarice an evil. To be sure, Aristotle and many other philosophers were avaricious; however, this was the result not of the nature or teachings of Philosophy but of a flaw in their habits or their warped characters. For Philosophy is the guide and mistress of the art of living the good life. She is a seeker of virtue, an expeller of vice. She does not honor misdeeds but censures them; she does not accord authority to crime but removes it. She teaches what is to be sought and what is to be avoided, so that the more one knows and understands Philosophy, the more the existence of vice in him should be criticized. Look how Philosophy reveals the strength of honor and the vigor of nature. Even if avarice is so common, so widespread, so implanted in everyone, as you assert, still, to this very day, no philosopher or author has been so rash that he has ever dared to serve as its advocate. Rather, I would openly maintain that no philosopher (who is indeed worthy of the name) has ever been an avaricious man. If he were avaricious, he would lack the appellation of philosopher, or if he were a true lover of wisdom, he would lack avarice. Now I will concede that an avaricious man may be acute, perspicacious, erudite, ingenious, learned and eloquent, but I will never admit that he can be a true lover of wisdom, that is, a good, impartial and just man. Contraries cannot be mixed, nor can virtue and avarice dwell together in the same house, where, as in a filthy gutter and fetid sewer, the splendor of virtue becomes soiled. But a little later I shall show clearly that a miser can never possess virtue.

Now you have adduced as an argument in favor of avarice the fact that many kings, princes, and republics have often been called avaricious. I shall demonstrate that this is not a defense of the vice but an exaltation of crimes. But those of high station are not afflicted by this vice alone. In the first place, there are always more evil men than good men among leaders, as there are among every sort and condition of men. Just because men are placed in high positions does not mean that they become more virtuous as a result. Nor does wisdom necessarily follow from the possession of power. In the second place, princes and lords are usually prideful, arrogant, quarrelsome, harsh, cruel and lustful, but their very power does not excuse such vices, which ought to be censured more in rulers than in a private citizen. It is possible, however, for rulers sometimes to conceal their vices. But, in fact, when one is in a position of power it is very difficult (and, indeed, beyond the abilities of most rulers) always to follow reason and be moderate. The tasks of ruling disturb the mind, inflame the intellect, upset reason, and incite various desires, so that it is no great wonder that when rulers are seized by anger or lust they feel that they should do whatever pleases them. Indeed, an avaricious king or prince is like a monster, for nothing harsher, nothing more perverted, nothing more criminal can be imagined than the avarice of sovereigns, which becomes the source of all evils. Private men can attribute their crime of avarice to fear of scarcity, and say that they are afraid they will starve and have to go begging in the future. But this same fear cannot arise in princes or kings in whose care, control, and protection are placed all the possessions of their subjects. What can avaricious rulers lack except loftiness of mind and good will? What drives them to avarice except a smallness of heart and malignity of mind? Indeed, the very same power and possession of great wealth also causes generosity.

The other vices take some stimulus and incitement from outside causes, to which even persons in high places are susceptible. Lust and pleasure arise from the delights of the senses. Anger comes from a desire for revenge, cruelty from immoderation in meting out punishment, hatred as a result of injuries. But avarice has no other stimulus than evil itself. It is born within, it has its roots within, and it is worst of all in a king or prince because it harms a great many people. But beware that you think that this evil harms only the rulers themselves. Avarice, of necessity, harms many and not just by accident but by design. Indeed, our Cicero has put the matter well (as he often does) in his work *On the Laws:*

> The avarice and vices of princes corrupt the entire city, for the sins of princes are not only evils themselves, but because they also serve as examples to the many imitators of princes. Therefore, princes are harmful not just because they are corrupt but also because they corrupt others, and they do more by their bad example than by their own sins. Hence, there is that fine saying of Plato's: "As the princes are in the state, so are the citizens bound to be."[38]

This quotation shows, Antonio, why avarice is so widespread, why it persists unpunished, and why it has assumed so much power. The stupid and ignorant consider that whatever they perceive has become an important concern of their princes must be good. So they imitate those customs that they think are good and pleasing to princes. But while the avarice of private men does not harm many, the same avarice in a prince brings plague and public ruin with it. Under an avaricious prince no laws, no rights, no justice are preserved. Crimes go unpunished if the rulers are paid off with gold. The innocent will be punished; the guilty will escape punishment. No crime will be so outrageous that the splendor of cash will not overshadow it. Robbers, thieves, and murderers will be free if they have the money to buy off the ruler. Everything will be

---

38. A paraphrase of Cicero *De legibus* 3.14.32, where Plato is quoted.

sold as from a public hawker. And isn't there even something worse? The avarice of princes becomes even more hateful as it works ever greater harm on the people spreading ruin everywhere.

But perhaps we should not call such men rulers, kings, and lords, since you can see that they are miserable slaves and contemptuous of every honorable act. The lower and more evil the master who is served, the more vile and abject becomes the condition of the servant. The avaricious man is clearly the slave of avarice, and that is the lowest of all the perversions of the mind. Therefore, he who serves avarice is not a lord but a most contemptible and abject slave. Would that such greedy kings and princes would suffer the fate of Perseus, the king of the Macedonians, or of the Roman emperor Galba. Now Galba was a man of the most sordid avarice (I shall discuss Perseus later), who used to order that leftover gruel or sometimes a half a lettuce, among other things, be saved for the next meal. Moreover, he only ate such vegetables, and he used to dole out money for household expenses one day at a time. As a result he soon earned the contempt and hatred of the Roman people, and after a few months he lost his empire and his life at the same time.[39] King Robert (if I am speaking of the same king you mentioned) was not a king but a tyrant; or if he were worthy of the title of king, then he was not a miser. It is impossible for a king to be a miser, for we call a king someone who provides diligently and well for the public good, who has the well-being of his subjects at heart, who performs every duty in order to enhance the comfort of the subjects over whom he rules. Whoever does these things can in no way be an avaricious man. And if someone did act as a greedy man, he should not be called a king but a tyrant, since a tyrant, by definition, is concerned with private gain. For what distinguishes a king from a tyrant is precisely this: The former pays attention to the needs of those he rules, while the latter only looks after his own interests. You have explained in your long speech that not just many but all (and "all" excludes no one) who are seized by a desire for gold are also seized by avarice. But let my two colleagues whose style of life is quite unsoiled by this vice refute you on this point. It is their task to live up to their good reputation.

39. Galba was a Roman emperor (A.D. 68–69), notorious for his parsimony; the anecdote derives from Suetonius *Galba* 12.3; 22.

Then Cencio said smiling: Perhaps when Antonio was discussing this topic he made the allusion to priests since for a long time now this evil has been so common among them that they have made it a part of their customs. It seems to me that from the very beginnings of our religion this vice has flourished among the priesthood. Even among the disciples, Judas betrayed the Savior in return for pieces of silver, and from his time onward this voracity for gold has persisted and continued, down to our own age. This trait is so deeply rooted among the clergy that it is rare to find a priest who is innocent of avarice. Saint Augustine reports that the most holy Cyprian, Bishop of Carthage, used to lament that in his age those in the Church were not only greedy men but robbers and usurers as well, and not only the laity but even the bishops.[40] If this happened when the fervor of the faith still glowed with youth, when the virtue of the martyrs flourished, when the world abounded with the sanctity of the faithful, what do you think is happening in this our squalid age with its perverted customs and corrupt men, now that the faith has begun to grow old? Francesco Petrarca, the best and most outstanding man of his age, has justly called the Church "a greedy Babylon."[41] He saw how deep-rooted was avarice in the human race, how infinite was men's greed, and how great their desire for material gain. Indeed, it has always seemed amazing to me that precisely those who can never lack anything (for they fight in the pay of Christ), who live with the greatest material abundance and never need look to the future, who are surrounded with wealth for their use, are yet always tormented by a perpetual thirst for gold, just as was Tantalus in Hell. The more possessions they actually obtain, the more they burn with avarice. They read but do not follow the advice of Isidore, who ordered man to avoid love of money since it is the basis of all crimes.[42]

40. St. Augustine's report on the laments of St. Cyrian, bishop of Carthage, in the middle of the third century, derives from Augustine's *Epistola* 108.10 (= *PL* 33.410).

41. Petrarch's criticism of the contemporary Church appeared frequently in his writings. He devoted two letters to the theme of the papal court at Avignon as a western Babylon: *Epistolae sine Nomine*, 8, 10; Latin text in P. Puir, *Petrarcas 'Buch ohne Name' und die päpstliche Kurie* (Halle, 1925), pp. 193–95, 197–201; English translation in N. P. Zacour, *Petrarch's Book without a Name* (Toronto, 1973), pp. 67–69, 71–73.

42. Cf. Isidore of Seville *Sententiarum tres libri* 2.41.3–4 (= *PL* 83.645–46).

But he was telling a tale to a deaf man. Indeed, on these matters I think it is better to remain silent than to say only a few words.

Andrea said: Let's abandon this topic, for this is not the place, nor did we intend to deplore the customs of our age, which, I realize, can be improved in many instances. Rather, let us return to Antonio's theme. In his discussion he had advanced many arguments and concluded that avarice is both useful and necessary. Let us see how much truth and seriousness there is in his argument. Antonio, you have said (and this really seemed ridiculous to me) that avaricious men benefit cities because they give assistance to many with their money and are of help to the state. With this argument you give approval to disease and plagues in our cities because many would grow rich from the inheritances of the dead. Thus poisoners, pillagers, and counterfeiters of wills will appear, since some men can get rich from false wills, pillaging, and poisoning. In fact, some crimes have occasionally brought with them private and public benefits. For example, the violence done to Lucretia brought freedom to the Roman people, and a great insurrection gave the office of tribunes to the Roman plebs.[43] But still we have not abolished laws that punish rape and insurrection harshly. Just because a crime may occasionally bring advantages, we do not, on that account, judge crimes as useful acts. If you had stated that we enjoy the wealth of those who have died, your statement would not have been wrong. The dead leave the wealth they have accumulated for the benefit of others because they can't take it with them. This is a source of great torment for misers since they are separated against their will from the gold and riches that they cherished and guarded so diligently. In our own age there was a miser who, on his death-bed, ordered a bag full of gold coins brought before him and, beseeching the gift and benefit of life from these coins, which he cherished as much as his own soul, he died muttering: "See here, to whom will I leave you?"

Therefore, it is not from the donations of misers but from their death that their property becomes useful to others. Hence, there is that popular proverb: Unless the miser dies, he does nothing right.

43. The legend of the rape of Lucretia, which caused the uprising of the Romans against the Tarquins, and the insurrection of the plebs, which created the office of the tribunes in the fifth century B.C., were probably known to Poggio from Livy *Ab urbe condita* 1.57–59, 2.32–33, respectively.

How, then, can we have esteem or love for a citizen whom we would rather see dead than alive? But you say the miser brings help to the indigent and bestows wealth on the poor. You ought to add: He does so by means of usury and by giving injury to those he seems to be helping. No one ever seeks out a miser, except unwillingly and driven by the direst need. For everyone knows that when he approaches a miser he is not taking refuge in a port but on a reef where he cannot help losing some of his possessions. Even when some misers do in fact help their cities, they do so complaining, compelled by some authority, or driven on by hope for gain. If one has need of something from a miser, he has to snatch it from him or wrench it away. A miser never gives freely, for he is tight-fisted, small of mind, and lacking in any goodwill. But to come to the aid of other citizens is the quality of a noble spirit—liberal, generous, high-minded. By Immortal God, how can a miser ever be a support and help to others when he won't even help himself? Who could think it possible to get money from someone who would prefer to lose his life rather than lose his coins? How could misers, who would prefer to remain in chains rather than pay their own ransom, ever be moved to ransom a fellow citizen held captive? Very true is that verse recorded by Seneca in one of his letters:

The miser is good to no one, he is worst to himself.[44]

Nothing can be truer than this. The miser is even crueler to himself than to others. Do not wonder that a miser who deserts himself will also desert others. Perseus, the king of the Macedonians (if indeed he were worthy of that title), was bequeathed a huge treasure that had been collected by his father, Philip, for use against the power of Rome.[45] He fought a war with the Romans, lost it, and was made prisoner because he would not pay the price agreed upon to many thousands of Bascanian cavalry and infantry when they came to his aid. If he had paid the agreed money to the mercenaries, he not only would have saved himself but would have been able to repel the Roman army. His greed was so great that

44. Seneca *Epistolae* 108.9, quoting a saying of Publilius Syrus.
45. The story of Perseus, a Macedonian king of the second century B.C., derives from Plutarch *Vitae Parallelae, Aemilius Paulus* 12.2–7.

whenever he had to pay out money he seemed to draw his last breath. Moreover, he paid other soldiers with golden vases instead of in coin, pretending that later he would pay them in cash if they would return the vases. When the soldiers returned the vases he paid nothing, and thus cheated them. Thus, in order to save money he stripped himself of every protection. Defeated in battle, deprived of treasure and kingdom, he came alive into the hands of Aemilius Paulus, and was led as a captive before the triumphant chariot. Who could be more abject than this man who was treated not as a king but as a vile beast? Here was a man who lost his kingdom in order to hold on to his gold, as if he intended to be as rich as possible when captured. I think the Romans really ought to thank him since he stood guard for them so diligently over such a quantity of gold and silver. Therefore, is any great hope to be placed in a miser's using his gold and treasure to help maintain the poor and wretched when he won't even use that treasure for his own protection? But this is, of course, necessary for him. He knows how to accumulate wealth, but he does not know how to spend it. The miser never spends at the right time. He moans and groans as though he's being tortured when he is separated from his coins.

You have stated that misers abound in friends and that their homes are filled with guests. I think that you said this so that, given this ridiculous assertion, all your other statements and opinions could be taken in the same vein. In fact, I was amazed that you were able to make such an assertion without laughing. For surely what is more deserted, what is lonelier than the home of misers? All mortals follow them with curses and maledictions. Everyone avoids them as they would their unlucky day. Only if goodwill is born of hatred would you find any friends there. If, in fact, friendship arises from love, and since the miser loves nothing but gold, it's only natural that no one loves him and would that he suffer even greater penalties! But you would have us believe that many men follow him. They are not seeking the man but his gold. In fact, they really wish that the miser would go to ruin. I shall not argue this point any longer, but surely you will not deny that no one who does not love his fellow man can expect to be loved by him. This affection of friends ought to be mutual. So that you can recognize that no one can be loved by the miser, listen, unless you reject the words of Chrysostom:

Whoever loves money will inflict countless evils on his neighbor and, at the same time, on himself. For the miser easily gets angry, heaps insults, calls out abuses, swears and swears falsely, and repudiates every precept of the ancient law. He who loves gold will never love his neighbor. Whoever loves money will not only not love his enemies, but will treat his friends as enemies. And are there any friends in this case? Those who love money repudiate nature itself, and they do not know any kind of relationship. They do not observe customs. They do not respect age. The miser hates everyone, and himself most of all, not just for having lost his soul, but for bringing infinite evils and afflictions down on his head.[46]

But why do I argue with you by quoting a noted authority? Reason itself, if it could speak, would exclaim in a loud voice: "The miser is in no way a friend to anyone; moreover, he is abusive and hostile to everyone." For whoever does everything out of greed, whoever is addicted to making money, will always turn to what is evil and will always lust after what is perverted and pernicious, since his desire is always for material gain. He will wish for the death of family and relatives, known and unknown, since he hopes that an inheritance will come his way. He will wish bad fortune on his neighbor since he wants his possessions. He will cause bankruptcies, murders, shipwrecks, and commit arson so that by harming others he can increase his future wealth. He will rejoice at scarcity and famine if he has stored up a lot of grain.

Remember that a certain miser used to say that one ought to look forward to that time when the child would come in tears begging for bread from his parents' table. He is really suggesting that one ought to look forward to a time of scarcity. What more atrocious, more inhumane expression could be attributed to anyone, who is not even a man but a savage monster? Who could want only that others will perish on account of his desires? You have also stated that the miser gives good advice to his country. But this is as impossible as for the miser not to want material gain. Surely a mind twisted with avarice and filled with greed can never give good advice. For whatever he may think, do, or say

46. St. John Chrysostom *Homiliae 87 in Johannem*, 3–4 (= PG 59.477).

always reflects his own self-interest. He will always think it best to do what will result in large additions to his treasury, even though this be counter to the public good. He will not worry about reducing the wealth of the city while he increases his own. For him nothing will be sacred, nothing religious, nothing fair, nothing just. He will even urge an unjust war, and one that is dangerous to his homeland, if he thinks that he can derive some personal advantage from it. He will argue for a ruinous and dishonorable peace when his house will be enriched by it. His words, deeds, and honor are always up for sale. He will plot against his homeland and aid the enemy for money. How many times, even in our own memory, have we known men who, corrupted by gold and for sale at a price, have attempted to betray their homeland. Thus, avarice makes them ruinous in their counsel and evil in their deeds. And you, Antonio, have even argued that misers ought to be invited to the city for the common good. If you indeed want to establish an asylum where all the wicked and evil men can assemble, then yours is a good suggestion! But if you are considering providing for the good of the city, your idea is terrible. A city should be full of good citizens, not bad men. Indeed, Plato, that wisest of the Greeks, considered that states would be happy if either the wise, or the students of wisdom, governed them.[47] But you would be happy if the cities were filled with the avaricious or the devotées of avarice, and what is more absurd than that? I ask you: Are you suggesting the establishment or the subversion of our cities? One or two greedy men, who are the common exploiters of everyone, can disrupt a city. What a devastation would occur if you were to bring in a great many avaricious men who would make an assault on our possessions like a charging batallion! And you call these men useful who, if they were numerous, would promptly destroy the cities!

But let's examine for a moment this question of the usefulness of avaricious men. If indeed they were useful to us, this would result from their possessing some virtue. First, no cultivation of justice (which is the firmest foundation of both public and private affairs) grows in him. Now, as Cicero has said, justice has two

47. An allusion to the famous description of the philosopher-king in Plato *Republica* 5.473D–E. This idea of the wise governing the state is developed at great length in books 5–7 of that work.

duties: to bring injury to no one and to serve the common good.[48] Moreover, it is the duty of justice to give each man his due; this means to distribute both penalties and rewards. But the miser does not distribute, he steals. He takes for himself the rewards of others since he is always after another man's property. For the right price he will refrain from inflicting a penalty. Thus he is remiss in bestowing reward and he is corrupt in meting out punishment. He will reward the guilty while he will punish the innocent. He will only consider what will bring him a profit. Thus he is devoid of both generosity and munificence, which are the most esteemed of virtues. For these qualities are quite foreign to avarice since they increase by making donations and rewarding merit, while avarice prospers by stealing. The miser will also lack magnificence and magnimity, for what can a weak, narrow, lax, and vile man do that is worthy of a lofty character? What great undertaking will be performed by one who hates the very word "contribution"? He who is afflicted with the love of money will never use it. He is the slave of money, not its master; its guardian, not its dispenser. A miser wants to accumulate money, but he never lets it leave his hands; he never lets go.

You may think that a possible exception is the man (whose name I won't mention), who seems to you to have acted with lofty motives for the benefit of his children. This man had, by his avarice, accumulated vast riches, and his adolescent children used to dine very sumptuously at home to the accompaniment of music and song. But the father, a man who rarely satisfied his hunger except at a poor table, was once so exasperated by the voices of the noisy supper guests that after he had kept silent with great difficulty for a long time, he finally burst forth from his little chamber very upset just like a man who had been let out of prison. And with his beak-nosed and menacing face, scarcely able to bear the light and looking at the merrymakers all around, he called his steward in a loud voice and said, wailing: "Since my children continue to consume my fortune that I have accumulated by my sweat in feasting and revelry, I also want to indulge myself and enjoy some pleasures. So now it's my turn. The children can look after themselves, and they will lose everything as they seem to

48. Cf. Cicero *De officiis* 1.7.20, 1.10.31.

wish. Meanwhile, I shall provide for myself." Then he took a
small bronze coin from his filthy pocket and said: "Take this and
ruin me while you still have time. Go and buy some lettuces so
that I may eat too." Believe me, he spoke these words with a show
of a lofty and high mind, for except for fear of the bad opinion
of the crowd, he would not have consented even to such a poor
allotment for household expenses. And I really think that he was
looking for praise for his moderation when, in fact, he was never
moderate; his outlook, attitude, and appetites all stemmed from
immoderation. Temperance observes the mean, while avarice is an
extreme. Now, can one find any courage in the man who said
this since avarice has so corrupted his mind and manly body? For
this Sallust is an important source and witness.[49]

Besides, such a man will be devoid of prudence, for whoever
lacks the other virtues will surely lack prudence, the moderator of
the others. The mind corrupted with greed will lack the capacity
to judge matters correctly. Therefore, this good man of yours,
deprived and destitute of any dignity or ornament of the virtues,
will not be useful in preserving the state but in destroying it. He
will not help to maintain cities but to ruin them. For greed brings
about the ruin of all good things. On this subject listen to what
Chrysostom (to whose opinions I readily turn as to a fertile field)
feels and thinks:

> Avarice is a ruinous thing. It dulls the vision and the hearing,
> and renders men more inhuman than wild beasts. It does not
> permit in any way the development of friendship, of fellow-
> ship, of the salvation of the soul itself. But shunning all these
> things, it enslaves, like a cruel tyrant, those whom it seizes,
> and, what is worse, the greedy man is forced to love the very
> author of his bitter slavery, and deceives like an incurable
> cancer. Avarice has caused ten thousand wars and filled the
> streets with blood and the cities with mourning.[50]

From this passage it is clear what will be the future utility of
this one who (leaving aside the other evils) will fill the cities with
blood and mourning. If it pleases you, invite the greedy man into

49. Poggio derived the notion of the debiltating quality of greed from
Sallust *Bellum Iugurthinum* 2.2–3.
50. St. John Chrysostom *Homilia 65 in Johannem* 3(= *PL* 59.363).

your state. (Our own city would not suffer any trouble in being deprived of these monstrous architects of cities.) If it were in my power, I would do just what Plato has described so well in his *Republic,* namely, to expel those who by their words and teachings seem to harm the development of the youth and the good morals of the cities.[51] Thus, if I had the consent of my auditors, I would banish by decree all greedy men from the cities, for these corrupt the minds of the citizens not by their words but by their deeds, not by their teachings but by their example.

Bartolomeo said: If I might answer for the others, we agree! For nothing more sacred can be sought, nothing more just can be imagined than what, if it be observed, would make republics immortal.

Cencio spoke: Would that misers together with kings had been expelled from Rome, and banned forever, that they had never again been welcomed there. The Roman state would still be vigorous, since it grew to its greatest size when there was no avarice. Later, however, avarice secretly seized Rome, and to this fact the saying of Jugurtha bears witness: "The empire has collapsed under the domination of avarice."[52]

Hence, I am amazed that Cicero (whom Augustine used to call the artisan of governing the state)[53] did not add to the laws that he had drawn up for the state this one: It is necessary to banish greedy men from the cities. Indeed, this would have been a much more necessary and important law than those that he established to observe sacred feasts and ceremonies or to create new magistracies. The promulgation of such a law would have been very useful, for it would have banished the very vice that brings about the corruption of every virtue. But this very prudent man probably submitted to the dictates of his age since he only required that a fine be levied for avarice and did not add a heavier penalty. We, on the other hand, exclude avarice entirely from dwelling in our cities, and we do not permit any vestige of such a terrible plague in them. Thus, we hold that this one law is more sacred than all the others: No greedy man shall reside in the cities, and if they do, let them be expelled by public edict.

Then Andrea said: I am happy that all approve my argument

51. Cf. Plato *Republica* 2.9. 400E–401D
52. Perhaps a paraphrase of Sallust *Bellum Iugurthinum* 81.
53. Cf. St. Augustine *De civitate Dei* 3.30.

and reject Antonio's. But I do want to refute the one statement of his that remains: that avarice in old men should be praised and is a matter of prudence. I shall simply remind you of a passage from Cicero against Antonio's position. You all know it, but I think that Antonio had forgotten it when he made his argument. Cicero says that he cannot understand "what purpose is served by avarice in the old, for can anything be more senseless in a traveler than to increase his baggage as he nears the end of his journey."[54]

It is not true that old men are greedy because they wish to help others or provide for a prosperous old age, as Antonio would have it; but they use this as an excuse to cover the guilt of their sin, so that it might appear to derive from this good motive rather than their own depravity. You have stated that avarice is a necessity, but it is evident that it is quite the opposite. Nothing that is useless and harmful is necessary, and nothing is more harmful than the vice from which all other evils arise. The Apostle Paul has proven that all evils arise from avarice, for there is his golden sentence: "Greed is the root of all evil."[55] He understands that this root is the very thing from which avarice arises. What truer thing was ever spoken? What harsher opinion could be expressed than that the root of avarice produces the seeds of all evils? Hence, if avarice is necessary, then every evil and vice that is contained in it exists of necessity. Indeed, if you were to find a single vice whose parent and progenitor is not avarice, you would have to overturn the mind, abolish reason, destroy true judgment, and inculcate false opinions, so that you could consider covetousness to be piety, usury a kind of benefit, and riches the wages of wisdom. But this particular evil, avarice, is almost the nurse of all the other evils, just as, according to the Apostle, when that virtue charity is missing, all the other virtues are lacking.[56] On charity St. Paul has gathered much praise: "Charity is not boastful, it is not envious, it is long-suffering, kind, it does not seek things that do not belong to it and things that are not its own."[57] Then he has added: "Whoever lacks this one virtue will come to lack all the others."[58]

54. Cicero *De senectute* 18.65–66.
55. 1 Tim. 6:10.
56. Cf. 1 Cor. 13:2–3.
57. 1 Cor. 13:4–5.
58. Cf. 1 Cor. 13:3.

Surely the heavenly voice has shown that the crime of avarice is as foreign to charity as it is to the other virtues. And Chrysostom affirms that no charity can dwell in the miser; the miser is never touched by mercy, never moved by love. Rightly and justly are charity and avarice always opposed.[59] Charity grows by giving, avarice by stealing; the former clothes the poor, the latter strips them. Charity frees paupers from prison, avarice throws them in. The one feeds the hungry, the other starves them. The one rejoices in goodwill, the other delights in spitefulness. The one has a heart filled with piety, the other with cruelty. And Chrysostom also proclaims: "Let us loath avarice, which St. Paul calls 'the root of all evils.'[60] Let us flee this sin. Greed has made this earthly world unstable, it has confused all things. It snatches us from the blessed service of Christ, for it is contrary to His teaching. For Christ says: 'Give to the poor.'[61] Avarice says: Rob those things belonging to the needy. Christ: 'Forgive those who do you harm.'[62] Avarice: 'Rain down blows on those who have done you no injury.' Christ: 'Be mild and merciful.'[63] Avarice: 'Be cruel and savage.' Let us abandon, therefore, love of money, and since we have recognized that all who have practiced avarice are as dead men, let us also cast out those who would profit from the labor of other men. For they are afflicted with torment and torture, and with every kind of evil. Is it not a condition of total madness that alive they are occupied in continual labor and dead they suffer intolerable suffering and torments?"[64]

Then Bartolomeo spoke: Chrysostom has spoken well and with great dignity and not at all without elegance. In fact, his words have pleased me so much that I should like to become more familiar with his works.

Andrea replied: You would praise him more if you had heard him in his ancient tongue. I have read many works by this most holy man, adorned with fine phrases and dignified in speech. But I have been quoting from Burgundio, a certain Pisan of little

---

59. An echo of the view expressed in St. John Chrysostom *Homilia 9 in Epistolam ad Ephesios* 3(= PG 62.73–74).

60. Cf. 1 Tim. 6:10.

61. Cf. Matt. 26:9.

62. Cf. Matt. 5:39.

63. Cf. Matt. 5:4, 7.

64. St. John Chrysostom *Homilia 40 in Johannem* 4(= PG 59.234).

eloquence, who made a Latin translation about two hundred and sixty years ago, and this conveys none of the original eloquence of the sermons.[65] Still, the dignity of the subject matter and the grandeur of the words are such that although the sermons lack all elegance in translation, one yet senses the splendor of Chrysostom's golden tongue. But I hope that one of you will give us a much more polished, elegant version of Chrysostom's writings, for there are now many scholars trained in Greek.

Bartolomeo said: It has certainly been very pleasing for us to hear these words from you, a man most learned in Greek, and they resound more richly in your mouth than in ours. Still, of all that we have heard the dignity of the words of the Apostle seem to surpass even what you have quoted.

Andrea said: This is so. But even as that saying of the Apostle surpasses the other author, so this saying is itself surpassed by another of his statements. For he says in another place: "Avarice is slavery to idols."[66] With this single statement all of Antonio's arguments are overturned, for the Apostle explains that the body of the miser is afflicted in this life with the miserable slavery in which he is bound, and his soul will be handed over to the torments of the devil, whom he chose as his patron when he was alive. Earlier the Apostle said that "the miser is a slave,"[67] and since slavery is made more tolerable by the status of the master, he called the miser the servant of the worst and most inhumane demon. Let others say what they will, no better, no bolder statement can be found. Could it be revealed more forcefully by some great circumlocution of words or with more dignity by the weight of many examples that avarice makes man into an idolater, that is, a servant of the devil? It is surely so. For the miser hoards gold and other precious things that he delights in, watches over, cultivates, and worships as a god; as a result, he is afraid to touch his treasure, as though it were holy. He thus separates himself from the worship of God, so that he serves false idols. For this reason

65. Giovanni Burgundio (d. 1194) was a Pisan natural scientist and physician who translated many of the works of Galen and of the Greek fathers, including John of Damascus and St. John Chrysostom, into literal, plain Latin. See J. A. Fabricius, *Bibliotheca latina mediae et infimae aetatis,* 6 vols. (Florence, 1858–59), 1:281–82.

66. Col. 3:5.

67. Eph. 5:5.

Augustine compares misers and heretics in his writings against the Donatists:

> I ask you, who sins more gravely: the man who unwittingly lapses in heresy, or the man who knowingly follows avarice? The latter, who consciously refuses to abstain from avarice, that is, from idolatry, is he not guilty of the crime of idolatry?[68]

Then he adds: "Therefore, just as heretics will not possess the kingdom of God, so misers will not enter into the kingdom of God."[69] O sacred opinion once offered by God's oracle! For how would anyone enter into the kingdom of God, how would he be saved who acts precisely against those commandments on which hang the law and the prophets? Now there are two commandments on which all the other laws depend: We should love God and our neighbor. God cannot in any way be loved by the miser since he is a slave to idols. Nor does the miser love his neighbor, as both reason and authority prove. What, then, remains but that we conclude clearly from what we have said above that the miser is a despicable man, past hope in this life, full of crimes, infamy, and evils. Nothing is unhappier than his life, for he is always tormented by various anxieties and troubles, and nothing is more miserable than his death, which brings him to his future reward. At least while they are alive they should be able to enjoy some pleasures of mind and body, some joy, some rest; but they are afflicted with constant evils and are placed beyond all good. Whoever knows them hates them, curses them, and pursues them with maledictions.

Augustine compares misers to heretics; they are seen by the Apostle as idolaters; Chrysostom calls them baser than the vilest pigs. They live, if it is living, trapped in the worst and lowest condition of life, always anxious, uncertain of mind, vacillating; they pile up wealth unceasingly, but they never use what they have acquired. They are complaining, groaning, nasty, difficult, and lacking in self-confidence. Hence, it seems to me that even the life and customs of Saracens are more tolerable than those of

68. St. Augustine *De baptismo contra Donatistas* 4.5.7 (= *PL* 43.158).
69. Ibid. 4.18.25 (= *PL* 43.170).

misers, who ought more eagerly to welcome death than to live such a horrid and miserable existence where there is no rest, no leisure, no joy, no pleasure. What shall I say of the worries that continually trouble the hearts of misers! What of the torments with which they are afflicted out of fear of losing their treasure? Like the whip of the Furies, they are forever seeing thieves and robbers before their eyes, so that they can never find any peace. That saying of the old man in Plautus' *Aulularia* comes to mind. There he warns how troubled is the heart of the miser, how afflicted and oppressed by fear. His nights are sleepless and his days busy and toilsome, since he alone is envious of everything because he lacks all good.[70]

I believe that we can invoke no greater evil on someone we hate than to wish that he becomes a miser because with this wish we curse him with all evils, that is, with the damnation of his body and soul. Nothing worse than this can be inflicted by God or by man. What indeed, by God Almighty, drives these rash and demented men? Is it their desire for gold and silver? But nothing results from that since they don't use it. Is it either the magnitude of riches and wealth or the desire to pile up ever so much more? But this is of no use because no hunger is ever satisfied, nor is the desire for plenty ever filled. Is it so they can leave their wealth to their offspring? But this will not last for long, and since it is evilly gained it will be even more quickly dissipated. Is it because they are seeking peace? But the piling up of money never brings peace. Is it because they are driven by power and a lust to rule? But it would be very unworthy for someone who has been placed in the worst slavery to rule others. Consider closely, therefore, this erroneous opinion, and consult for a while your reason and obey its prescriptions. Reason teaches you that you are a man, that is, as Horace says, "shadow and ashes."[71]

But you are endowed with an immortal soul and it ought to be enriched, cultivated, embellished, and no great effort ought to be expended on other things. Material wealth should be used for provisioning this very short and transitory life. What do you really seek, most miserable of mortals? What mind, what intellect leads those astray so far from the truth? If you wish to become

70. Cf. Plautus *Aulularia* 70–74.
71. Horace *Carmina* 4.7.16: "pulvis et umbra sumus."

rich, you can obtain wealth quicker and more easily by despising it than by lusting after it. If you desire quiet, this should be sought by other means. The pure and sincere mind will find peace and quiet, but not in the treasure room where great riches have been accumulated to the point that you are embroiled in even greater troubles. If you want peace of heart, you will find it not in gold but in virtue, which has been placed beyond every fear. If you want to be ennobled, an excellent character and rejoicing in its virtue will make you noble. If you are concerned with leaving a fine inheritance for your children and grandchildren, you can bequeath them nothing more outstanding, nothing more solid than virtue and glory. If power pleases you, a man who can govern himself will be able to govern anyone. The good mind will possess the kingdom. Seeking money will make you weak, ignoble, timid, restless, and poor. Therefore, because evil desires blind you and lead you astray, you can see nothing that is just, nothing honorable. Why do you abandon virtue—a firm and stable quality within the power of our will—and chose those things of the appetites whose transient and certain qualities are under the influence of Fortune? Those things you seek with so much toil and trouble, on which you have expended so much effort and spent your entire life—I mean wealth, riches, farms, houses, and other possessions—in short, those things that you consider so valuable are really quite fragile and fleeting. Material goods are possessed on loan, and no possession will last with you for a long time, and nothing will go with you at death. When you depart this life, you will leave these things behind. Naked, impoverished, deserted, you will descend into Hell to plead your case, without the aid of a lawyer, and you will tremble before a judge who cannot be corrupted by gold. You will find no aid, no defense, no advocate. The only thing that will count is your own virtue, if you acted justly when you were alive.

Then Bartolomeo spoke: You should add to this both what your Lucian said on this matter and what we have from the noble poet Silius Italicus. On this Lucian said:

O fools, why are you wandering about this earthly place? At some time seek rest, for you are surely going to die. Of those things now with us, nothing is eternal. No one can take it with him when he dies, but stripped and naked he will go below.[72]

Indeed Silius, addressing a rich miser who died in war, added this passage:

O high-born Volunx, you lie low. What availed him now, all his treasure locked up in secret chambers, or his royal palace, once shining with ivory, or whole villages belonging to him, or the thirst for gold that men can never quench? The man whom Fortune favored once and crammed with piled-up wealth and rich gifts—him now shall Charon's boat convey naked to Tartarus.[73]

Then Andrea spoke: These passages and much more were written by them. But these are not statements of one author or another; these are the voices of nature and truth itself. And if men will only heed these voices, no doubt they will, for a time, stand firm. Thus, they will not set sail, blind and headlong, on the sea of greed. But it is strange that despite the counsel of many fine men, despite so many authoritative opinions and sober judgments placed before our eyes, which ought to affect the minds of mortals, still there are those who, impervious to every argument, continue to dedicate themselves to avarice and worship it as a god. Let them repent while there is still time and attend to their future life. They should listen to the opinion of the wisest men and heed the advice of the learned. They especially ought to have inscribed in their minds and carry in their hearts this saying of Cicero's:

For there is nothing so characteristic of narrowness and small-ness of soul as the love of riches, and there is nothing more honorable and noble than to be indifferent to money if one does not possess it, and to devote it to beneficence and gen-erosity if one does possess it.[74]

72. Cf. Lucian *Hermotimus* 6–7.
73. Silius Italicus *Punica* 5.261–67, a text that Poggio had discovered in 1417, probably in the monastery at St. Gall.
74. Cicero *De officiis* 1.26.92.

When this was said, Antonio spoke: I am glad that I took the miser's part so we might hear these arguments from you.

Bartolomeo said: I hope they are worthy to your ears. If you approve them, I shall have nothing to fear from other critics. But we have discussed long enough, and night is coming on. I think we ought to leave.

Then they all stood up.

ANGELO
POLIZIANO

Introduction

ELIZABETH B. WELLES

By April 1478, the time of the Pazzi Conspiracy, Lorenzo de' Medici had been the unofficial head of the Florentine Republic for slightly more than eight years.[1] These were years in which the brilliant artistic and intellectual life that surrounded Lorenzo and his younger brother, Giuliano, was on the rise. The city was at peace; even Italy was at peace, enjoying the delicate balance of power maintained by Milan, Venice, Florence, and Naples.

Into this stimulating and sophisticated ambience Angelo Ambrogini (1454–94) was sent from his little hill town of Montepulciano, whence he was called Poliziano, to be educated. His father had been recently murdered, and at the age of ten he found himself penniless and alone. In spite of these dismal facts, he pursued his studies with such intensity that by a precocious sixteen the young man was able to attract the attention of the Medici by his translation into Latin hexameters of book 2 of the *Iliad*.[2]

1. Piero, his father, died on 2 December 1469. Lorenzo took over almost immediately.

2. Poliziano started this project in 1470 but never finished it. Book 3 was completed in 1471–72, book 4 in 1473, book 5 in 1475. Translating Homer was a challenge of particular interest to Renaissance scholars since Greek had come into the curriculum only at the beginning of the fifteenth century. Poliziano's effort followed that of Carlo Marsuppini to whom the project had been entrusted by Pope Nicolas V and who died after completing book 1 in 1453. Other translators of Homer in the Quattrocento included Leonardo Bruni, Lorenzo

Poliziano's efforts eventually won him, in 1473, a place in the Medici household as preceptor to the children, as confidant to Lorenzo, but, most important, as poet. Although he was undoubtedly attached to Lorenzo by ties of genuine affection, their relationship was always controlled by the limitations of patronage: he was constantly at the beck and call of Lorenzo and his difficult wife, Clarice. However, his benefactor treated him well, giving him in 1477 the benefice of the priory of San Paolo, which saved him from absolute penury, and in 1483 a villa in Fiesole, which provided him leisure for study and writing. During this early period before the conspiracy, Poliziano was the author of poetry in Greek and Latin, though better known for his lyric poems in Italian. In the later part of his life, after 1480, he seems to have given up poetry in Italian and devoted himself to scholarship as a lecturer at the Studium. As a poet, his greatest ambition was to follow in Vergil's footsteps, to write an epic on contemporary historical event[3]; the closest he came was the *Stanze per la Giostra.*

This poem, though unfinished, is considered Poliziano's masterpiece. Written to celebrate the tournament in honor of the new Florentine alliance with Milan and Venice, it was supposed to immortalize that festival but immortalized instead youth, beauty, and the moment in which they could be enjoyed. Giuliano de' Medici and his lady, Simonetta Vespucci, were the chief protagonists of both the tournament and the poem, in which they become admirable idealizations of youthful, ephemeral beauty. The beginning of the poem follows a hunting party in a wood outside the city, another section takes place in the garden of Venus, but the real place of reference is "Fiorenza," which under Lorenzo "lieta in pace si riposa" (*Stanze,* 4). The evocation of the Golden Age in Venus's garden and Giuliano's "verde etate" (*Stanze,* 8) supply the imagery that can be applied to that springtime of the Golden Age in Florence.

Simonetta died of consumption in 1476, and Giuliano was murdered by the Pazzi two years later. Whether it was their deaths

---

Valla, Giovanni Aurispa, Guarino da Verona, and Pier Candido Decembrio. See Ida Maier, *Ange Politien: la formation d'un poète humaniste (1469–1480)* (Geneva, 1966), pp. 84–85.

3. In the dedication of book 3 of the *Iliad,* Poliziano proposed an epic on the sack of Volterra, which turned out, along with the revenge against the Pazzi, to be one of Lorenzo's worst acts. See Maier, *Ange Politien,* p. 103.

or exhaustion of interest, work on the *Stanze* ceased. Poliziano never got to the description of the tournament at all, for such a frivolous undertaking could hardly find inspiration in the grim and lugubrious atmosphere that was the aftermath of the Pazzi Conspiracy. The poet turned instead to writing in serious Latin prose about that iniquitous incident that so wholly occupied not only the Medici but all of Florence.

The Pazzi Conspiracy was a shocking and violent affair that had its chief causes in hatred and jealousy aroused by Medici prosperity. The more specific and political causes are to be found in the machinations of the pope, Sixtus IV (Francesco della Rovere). He had allowed himself to be convinced by Francesco de' Pazzi, head of the Pazzi bank in Rome, to withdraw his abundant account from the Medici in favor of the Pazzi. With their aid he was able to buy the Signoria of Imola and put his favorite nephew, Girolamo Riario, at its head. Imola was strategically important to Florence, and Lorenzo's efforts to encourage local resistence to the new ruler enraged both the pope and Girolamo. In Florence itself, Giovanni de' Pazzi was further tried by the influence of the Medici. He had married a Borromeo (cousins of the Medici), who stood to inherit her father's considerable estate until a law, newly created by Lorenzo, cheated him out of it by ruling that male nephews had rights before daughters. Furthermore, Pazzi pride was continually being wounded by what they took to be the haughty, overbearing attitude of the Medici.

Not long after the purchase of Imola, the pope appointed as archbishop of Pisa a Medici enemy, Francesco Salviati. To extreme annoyance of the would-be archbishop, Lorenzo managed to keep him from assuming his position for three years since, by previous agreement with the pope, the Church was to consult Florence on all its appointments in Tuscany. Therefore, Francesco and Girolamo, who saw their own future gains only in terms of the demise of the Medici, drew Salviati in with them. These three proceeded to formulate plans to destroy Medici power—which could only mean destroy the Medici in power—so that the plot that took shape in their minds was chiefly to arrange for the murder of Lorenzo and Giuliano. They hired Montesecco, a papal soldier, to work out many of the practical details and, most important, to kill Lorenzo. The extent of the involvement of the pope is clear. Montesecco's confession, written the day before his execution (4 May 1478) documents the collusion of Sixtus, who said in the presence of Riario, the archbishop, and Montesecco: "I do not wish the death of anyone at all, because it is not our duty to consent to the death of anyone, and even if Lorenzo is a villain and behaves badly towards us, I still do not want his death for anything, but the change of the State, yes." He thus washed his hands of the murders in advance while asking for the impossible, for the Florentine state could not be changed without the annihilation of the Medici. Montesecco told him: "These things can be done badly without the death of Lorenzo and Giuliano."[4]

The execution of the ill-starred plot was full of difficulties. The conspirators knew that to be successful they had to kill both brothers, and their plans were foiled several times. The first dinner planned in honor of the young Cardinal Riario at Fiesole failed because Giuliano was ill and did not attend. Another banquet was contrived at the Medici Palace in Florence to be held after mass on Sunday, 26 April, but Francesco de' Pazzi understood that Giuliano again was ill and would not attend. A new plan had to be immediately improvised so that the double assassination would take place during the mass itself. This marked the real downfall of the conspirators,[5] since under these circumstances Montesecco refused to have any part of it, and his substitutes, two monks, proved themselves incompetent. Lorenzo lived, and, exactly as the conspirators had predicted, the plot failed.

The conspiracy, bloody in its conception, was worse in its result. Lorenzo's revenge was swift and thorough. Machiavelli commented

4. The pope repeated at least four times that he wished the state to change without death, but in the end he said "andate e fate chome pare a voi, purchè non cie intervengha morte (Go and do as it seems best to you, provided that death does not interfere)." "Io non voglio la morte de niun per niente, perchè non è offitio nostro aconsentire alla morte de persona; e bene che Lorenzo sia un villano e con noi se porte male, pure io non vorria la morte sua per niente, ma la mutatione dello Stato sì." Quoted in Gino Capponi, *La storia di Firenze,* 2 vols. (Florence, 1876), 2:514.

5. Montesecco had only consented to the murder on the say-so of Girolamo Riario, who assured him of the pope's complicity. Montesecco replied ". . . diavolo, egl'è gran facto che el consente! Me respuse: Non sa' tu, che gle famo fare quello volimo noi? Basta che le cose andranne bene (. . . the Devil, it is a great thing that he consents. He answered me: Don't you know that we do what we want? It's enough if things go well.)" Quoted in ibid., p. 516.

that "such conspiracies, because unlikely to succeed, usually produce ruin for those who form them, but greatness for those against whom they are directed."[6] All the conspirators and their cohorts were killed or punished, the Pazzi name was officially abolished; their arms were cancelled; and they were not permitted to marry or own property.

The period that followed the conspiracy was hardly comfortable for the Medici either. The pope excommunicated Lorenzo[7] and then the entire city. Two years of war ensued between Florence and Sixtus IV, allied with Naples; it was ended only when Lorenzo, in December 1479, went to Naples and by the sheer force of his own personality was able to make a treaty with King Ferrante. Though Lorenzo lamented much the loss of his brother, it also left him with his hands free. Guicciardini noted: "His brother Giuliano, with whom he would have had to divide his property and contend for power, was now dead. His enemies were removed gloriously, and by the public arm; whatever resentment and suspicion there was against him disappeared too."[8] His position in Florence was stronger and his prestige abroad greater than ever before. Yet something had happened to spoil the golden days of festive security. The threat of evil and death, always menacing, had been realized, and men were once more made aware of their own vulnerable mortality.

The *Coniurationis Commentarium*[9] was composed almost im-

6. N. Machiavelli, *The History of Florence*, book 8, chap. 1, trans. Allan Gilbert, *Machiavelli, The Chief Works and Others*, 3 vols. (Durham, N.C., 1965), 3:1383; Italian text in *Istorie fiorentine*, ed. F. Gaeta (Milan, 1962), p. 509.

7. Ferdinand Schevill, *The Medici* (New York, 1949), p. 130, comments that the pope's action was "to all appearances for unlawful resistance to murder," although Sixtus claimed it was for the death of the archbishop and his nephew's imprisonment.

8. F. Guicciardini, *The History of Florence*, trans. M. Domandi (New York, 1972), p. 38; Italian text in *Storie fiorentine*, ed. R. Palmarocchi (Bari, 1931), p. 37.

9. But of course Poliziano's was not the only account. A contemporary history against the Medici is Alamanno Rinuccini, "De libertate," ed. F. Adorno, *Atti e Memorie dell'Accademia Toscana di Scienze e Lettere, La Colombaria* 22 (1957):207–303. Montesecco's detailed confession was published on 11 August 1478; another eyewitness account was by Filippo Strozzi: both was published in Capponi, *Storia di Firenze*, 2:508–20. The conspiracy was described in Piero Parenti, *Storia Fiorentina* (1496), available as an appendix in Poliziano, *Della*

mediately after the debacle. Lorenzo, having decided to face the critical moment vigorously, had organized a large propaganda campaign. On the one hand he sought the aid of the law, both canon and secular, to prove the pope's charges unjust and, on the other, he enlisted services of humanists and artists: Ficino wrote two letters to the Pope;[10] Botticelli was paid on July 21 for painting the hanged conspirators on the Palazzo Vecchio;[11] and, not the least of these, Poliziano composed a history of the event. It was the poet's first work written specifically for publication, to insure, one assumes, its wide distribution, and thus Poliziano was given the opportunity to serve his patrons publicly. It is ironic that his ambition to celebrate the Medici in an epic about a contemporary event was realized in an idyll about a mock war, the *Stanze,* and in a prose work of history in Latin, the *Commentarium.*

The aim of the work is clearly to show the Medici in the best possible light, as innocent victims of evil men. To this end Poliziano used ancient authors not merely as models of style but as pointed references to the case at hand. His chief source was Sallust, who, with Livy and Tacitus, was the Roman historian most respected by the humanists. Sallust's *War with Catiline* was exceedingly appropriate for the cause since with it he could easily imply the comparison between ancient Rome, which had withstood the menace of conspiracy, and modern Florence, which, in consequence, would also. Furthermore, Catiline had a special meaning for the Florentines. Dante followed the tradition that he had fled to Fiesole and caused it to revolt against Rome. The Romans were true founders of Florentine nobility, while Catiline's descendents, *"quello ingrato popolo maligno"* (*Inferno* 15:68), common peo-

congiura dei Pazzi (*Coniurationis Commentarium*), ed. A. Perosa (Padua, 1958), pp. 69–76; and there is a brief account in Luca Landucci, *A Florentine Diary from 1450 to 1516,* trans. A. Jervis (New York, 1969), pp. 15–20. Machiavelli's *History of Florence,* book 8, chaps. 1–9, and Guicciardini's *History of Florence,* chap. 4, are well-known anti-Medici versions by two great historians.

10. Marsilio Ficino, *Epistolae,* book 8, nos. 1, 9, in his *Opera omnia* (Turis, 1962), 1: 808–10, 813–15.

11. "Item servatis, etc., deliberaverunt et stantiaverunt Sandro Botticello pro eius labore in pingendo proditores flor. quadraginta largos," cited in J. A. Crowe and G. B. Cavalcaselle, *A History of Painting in Italy* (New York, 1911), 4:251, from a document in the Archivio di Stato, Florence, published in *Giornale storico degli Archivi Toscani* 6(1862):5n. The frescoes were removed after the fall of the Medici in 1494; see also M. Levey and G. Mandel, *The Complete Paintings of Botticelli* (New York, 1967), p. 83.

ple, were *"avara, invidiosa e superba."* Thus, when Poliziano begins with two references to the beginning of Sallust's *War with Catiline,* the point about the conspirators is made.

Also for purpose of propaganda, he telescopes events so that he does not need to explain the immediate causes, except for the innate jealousy of the Pazzi. The Medici entanglement with the pope over Imola, which Lorenzo had wanted as much for himself as Sixtus had, and the incident over the Borromeo inheritance are left out. The narrative proceeds completely out of context so that there is no possibility that the reader's sympathies might be enlisted by any just cause of the Pazzi. Also missing is any mention of the pope or Girolamo Riario, perhaps in order not to strain relations between the Church and Lorenzo any further.

Poliziano further simplifies the action by describing the two sides in absolute moral terms. *Omnes boni,* all the good people, were on the side of the Medici, and those who opposed them, the Pazzi and Salviati were the bad. There is no middle ground here, and the drama results from the collision of the opposites. The author had some trouble, however, with Giovanni Battista Montesecco, who was by all accounts a good man who happened to be on the wrong side. He solved the dilemma by presenting the soldier in generalities—"He was a man of great talent, judgement, and astuteness, and very skillful at accomplishing his purpose . . ."— and then by showing him no compassion at his execution—". . . a few days later Giovanni Battista was punished." Poliziano does not even mention his honest and invaluable confession, which itself was published August 11 of that year.

The work is framed with a series of portraits: at the beginning the conspirators, and at the end Giuliano. This emphasis on portraiture bears out the Plinian dictum, adopted by medieval and Renaissance rhetoric, that the physiognomy reflects the moral condition of the man. Therefore, Poliziano made Pazzi as ugly and unappealing as possible and, when he neglected their physical aspects, dwelt upon other proofs of their bad character, exaggerating and even lying for the desired effect. The most flagrant example of this disregard for truth was his description of Renato Pazzi, to whom he attributes dissimulation and cowardice, while both Guicciardini and Machiavelli considered him wise, benevolent, and without pride. To Jacopo de' Pazzi he gives several of Catiline's vices, avarice and prodigality in a style syntactically reminiscent of

Sallust. In this way he makes Jacopo the true son of Catiline, and the *"ingrato popolo maligno."*

In general, Renaissance historiography did not hold strict respect for objective facts but was more concerned with producing work of literary merit that would provide lessons for future generations. Poliziano stretches the truth further than perhaps was acceptable even then—though we must remember it was truth in the service of the Medici—but he adhered to the precepts of literary standards and moral purpose. For elevation of style he turns of course, to the Romans—Livy, Cicero, Caesar, Suetonius—but again mostly to Sallust. From him he took the direct, terse style, formulas of transition, and the use of infinitives to accelerate the action.

The structure is simple, built up from an equilibrium or conflict of opposites—the good versus the bad. The portraits of the conspirators in the beginning (a device taken from Sallust who began with a description of Catiline) is balanced by a longer single portrait of Giuliano at the end, just as the single murder of Giuliano is balanced but also multiplied by the numerous executions of the conspirators. A kind of rhythm is established of the bad (conspirators), the good (Medici), the bad (plot and executions), the good (Giuliano), which corresponds to a numerical proportion—many conspirators, few Medici, one murder, many executions. Thus the whole is held together by a kind of dramatic action in tension that results in almost static dynamism. The symmetry is plausible as it is provided by the facts themselves. The author could maintain (also because he eliminated much relevant material about causes) classic dramatic unities of time, place, and action. The action is complete, for all the characters are dead or accounted for in the end. Poliziano may have intended that the reader be reminded of a classical tragedy that would have come true if Lorenzo had not lived.

Within the narrative are another pair of opposites that demonstrate the favorite Renaissance theme: *virtù* and *fortuna*. The primary example, the archbishop Salviati, shows that men who depended too much upon fortune's favor without merit of their own were quickly cast down. He stands in contrast to Lorenzo whose marvelous *virtù* shines forth from the vicissitudes following the plot and to Giuliano, with whose evocation as the humanist ideal of physical and moral perfection the work closes. Poliziano begins the description of Giuliano with ruminations on the "fickleness of fortune," implying that not only Giuliano's death but the whole "upheaval of human affairs" were the result of fortune. The death of Giuliano leaves the reader with the idea that *fortuna* has been victorious, but, referring to the last line of Vergil's first Georgic, he expresses the hope that Lorenzo, like Augustus after the death of Caesar, will be able to bring order to the disrupted world. This last sentence reaffirms his faith in human potential and accomplishment.

This optimistic concluding sentence, however, follows upon many grim paragraphs in which the real concern is death. Lorenzo's extreme and bloody revenge upon the Pazzi was considered a blot on his record, but Poliziano does not censure it. Rather, he sees it as the sad result of Giuliano's murder. It may seem surprising that our poet did not shirk from describing the most gruesome details of this aftermath. He came voluntarily out of the safety of the Medici palace to watch conspirators hung and bodies chopped up. This morbid curiosity and fondness for the grotesque[12] runs parallel to his fascination for beauty and nature, which was the subject of his better known poetry. As in any true poet, his sensibility was not limited but inclusive of all human experience, and his powers of observation—he is almost a voyeur here—were always at work. He knew that the menace of death was always present, always lurking just on the other side of the gay, fervished *carpe diem* that we associate with Lorenzo's circle. Life, which fled so elegantly through Poliziano's and Lorenzo's verse, must inevitably end and was often cut short at its best moment, as it was for Simonetta and Giuliano. In the *Orfeo*, his last work in Italian, the beautiful young Eurydice is killed by a snake. Orpheus begging Pluto, meditates on death:

> All living things return to you at last
> Each mortal life falls back to you again,
> Whatever lies under the circling moon,
> Must finally arrive in your domain
> But everyone must take these roads at last.
>
> *Orfeo* 262–67

It is the gloomy epilogue to a whole period.

---

12. See Julia Cotton Hill, "Death and Politian," *Durham University Journal* 46(1953–54):96–105.

The wake of the conspiracy and the war that followed were sad years for Poliziano. Tuscany was besieged by the Duke of Calabria (Ferrante's son) and endured famine, pestilence, and dreary rains. To escape the dangers of the city, Lorenzo sent his family to live in various villas outside of Florence. The poet suffered from conflicts with Clarice, Lorenzo's wife, and from boredom. He wrote in a letter (18 December 1478) from Cafaggiolo that he was alone and bored and often given to meditation "upon deaths and wars, the sadness of the past and fear of the future."[13] It was a year later that Lorenzo left for Naples. Poliziano asked to go with him but was finally left behind because he kept changing his mind. Hurt and unhappy, he left the city and wandered through northern courts. He settled briefly at Mantua during the spring, where he wrote the *Orfeo*. By June 1480, after peace was concluded, Lorenzo returned triumphantly to Florence, and Poliziano was recalled to teach in the *Studium*. Although peace and security reigned for the next twelve years until Lorenzo's death, it was never quite the same. The *lieta pace* had gone forever.

BIBLIOGRAPHY

Angelo Poliziano: Principal Editions

Opera omnia. Edited by Ira Maier. 3 vols. Turin, 1970–71.

Della Congiura dei Pazzi (Coniurationis Commentarium). Edited by A. Perosa. Padua, 1958.

Prose volgari inedite e poesie latine e greche edite e inedite. Edited by Isidore Del Lungo. Florence, 1867.

Le Rime. Edited by N. Sapegno. Rome, 1949.

Le Selve e la Strega, Prolusioni nello Studio Fiorentino (1482–1492). Edited by Isidore Del Lungo. Florence, 1925.

Stanze cominciate per la giostra di Giuliano de' Medici. Edited by V. Pernicone. Turin, 1954.

Studies

Biasin, G. P. " 'Messer Jacopo giù per Arno se ne va...'." *Modern Language Notes* 79(1964):1–13.

13. Poliziano, *Prose volgari inedite e poesie latine e greche edite e inedite*, ed. I. Del Lungo (Florence, 1867), p. 68, my translation.

Bigi, E. "Ambrogini, Angelo, detto il Poliziano." *DBI* 2(1960):691–702.

Carducci, G. "Delle poesie toscane di Messer Angelo Poliziano, Discorso." In Angelo Poliziano. *Le Stanza, l'Orfeo e le Rime*, pp. 2–244. Bologna, 1912.

Donato, Eugenio. "Death and History in Poliziano's *Stanze.*" *Modern Language Notes* 80(1965):27–40.

Ferruolo, A. "A Trend in Renaissance Thought and Art: Poliziano's *Stanze per la Giostra.*" *Romanic Review* 44(1953):246–56.

Garin, Eugenio. "The Cultural Background of Politian." In *Portraits from the Quattrocento*, pp. 161–89. New York, 1972.

Hill, Julia Cotton. "Death and Politian." *Durham University Journal* 46(1953–54):96–105.

Maier, B. "Angelo Poliziano." In *Letteratura Italiana, I Maggiori*, 1:243–305. Milan, 1956.

Maier, Ida, *Ange Politien: La formation d'un poète Humaniste (1469–1480)*. Geneva, 1966.

———. *Le Manuscrits d'Ange Politien: Catalogue descriptif*. Geneva, 1965.

Malagoli, Luigi. *Le Stanze e l'Orfeo e lo spirito del Quattrocento*. Rome, 1941.

Momigliano, Attilio. "Il motivo dominante della poesia del Poliziano." In Angelo Poliziano. *Le Stanze, l'Orfeo e le Rime*, pp. 7–39. Turin, 1921.

Mutini, Claudio. *Interpretazione del Poliziano*. Rome, 1972.

Perosa, Alessandro. "Febris: A Poetic Myth Created by Poliziano." *Journal of the Warburg and Courtauld Institutes* 9(1946):74–95.

———. *Mostra del Poliziano nella Biblioteca Medicae Laurenziana, Catalogo*. Florence, 1955.

Picotti, G. B. "Studi Polizianeschi." In *Ricerche umanistiche*, pp. 1–176. Florence, 1955.

Il Poliziano e il suo tempo. Atti del IV Convegno internazionale di Studi sul Rinascimento, 1954. Florence, 1957.

Ramat, R. *La Poesia toscana del Poliziano*. Florence, 1962.

Scaglione, Aldo. "The Humanist as Scholar and Politian's Conception of the 'grammaticus.'" *Studies in the Renaissance* 8(1961):49–70.

Welliver, Warman. "The Subject and Purpose of Poliziano's *Stanze.*" *Italica* 48(1971):34–50.

ANGELO POLIZIANO
*The Pazzi Conspiracy**

Translated by ELIZABETH B. WELLES

I am resolved to describe briefly the Pazzi Conspiracy, a crime most worthy of record that occurred in my own times, for indeed it almost overthrew the whole Florentine Republic from within.[1]

The state of this city was then that while all the good people were on the side of the brothers Lorenzo and Giuliano[2] and the rest of the Medici family, a branch of the Pazzi family and some of the Salviati began, first in secret and then even openly, to oppose the existing government. They envied the power of the Medici family in public affairs and its brilliance in private ones, and they sought to destroy it as much as they could.

The Pazzi family was hated by citizens and common people alike. Moreover, they were all extremely greedy, and none could stand their outrageous and insolent nature. The head of the family,

---

* Translated from *Della Congiura dei Pazzi* (*Coniurationis Commentarium*), edited by A. Perosa (Padua, 1958), which includes extensive notes and a discussion of the manuscript tradition.

1. Cf. Sallust *Bellum Cataline* 4.2–3. Poliziano recalls the beginning of Sallust's work on the Catiliniam conspiracy by specific references. Compare, for example, "statui res gestas populi Romani . . . perscribere . . ." of Sallust to Poliziano's "Pactianum coniurationem paucis describere instituo."

2. Lorenzo de' Medici (1449–92), called il Magnifico, and Guiliano de' Medici (1453–78). They were the sons of Piero and the grandsons of Cosimo the Elder.

Jacopo,[3] a knight, had time only for gambling day and night, and if it happened that the die was thrown badly, he swore fearfully at God and man and very often he would in anger blindly hurl whatever was nearby at the dealer or anyone else around. He was pale and bloodless, always twitching his head and, what should be great proof of his shiftiness, never kept his mouth, nor his eyes, nor his hands still. He had two inborn vices, and, what is incredible, they were conspicuously contrary; he was extremely avaricious, but he took great pleasure in wasting his patrimony.[4] He tore down the magnificently built palace he inherited from his father and undertook to build it entirely new from its foundation.[5] Often he hired day laborers, but he did not pay them in full, and cheated the poor men badly who eked out a mean living by the work of their hands, by giving them tough rotten pork. For these reasons he was disliked by everyone, and neither he nor his forefathers were ever in favor with the people. He had, moreover, no legitimate children; therefore his relatives courted him like fortune-hunters. He was very careless and was especially negligent in family matters. Since this was his character, it seemed easy to him to overturn the state, and it was a spur and incitement to him to hasten this very evil undertaking. A man both insolent and ambitious for bankruptcy, he did not imagine that he might bring disgrace on anyone, and he therefore worked hard to reduce both himself and Florence to ashes with a single fire.

Francesco Salviati,[6] moreover, a man suddenly fortunate who had obtained the archbishopric of Pisa only recently, understood little about himself or his fortune, began to grow incredibly

3. Jacopo di Andrea de' Pazzi (1422–78) was considered the head of the Pazzi family.

4. Cf. Sallust *Cataline* 5.4–8. Sallust says the same sort of thing about Cataline and the corruption of public morals.

5. It is possible that Jacopo was carrying out plans that Brunelleschi had made for Andrea, his father. Documents show only, however, that the palace on the corner of Borgo degli Albizzi and Via Proconsul underwent enlargement after 1462. See Cornelius von Fabriczy, *Filippo Brunelleschi* (Stuttgart, 1892), pp. 129, 136.

6. Francesco di Bernardo Salviati was made archbishop of Pisa in 1474 but was prevented from assuming the position by Lorenzo for three years. Poliziano seems once to have had a different opinion of Salviati, for he had sent his "Dolce Salviati" (1473), a Latin epigram requesting a favor. See Poliziano, *Prose volgari inedite e poesie latine e greche edite e inedite* ed. I. Del Lungo (Florence, 1867), p. 113.

haughty and to presume for himself all sorts of things due to his good luck. This Francesco was, both the gods and men know, an ignorant disparager of every law, human and divine. Ruined by an excess of lust and infamous for pandering, he was guilty of every sort of shameful act.[7] He was devoted to gambling and was, furthermore, a great flatterer, very frivolous, very vain, but bold, headlong, cunning, and impudent. With these arts (and he did not shame Fortune), he acquired the archbishopric and tried to gain heaven itself with his prayers.

On account of his innate vanity, he, along with Francesco Pazzi, proposed this monstrous scheme and had, it is said, discussed plans for killing Lorenzo and Giuliano and taking over the government long before. Finally, at Jacopo Pazzi's villa, called Montughi, near Florence, all the conspirators planned this evil deed. Salviati himself formulated the terms of the plot.

The principal conspirators after Salviati were Jacopo and Francesco Pazzi.[8]

Francesco,[9] a man of willful nature from which arose his enormous arrogance and pride, was the son of Antonio Pazzi, Jacopo's brother. He was exceedingly indignant that the Medici family surpassed his own. He would always disparage Lorenzo and Giuliano and parade these insults about everywhere, forbearing no curse, no abuse; he had no thought except to injure them as much as possible. He stayed in Rome most of the time at the Pazzi banking house because he knew his influence was of no value in Florence in comparison to the Medici brothers, who showed him up by their kindness, virtue, and good character. Moreover, he was, like all the Pazzi, prone to unbelievable tantrums. He was small of stature, with a puny body, livid complexion, blond hair, the care of which immoderately preoccupied him. As were his appearance and bearing, so were his gestures, in such a way that everyone perceived his incredible insolence, which he endeavored greatly to cover up at first encounters; but he did not succeed as he wished. He was,

7. Cf. Sallust *Cataline* 21.1.
8. Cf. Sallust *Cataline* 43.1.
9. Francesco d'Antonio de' Pazzi (1444–78) was Jacopo's nephew, and, according to Poliziano, the chief instigator of the plot. The description of him is hardly flattering, but Guicciardini concurs that he was small and thin as well as "very restless, spirited, and ambitious." F. Guicciardini, *Storie fiorentine,* edited by R. Palmarocchi (Bari, 1931), pp. 31–32.

besides, a bloodthirsty man, who set out to accomplish whatever entered his mind and was not stopped by respect for any honor, any religion, any reputation, or any name.

Jacopo Salviati,[10] on the other hand, was bent entirely on gaining other men's favor. Always with a smile on his lips,[11] he gave everyone a sumptuous welcome, eager to offer them both prostitutes and comestibles. He was also said, however, to be skillful and active in commerce.

The third in this company was Jacopo,[12] the son of the learned Poggio Bracciolini. He was, on account of his family's straightened circumstances, his debts (of which he had made a great many), and his natural vanity, eager for change of government.[13] He was especially skilled at abusive talk, and in this alone did he resemble his father, a very scurrilous man. He was constantly attacking eminent men at every turn, and he either slandered their behavior indiscriminately or tore apart the writings of the learned, without sparing anyone. He was incredibly proud of reciting many stories from memory, pushing them upon any circle or company to the annoyance of his listeners. He had inherited from his father a large patrimony that he had completely squandered in a few years. Thus, compelled by his destitute state, he surrendered himself wholly to the Pazzi and to Salviati; he was as he had always been, up for sale to whoever would buy.

The fourth of the conspirators was Jacopo,[14] the brother of the archbishop and an altogether obscure and sordid person. And

10. Jacopo di Jacopo Salviati, cousin of the archbishop.

11. Cf. Terence *Adelphoe* 863–64: "Ille suam semper egit vitam in otio, in conviviis, / clemens placidus, nulli laedere os, adridere omnibus." Poliziano: "Semper is arridere os omnibus, laute omnes accipere, scortis et comessationibus intentus agere. . . . "

12. Jacopo di Poggio Bracciolini (1442–78) was the son of Poggio, author of *On Avarice,* translated in this volume, once chancellor of Florence, and famous for the discovery of many ancient texts and for his biting wit. Jacopo was himself a scholar and a member of the Platonic Academy. Poliziano assumes that he joined the conspiracy on account of his poverty, but he was probably also influenced by his ties to the archbishop, since he had lately become secretary to Cardinal Raffaello Riario Sansoni (Girolamo's nephew), who was in the care of Salviati in Pisa.

13. Cf. Sallust *Cataline* 48.1.

14. Jacopo di Bernardo Salviati, the brother of the archbishop. Nothing else about him is known.

Besides him there was Bernardo Bandini,[15] desperate, bold, and fearless, who, having ruined the affairs of his family, cast himself headlong into every sort of scandal.

There were seven Florentines[16] who undertook the evil deed. Added to their number were Giovanbattista, from Montesecco[17] and the family of the counts of Girolamo, and Antonio da Volterra,[18] who either by hatred of his country or his slippery readiness to please others, was induced to join the evil activity. Besides these there was Stefano,[19] a priest, Jacopo Pazzi's secretary, a lewd and evil man who gave ear to every crime and who, it is said, hardly behaved decently in his master's house, where he taught his only and illegitimate daughter her letters.

It has also been discovered that Renato[20] and Guglielmo Pazzi[21] were not ignorant of the conspiracy. Guglielmo had married Bianca,

15. Bernardo di Giovanni Bandini de' Baroncelli, assigned along with Francesco Pazzi to Giuliano's murder, was the first to stab Giuliano, and he killed Nori, Lorenzo's defender. He was probably induced to join the plot by hopes of financial gain.

16. Jacopo and Francesco Pazzi; Francesco, Jacopo di Jacopo and Jacopo di Bernardo Salviati, Jacopo Bracciolini, Bernardo Bandini.

17. Giovanni Battista da Montesecco from the Marches, an outstanding Condottiere, known as a prudent, able, and intelligent man, was an officer in the forces of Pope Sixtus IV. He had been reluctant to join the plot at the outset because it was both dangerous and difficult. Urged by the pope himself and persuaded by Riario, he consented, however, and took an active part in the planning. N. Machiavelli, *Istorie fiorentine,* book 8, chap. 4, edited by F. Gaeta (Milan, 1962), pp. 513–15.

18. Antonio di Gherardo Maffei of Volterra was a scribe in the Apostolic Camera. Poliziano's impression that he took part in the plot in order to get back at the Medici for the sack of Volterra in 1472 is borne out in *Commentari Urbani* of Volterrano.

19. Stefano di Ser Niccolo da Bagnone served as secretary to Jacopo Pazzi and tutor to his one illegitimate daughter, Caterina. At the last minute, he was, with Antonio of Volterra, assigned to the murder of Lorenzo.

20. Renato di Pietro di Andrea de' Pazzi (1442–78) is described by Poliziano as treacherous, cowardly, and greedy. However, he had held important posts in the government and both Machiavelli and Guicciardini saw him as wise, prudent, and studious. He is known also to have opposed the conspiracy until the end.

21. Guglielmo di Antonio di Andrea de' Pazzi, Francesco's brother (1437–78), was married to Lorenzo's sister, Bianca de' Medici. Cosimo, her grandfather, had hoped the match would heal some of the enmity between the two houses. It is difficult to say whether he was directly involved in the plot. He is named in the *Sentenze del Podestà* along with the other guilty members of his family, but had been heard by others to have claimed his innocence.

Lorenzo de' Medici's sister, and she had born him many children, whereby he was thought to sit, as it is said, in two saddles.[22] He was the older brother of Francesco, of whom we have often spoken, and Renato, son of Pietro, a nobleman, Jacopo and Antonio's brother and thus a cousin on his father's side to Guglielmo and Francesco. This man was a great dissimulator[23] and very adept at hiding evil deeds. Although neither bold nor courageous, he hastened to act on everything that came into his head. At the same time he was stingy and greedy for money of others, which caused him to be unpopular with the people. Besides these there was Napoleone Franzesi,[24] a man in Guglielmo's pay, who was not the least important part in this affair.

Some other persons of no account entered into this villainy, some from the archbishop and some from the Pazzi. Among these was a certain Brigliano,[25] a man of the vilest condition and Nanni,[26] a Pisan notary, both factious and bad.

But the one among the non-Florentines to take upon himself the most important role was Giovanni Battista, from the family of the counts of Girolamo whom we have mentioned before. He had deferred the whole business, which had been planned for two years, to 5 May 1478,[27] the Sunday before Ascension Day. He was a man of great talent, judgement, and astuteness, and very skillful at accomplishing his purpose, although he had not frequently practiced in things of this sort. Salviati, as well as all the other conspirators, had great faith in him.

Now the situation demands that we explain the plan of the conspiracy.[28]

22. Seneca *Controversiae* 7.3.9: "atqui soles duabus sellis sedere." The expression, which points to Guglielmo's ambiguous attitude toward the plot, had probably become proverbial. Poliziano probably knew the saying from Macrobius *Saturnalia* 2.3.10, rather than directly from the Seneca text, which has only recently been discovered.

23. Cf. Sallust *Cataline* 5.4.

24. Napoleone di Antonio di Niccolo Franzesi da Staggia was a follower of the Pazzi.

25. Giovanni di Domenico, called Il Brigliano or Il Cagnotto (dog), was a hired bully of the Pazzi.

26. Nanni, a Pisan notary, was probably of the archbishop's suite.

27. Poliziano is in error about the date. The conspiracy took place on Sunday, 26 April.

28. Again in imitation of Sallust, who first gave a portrait of Catiline before

The Medici family was splendid and magnificent in all their undertakings, especially in receiving famous personages. No famous man either came to Florence or Florentine territory whom that household did not treat with this sort of magnificence. When, therefore, as soon as the Cardinal Raffaello,[29] the son of Count Girolamo's sister, had arrived at Jacopo's country villa outside the city, where, we have shown, the conspiracy was planned, the conspirators seized the opportunity for the evil deed. They announced the cardinal to the brothers so that they might receive him at their villa in Fiesole. There Lorenzo and I, with his son Piero, went; Giuliano stayed home because he was hindered by the state of his health, which delayed the matter to the day that we have mentioned. Then they wrote anew [to Lorenzo] more familiarly,[30] that the Cardinal very much wanted to be received at a banquet in Florence to see the ornaments of the palace; the hangings, tapestries, gems, silver, and all the other precious objects. The two excellent young men suspected no trickery; they prepared the house; they got out the ornaments, spread out the tapestries, arranged the silver, statues, and paintings for public view, put out the gems in their cases, and had a most magnificent banquet prepared.

And then, before long, the conspirators began to ask where Lorenzo and Giuliano were. They found out that they had both gone to Santa Reparata, so they hurried off.[31] The Cardinal was led,

describing the events, Poliziano uses wording ("Res ipsa iam postulat") based on a passage from Sallust *Cataline* 5.9 ("Res ipsa hortari videtur") to mask the end of the introduction of characters and the beginning of the narrative.

29. Raffaello Riario Sansoni (b. 1460), the nephew of the pope's favorite Girolamo, was made cardinal by Sixtus in 1477. He had no active part in the conspiracy except as he was used by others as a decoy.

30. Since the first attempt at Fiesole had failed on account of Giuliano's absence, the conspirators decided to try again. They had the young cardinal invited to the Medici palace in Florence on the pretext of seeing their collection of art.

31. Actually, the cardinal was expected to go straight to the church but went first to the Medici palace to change his clothes. When the Medici found this out, they returned as quickly as possible from the cathedral in order to do him homage, and they met him just as he was setting out. The original plan, which Poliziano does not mention, to kill both brothers at the banquet had to be modified because Giuliano did not intend to go to dinner. Machiavelli says that Giuliano had not yet arrived at the church when mass began, so that Francesco Pazzi and Bernardo Bandini, his murderers, went to fetch him from his house. They accompanied him to the church with a great show of friendliness, "hugging

according to custom, onto a platform in the choir. While the
Eucharist was being celebrated, the archbishop, along with Jacopo
di Poggio, the two Jacopo Salviati, and several companions, went
to the Palazzo Vecchio[82] in order to throw the rulers of Florence
out of their citadel and take over the palace. The rest stayed in the
church to carry out their evil work. Although assigned to Lorenzo's
murder, Giovanni Battista[33] had withdrawn from the crime, and
Antonio da Volterra had taken it over; the rest were attending to
Giuliano.

As soon as the communion of the priest was over and the signal
had been given,[34] Bernardo Bandini, Francesco Pazzi, and other
conspirators surrounded Giuliano in a circle. First Bandini struck
the young man, forcing his sword through his chest. Giuliano,
dying, fled a few steps; they followed. Gasping for breath the
youth fell to the ground. Francesco stabbed him again and again
with his dagger. Thus this upright young man was murdered. His
servant, breathless with terror, flung himself into hiding in a most
contemptible fashion.

Meanwhile, the chosen assassins attacked Lorenzo, and Antonio,
first laying a hand on his left shoulder, aimed his dagger at
Lorenzo's throat. The latter, undaunted, let his mantel fall and
wrapped it around his left arm, drawing his sword out of its scab-
bard at the same time; however, he received one more blow, and,
as he freed himself, was wounded in the neck. Then, as a man both
astute and brave, he turned upon his murderers with his unsheathed
sword, watching carefully and guarding himself. They were terri-

him with their hands and arms, to see if he wore a cuirass or similar kind of
defense." See Machiavelli, *Istorie fiorentine*, book 8, chap. 5–6, ed. Gaeta, pp.
517–18.

32. The archbishop left, saying he was going to visit his mother whom he
hadn't seen in a long time.

33. Montesecco withdrew from the plot when he found it was to be executed
in the church. The task of murdering Lorenzo, to which he had been originally
assigned, may have been particularly odious to him since he had been well received by Lorenzo personally. Lorenzo's escape marked the failure of the plot,
which, in the opinion of both Machiavelli and Guicciardini, was caused largely by
Montesecco's withdrawal. The two to whom the task was given were too weak-
hearted and inept to carry it out.

34. Reports of the exact moment of the signal differ; some say it was the
elevation of the host, others say it was a little after, at the communion of the
priest. Probably it was between the priest's communion and the *ita missa est,*
when the congregation was preparing to leave and their attention was elsewhere.

fied and took flight while his two courtiers, Andrea and Lorenzo Cavalcanti, were quick to defend him. Lorenzo was wounded in the arm; Andrea came through safely.

The panic of the people was something to be seen: men, women, and children fleeing everywhere, wherever their feet took them. The whole place was filled with roaring and groaning, yet you could not hear anything clearly that was said, and there were some who thought the church would collapse.

Bernardo Bandini, who had already slaughtered Giuliano, not content with that assignment, went after Lorenzo, who in the nick of time had taken refuge with a few companions in the sacristy. Bandini, however, met up with Francesco Nori,[35] an overseer of Medici interests and a prudent man, and after running him through the stomach with his sword, slew him with a single blow. Nori's body was carried, still breathing, into the sacristy where Lorenzo had retreated.

Then I, who had withdrawn to the same place with some others, shut the bronze doors. Thus we warded off the danger that assailed us from Bandini. While we guarded the doors, others within began to worry about Lorenzo's wound. Antonio Ridolfi,[36] Jacopo's son and a worthy young man, sucked the wound. Lorenzo, however, had no concern for his own safety but kept asking eagerly how Giuliano fared; alternately enraged at being so threatened, and raging against those who had endangered his life with such unequal advantage. A group of young men faithful to the Medici were gathering with their weapons outside the sacristy doors. They shouted that they were all friends or relatives of Lorenzo and that he should come out before his enemies became stronger. We inside were anxious, not knowing if these were friends or enemies, and asked if Giuliano were alone. To this they answered nothing. Then Sigismondo della Stufa,[37] a valiant young man, bound to Lorenzo

35. Francesco di Antonio Nori, a merchant and an agent of the Medici, gained much fame by his action here. Leo X (Giovanni de' Medici) gave perpetual indulgence to those who, on the last Sunday of April, prayed for Nori's soul because he had saved Lorenzo, his father.

36. Antonio di Jacopo Ridolfi (1454–99), one of the most faithful of the Medici followers, sucked the wound for fear it was poisoned. Poliziano himself was closed up in the Sagrestia Nuova with Lorenzo so that he could relate events to which none of the others who wrote about the conspiracy had access.

37. Sigismondo di Angelo della Stufa had been the Gonfaloniere of Justice in

by many ties of love and duty since childhood, went up the stairs to where the organ was and sought hurriedly a small window that looked out into the church. When he saw the corpse of Giuliano lying there he understood what evil had transpired. He saw that those who were waiting outside the doors were friends, and he ordered the doors open. They took Lorenzo in the midst of a group of armed men and led him through the streets in such a way that he would not encounter the corpse of Giuliano.

I went straight to the house by the shortest route and came across Guiliano's body wretchedly lying there, fouled with the blood of many wounds. Trembling, and hardly in possession of myself for the grief, I was supported by some friends and taken home.

The whole house was full of armed men and full of cries in favor of the Medici, which resounded off the roof in a great din. It was something to see: boys, old men, young men, priests, and laymen seizing arms to defend the Medici house as though it were the public safety.

Meanwhile, the Archbishop of Pisa[38] called Cesare Petrucci, the Gonfaloniere of Justice, as they say, into council, so that he could kill him, although he said he had something to tell him from the Pope. Certain of the exiles from Perugia who accompanied him into the Palazzo Vecchio knew about the evil affair. They met in the chancellery so that they would hold an advantageous position, but when they closed the doors of the room, they could not open them when it was necessary[39]; thus they were no help either to themselves or their own side. But Petrucci, as he gazed at the faltering Salviati, suspected the plot and called the guards to arms. Salviati, much upset and scared, rushed out of the room, whereupon Petrucci met up with Jacopo di Poggio and with great courage grabbed him by the hair, threw him to the ground, and called guards to watch him. Then he ran hastily into the high tower of

---

1478, but he is better known as the fiancé of the beautiful Albiera degli Albizzi, who died in 1473, before the marriage. The death inspired many poems, not the least of which was Poliziano's own.

38. Salviati left the church with a group of followers to take over the Palazzo Vecchio, where he pretended to have something to tell the Gonfaloniere, Petrucci, in secret: that the pope wanted to do something for his son. Salviati was in such a state that Petrucci, suspecting something was wrong, acted immediately to combat the conspirators.

39. When they closed the doors they could not open them again without a key. Thus the Perugians had unwittingly imprisoned themselves.

the palazzo with a band of all of the magistrates. There, as best he could, he guarded the doors with a spit snatched from the kitchen (fear and anger had provided him with this weapon) and fiercely defended his own and the public safety. The others fought likewise bravely for their lives. The Palazzo Vecchio has numerous doors, and these were closed by guards so that the chiefs of the conspirators were separated. Thus divided, they lost much of the momentum of their attack. Meanwhile, there was a low murmuring noise throughout the Palazzo where some of the citizens had gathered.

Jacopo Pazzi,[40] however, when he understood that his hope for killing Lorenzo had failed, admitted with full knowledge how evil he was, striking his face with one hand, then the other, and he ran out of the church to his house, where he collapsed on the floor in great anguish. At length, when he saw that his predicament was critical, he began to tempt fate again. With a few relatives he went right into the piazza and called the people to arms. He had no success, and in fact, everyone called him an evil man; indeed, his voice was so broken by terror that he could scarcely be heard, and all men held him in contempt and cursed his crime. When he saw that there was no backing from the people, he began to tremble and lose courage. Those who had taken themselves to the bulwark on top of the Palazzo Vecchio hurled spears and large stones at him. Thus terrified, he went back to his house. Francesco, badly wounded in the fray, had already fled in haste to that same place.

Meanwhile, Lorenzo's sympathisers regained the Palazzo Vecchio. The Perugian conspirators broke down their door and were slaughtered.[41] In this way the Medici supporters vented their rage upon the rest. They hung Jacopo di Poggi from the windows; they led the captive cardinal to the Palazzo with a large guard and had

40. Jacopo first went home, where he found Francesco with a wound in one leg (possibly inflicted by himself in his fury in killing Giuliano); that was so grave that he asked Jacopo to go and rouse the people to arms. According to Machiavelli, Jacopo "although old and not adept in such tumultuous matters . . . mounted a horse, with perhaps a hundred armed men already prepared for such an undertaking, went into the Piazza della Signoria calling for help upon the people and upon liberty. But since the former had been made deaf by fortune and by the liberality of the Medici, and the latter was unknown in Florence, there was no answer." *Istorie fiorentine* book 8, chap. 8, ed. Gaeta, p. 521.

41. The first to be killed were the Perugians, who has locked themselves in. After they broke down the door, they were cut to pieces as they tried to escape.

much difficulty in protecting him from an attack by the people.[42] Most of those who followed him were killed by the crowd, all torn apart, their bodies mangled cruelly; in front of Lorenzo's doors someone brought, now a head fixed on a spear, now a shoulder. Nothing else was heard besides the voices of the people shouting "Palle, Palle"[43]—for that is the Medici insignia.

But Jacopo Pazzi decided to take flight, and with an armed band he made for the Porta alla Croce and escaped.

The people, meanwhile, were gathering at the Medici palace with incredible excitement and demonstration of support. They demanded that the traitors be handed over to them for punishment and spared no threat or abuse until they forced the criminals to be arrested.[44] The house of Jacopo Pazzi was barely defended from plunder, and Francesco, naked and wounded, was taken almost half dead to the hangman by the company of Pietro Corsini;[45] for it was not easy, or even possible, to control the fury of the crowd. From the same window as Francesco Pazzi, the archbishop of Pisa was also hung directly above the dead body itself. When he had been cut down (I witnessed in the amazed faces of the crowd what happened, and it was unknown to none at the time), either by chance or anger he bit Franceso's corpse in the chest, and even as he was strangled by the noose, his eyes wide open in rage, he hung onto it with his teeth. After this the necks of the two Jacopos Salviati were broken by hanging.

I remember that I came then into the piazza (for things were quiet now at the Medici palace), where I saw many corpses strewn about, foully mangled and greatly mocked and scorned by the people, for the House of the Medici had earned the gratitude of the people for many reasons. Everyone abhorred the death of

42. Cardinal Riario, Salviati's pawn, was barely saved but was treated with much suspicion. He was not permitted to leave Florence until 12 June, after Sixtus had excommunicated Lorenzo.

43. The Medici coat of arms was five red rondels on a shield. Although reminiscent of the pawnbroker's three gold balls, these arms had probably been used by the family long before they were associated with banking. See Raymond de Roover, *The Rise and Decline of the Medici Bank* (Cambridge, Mass., 1963), p. 15.

44. Lorenzo asked the crowd to restrain itself in order not to punish the innocent as well as the guilty.

45. Pietro Corsini (1441–99) was an important political figure and became an enemy of the Medici after their expulsion from the city.

While these things were going on, it was announced that Gian Francesco da Tolentino, the governor of Forlì, had broken into our territory with a band of selected men from the very borders of Forlì. Soon Lorenzo di Amadeo from Città di Castello did the same from the border dividing Florentine from Sienese territory, which we were warned about by many letters and messengers, but when they had been repelled by our men, both bands of invaders went back home.[47] At night guards were stationed throughout, Lorenzo's house being guarded with particular care; sentries of armed men were placed at the crossroads, in the piazza and around the whole city. The next day Giovanni Bentivolgio, a knight of Bologna and head of his republic, a man obligated to the Medici on many accounts, had arrived on the Mugello in aid with some troops of horsemen and many of infantry, but the city was already full of soldiers. However, the Board of Eight, worrying that the excited troops would make an uproar, chose some to remain as guards in the city and ordered the others home (or wherever they were useful) as soon as they arrived.

Meanwhile, Renato de' Pazzi, who the day before the crime had retired to his villa on the Mugello to collect soldiers,[48] was taken captive with his two brothers, Giovanni and Niccolò.[49] Giovanni de' Pazzi,[50] the brother of Guglielmo and Francesco, was seized in a garden near his house. Those who went after Jacopo, who was now abandoned by everyone, arrested him in Castagneto. The first to come upon him was a certain Alexander, a farmer of barely more than twenty. He laid his hands on the man, but Jacopo took out seven gold florins and began to beg the peasant to put him to death; he did not persuade him. The more he begged, the more Alexander's brother (who had joined the fray) hit him with his staff. Finally the wretch understood the saying: "The fates lead

47. They were not actually defeated by the Florentines, but when they understood the outcome of the plot, they turned back. Both were condemned as rebels.

48. Poliziano's is the only account that says that Renato intended to gather soldiers. It seems that works to imply Renato's involvement, which in fact was minimal.

49. Giovanni and Niccolò were sons of Piero de' Pazzi.

50. This Giovanni de' Pazzi was the son of Antonio and brother of Francesco and Guglielmo. He was married to Beatrice Borromeio and stood to inherit her patrimony, except for a Medici law which then allowed male nephews to inherit before a female. This was another cause of the bitterness between the two families.

those willing, and push those unwilling."[51] Then he was led to Florence with the bodyguard of the Board of Eight, so that he would not be torn to pieces by the crowd; and at the Palazzo Vecchio, after he had given his full confession without torture, he was hanged within a few hours. Now near death, he acted not inconsistently with his violent and angry nature, and shouted that he gave his departed soul to the devil. After him Renato's punishment was exacted. The rest of the brothers were thrown in chains.[52] The youngest of these was Galeotto, still a boy, who was wrapped in woman's clothing; terrified, he made an attempt to flee, and when he was recognized, he was thrown in the same prison. Thus, a little later, they also dragged Andrea, Renato's brother, back from flight.

Bandini fled to Città di Castello, where he was received by his own soldiers, and so pressed through to Siena.[53] Napoleone, aided by the knight Pietro Vespucci, accordingly decided to flee.[54] A few days later Giovanni Battista[55] was punished. Antonio da Volterra, who had wounded Lorenzo, and Stefano hid in the Badia for a few days. When this was discovered a throng of people gathered quickly, scarcely keeping their hands off the monks who, because of the requirements of their vows, would not reveal the fugitives. But after they had seized the murderers, the people mutilated them horribly; they cut off their noses and their ears, hacked at them with many blows, and, after they had made their confession to the crime, the criminals were carried off to the gallows.[56] Then a reward was announced by public decree and public crier for him who killed or brought in as living captives Bandini and Napoleone. Guglielmo de' Pazzi, trusting in his family ties, had found refuge

51. Seneca *Epistulae* 107.11, virtually a proverb.

52. The brothers of Renato, Andrea, Giovanni, Niccolò, and Galeotto di Piero were, along with their cousin, Giovanni di Antonio, condemned to life imprisonment in the Stinche in Florence.

53. Bandini fled to Constantinople but was arrested about a year later and sent back to Florence by Mohammed II. The culprit was hanged in December 1479, still dressed in his Turkish clothes.

54. Napoleone Franzesi fled but died during the next year in the camp of the Duke of Calabria.

55. Montesecco was examined on 4 May and wrote an invaluable confession. He was executed that night at the door of the Palazzo del Podestà.

56. No other source includes these gruesome details. They were hung from the windows of the Palazzo del Podestà.

in Lorenzo's palace and was confined with his children to within the fifth and twentieth mile from the city.

As soon as it was discovered that Pietro Vespucci had helped Napoleone, he was seized without delay. From boyhood he had squandered his father's property, and, in accordance with his father's testament and by law, he had been disinherited. At home he was poor and abroad he had great debts; thus he was offended by the present government and desired a new one. As soon as he saw that all the common people and all the citizens were with Lorenzo, he ran directly to pillage the Pazzi house and found soldiers gaping eagerly at the booty; but if that valorous young Pietro Corsini had not opposed them fiercely, Vespucci would have put all the citizens and everything sacred and profane in the greatest danger; in fact, this precipitous and frenzied young man roused both the people and soldiers to desire the booty. Finally, he was himself thrown into jail, and his son, Marco, was banished to live at least five miles from the city of Florence.[57]

Besides these there followed many killings, and all the conspirators were either dead, held in chains, or exiled.

When the event was announced at Rome there was great sadness; but ambassadors from many countries were happy about the miraculous salvation of Lorenzo.

For Giuliano a funeral was most splendidly conducted in San Lorenzo and due ceremonies performed for his soul. The greater part of Florentine youth put on mourning. He himself had been pierced with nineteen wounds. He had lived for but five and twenty years.

After a few days, when unseasonable rains began, a great many men from all the outlying districts streamed all of a sudden into the city. They said that it was an abomination that the body of Jacopo Pazzi had been buried in sacred ground; that this was why it had rained so long, since he was an evil man who had no respect for God or religion even in death; that it was against human and divine law that he be buried in church; and that this had interfered, according to an old peasant superstition, with the production of

---

57. Pietro Vespucci was the father of Marco whose wife, "La Bella Simonetta," was the airy heroine of Poliziano's *Stanze* and Giuliano's lady love. The attention given here is far greater than his actual importance in the crime. Pietro was sent to prison; Marco to perpetual banishment.

milk and grain. All the people, as usually happens in such cases, confirmed this indiscriminately. A great crowd then gathered at the gravesite itself, took out the corpse, and buried it outside the city walls.[58]

The next day monstrous events occurred; a huge crowd of young boys, as if fired up by certain mysterious torches of the Furies, dug up the buried corpse again. They almost stoned to death a man, I know not who, who interfered. Then they seized the dead man by the noose with which he had been strangled, and with much abuse and ridicule they dragged him all over the streets of the city. Some, for a joke, went on ahead and ordered everyone they met to make way, saying that they led forth a great knight; others, poking him with sticks and pointed stakes, warned him not to make a fool of himself in front of the citizens awaiting him in the piazza. Eventually they brought the corpse to his own doorstep, where they forced him to knock on the door with his head while they shouted, "Is there anyone home? Is there anyone to welcome the master returning with his great retinue?" Since they were forbidden to come into the piazza, they went off to the Arno and threw the body in it. When it floated, a huge crowd of peasants showered it with abuse, from which, it is reported, this jest was invented: that all his plans would have come out well if he had kept the same company in life that he kept in death.

From this great upheaval of human affairs I am directly warned about the fickleness of fortune, and I marvel at the incredible grief caused by the death of Giuliano. In what consisted the beauty of his body, what were his bearing and manners, I shall discuss but little.[59] He was of tall stature, well proportioned, with a large and prominent chest, shapely muscular arms, stout limbs, flat belly, full thighs, equally full calfs, keen eyes, a lively face with a fairly dark

58. According to popular legend, the sun came out as soon as the body was moved to unconsecrated ground.

59. The tract ends with the description in praise of Giuliano, who was handsome, charming, and devout. He belonged to the confraternity of the Magi called San Paolo. He was active in the Platonic Academy. Of his poetry there remains none, though Lorenzo mentions in a letter (1477) to Poliziano that he is pleased with his brother's literary progress. *Epistole inedite di Angelo Poliziano*, ed. L. D'Amore (Naples, 1909), pp. 10, 5. The portrait owes much to Suetonius in its handling of varied material which exemplifies his subject's character and bearing.

complexion, a thick mane of long black hair combed back from the front to the back of his head. He was expert at riding and throwing a javelin, excellent at jumping and wrestling, and took more than usual pleasure in hunting. He was charitable and loyal, an observer of religion and morality; he enjoyed painting, music, and all sorts of elegant activity. His talent at poetry was not small; he wrote some wonderfully dignified Tuscan poems, full of significance, and he read love poems gladly. He was eloquent and prudent, and no less astute; he loved wit and was himself not unwitty. But above all he hated liars and those who bore grudges. In the care of his person he was moderate, but elegant and neat. He bore great reverence, humanity, and respect for his brother, and he was of great strength and valor. These and other things made him dear to his people and to his family while he lived, and these same things leave for all of us a sorrowful and bitter memory of this illustrious young man. We pray to God most high and most good "that at least that this young man [Lorenzo] be not hindered from helping this shipwrecked age."[60]

60. The closing line, taken from Vergil's *Georgica* 1.500, implies a comparison of Giuliano and Lorenzo with Caesar and Augustus.

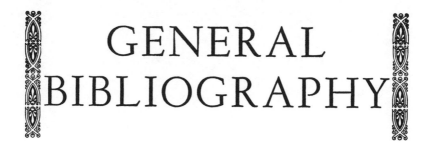

GENERAL BIBLIOGRAPHY

STUDIES

Baron, Hans. "Cicero and the Roman Civic Spirit in the Middle Ages and Early Renaissance." *Bulletin of the John Rylands Library* 22(1938):72–97. Reprinted in *Lordship and Community in Medieval Europe*, edited by F. L. Cheyette, pp. 291–314. New York, 1968.

———. *Crisis of the Early Italian Renaissance.* 2 vols. Princeton, 1955, rev. ed. 1966.

———. "Franciscan Poverty and Civic Wealth as Factors in the Rise of Humanistic Thought." *Speculum* 13(1938):1–38.

———. *From Petrarch to Leonardo Bruni.* Chicago. 1968.

———. *Humanistic and Political Literature in Florence and Venice at the Beginning of the Quattrocento.* Cambridge, Mass., 1955.

———. "Secularization of Wisdom and Political Humanism in the Renaissance." *Journal of the History of Ideas* 21(1960):131–50.

Becker, Marvin B. *Florence in Transition.* 2 vols. Baltimore, 1967–68.

Bouwsma, William J. "The Two Faces of Humanism: Stoicism and Augustinianism in Renaissance Thought." In *Itinerarium Italicum,* edited by Heiko A. Oberman and T. A. Brady, Jr., pp. 3–60. Leiden, 1975.

Brucker, Gene A. *The Civic World of Early Renaissance Florence.* Princeton, 1977.

———. *Renaissance Florence.* New York, 1969.

Burckhardt, Jacob. *The Civilization of the Renaissance in Italy.* London, 1944.

Burke, Peter. *Culture and Society in Renaissance Italy, 1420–1540.* New York, 1972.

Garin, Eugenio. *Italian Humanism: Philosophy and Civic Life in the Renaissance.* Translated by P. Munz. New York, 1966.

———. *Portraits from the Quattrocento.* Translated by V. and E. Velen. New York, 1972.

Gray, Hanna H. "Renaissance Humanism: The Pursuit of Eloquence." *Journal of History of Ideas* 24(1963):497–514. Reprinted in *Renaissance Essays,* edited by P. O. Kristeller and P. P. Weiner, pp. 199–216. New York, 1968.

Hay, Denys. *The Italian Renaissance in Its Historical Background.* 2nd ed. Cambridge, 1977.

Holmes, George. *The Florentine Enlightenment, 1400–1450.* New York, 1969.

Hyde, J. K. *Society and Politics in Medieval Italy. The Evolution of the Civil Life 1000–1350.* New York, 1973.

Kristeller, P. O. *Renaissance Thought: The Classic, Scholastic and Humanist Strains.* New York, 1961.

———. *Renaissance Thought II.* New York, 1965.

———. *Studies in Renaissance Thought and Letters.* Rome, 1956.

Lane, Frederic C. *Venice, A Maritime Republic.* Baltimore, 1973.

Larner, John. *Culture and Society in Italy, 1290–1420.* New York, 1971.

Lindholm, Gudrun. *Studien zum mittellateinischen Prosarhythmus.* Stockholm, 1963.

Logan, G. M. "Substance and Form in Renaissance Humanism." *Journal of Medieval and Renaissance Studies* 7(1977):1–34.

Martin, Alfred von. *Sociology of the Renaissance.* Introduction by W. K. Ferguson. New York, 1963.

Martines, Lauro. *The Social World of the Florentine Humanists.* Princeton, 1963.

Panofsky, Erwin. *Renaissance and Renascences in Western Art.* Stockholm, 1960.

Rossi, Vittorio. *Il Quattrocento.* 8th ed. Milan, 1964.

Sabbadini, Remigio. *Il metodo degli umanisti.* Florence, 1920.

———. *Le scoperte dei codici latini e greci ne' secoli XIV e XV.* 2 vols. 1905–14. Reprint ed. Florence, 1967.

Saitta, Giovanni. *Il pensiero italiano nell'Umanesimo e nel Rinascimento.* 3 vols. 2d. ed. Florence, 1961.

Schevill, Ferdinand. *A History of Florence.* New York, 1936.

Seigel, J. E. *Rhetoric and Philosophy in Renaissance Humanism.* Princeton, 1968.

Struever, Nancy S. *The Language of History in the Renaissance.* Princeton, 1970.

Tateo, Francesco. *Tradizione e realtà nell'Umanesimo italiano.* Bari, 1967.

Trinkaus, Charles. *Adversity's Nobleman: The Italian Humanists on Happiness.* 1940. Reprint ed. New York, 1965.

———. *In Our Image and Likeness: Humanity and Divinity in Italian Humanist Thought.* 2 vols. Chicago, 1970.

Ullman, B. L. *Studies in the Italian Renaissance.* 2d. ed. Rome, 1973.

Ullmann, Walter. *Medieval Foundations of Renaissance Humanism.* London, 1977.

Varese, Claudio. *Storia e politica nella prosa del Quattrocento.* Turin, 1961.

Vasoli, Cesare. *La dialetta e la rettorica dell'Umanesimo.* Milan, 1968.

Voigt, Georg. *Die Wiederbelebung des classischen Alterthums.* 3rd ed. 2 vols. Berlin, 1893.

Weiss, Robert. "The Dawn of Humanism in Italy." *Bulletin of the Institute of Historical Research* 42(1969):1–16.

———. *The Renaissance Discovery of Classical Antiquity.* Oxford, 1969.

Wilcox, Donald J. *The Development of Florentine Humanist Historiography in the Fifteenth Century.* Cambridge, Mass., 1969.

SOURCES AND TRANSLATIONS

Cassirer, Ernst, *et al.,* eds. *The Renaissance Philosophy of Man, Selections in Translation.* Chicago, 1948.

Emerton, Ephraim. *Humanism and Tyranny, Studies in the Italian Trecento.* Cambridge, Mass., 1925.

Garin, Eugenio, ed. *Prosatori latini del Quattrocento.* Milan and Naples, 1952.

Gragg, Florence A. *Latin Writings of the Italian Humanists.* New York, 1927.

Guarino Veronese. *Epistolario.* Edited by R. Sabbadini. 3 vols. Venice, 1915–19.

Müllner, Karl. *Reden und Briefe italienischer Humanisten.* Vienna, 1899.

Ross, J. B. and M. M. McLaughlin, eds. *The Portable Renaissance Reader.* New York, 1953.

Thompson, David, and A. F. Nagel, eds. *The Three Crowns of Florence: Humanist Assessments of Dante, Petrarca and Boccaccio.* New York, 1972.

Vergerio, Pier Paolo. *Epistolario.* Edited by L. Smith. Rome, 1934.

Vespasiano da Bisticci. *Memoirs.* Translated by W. George and E. Waters, London, 1926.

Whitcomb, Merrick. *A Literary Source-Book of the Italian Renaissance.* Philadelphia, 1898.

INDEX